Fundamentals
of Meal Management

FIFTH EDITION

Fundamentals of Meal Management

Margaret McWilliams, Ph.D., R.D.

Professor Emeritus
California State University, Los Angeles

PEARSON
Prentice Hall

Upper Saddle River, New Jersey 07458

Library of Congress Cataloging-in-Publication Data

McWilliams, Margaret.
   Fundamentals of meal management / Margaret McWilliams. — 5th ed.
     p. cm.
   Includes bibliographical references and index.
   ISBN-13: 978-0-13-514086-4 (alk. paper)
   ISBN-10: 0-13-514086-2 (alk. paper)
   1. Food. 2. Grocery shopping. 3. Nutrition. I. Title.

TX354.M29 2009
641.3—dc22

                                        2007044213

Executive Editor: Vernon R. Anthony
Editorial Assistant: Sonya Kottcamp
Director of Marketing: David Gesell
Marketing Manager: Jimmy Stephens
Marketing Assistant: Les Roberts
Production Manager: Wanda Rockwell
Creative Director: Jayne Conte
Cover Design: Bruce Kenselaar
Cover Illustration/Photo: Plycon Press
Full-Service Project Management/Composition: Integra
Printer/Binder: Hamilton Printing Company
Cover Printer: Phoenix Color Corp.

Credits and acknowledgments borrowed from other sources and reproduced, with permission, in this textbook appear on appropriate page within text.

Pearson Education LTD.
Pearson Education Singapore, Pte. Ltd
Pearson Education, Canada, Ltd
Pearson Education–Japan

Pearson Education Australia PTY, Limited
Pearson Education North Asia Ltd
Pearson Educación de Mexico, S.A. de C.V.
Pearson Education Malaysia, Pte. Ltd

10 9 8 7 6 5 4 3 2 1
ISBN-13: 978-0-13-514086-4
ISBN-10:   0-13-514086-2

Brief Contents

Contents

Preface

Today's news is dominated by the war against terrorism and the continuing violence in Iraq and Afghanistan, as well as critical problems in Africa. Against this backdrop, thoughts of pleasant and nourishing meals provide an increasingly important dimension to people's lives. Sociability and good health are promoted when people eat nourishing, well-prepared, and appetizing meals in a pleasant setting.

Eating is one of the great pleasures in life. Not only is it essential as the source of all of the nutrients we need for growth and health, but it also contributes greatly to our feelings of comfort and well-being. The challenge in meal management is to prepare foods that meet our physical and psychological needs while also helping to achieve and maintain a healthy weight. The recognized threat of the obesity epidemic in the United States today clearly underlines the importance of meeting this challenge.

This edition is designed to help students learn key aspects of meal planning and management so they will be able to enhance the dining experiences of their clients, family, and friends. It is divided into four sections. Section I introduces the overall subject of meal management. Included in the first two chapters are discussions about defining and implementing values and goals for managing meals, an overview of nutrient requirements, and ideas to help use this information in planning menus. Menu planning factors (types, demographics, resources, nutrition, and food selection), the structure of meal plans, and refinement to the finished menus are explored in depth in Chapter 3.

Food buying is the broad topic of Section II, which begins by examining the many types of food markets and factors to consider when deciding where to shop. Shopping tools (an accurate and complete shopping list, efficiencies in shopping, and use of labeling and product dating) are also examined. The remaining five chapters in this section examine issues and product choices in shopping for the various categories of foods.

Management arenas of particular importance in meal management are considered in Section III. Food safety is a key concern at all levels, beginning with government oversight and regulation of the safety of the food supply and ultimately with the people who prepare and serve food to consumers. Several of the particularly dangerous types of food infections, sources of these foodborne illnesses, and techniques to minimize their risk are the focus of Chapter 10. Kitchen planning and management of time and energy are other aspects of management included in this section.

Service and hospitality, the central focus of Section IV, are the aspects of meal management that can transform a meal from being simply a matter of eating into an occasion that provides psychological satisfaction, sociability, and lasting pleasure. The basics involved in setting the table (including descriptions of various table appointments and their selection), a look at different styles of meal service, and ways to create a lovely dining experience are examined in this section. Aspects of presenting buffets, receptions, dinners, formal teas, and informal teas are also discussed. At the request of several professors, I added a final chapter that discusses etiquette and cultural aspects of manners.

Features called "Food Insights" on a variety of topics related to the content of each chapter are a new element in this edition. They are written to add breadth and interest to your *exploration* of meal management.

Because of space, this book focuses on meal management, rather than on preparation of the foods being served. My books *Food Fundamentals* and the accompanying manual, *Illustrated Guide to Food Preparation,* provide this information; both also are published by Prentice Hall. I am sure these books will be useful parts of your study of meal management, foods, and nutrition.

I hope you will share with me the joy of being comfortable in preparing meals and entertaining friends and associates in your home or other settings. Through food, we can all help to bring feelings of friendship and pleasure to others.

Margaret McWilliams
Redondo Beach, California

Acknowledgments

A true test of friendship is willingness to proofread numerous pages of a book, so it is with sincere appreciation that I thank Dr. Toni Empringham and Pat Chavez for their dedication to eliminating typos in this edition. Dr. Empringham has also provided useful editorial insights. Special thanks for their professional suggestions and encouragement go to my reviewers Vala Jean Stults, Allison H. Worthen, and Jamie D. Haritz.

Margaret McWilliams
Redondo Beach, California

SECTION

Planning Meals

I

CHAPTER

1

Defining Menu Parameters

INTRODUCTION

Food is absolutely essential to life. It is the source of the nutrients that we all need for our health and survival. Fortunately, it also can bring considerable pleasure and comfort. The beauty of food appeals to the eye, and the flavor and aroma engage the senses of taste and smell; texture adds yet another dimension to the dining experience. The setting in which food is eaten also contributes to the dining experience. In this book, we explore ways to integrate eating pleasure and good nutrition.

Fine dining is a favorite hobby and/or a way of life for some people. For others, eating is just a required part of life. Still others are dealing with weight control and health problems that dictate adjustments in their food patterns and lifestyles. Limited incomes add to the feeding challenges for some people, whereas others are limited by their knowledge of nutrition and food preparation that would enhance their meals.

Clearly, healthful and pleasant food experiences can be an important part of life if people have adequate time, knowledge, and income. This book deals with the challenges involved in eating healthfully and well. Good meals require planning and management, as well as the knowledge and skills needed for obtaining, preparing, and serving food safely, attractively, and palatably. Food professionals can help people gain the knowledge and skills needed to optimize dining pleasure and health.

Food and nutrition professionals play key roles in helping ensure that people are able to eat safely and with pleasure. Among the food professionals involved in helping people eat safe food are personnel in such federal government agencies as the Food and Drug Administration, the Department of Agriculture, and Health and Human Services, as well as in similar departments in all 50 states. Dietitians, food scientists, food technologists, nutritionists, and foods teachers are in positions where they provide products, services, and knowledge to individuals and families to help them optimize their health and pleasure from food.

Dietitians have the professional expertise needed to interpret dietary requirements to clients. Their responsibility is to identify special dietary needs of individual clients with diabetes, heart conditions, or other diagnoses requiring modifications in eating patterns. They also can work with the general public to help people learn about healthful eating, including achieving and maintaining recommended weight. Part of a dietitian's role is to translate dietary recommendations into reality by explaining to clients how to select, buy, and prepare foods and meals that fit the individual's and/or family's situation and needs.

Professionals in food service are responsible for planning and preparing foods and meals that meet the dietary needs of their clientele, whether in a restaurant, institutional, or hospital setting. The challenge is great if the food is to meet consumer expectations within budgetary restrictions. Creativity needs to be blended with a scientific knowledge of food, smart buying, personnel management, and understanding of the audience to be fed.

Food scientists and technologists are charged with the task of creating safe food products that are tailored to the lifestyles, health needs, and food preferences of consumers. This is a huge challenge because today's consumers vary widely in such aspects as ethnicity, income, food preferences, time pressures, family situation, and interest in food and its preparation.

For all of these professionals, food is their medium for bringing their knowledge and expertise to their clientele. To be effective in their careers, they need to develop an understanding of who their clients are and what and how they want to eat. Not only is it important for these various food experts to really know food, but they also have to step away from their own biases and see food from their client's perspective.

Now is your opportunity to build a breadth of knowledge about food, its planning, preparation, and service. This base includes an awareness of the expectations and needs of those who will be eating your food. Whether the diner will be you, your family, clients, or other consumers, your success in the field of foods begins with selection of the foods themselves and then integrates the science involved in preparing and combining them into a diet that provides adequate nutrition for the body and the mind. In other words, food needs to provide a feeling of pleasure as well as optimal health. That is an ever-changing challenge, but is one of the reasons that your career will continue to be satisfying and rewarding.

A CHANGING SCENE

In a world dominated by concerns about terrorism, food is emerging as both a source of comfort and a potential threat to health. Meals shared with other family members or friends can be relaxing and provide a soothing respite from the pressures of the day. When the foods being eaten are personal favorites and perhaps reflect cultural heritage as well, subtle feelings of security and pleasure naturally emerge.

Unfortunately, food habits may gradually over the years contribute to long-term health consequences, such as obesity and heart disease. Weight control is a significant public health issue at the present time because of the relationship between obesity and such conditions as diabetes. Research efforts are aimed at uncovering underlying causes of overweight and appetite control, as well as developing new food products for dieters. Greater emphasis is being placed on increasing consumption of plant foods because of possible links between components in foods and protection against cancer and other diseases.

Food sometimes carries health risks in the form of microorganisms that cause illnesses that may strike quickly and briefly. Other food-borne illnesses may continue for an extended period or even cause death. Considerable effort is being directed toward ensuring the safety of the nation's food supply.

Today's consumers are faced with the problem of feeding themselves in a way that adds pleasure to their lives and also promotes good health. That task is a challenging one in today's complex world. Time pressures may crowd thoughts about wholesome

---

BOX 1.1

Food Insights: Spinach Surprise?

In the late summer and early fall of 2006, many people were sickened from ingesting *E. coli* 0157:H7 that was present in fresh spinach. Three people died and more than 200 cases of the illness were reported across the nation in 26 states. The source of the outbreak was traced to fresh baby spinach packaged in sealed bags of various ready-to-eat salads. A broad recall of these salads from three different packers was done to halt the spread of the bacteria, but not before one person had died from eating contaminated fresh spinach.

Needless to say, the financial impact on the growers and others along the supply chain was devastating. At least one of the probable sources of the contamination was cow manure in fields adjacent to the fields of spinach. Water runoff from the contaminated fields apparently seeped into the fields where crops are grown. This is one illustration of the need for constant vigilance to protect and deliver a safe supply of food to consumers.

meals to a low priority, and the day's food choices are made in response to immediate hunger rather than long-term health needs. Resolutions to do better tomorrow may become merely token gestures toward eating for good health. Many consumers are making some changes in their food choices, but not always for the better. Sometimes information influencing these changes is not accurate and may even have negative health consequences. Clearly, consumers can use some professional help so they can feed themselves well.

When viewed from a national perspective, the food habits of Americans are a cause for concern because overweight and obesity are increasing nationwide among males and females in all age groups (Figure 1.1). Not only does this high incidence have an impact on self-image and activity patterns, but it also increases the risk of these conditions:

- Hypertension
- Dyslipidemia (for example, high total cholesterol or high levels of triglycerides)
- Type 2 diabetes
- Coronary heart disease
- Stroke
- Gallbladder disease
- Osteoarthritis
- Sleep apnea and respiratory problems
- Some cancers (endometrial, breast, and colon)

The high costs of excess weight psychologically, physically, and economically are being recognized nationally, and government agencies, dietitians and other health workers, and the food industry are working together to try to reverse the trend.

FIGURE 1.1   The goals established for meal management need to fit the lifestyle, values, and philosophy of the family, group, or individual.

TABLE 1.1   Risk of cardiovascular disease, hypertension, and type 2 diabetes among overweight and obese people compared with normal persons[a]

Category (Body Mass Index)	Disease risk and waist circumference	
	Men (<40") Women (<35")	Men (>40") Women (>35")
Overweight		
25.0–29.9	Increased	High
Obese		
30.0–34.9	High	Very high
35.0–39.9	Very high	Very high
Extremely obese		
>40	Extremely high	Extremely high

[a] *Adapted from* Preventing and Managing Global Epidemics of Obesity. *Report of the World Health Organization Consultation of Obesity. WHO. Geneva. June 1997.*

Consumers also will need to work hard to modify their eating behaviors if they are to be successful individually in achieving and maintaining a healthful weight. Meal management clearly has an important role to play in weight control efforts.

THE CURRENT SITUATION

Studies of American eating habits are continually in progress to aid food and nutrition professionals in knowing how to design programs and products to meet consumer needs. Many years ago, the pattern of three meals eaten at home every day described virtually the entire population. Societal changes in recent decades have altered the situation, due in part to increasing cultural diversity and changes in work locations and marketplaces. However, Americans still ate an average of 941 meals (>2.5 daily) at home in 2000 (NPD Group/Crest, 2000). More people ate breakfast and lunch at home than in any other place. Dinner was eaten at home an average of five times weekly in the majority of households described as married with children (NPPC, 2000). Overall patterns of dinner consumed at home (NPD Group, 2000) have varied slightly between 1984 and 2000, with a high of 70 percent in 1992 and a low of 66 percent each year between 1998 and 2000.

In 2005, 56 percent of people between ages 52 and 60 and 58 percent 65 or older ate meals prepared at home five or more days a week. When meals are eaten at home, they may range from elaborate meals prepared by someone in the family (including children in many cases) to simple preparations or ready-to-eat items (including heat-and-serve foods) from grocery delicatessens or restaurants.

Takeout meals from restaurants and fast-food outlets increased from an annual average of 43 meals per person in 1984 to 72 in 2000 (NPD Group, 2000). Reasons for consumers opting to use easy-to-prepare and/or preprepared foods at home vary with the household, but one survey (Stouffer's, 1999) found that almost three in four respondents did not have enough time to do the cooking themselves. Less than half said they did not want to do the clean up or had other uses for their time (42 percent and 41 percent, respectively). About one in five indicated that cooking was not enjoyable.

Snacks are an important source of calories (about 20 percent of the typical daily intake), with four or more snacks being eaten each day by more than 30 percent of Americans. Whether snacks are used as a way for including enough fruits and vegetables in the diet or whether they are primarily sources of sugar and fat depends on the individual. Any food (regardless of nutritional value) eaten between meals is considered to be a snack. With such a high incidence of snacking, it is evident that daily menu planning needs to include snacks if they are a part of the eating pattern for the person or family.

Lifestyles today run the gamut from the very wealthy to the homeless, from single households to large and/or extended families, and from native born to recent immigrants. The money available for food and the foods preferred clearly are influenced by the situations in which individuals and families are living. Long commutes are part of the day's schedule that many families face to obtain affordable or suitable housing. Career demands and the complicated schedules of children involved in school-related activities add to the challenge of feeding families healthfully.

A MATTER OF PHILOSOPHY

The context in which families and individuals wish to eat determines how meals can be managed for the greatest satisfaction. No single pattern can be expected to be best for all people. Instead, the person or group needs to identify the philosophy, values, and goals that provide an appropriate foundation for effective meal management.

Each group may have some unique factors to consider, but certain questions usually contribute in major ways to developing a philosophical basis for meal planning. These questions include:

1. What can mealtime contribute to family communication?
2. How important is cost control in the food budget?
3. Can family meals enhance social skills of individuals?
4. How can family meals promote the health of various family members?
5. Can various family members develop creativity by helping in meal preparation and service?
6. In what other ways can family meals add to the quality of life in a family, as a group, or as individuals?

Obviously, the answers to these and other questions vary from family to family or between individuals. There are no right or wrong answers to these questions. They are designed to stimulate thoughts about how meals can be a pivotal and positive point in the lives of individuals and their families. When a philosophy has been identified, it provides the background for managing meals that fit the situation and improve the quality of life.

Values

Value
Something considered very desirable and significant.

Values represent the philosophical and attitudinal orientation of a family toward characteristics or ideals to which they willingly and enthusiastically are committed. These values may not necessarily have been expressed but rather may seem quite intangible; nevertheless, they are of importance to individuals and the family as a whole.

A value may be defined as something intrinsically desirable, of relative worth, or of importance. One of the characteristics that families value is good health for all members. This state of physical well-being is considered to be important because good health is vital to the achievement of many individual and family goals. It also is an important aspect of the quality of life families usually are seeking. Because of the value placed on health, the area of prevention is being stressed increasingly, both in medicine and in dentistry. People value good health so much that they are willing to take preventive measures, such as a modest increase in exercise or minor dietary modifications, to promote and prolong their present state of health. Health insurance is another manifestation of the value families place on maintaining good health.

In the realm of preventive measures to protect health, the establishment of dietary patterns that ensure good nutrition throughout life is key. Meal management, in its broad definition, affords an excellent opportunity to support the value of good health. The menus planned, the manner in which the food is prepared, and the environment in which meals are served all play a part in achieving an appropriate food intake and a well-nourished body.

In many families, meals and food possess social value. The clarification of this value is different in various families, with some viewing food as the setting or background for social experiences, either within the family or with friends in the home. The meal situation is valued or appreciated as a means of creating a relaxing and interesting vehicle for stimulating conversation and the exchange of ideas. In a sense, these families value food for its ability to nourish the mind as well as the body.

Some people place a different social value on food. Families experiencing a sudden reduction in income may seek to build their confidence and sense of stability by continuing to eat just as they did when they had a comparatively high income. To give up relatively expensive foods that previously were common parts of their food pattern may be a painful reminder of personal values attached to specific foods.

In the reverse situation, families with increasing incomes and a rising standard of living may deliberately alter food choices to include items deemed to be appropriate for the change in social position. Food is seen as a visible manifestation of social stature and income level. This alteration in food selection in relation to income may be important only to the individual, but it often may be used as a statement to the world as well. For some people, the food served says much about the circumstances of a family. Some families do not feel that it is important to make such statements, but others who equate expensive meals with social or economic status may place a high value on their quality.

Food can also carry cultural values for families wishing to maintain their identity with their culture. Preparation and service of ethnic and cultural foods may be valued highly because of the memories and associations evoked when these foods are prominent in meal patterns. In some instances, these foods may convey a negative value to a family rather than a positive one. This may be of importance when a family moves into a new region and is eager to become an integral part of the new environment.

Another value held by some is the effective management of time, energy, or a combination of these resources. In homes where all of the adults are employed, time often is of prime importance, for this may be the resource in shortest supply. If a higher value is placed on the time required to prepare meals than on the social value they provide, menu plans may be quite different than when these values are reversed. The trade-offs involved in integrating meal management with the hierarchy of pertinent values will become apparent in the following chapters.

Money and its conservation may be a high value for many families faced with the economic realities of a stalled national economy and the uncertainties generated by a weak stock market amid the possibility of terrorism. The relative importance of expenditures on expensive cuts of meat or other costly food items needs to be weighed against essential nonfood purchases when planning menus. Within the realm of menu planning and food shopping, there are many opportunities to exercise judgments that can greatly influence the amount spent for food in a year. For some people, skillful management of money is of great importance, whereas for others, this simply is not a meal management priority.

Energy conservation, whether in the form of electrical, gas, or human energy, is an individual and national priority for many people. Meals that feature short-time cooking methods or one-dish menus are ways of helping conserve existing resources. The commitment to energy conservation varies considerably among people. It may be a motivating value to some, whereas others give it little more than a passing thought.

The value of human energy merits considerable thought if the person doing meal preparation has physical limits and/or has many other demands, which may include demanding jobs, child care, and/or volunteer work. Modifications in menus and the type of service can result in considerable savings in human energy. Meals featuring home-prepared products, perhaps even the bread, require considerable energy to prepare and serve them graciously. In comparison, very little energy is required to heat a frozen dinner and serve it in its container, accompanied by a paper napkin. For people on a very demanding schedule and with little interest in food other than as a means of survival, the frozen dinner option may be an appropriate way of supporting the identified value of saving energy.

Many people highly value creativity. Food certainly affords inviting opportunities for expressing this valued characteristic. The colors, shapes, textures, flavors, and aromas afford rare opportunities to appeal to all of the senses through a single experience. For people who place a high value on creativity, meal management may assume a very different mode than it does in the hands of those with little interest in exploring the artistic opportunities afforded by food.

Education is a value in many families. Food can be the means of increasing knowledge about a wide range of topics. Very young children can learn about the aromas and flavors of various foods. Older children can learn about how plants grow and how food crops are farmed. Families can learn about the geography, culture, and foods of countries around the world when they prepare and serve dishes typical of a foreign nation (Figure 1.2).

These are but some examples of values held by families and their individual members. The esteem in which values are held will influence how meals are managed. Even

FIGURE 1.2 Meals that introduce foods from other cultures provide a flavorful education.

when values have not been assessed consciously, the accepted attitudes toward underlying values will influence the total manner in which food is planned, prepared, served, and eaten.

Goals

Goal
An objective worthy of considerable effort to achieve it.

Goals are aims or objectives that people try to reach. Values can become tangible when goals are developed that support the values. In terms of meal management, goals can be expressed in specific, measurable ways. For example, the value of good health can be supported by the goal of preparing three meals daily that conform to MyPyramid. Here are some other goals that might be developed to aid in meeting the goal of good health:

- Serving fish or poultry at least four times weekly to help reduce serum cholesterol.
- Controlling portion sizes by preparing smaller amounts of food to aid in weight reduction.
- Preparing a rich dessert no more than once a week (again to help control weight).
- Serving breakfast early enough for people to eat unhurriedly before leaving for school or work.

These are but a few examples of realistic, practical goals that can be established to support the value of good health.

These goals are stated in terms that make it easy to determine whether or not they have been met. Behavioral objectives are goals that can be measured. Such goals can provide the framework needed for successful meal management. When goals are set and the performance subsequently is evaluated, a feeling of accomplishment and pride will develop. Such achievements are important psychologically in managing meals as well as other aspects of life. The seemingly never-ending responsibility of meal management can weigh heavily on people who have not found ways of measuring management successes. Whether meal management is viewed as a managerial success or simply another pile of dirty dishes is very much in the hands of the person responsible for meals. Creative meal management can add pleasure and satisfaction to people's lives.

Meal management goals to support a social value may be difficult to state in terms that can be measured. When possible, goals should be stated in behavioral (measurable) terms so progress toward the goal can be seen. However, important goals should be stated to show the relationship to defined goals even when behavioral objectives cannot be drafted.

THE PROCESS OF MANAGEMENT

Overall, management consists of six steps:

- Planning
- Organizing
- Delegating
- Implementing
- Supervising
- Evaluating

Each of these steps is part of the management process, but the emphasis placed on each step varies depending on the circumstance. Certainly, this is true in meal management. Planning, organizing, implementing, and evaluating are vital parts of meal management regardless of whether the meal is being prepared in a home, a restaurant,

FIGURE 1.3 This kitchen, with its counter opening to the adjacent family room, is efficient for organizing food preparation and service.

or an institutional kitchen. Delegating and supervising are key management tasks in situations where employees are involved in various aspects of meal management. These tasks also are important in managing family meals at home except in one-person households.

Menu planning is a key task of meal management, one that requires consideration of such factors as nutritional quality, aesthetic and gustatory appeal, food availability, cost control, facilities, time, and energy. Clearly, this is a vital part of meal management. Related planning tasks include kitchen planning and time management so food shopping, preparation, service, and cleanup are managed effectively.

Organization is essential to having meal production proceed efficiently and with optimal use of resources. For example, efficient arrangement of work and storage areas in the kitchen can save the energy and time of workers (Figure 1.3). An organized shopping list provides similar savings when shopping for food. Other aspects of meal management also afford opportunities to develop and utilize organizational skills.

When workers or family members are available to help, delegation of tasks can be done to speed meal preparation and service. The skills and capabilities of the available workers need to be considered so optimal results are obtained and time is not wasted. Clear communication regarding the tasks assigned is essential to successful delegation. This can be a particular challenge if the supervisor and worker do not speak the same language.

Implementing a meal management plan involves actual shopping for the food, appropriate and safe storage and handling of food, preparation, service, and cleanup. Knowledge of food safety, food selection, preparation techniques, types of service, and kitchen sanitation must all be involved to manage a meal successfully.

Supervision of employees or family members is an essential part of the management process to achieve successful meal management and to develop the skills of those being supervised. Employee morale is a key component of management success. Adequate training, clear directions, and recognition of good work are important components of supervision.

Evaluation is very important in meal management. Assessment of the various factors of a meal gives a manager information regarding changes that could be made to improve the meal at another time. Equally important is recognition of the aspects that were of high quality and what was done to reach this level. Careful analysis of a meal can provide useful ideas for improvement and also build confidence in managing meals.

Summary

Food is a key element of life and essential to good health and life itself. Food professionals (e.g., dietitians, food scientists, food technologists, nutritionists, food service personnel, and restaurateurs) provide the expertise and knowledge to help consumers with food choices and preparation that will give them optimal health and satisfaction. The time pressures and societal scene of life today significantly influence the way people are eating. Despite the challenges, healthy meals are recognized as being very important for everybody.

Meal management is a vital aspect of daily living; it has the potential for enhancing the quality of life for individuals and families. A philosophy of meal management can be developed to be consistent with specific parameters, such as lifestyle and economics. Because there are many different approaches to meal management, it is helpful to identify the values attached to meals and their management. Goals then can be developed to aid in strengthening and supporting these values. Goals can increase satisfaction in managing meals by providing a framework for evaluating and achieving management success. The management process consists of planning, organizing, delegating, implementing, supervising, and evaluating.

Study Questions

1. What food career is particularly interesting to you? How do you think knowledge of meal management will help you in your career?

2. Write down each meal and snack that you ate yesterday. Is this typical of the way you usually eat? Are there changes you could make that would be healthier for you? Is it possible to make these changes? If not, identify the reasons they would be difficult to make.

3. What is the difference between a value and a goal?

4. Interview a student from a background different from yours to learn about (a) what meals are eaten with family members, (b) who prepares and helps prepare family meals, and (c) what is a favorite dinner menu. Compare the findings from this interview with your responses to the same questions.

5. Interview a working mother with at least one child at home and ask her (a) what meals are eaten with family members, (b) who prepares and who helps prepare family meals, (c) what is a favorite dinner menu, and (d) how do meals change on the weekends. What are the differences, if any, that can be seen between her answers and those found in the preceding question? How do work and the responsibility for feeding children influence her responses regarding meal management?

6. State a goal for managing each of the following processes in a meal: (a) planning, (b) organizing, (c) delegating, (d) implementing, (e) supervising, and (f) evaluating.

Suggested Websites

www.mindtools.com
Information on various management topics.

http://hp2010.nhlbihin.net/menuplanner/menu.cgi
Menu planning aid sponsored by the National Heart,
Lung, and Blood Institute.

http://health.nih.gov
Recommendations for eating 5-a-Day and other topics
on food, nutrition, and health.

http://www.khake.com/page30.html
Information on many different careers in food, food science, and nutrition.

http://www.foodindustryjobs.com/
Career opportunities and placement.

http://www.cdc.gov/nccdphp/dnpa/obesity/index.htm
Information on health risks of overweight
and obesity.

http://aje.oxfordjournals.org/cgi/content/abstract/158/1/85
Article on association between eating patterns and obesity in a free-living U.S. adult population.

http://www.nrdc.org/media/pressreleases/060622b.asp
Rulings on controlling animal waste pollution from
farms.

Bibliography

Blackburn, G. L. 2002. The American obesity epidemic is
    getting worse. *Food Technol.* 56 (6): 148.

Boddy, D. 2005. *Management: An Introduction.* Prentice
    Hall. Upper Saddle River, NJ.

Clark, P. 2005. Diet trends affect processing. *Food
    Technol.* 59 (3): 59.

Cullen, K. W., et al. 2001. Using goal setting as a strategy for
    dietary behavior change. *J. Am. Dietet. Assoc.* 101 (5): 562.

Frazao, E. (ed.). 1999. *America's Eating Habits: Changes
    and Consequences.* Ag. Info. Bull. 750. Washington, DC.

Neuhouser, M. L., et al. 2000. Do consumers of savory
    snacks have poor-quality diets? *J. Am. Dietet. Assoc.*
    100 (5): 576.

NPD Group. 2000. *National Eating Trends Survey.* NPD
    Group. Rosemont, IL.

NPD Group. 2001. *The Skinny on the Weight Loss
    Market.* NPD Group. Rosemont, IL.

NPD Group/Crest. 2000. *Food Service.* Crest Information
    Services, NPD Group. Rosemont, IL.

NPPC. 2000. *Consumer Kitchen Survey.* National Pork
    Producers Council. Des Moines, IA.

NRA. 2000. *Takeout Food: Consumer Study of Carry-
    Out and Delivery.* National Restaurant Assoc.,
    Washington, DC.

NRA. 2001. *Restaurant Industry Forecast.* National
    Restaurant Assoc., Washington, DC.

Sloan, A. E. 2001. Top 10 trends to watch and work on.
    Food Technol. 55 (4): 38.

Sloan, A. E. 2005. Demographic directions: mixing of the
    market. *Food Technol.* 59 (7): 34.

Sloan, A. E. 2006. Consumer trends. *Food Technol.*
    60 (5): 19.

Sloan, A. E. 2006. Top 10 functional food trends. *Food
    Technol.* 60 (4): 22.

Stouffer's. 1999. *Consumer Attitudes on Meal
    Preparation and Packaged Meals.* Stouffer's.
    Solon, OH.

Tseng, M., and DeVellis, R. F. 2001. Fundamental dietary
    patterns and their correlates among US whites. *J. Am.
    Dietet. Assoc.* 101 (8): 929.

Wiecha, J. M., et al. 2001. Differences in dietary patterns
    of Vietnamese, White, African-American, and Hispanic
    adolescents. Worcester, MA. *J. Am. Dietet. Assoc.*
    101 (2): 248.

Zoumas-Morse, C., et al. 2001. Children's patterns of
    macronutrient intake and associations with
    restaurant and home eating. *J. Am. Dietet. Assoc.*
    101 (8): 923.

CHAPTER

Nutrition in Meal Planning

2

Introduction
Dietary Guidelines for Americans
MyPyramid
National Variations
Dietary Reference Intakes
Food Labeling
    Ingredient Labeling
Food Insights: Allergen Alert
    Nutrition Labeling
Integrating Nutrition into Menus
Summary
Study Questions
Suggested Websites
Bibliography

INTRODUCTION

Menu planning is done on the basis of a meal (e.g., breakfast, lunch, dinner), but these meals and any snacks during the day need to include enough of each of the nutrients required for good health without providing too many calories. Variety, particularly in fruits and vegetables, helps obtain necessary vitamins and minerals while also keeping calories under control. The ways in which foods are to be prepared (e.g., fried versus broiled) can be adjusted to modify energy intake. Another key element for planning healthy meals is portion control. Although menu plans do not indicate portion size, the recipes and shopping list for the menus need to focus on serving sizes if weight control is a necessary part of the total picture.

DIETARY GUIDELINES FOR AMERICANS

Nutrition and Your Health: Dietary Guidelines for Americans
Guidelines for healthful eating developed by the USDA and HHS and revised approximately every five years.

In 1985, the U.S. Departments of Agriculture (USDA) and Health and Human Services (HHS) joined forces to produce the first edition of **Nutrition and Your Health: Dietary Guidelines for Americans**. The most recent edition was released in 2005. These guidelines are intended to serve as the basis for professionals to educate consumers about nutrition and for consumers to apply the guidelines to improve their own diets. Evaluation of menus and dietary patterns using these guidelines can be helpful in planning menus that will improve nutritional adequacy.

When *Dietary Guidelines for Americans* 2005 was being developed, the public health problem of weight control was well documented. Therefore, the guidelines were developed in the context of the need for meals and snacks that are high in nutrients but low to moderate in calories. The guidelines are intended to promote diets that support normal growth and development of children and optimal health for people of all ages, including reducing risk of many chronic diseases.

Assumptions underlying the guidelines included the following:

- Recommended diets should provide all the nutrients needed for growth and health.
- Nutrients should come primarily from foods.

The nutrients that were recognized as being of particular concern for adults were fiber, vitamins A (carotenoids), C, and E, and some specific minerals (calcium, potassium, and magnesium). For children and adolescents, the nutrients of concern were calcium, potassium, magnesium, fiber, and vitamin E. These two key recommendations stated in the guidelines help provide these and also the other nutrients:

- Consume a variety of nutrient-dense foods and beverages within and among the basic food groups while choosing foods that limit the intake of saturated and trans fat, cholesterol, added sugars, salt, and alcohol.
- Meet recommended intakes within energy needs by adopting a balanced eating pattern, such as the USDA Food Guide or the DASH eating plan.

Recommendations for specific population groups also were made:

- ***People over age 50:*** Consume vitamin B_{12} in its crystalline form (i.e., fortified foods or supplements).
- ***Women of childbearing age who may become pregnant:*** Eat foods high in heme-iron and/or consume iron-rich plant foods or iron-fortified foods with an enhancer of iron absorption, such as food rich in vitamin C.
- ***Women of childbearing age who may become pregnant and those in the first trimester of pregnancy:*** Consume adequate synthetic folic acid daily (from fortified foods or supplements) in addition to food forms of folate from a varied diet.

- *Older adults, people with dark skin, and people exposed to insufficient ultraviolet band radiation (i.e., sunlight):* Consume extra vitamin D from food fortified with vitamin D and/or supplements.

Two eating plans, the USDA Food Guide and DASH Eating Plan, have been developed to guide consumers toward healthy diets. Since 1985, the USDA has published its **USDA Food Guide** as a means of helping consumers put guidelines into practice. The guide is revised approximately every five years to incorporate appropriate changes based on relevant and current research findings. The current edition, the sixth, was released in 2005 (Table 2.1). The National Heart, Lung, and Blood Institute (in HHS) developed its own diet guide, the **DASH Eating Plan**. The DASH name is an acronym for the actual name, "Dietary Approach to Stop Hypertension." Table 2.2 compares the two plans.

Discussion of the USDA Food Guide is centered on basic points to help guide selection of foods:

USDA Food Guide
Recommendations for healthful eating based primarily on vegetables, fruits, breads and cereals, milk and milk products, and meats and legumes.

DASH Eating Plan
"Dietary Approach to Stop Hypertension," the recommended eating plan developed by the Heart, Lung, and Blood Institute.

1. Meeting recommended intakes within energy needs:
   - More dark green and orange vegetables, legumes, fruits, whole grains, and reduced-fat milk and milk products are recommended.
   - Intake of total fats (particularly trans and saturated fats and cholesterol), added sugars, refined cereals, and extra calories should be reduced.
   - Lean meats, fish, poultry, beans, eggs, and nuts should be included.
2. Variety among and within food groups: All food groups need to be included because of the unique nutrient contributions of each group. Variety within each group is recommended to take advantage of the broadened array of nutrients available.
3. Nutrient-dense foods: Foods containing little except calories quickly meet energy needs but contribute little to meeting nutrient requirements. Vegetables and nonfat milk are examples of nutrient-dense foods that provide significant levels of essential nutrients but relatively few calories.
4. Nutrients of concern: Adults need to focus on getting enough calcium, potassium, magnesium, fiber, and vitamins A, C, and E. Children need to be sure to consume enough calcium, potassium, magnesium, fiber, and vitamin E.
5. Considerations for specific population groups:
   - People older than 50 years need to get vitamin B_{12} from fortified cereals or a crystalline B_{12} supplement.
   - Women need heme-iron from meats or iron-fortified foods or iron-rich vegetables accompanied by orange juice or other source of vitamin C.
   - Pregnant women or women who may become pregnant need adequate folic acid from folate-fortified foods or a supplement.
   - The elderly, people with dark skin, and those exposed to little sunlight need a vitamin D supplement or an intake of 1,000 international units (IUs) of vitamin D daily.
6. Fluid: People usually drink enough fluid with and between meals when drinking according to thirst. In times of heat stress or vigorous activity, purposeful drinking is needed to prevent dehydration.
7. Flexibility of food patterns for varied food preferences:
   - Vegetarians need to pay special attention to their intakes of iron, vitamin B_{12}, and protein. In addition, if milk is not being consumed, calcium and vitamin D levels in the diet will be low. Eggs are useful as a protein source that also provides some iron. Substitutions for 1 ounce of meat can be made using 1 egg, 1/2 ounce of nuts, or 1/4 cup legumes. For a day, a person eating 2,000 calories would need to include 5.5 times these substitution figures.
   - Milk consumption provides more than 70 percent of the calcium Americans consume. Lack of milk consumption has a negative impact on the intake not only of calcium but also potassium, magnesium, zinc, riboflavin, vitamins A, D, and folate.

TABLE 2.1 USDA Food Guide

Daily Amount of Food from Each Group (vegetable subgroup amounts are per week)

Calorie Level	1,000	1,200	1,400	1,600	1,800	2,000	2,200	2,400	2,600	2,800	3,000	3,200
Food Group	Food group amounts shown in cup (c) or ounce-equivalents (oz-eq), with number of servings (srv) in parentheses when it differs from the other units. See note for quantity equivalents for foods in each group.											
	Oils are shown in grams (g).											
Fruits	1 c (2 srv)	1 c (2 srv)	1.5 c (3 srv)	1.5 c (3 srv)	1.5 c (3 srv)	2 c (4 srv)	2 c (4 srv)	2 c (4 srv)	2 c (4 srv)	2.5 c (5 srv)	2.5 c (5 srv)	2.5 c (5 srv)
Vegetables	1 c (2 srv)	1.5 c (3 srv)	1.5 c (3 srv)	2 c (4 srv)	2.5 c (5 srv)	2.5 c (5 srv)	3 c (6 srv)	3 c (6 srv)	3.5 c (7 srv)	3.5 c (7 srv)	4 c (8 srv)	4 c (8 srv)
Dark green veg.	1 c/wk	1.5 c/wk	1.5 c/wk	2 c/wk	3 c/wk	3 c/wk	3 c/wk	3 c/wk	3 c/wk	3 c/wk	3 c/wk	3 c/wk
Orange veg.	.5 c/wk	1 c/wk	1 c/wk	1.5 c/wk	2 c/wk	2 c/wk	2 c/wk	2 c/wk	2.5 c/wk	2.5 c/wk	2.5 c/wk	2.5 c/wk
Legumes	.5 c/wk	1 c/wk	1 c/wk	2.5 c/wk	3 c/wk	3 c/wk	3 c/wk	3 c/wk	3.5 c/wk	3.5 c/wk	3.5 c/wk	3.5 c/wk
Starchy veg.	1.5 c/wk	2.5 c/wk	2.5 c/wk	2.5 c/wk	3 c/wk	3 c/wk	6 c/wk	6 c/wk	7 c/wk	7 c/wk	9 c/wk	9 c/wk
Other veg.	4 c/wk	4.5 c/wk	4.5 c/wk	5.5 c/wk	6.5 c/wk	6.5 c/wk	7 c/wk	7 c/wk	8.5 c/wk	8.5 c/wk	10 c/wk	10 c/wk
Grains	3 oz-eq	4 oz-eq	5 oz-eq	5 oz-eq	6 oz-eq	6 oz-eq	7 oz-eq	8 oz-eq	9 oz-eq	10 oz-eq	10 oz-eq	10 oz-eq
Whole grains	1.5	2	2.5	3	3	3	3.5	4	4.5	5	5	5
Other grains	1.5	2	2.5	2	3	3	3.5	4	4.5	5	5	5
Lean meat and beans	2 oz-eq	3 oz-eq	4 oz-eq	5 oz-eq	5 oz-eq	5.5 oz-eq	6 oz-eq	6.5 oz-eq	6.5 oz-eq	7 oz-eq	7 oz-eq	7 oz-eq
Milk	2 c	2 c	2 c	3 c	3 c	3 c	3 c	3 c	3 c	3 c	3 c	3 c
Oils	15 g	17 g	17 g	22 g	24 g	27 g	29 g	31 g	34 g	36 g	44 g	51 g
Discretionary calorie allowance	165	171	171	182	195	267	290	362	410	426	512	648

TABLE 2.2   Sample USDA Food Guide and the DASH Eating Plan at the 2,000-Calorie Level[a]

Food Groups and Subgroups	USDA Food Guide Amount[b]	DASH Eating Plan Amount	Equivalent Amounts
Fruit Group	2 cups (4 servings)	2 to 2.5 cups (4 to 5 servings)	$\frac{1}{2}$ cup equivalent is: • $\frac{1}{2}$ cup fresh, frozen, or canned fruit • 1 med fruit • $\frac{1}{4}$ cup dried fruit • $\frac{1}{2}$ cup fruit juice
Vegetable Group • Dark green vegetables • Orange vegetables • Legumes (dry beans) • Starchy vegetables • Other vegetables	2.5 cups (5 servings) 3 cups/week 2 cups/week 3 cups/week 3 cups/week 6.5 cups/week	2 to 2.5 cups (4 to 5 servings)	$\frac{1}{2}$ cup equivalent is: • $\frac{1}{2}$ cup of cut-up raw or cooked vegetable • 1 cup raw leafy vegetable • $\frac{1}{2}$ cup vegetable juice
Grain Group • Whole grains • Other grains	6 ounce-equivalents 3 ounce-equivalents 3 ounce-equivalents	6 to 8 ounce-equivalents (6 to 8 servings[c])	1 ounce-equivalent is: • 1 slice bread • 1 cup dry cereal • $\frac{1}{2}$ cup cooked rice, pasta, cereal • DASH: 1 oz dry cereal ($\frac{1}{2}$–$1\frac{1}{4}$ cup depending on cereal type—check label)
Meat and Beans Group	5.5 ounce-equivalents	6 ounces or less meats, poultry, fish 4 to 5 servings per week nuts, seeds, and legumes[d]	1 ounce-equivalent is: • 1 ounce of cooked lean meats, poultry, fish • 1 egg[e] • USDA: $\frac{1}{4}$ cup cooked dry beans or tofu, 1 Tbsp peanut butter, $\frac{1}{2}$ oz nuts or seeds • DASH: $1\frac{1}{2}$ oz nuts, 2 Tbsp peanut butter, $\frac{1}{2}$ oz seeds, $\frac{1}{2}$ cup cooked dry beans
Milk Group	3 cups	2 to 3 cups	1 cup equivalent is: • 1 cup low-fat/fat-free milk, yogurt • $1\frac{1}{2}$ oz of low-fat, fat-free, or reduced fat natural cheese • 2 oz of low-fat or fat-free processed cheese
Oils	27 grams (6 tsp)	8 to 12 grams (2 to 3 tsp)	DASH: 1 tsp equivalent is: • 1 tsp soft margarine • 1 Tbsp low-fat mayo • 2 Tbsp light salad dressing • 1 tsp vegetable oil

Discretionary Calorie Allowance
• Example of distribution:
   Solid fat[f]
   Added sugars
	
	267 calories
	18 grams
	8 tsp
		
		~2 tsp of added sugar (5 Tbsp per week)
			DASH: 1 Tbsp added sugar equivalent is:
			• 1 Tbsp jelly or jam
			• $\frac{1}{2}$ cup sorbet and ices
			• 1 cup lemonade

[a] All servings are per day unless otherwise noted. USDA vegetable subgroup amounts and amounts of DASH nuts, seeds, and dry beans are per week.
[b] The 2,000-calorie USDA Food Guide is appropriate for many sedentary males 51 to 70 years of age, sedentary females 19 to 30 years of age, and for some other gender/age groups who are more physically active. See table 3 for information about gender/age/activity levels and appropriate calorie intakes. See appendixes A-2 and A-3 for more information on the food groups, amounts, and food intake patterns at other calorie levels.
[c] Whole grains are recommended for most grain servings to meet fiber recommendations.
[d] In the DASH Eating Plan, nuts, seeds, and legumes are a separate food group from meats, poultry, and fish.
[e] Since eggs are high in cholesterol, limit egg yolk intake to no more than 4 per week; 2 egg whites have the same protein content as 1 oz of meat.
[f] The oils listed in this table are not considered to be part of discretionary calories because they are a major source of the vitamin E and polyunsaturated fatty acids, including the essential fatty acids, in the food pattern. In contrast, solid fats (i.e., saturated and trans fats) are listed separately as a source of discretionary calories.

- People who cannot drink milk because of allergies, cultural beliefs, or other reasons need to eat rich sources of calcium, vitamins A and D, potassium, and magnesium.
- Lactose intolerance causes some people to avoid milk because of discomfort from digestive problems. Lactose-reduced milk products, consumption of small amounts several times during the day, or taking a lactose-digesting enzyme before drinking or eating milk and milk products are techniques for consuming adequate quantities of milk and its nutrients without discomfort.

MYPYRAMID

MyPyramid
Visual developed by the USDA to be used as a teaching tool in nutrition education.

The U.S. Department of Agriculture developed **MyPyramid** as the visual to help people visualize the importance of a varied diet and exercise (Figure 2.1). This pyramid emphasizes the importance of activity by showing a figure climbing the steps from the left of the pyramid up toward the apex. The pyramid itself is comprised of multicolored stripes that are broad at the base and taper toward the top. Each stripe represents a food group, and the width of each stripe indicates the relative amount of each group that needs to be eaten daily. The grains group, the orange band on the left, is the widest. Next is the vegetable group, represented by a green stripe, then a red stripe for fruits, a very narrow yellow stripe for oils, a blue stripe for milk, and finally a purple stripe for meat and beans.

MyPyramid is available as an interactive website (www.MyPyramid.gov) that is designed so individuals can enter their information and obtain a diet plan tailored specifically to their age, sex, and activity level. The serving sizes and numbers of servings recommended for the groups are included in the plan. Although the basic plan for the day is described, individuals are to devise the actual menus for the day. This helps people develop meals that are nourishing and will help form permanent eating patterns that promote health.

NATIONAL VARIATIONS

Various countries around the world have developed visuals to use in communicating nutrition recommendations to their people.

- Canada has created a visual resembling half a rainbow with four colored bands: The outer yellow band depicts grain products, the next green-colored band is vegetables and fruits, next is the blue band representing milk products, and the innermost red band represents meats and alternatives (Figure 2.2).
- China has a five-tiered pagoda with cereals on the bottom, vegetables and fruits on the next level, then meat, poultry, fish, shrimp, and eggs at the middle level, then a layer of milk and milk products and bean and bean products next to the top, and fats and oils at the very top (Figure 2.3).
- Puerto Rico has developed its Piramide Alimentaria para Puerto Rico, a graphic that includes water in recognition of the need for it in the hot climate there (Figure 2.4).

These are but a few of the visuals used in other countries. The foods sketched in each of these visuals are foods typical of the country and consistent with the food patterns generally recommended in each country. Dietitians and other health professionals who are counseling people from other cultures about their diets and other aspects of meal management need to become familiar with the food practices of the cultural groups with whom they are working (McWilliams, 2007).

Although the specific foods selected and the graphic presentations of the recommendations differ among countries, certain basic concepts are common to the plans (Painter et al., 2002). Among these common concepts is the need for a comparatively

FIGURE 2.1   MyPyramid logo suggests exercise and food groups (grains, vegetables, fruits, milk, meat and beans), and oils on a daily basis.

Health   Santé
Canada   Canada

Grain Products
Choose whole grain
and enriched
products more often.

Vegetables and Fruit
Choose dark green and
orange vegetables and
orange fruit more often.

Milk Products
Choose lower-fat milk
products more often.

Meat and Alternatives
Choose leaner meats,
poultry and fish, as well
as dried peas, beans
and lentils more often.

FIGURE 2.2   Canada's Food Guide for Healthy Eating.

large amount of grains, and there is also a strong reliance on fruits and vegetables. Smaller amounts of foods from the meat group and also from milk and dairy are common concepts too.

DIETARY REFERENCE INTAKES

A key goal of menu planning is to include foods that will provide adequate amounts of all of the nutrients essential to meet the physical needs of the individual on a daily basis. The levels of the various nutrients needed by males and females of various ages have been studied extensively for many years, and tables of the recommendations have been

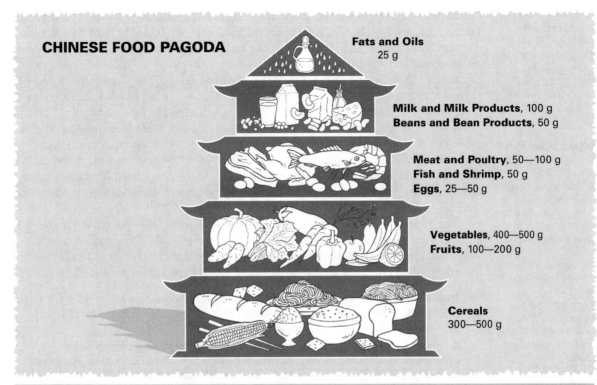

FIGURE 2.3 Food Guide Pagoda for Chinese Residents. Developed by the Chinese Nutrition Society. 1999.

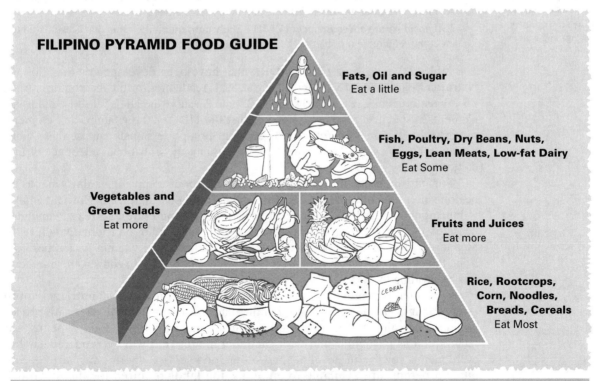

FIGURE 2.4 Pyramide Alimentaria para Puerto Rico. Developed by the University of Puerto Rico with the U.S. Department of Agriculture. 2nd ed. 1995.

issued periodically since 1941. The earlier tables were identified as the Recommended Dietary Allowances (RDA), commonly referred to as the RDA. In the 1990s, significant changes were initiated, however, and the terminology for the recommendations was modified and expanded.

Rather than delay the release of the revisions until all of the nutrients had been reviewed, values for various nutrients were released in a planned sequence as the reviews were completed. The first nutrients presented in the new format were calcium, phosphorus, magnesium, vitamin D, and fluoride. These values were made available in 1997. The B vitamin values (thiamin, riboflavin, niacin, vitamin B_6, folate, vitamin B_{12}, pantothenic acid, biotin, and choline) were released in the new format in 1998. In 2000, vitamins C and E, selenium, and the carotenoids were announced. Vitamins A and K, arsenic, boron, chromium, copper, iodine, iron, manganese, molybdenum, nickel, silicon, vanadium, and zinc recommendations were published in 2001.

These recent tables, which were developed under the guidance of the Food and Nutrition Board of the Institute of Medicine in the National Academies in Washington, are identified as Dietary Reference Intakes (DRI). These four terms have been defined carefully for use in clarifying the basis of the values presented in the tables:

- *Recommended Dietary Allowance* **(RDA)** — Average daily intake level that is sufficient to meet the nutrient requirement of nearly all (97 to 98 percent) healthy individuals in a particular life stage and gender group.
- *Adequate Intake* **(AI)** — The recommended intake value based on observed or experimentally determined approximations of estimates of nutrient intake by a group (or groups) of healthy people that are assumed to be adequate; used when an RDA cannot be determined.
- *Tolerable Upper Intake Level* **(UL)** — The highest level of daily nutrient intake that is likely to pose no risk of adverse health effects for almost all individuals in the general population. As intake increases above the UL, the potential risk of adverse effects increases.
- *Estimated Average Requirement* **(EAR)** — Daily nutrient intake value that is estimated to meet the requirement of half of the healthy people in a life stage and gender group.

Tables 2.3 and 2.4 present the DRIs that have been developed by the Food and Nutrition Board, Institute of Medicine, National Academies for the macronutrients and energy requirements, respectively. Tables 2.5 and 2.6 show the DRIs for the vitamins and elements, respectively. Tables 2.7 and 2.8 list the ULs for the vitamins and elements, respectively. Dietitians and other food and nutrition professionals can use these tables, particularly Tables 2.3, 2.4, 2.5, and 2.6, to evaluate the nutritional adequacy of their daily menus.

Comparison of the nutrients provided by the foods comprising a day's menus can be done after the nutrient analysis of the menus has been completed. Nutrient analysis is done using standard references in either print or computer formats (e.g., Pennington, 2007, or the USDA, Agricultural Research Service 2001 Nutrient Database for Standard Reference, Release 14). To interpret the intake of vitamin A as reported in some tables of food composition with the DRI, it is necessary to convert the number of IUs by dividing by 3.33.

If the menus planned for a day are low in any of the essential nutrients, appropriate changes can be incorporated in the plans to rectify inadequacies. This process is time-consuming, but is effective in ensuring nutritionally adequate menus. This technique has particular merit for planning menus that will be repeated, such as cycle menus for use in hospitals and other food service operations. Various computer programs are available to minimize the labor required for the nutritional analysis of menus.

TABLE 2.3   Dietary Reference Intakes (DRIs): Recommended Intakes for Individuals, Macronutrients

Food and Nutrition Board, Institute of Medicine, National Academies

Life Stage Group	Total Water[a] (L/d)	Carbohydrate (g/d)	Total Fiber (g/d)	Fat (g/d)	Linoleic Acid (g/d)	α-Linoleic Acid (g/d)	Protein[b] (g/d)
Infants							
0–6 mo	0.7*	60*	ND	31*	4.4*	0.5*	9.1*
7–12 mo	0.8*	95*	ND	30*	4.6*	0.5*	**11.0**[c]
Children							
1–3 y	1.3*	**130**	19*	ND	7*	0.7*	**13**
4–8 y	1.7*	**130**	25*	ND	10*	0.9*	**19**
Males							
9–13 y	2.4*	**130**	31*	ND	12*	1.2*	**34**
14–18 y	3.3*	**130**	38*	ND	16*	1.6*	**52**
19–30 y	3.7*	**130**	38*	ND	17*	1.6*	**56**
31–50 y	3.7*	**130**	38*	ND	17*	1.6*	**56**
51–70 y	3.7*	**130**	30*	ND	14*	1.6*	**56**
> 70 y	3.7*	**130**	30*	ND	14*	1.6*	**56**
Females							
9–13 y	2.1*	**130**	26*	ND	10*	1.0*	**34**
14–18 y	2.3*	**130**	26*	ND	11*	1.1*	**46**
19–30 y	2.7*	**130**	25*	ND	12*	1.1*	**46**
31–50 y	2.7*	**130**	25*	ND	12*	1.1*	**46**
51–70 y	2.7*	**130**	21*	ND	11*	1.1*	**46**
> 70 y	2.7*	**130**	21*	ND	11*	1.1*	**46**
Pregnancy							
14–18 y	3.0*	**175**	28*	ND	13*	1.4*	**71**
19–30 y	3.0*	**175**	28*	ND	13*	1.4*	**71**
31–50 y	3.0*	**175**	28*	ND	13*	1.4*	**71**
Lactation							
14–18 y	3.8*	**210**	29*	ND	13*	1.3*	**71**
19–30 y	3.8*	**210**	29*	ND	13*	1.3*	**71**
31–50 y	3.8*	**210**	29*	ND	13*	1.3*	**71**

Note: This table presents Recommended Dietary Allowances (RDAs) in **bold** *type and Adequate Intakes (AIs) in ordinary type followed by an asterisk (*). RDAs and AIs may both be used as goals for individual intake. RDAs are set to meet the needs of almost all (97 to 98 percent) individuals in a group. For healthy infants fed human milk, the AI is the mean intake. The AI for other life stage and gender groups is believed to cover the needs of all individuals in the group, but lack of data or uncertainty in the data prevent being able to specify with confidence the percentage of individuals covered by this intake.*
[a]Total water includes all water contained in food, beverages, and drinking water.
[b]Based on 0.8 g/kg body weight for the reference body weight.
[c]Change from 13.5 in prepublication copy due to calculation error.

Dietary Reference Intakes (DRIs): Additional Macronutrient Recommendations

Food and Nutrition Board, Institute of Medicine, National Academies

Macronutrient	Recommendation
Dietary cholesterol	As low as possible while consuming a nutritionally adequate diet
Trans fatty acids	As low as possible while consuming a nutritionally adequate diet
Saturated fatty acids	As low as possible while consuming a nutritionally adequate diet
Added sugars	Limit to no more than 25% of total energy

Source: Dietary Reference Intakes for Energy, Carbohydrate, Fiber, Fat, Fatty Acids, Cholesterol, Protein, and Amino Acids (2002).

TABLE 2.4 Dietary Reference Intakes (DRIs): Estimated Energy Requirements (EER) for Men and Women 30 Years of Age[a]

Food and Nutrition Board, Institute of Medicine, National Academies

Height (m [in])	PAL[b]	Weight for BMI[c] of 18.5 kg/m² (kg [lb])	Weight for BMI of 24.99 kg/m² (kg [lb])	EER, Men[d] (kcal/day) BMI of 18.5 kg/m²	BMI of 24.99 kg/m²	EER, Women[d] (kcal/day) BMI of 18.5 kg/m²	BMI of 24.99 kg/m²
1.50 (59)	Sedentary	41.6 (92)	56.2 (124)	1,848	2,080	1,625	1,762
	Low active			2,009	2,267	1,803	1,956
	Active			2,215	2,506	2,025	2,198
	Very active			2,554	2,898	2,291	2,489
1.65 (65)	Sedentary	50.4 (111)	68.0 (150)	2,068	2,349	1,816	1,982
	Low active			2,254	2,566	2,016	2,202
	Active			2,490	2,842	2,267	2,477
	Very active			2,880	3,296	2,567	2,807
1.80 (71)	Sedentary	59.9 (132)	81.0 (178)	2,301	2,635	2,015	2,211
	Low active			2,513	2,884	2,239	2,459
	Active			2,782	3,200	2,519	2,769
	Very active			3,225	3,720	2,855	3,141

[a]For each year below 30, add 7 kcal/day for women and 10 kcal/day for men. For each year above 30, subtract 7 kcal/day for women and 10 kcal/day for men.
[b]PAL = physical activity level.
[c]BMI = body mass index.
[d]Derived from the following regression equations based on doubly labeled water data:
   Adult man: EER = 662 − 9.53 × age (y) + PA × (15.91 × wt [kg] + 539.6 × ht [m])
   Adult woman: EER = 354 − 6.91 × age (y) + PA × (9.36 × wt [kg] + 726 × ht [m])
Where PA refers to coefficient for PAL

PAL = total energy expenditure + basal energy expenditure
   PA = 1.0 if PAL ≥ 1.0 < 1.4 (sedentary)
   PA = 1.12 if PAL ≥ 1.4 < 1.6 (low active)
   PA = 1.27 if PAL ≥ 1.6 < 1.9 (active)
   PA = 1.45 if PAL ≥ 1.9 < 2.5 (very active)

Dietary Reference Intakes (DRIs): Acceptable Macronutrient Distribution Ranges

Food and Nutrition Board, Institute of Medicine, National Academies

Macronutrient	Range (percent of energy) Children, 1–3 y	Children, 4–18 y	Adults
Fat	30–40	25–35	20–35
ω-6 polyunsaturated fatty acids[a] (linoleic acid)	5–10	5–10	5–10
ω-3 polyunsaturated fatty acids[a] (α-linolenic acid)	0.6–1.2	0.6–1.2	0.6–1.2
Carbohydrate	45–65	45–65	45–65
Protein	5–20	10–30	10–30

[a]Approximately 10% of the total can come from longer-chain n-3 or n-6 fatty acids.
Source: Dietary Reference Intakes for Energy, Carbohydrate, Fiber, Fat, Fatty Acids, Cholesterol, Protein, and Amino Acids (2002).

TABLE 2.5   Dietary Reference Intakes (DRIs): Recommended Intakes for Individuals, Vitamins
Food and Nutrition Board, Institute of Medicine, National Academie

Life Stage Group	Vit A (µg/d)[a]	Vit C (mg/d)	Vit D (µg/d)[b,c]	Vit E (mg/d)[d]	Vit K (µg/d)	Thiamin (mg/d)	Riboflavin (mg/d)	Niacin (mg/d)[e]	Vit B$_6$ (mg/d)	Folate (µg/d)[f]	Vit B$_{12}$ (µg/d)	Pantothenic Acid (mg/d)	Biotin (µg/d)	Choline[g] (mg/d)
Infants														
0–6 mo	400*	40*	5*	4*	2.0*	0.2*	0.3*	2*	0.1*	65*	0.4*	1.7*	5*	125*
7–12 mo	500*	50*	5*	5*	2.5*	0.3*	0.4*	4*	0.3*	80*	0.5*	1.8*	6*	150*
Children														
1–3 y	300	15	5*	6	30*	0.5	0.5	6	0.5	150	0.9	2*	8*	200*
4–8 y	400	25	5*	7	55*	0.6	0.6	8	0.6	200	1.2	3*	12*	250*
Males														
9–13 y	600	45	5*	11	60*	0.9	0.9	12	1.0	300	1.8	4*	20*	375*
14–18 y	900	75	5*	15	75*	1.2	1.3	16	1.3	400	2.4	5*	25*	550*
19–30 y	900	90	5*	15	120*	1.2	1.3	16	1.3	400	2.4	5*	30*	550*
31–50 y	900	90	5*	15	120*	1.2	1.3	16	1.3	400	2.4	5*	30*	550*
51–70 y	900	90	10*	15	120*	1.2	1.3	16	1.7	400	2.4[i]	5*	30*	550*
> 70 y	900	90	15*	15	120*	1.2	1.3	16	1.7	400	2.4[i]	5*	30*	550*
Females														
9–13 y	600	45	5*	11	60*	0.9	0.9	12	1.0	300	1.8	4*	20*	375*
14–18 y	700	65	5*	15	75*	1.0	1.0	14	1.2	400[i]	2.4	5*	25*	400*
19–30 y	700	75	5*	15	90*	1.1	1.1	14	1.3	400[i]	2.4	5*	30*	425*
31–50 y	700	75	5*	15	90*	1.1	1.1	14	1.3	400[i]	2.4	5*	30*	425*
51–70 y	700	75	10*	15	90*	1.1	1.1	14	1.5	400	2.4[h]	5*	30*	425*
> 70 y	700	75	15*	15	90*	1.1	1.1	14	1.5	400	2.4[h]	5*	30*	425*
Pregnancy														
14–18 y	750	80	5*	15	75*	1.4	1.4	18	1.9	600[j]	2.6	6*	30*	450*
19–30 y	770	85	5*	15	90*	1.4	1.4	18	1.9	600[j]	2.6	6*	30*	450*
31–50 y	770	85	5*	15	90*	1.4	1.4	18	1.9	600[j]	2.6	6*	30*	450*
Lactation														
14–18 y	1,200	115	5*	19	75*	1.4	1.6	17	2.0	500	2.8	7*	35*	550*
19–30 y	1,300	120	5*	19	90*	1.4	1.6	17	2.0	500	2.8	7*	35*	550*
31–50 y	1,300	120	5*	19	90*	1.4	1.6	17	2.0	500	2.8	7*	35*	550*

This table (taken from the DRI reports, see www.nap.edu) presents Recommended Dietary Allowances (RDAs) in **bold type** and Adequate Intakes (AIs) in ordinary type followed by an asterisk (*). RDAs and AIs may both be used as goals for individual intake. RDAs are set to meet the needs of almost all (97 to 98 percent) individuals in a group. For healthy breastfed infants, the AI is the mean intake. The AI for other life stage and gender groups is believed to cover needs of all individuals in the group, but lack of data or uncertainty in the data prevent being able to specify with confidence the percentage of individuals covered by this intake.

[a]*As retinol activity equivalents (RAEs). 1 RAE = 1 µg retinol, 12 µg β-carotene, 24 µg α-carotene, or 24 µg β-cryptoxanthin. The RAE for dietary provitamin A carotenoids is twofold greater than retinol equivalents (RE), whereas the RAE for preformed vitamin A is the same as RE.*
[b]*As cholecalciferol. 1 µg cholecalciferol = 40 IU vitamin D.*
[c]*In the absence of adequate exposure to sunlight.*
[d]*As α-tocopherol. α-Tocopherol includes RRR-α-tocopherol, the only form of α-tocopherol that occurs naturally in foods, and the 2R-stereoisomeric forms of α-tocopherol (RRR-, RSR-, RRS-, and RSS-α-tocopherol) that occur in fortified foods and supplements. It does not include the 2S-stereoisomeric forms of α-tocopherol (SRR-, SSR-, SRS-, and SSS-α-tocopherol), also found in fortified foods and supplements.*
[e]*As niacin equivalents (NE). 1 mg of niacin = 60 mg of tryptophan; 0–6 months = preformed niacin (not NE).*
[f]*As dietary folate equivalents (DFE). 1 DFE = 1 µg food folate = 0.6 µg of folic acid from fortified food or as a supplement consumed with food = 0.5 µg of a supplement taken on an empty stomach.*
[g]*Although AIs have been set for choline, there are few data to assess whether a dietary supply of choline is needed at all stages of the life cycle, and it may be that the choline requirement can be met by endogenous synthesis at some of these stages.*
[h]*Because 10 to 30 percent of older people may malabsorb food-bound B$_{12}$, it is advisable for those older than 50 years to meet their RDA mainly by consuming foods fortified with B$_{12}$ or a supplement containing B$_{12}$.*
[i]*In view of evidence linking folate intake with neural tube defects in the fetus, it is recommended that all women capable of becoming pregnant consume 400 µg from supplements or fortified foods in addition to intake of food folate from a varied diet.*
[j]*It is assumed that women will continue consuming 400 µg from supplements or fortified food until their pregnancy is confirmed and they enter prenatal care, which ordinarily occurs after the end of the periconceptional period—the critical time for formation of the neural tube.*

TABLE 2.6 Dietary Reference Intakes (DRIs): Recommended Intakes for Individuals, Elements

Food and Nutrition Board, Institute of Medicine, National Academies

Life Stage Group	Calcium (mg/d)	Chromium (µg/d)	Copper (µg/d)	Fluoride (mg/d)	Iodine (µg/d)	Iron (mg/d)	Magnesium (mg/d)	Manganese (mg/d)	Molybdenum (µg/d)	Phosphorus (mg/d)	Selenium (µg/d)	Zinc (mg/d)	Potassium (g/d)	Sodium (g/d)	Chloride (g/d)
Infants															
0–6 mo	210*	0.2*	200*	0.01*	110*	0.27*	30*	0.003*	2*	100*	15*	2*	0.4*	0.12*	0.18*
7–12 mo	270*	5.5*	220*	0.5*	130*	11	75*	0.6*	3*	275*	20*	3	0.7*	0.37*	0.57*
Children															
1–3 y	500*	11*	340	0.7*	90	7	80	1.2*	17	460	20	3	3.0*	1.0*	1.5*
4–8 y	800*	15*	440	1*	90	10	130	1.5*	22	500	30	5	3.8*	1.2*	1.9*
Males															
9–13 y	1,300*	25*	700	2*	120	8	240	1.9*	34	1,250	40	8	4.5*	1.5*	2.3*
14–18 y	1,300*	35*	890	3*	150	11	410	2.2*	43	1,250	55	11	4.7*	1.5*	2.3*
19–30 y	1,000*	35*	900	4*	150	8	400	2.3*	45	700	55	11	4.7*	1.5*	2.3*
31–50 y	1,000*	35*	900	4*	150	8	420	2.3*	45	700	55	11	4.7*	1.5*	2.3*
51–70 y	1,200*	30*	900	4*	150	8	420	2.3*	45	700	55	11	4.7*	1.3*	2.0*
>70 y	1,200*	30*	900	4*	150	8	420	2.3*	45	700	55	11	4.7*	1.2*	1.8*
Females															
9–13 y	1,300*	21*	700	2*	120	8	240	1.6*	34	1,250	40	8	4.5*	1.5*	2.3*
14–18 y	1,300*	24*	890	3*	150	15	360	1.6*	43	1,250	55	9	4.7*	1.5*	2.3*
19–30 y	1,000*	25*	900	3*	150	18	310	1.8*	45	700	55	8	4.7*	1.5*	2.3*
31–50 y	1,000*	25*	900	3*	150	18	320	1.8*	45	700	55	8	4.7*	1.5*	2.3*
51–70 y	1,200*	20*	900	3*	150	8	320	1.8*	45	700	55	8	4.7*	1.3*	2.0*
>70 y	1,200*	20*	900	3*	150	8	320	1.8*	45	700	55	8	4.7*	1.2*	1.8*
Pregnancy															
14–18 y	1,300*	29*	1,000	3*	220	27	400	2.0*	50	1,250	60	12	4.7*	1.5*	2.3*
19–30 y	1,000*	30*	1,000	3*	220	27	350	2.0*	50	700	60	11	4.7*	1.5*	2.3*
31–50 y	1,000*	30*	1,000	3*	220	27	360	2.0*	50	700	60	11	4.7*	1.5*	2.3*
Lactation															
14–18 y	1,300*	44*	1,300	3*	290	10	360	2.6*	50	1,250	70	13	5.1*	1.5*	2.3*
19–30 y	1,000*	45*	1,300	3*	290	9	310	2.6*	50	700	70	12	5.1*	1.5*	2.3*
31–50 y	1,000*	45*	1,300	3*	290	9	320	2.6*	50	700	70	12	5.1*	1.5*	2.3*

*This table presents Recommended Dietary Allowances (RDAs) in **bold type** and Adequate Intakes (AIs) in ordinary type followed by an asterisk (*). RDAs and AIs may both be used as goals for individual intake. RDAs are set to meet the needs of almost all (97 to 98 percent) individuals in a group. For healthy breastfed infants, the AI is the mean intake. The AI for other life stage and gender groups is believed to cover needs of all individuals in the group, but lack of data or uncertainty in the data prevent being able to specify with confidence the percentage of individuals covered by this intake.*

Sources: Dietary Reference Intakes for Calcium, Phosphorous, Magnesium, Vitamin D, and Fluoride (1997); Dietary Reference Intakes for Thiamin, Riboflavin, Niacin, Vitamin B₆, Folate, Vitamin B₁₂, Pantothenic Acid, Biotin, and Choline (1998); Dietary Reference Intakes for Vitamin C, Vitamin E, Selenium, and Carotenoids (2000); Dietary Reference Intakes for Vitamin A, Vitamin K, Arsenic, Boron, Chromium, Copper, Iodine, Iron, Manganese, Molybdenum, Nickel, Silicon, Vanadium, and Zinc (2001); and Dietary Reference Intakes for Water, Potassium, Sodium, Chloride, and Sulfate (2004). These reports may be accessed via http://www.nap.edu.

TABLE 2.7 Dietary Reference Intakes (DRIs): Tolerable Upper Intake Levels (UL[a]), Vitamins

Food and Nutrition Board, Institute of Medicine, National Academies

Life Stage Group	Vitamin A (μg/d)[b]	Vitamin C (mg/d)	Vitamin D (μg/d)	Vitamin E (mg/d)[c,d]	Vitamin K	Thiamin	Riboflavin	Niacin (mg/d)[d]	Vitamin B_6 (mg/d)	Folate (μg/d)[d]	Vitamin B_{12}	Pantothenic Acid	Biotin	Choline (g/d)	Carotenoids[e]
Infants															
0–6 mo	600	ND[f]	25	ND	ND	ND	ND	ND	ND	ND	ND	ND	ND	ND	ND
7–12 mo	600	ND	25	ND	ND	ND	ND	ND	ND	ND	ND	ND	ND	ND	ND
Children															
1–3 y	600	400	50	200	ND	ND	ND	10	30	300	ND	ND	ND	1.0	ND
4–8 y	900	650	50	300	ND	ND	ND	15	40	400	ND	ND	ND	1.0	ND
Males, Females															
9–13 y	1,700	1,200	50	600	ND	ND	ND	20	60	600	ND	ND	ND	2.0	ND
14–18 y	2,800	1,800	50	800	ND	ND	ND	30	80	800	ND	ND	ND	3.0	ND
19–70 y	3,000	2,000	50	1,000	ND	ND	ND	35	100	1,000	ND	ND	ND	3.5	ND
>70 y	3,000	2,000	50	1,000	ND	ND	ND	35	100	1,000	ND	ND	ND	3.5	ND
Pregnancy															
14–18 y	2,800	1,800	50	800	ND	ND	ND	30	80	800	ND	ND	ND	3.0	ND
19–50 y	3,000	2,000	50	1,000	ND	ND	ND	35	100	1,000	ND	ND	ND	3.5	ND
Lactation															
14–18 y	2,800	1,800	50	800	ND	ND	ND	30	80	800	ND	ND	ND	3.0	ND
19–50 y	3,000	2,000	50	1,000	ND	ND	ND	35	100	1,000	ND	ND	ND	3.5	ND

[a]UL = The maximum level of daily nutrient intake that is likely to pose no risk of adverse effects. Unless otherwise specified, the UL represents total intake from food, water, and supplements. Due to lack of suitable data, ULs could not be established for vitamin K, thiamin, riboflavin, vitamin B_{12}, pantothenic acid, biotin, carotenoids. In the absence of ULs, extra caution may be warranted in consuming levels above recommended intakes.

[b]As preformed vitamin A only.

[c]As α-tocopherol; applies to any form of supplemental α-tocopherol.

[d]The ULs for vitamin E, niacin, and folate apply to synthetic forms obtained from supplements, fortified foods, or a combination of the two.

[e]β-Carotene supplements are advised only to serve as a provitamin A source for individuals at risk of vitamin A deficiency.

[f]ND = Not determinable due to lack of data of adverse effects in this age group and concern with regard to lack of ability to handle excess amounts. Source of intake should be from food only to prevent high levels of intake.

Sources: Dietary Reference Intakes for Calcium, Phosphorous, Magnesium, Vitamin D, and Fluoride (1997); Dietary Reference Intakes for Thiamin, Riboflavin, Niacin, Vitamin B_6, Folate, Vitamin B_{12}, Pantothenic Acid, Biotin, and Choline (1998); Dietary Reference Intakes for Vitamin C, Vitamin E, Selenium, and Carotenoids (2000); and Dietary Reference Intakes for Vitamin A, Vitamin K, Arsenic, Boron, Chromium, Copper, Iodine, Iron, Manganese, Molybdenum, Nickel, Silicon, Vanadium, and Zinc (2001). These reports may be accessed via http://www.nap.edu. Copyright 2004 by the National Academy of Sciences. All rights reserved.

TABLE 2.8 Dietary Reference Intakes (DRIs): Tolerable Upper Intake Levels (UL[a]), Elements

Food and Nutrition Board, Institute of Medicine, National Academies

Life Stage Group	Arsenic[b]	Boron (mg/d)	Calcium (g/d)	Chromium	Copper (µg/d)	Fluoride (mg/d)	Iodine (µg/d)	Iron (mg/d)	Magnesium (mg/d)[c]	Manganese (mg/d)
Infants										
0–6 mo	ND[f]	ND	ND	ND	ND	0.7	ND	40	ND	ND
7–12 mo	ND	ND	ND	ND	ND	0.9	ND	40	ND	ND
Children										
1–3 y	ND	3	2.5	ND	1,000	1.3	200	40	65	2
4–8 y	ND	6	2.5	ND	3,000	2.2	300	40	110	3
Males, Females										
9–13 y	ND	11	2.5	ND	5,000	10	600	40	350	6
14–18 y	ND	17	2.5	ND	8,000	10	900	45	350	9
19–70 y	ND	20	2.5	ND	10,000	10	1,100	45	350	11
>70 y	ND	20	2.5	ND	10,000	10	1,100	45	350	11
Pregnancy										
14–18 y	ND	17	2.5	ND	8,000	10	900	45	350	9
19–50 y	ND	20	2.5	ND	10,000	10	1,100	45	350	11
Lactation										
14–18 y	ND	17	2.5	ND	8,000	10	900	45	350	9
19–50 y	ND	20	2.5	ND	10,000	10	1,100	45	350	11

[a]UL=The maximum level of daily nutrient intake that is likely to pose no risk of adverse effects. Unless otherwise specified, the UL represents total intake from food, water, and supplements. Due to lack of suitable data, ULs could not be established for arsenic, chromium, silicon, potassium, and sulfate. In the absence of ULs, extra caution may be warranted in consuming levels above recommended intakes.

[b]Although the UL was not determined for arsenic, there is no justification for adding arsenic to food or supplements.

[c]The ULs for magnesium represent intake from a pharmacological agent only and do not include intake from food and water.

[d]Although silicon has not been shown to cause adverse effects in humans, there is no justification for adding silicon to supplements.

[e] Although vanadium in food has not been shown to cause adverse effects in humans, there is no justification for adding vanadium to food and vanadium supplements should be used with caution. The UL is based on adverse effects in laboratory animals and this data could be used to set a UL for adults but not children and adolescents.

[f] ND = Not determinable due to lack of data of adverse effects in this age group and concern with regard to lack of ability to handle excess amounts. Source of intake should be from food only to prevent high levels of intake.

Sources: Dietary Reference Intakes for Calcium, Phosphorous, Magnesium, Vitamin D, and Fluoride (1997); Dietary Reference Intakes for Thiamin, Riboflavin, Niacin, Vitamin B$_6$, Folate, Vitamin B$_{12}$, Pantothenic Acid, Biotin, and Choline (1998); Dietary Reference Intakes for Vitamin C, Vitamin E, Selenium, and Carotenoids (2000); Dietary Reference Intakes for Vitamin A, Vitamin K, Arsenic, Boron, Chromium, Copper, Iodine, Iron, Manganese, Molybdenum, Nickel, Silicon, Vanadium, and Zinc (2001); and Dietary Reference Intakes for Water, Potassium, Sodium, Chloride, and Sulfate (2004). These reports may be accessed via http://www.nap.edu.

FOOD LABELING

Ingredient Labeling

Federal legislation requires ingredient labeling on all packaged foods and nutrition labeling on any of these foods that are meaningful sources of calories or nutrients or that make nutritional claims. Fresh produce or other foods sold from bins may be labeled in a location convenient to consumers. Regulations regarding specifications for the labeling are defined very specifically; the U.S. Food and Drug Administration (FDA) is the enforcing agency for most foods, although the USDA has authority on meat labeling.

Ingredient labels list the content of all food mixtures containing more than one ingredient. The listing begins with the ingredient that is present in the greatest amount

TABLE 2.8   Dietary Reference Intakes (DRIs): Tolerable Upper Intake Levels (UL), Elements

Molybdenum (µg/d)	Nickel (mg/d)	Phosphorus (g/d)	Potassium	Selenium (µg/d)	Silicon[d]	Sulfate	Vanadium (mg/d)	Zinc (mg/d)[e]	Sodium (g/d)	Chloride (g/d)
ND	ND	ND	ND	45	ND	ND	ND	4	ND	ND
ND	ND	ND	ND	60	ND	ND	ND	5	ND	ND
300	0.2	3	ND	90	ND	ND	ND	7	1.5	2.3
600	0.3	3	ND	150	ND	ND	ND	12	1.9	2.9
1,100	0.6	4	ND	280	ND	ND	ND	23	2.2	3.4
1,700	1.0	4	ND	400	ND	ND	ND	34	2.3	3.6
2,000	1.0	4	ND	400	ND	ND	1.8	40	2.3	3.6
2,000	1.0	3	ND	400	ND	ND	1.8	40	2.3	3.6
1,700	1.0	3.5	ND	400	ND	ND	ND	34	2.3	3.6
2,000	1.0	3.5	ND	400	ND	ND	ND	40	2.3	3.6
1,700	1.0	4	ND	400	ND	ND	ND	34	2.3	3.6
2,000	1.0	4	ND	400	ND	ND	ND	40	2.3	3.6

(by weight) and continues in descending order through all of the ingredients. Clarification of the reason for various additives is included on the ingredient label.

A few specific requirements need to be met when certain ingredients are used. For example, FDA-certified food color additives must be listed by name. Sources of protein hydrolysates must be listed. In foods (e.g., coffee whiteners) claiming to be nondairy but containing caseinate, the ingredient label must state that caseinate is a milk derivative.

BOX 2.1

Food Insights: Allergen Alert

In 2006, a new facet of ingredient labeling, allergen labeling, became a requirement because of cases involving serious health risks due to people ingesting food allergens. Proteins in milk, eggs, peanuts, tree nuts, fish, shellfish, soy, and wheat were the cause of the most serious allergic reactions among people with specific allergic sensitivities. This is why allergen labeling is required if any proteins from milk, eggs, peanuts, tree nuts (such as walnuts, cashews, almonds), fish (bass, cod, flounder), shellfish (crab, shrimp, lobster), soy, and wheat are in the food product. Allergens in food coloring, flavorings, or other additives also have to be listed by name to alert affected people to their presence.

After the listing of ingredients on the product label, there must be a statement "Contains (the name of the food source of the allergen)" either immediately below or adjacent to the ingredients, and the type size must be no smaller than the type size used for listing ingredients.

These specific items are required on the ingredient label if they are present because of their potential to harm consumers sensitive to them. To aid consumers in knowing how much of a beverage is fruit juice, the percentage of fruit juice must be stated on the label, and the product must be identified as being flavored with a juice when the actual juice is a minor constituent. As a further aid to consumers, the print size on food labels is mandated so it is large enough to be read easily.

Nutrition Labeling

Nutrition labeling appears on packages today in a specified format and is titled "Nutrition Facts." The format is prescribed very precisely, and terms are defined in relation to their use on the label (see Figure 2.5). Serving size, which is the first listing on the label, is defined in terms of a typical serving. Specifics are written to help all food manufacturers state the serving size using a consistent standard. This requirement is intended to avoid the confusion consumers had previously when manufacturers arbitrarily declared the serving size for their particular product package. Comparison between products previously was challenging for consumers. Standardized definitions of serving sizes for various food products today serve as a consumer aid and also as the basis for calculating the number of servings per container. However, many consumers glance at the calories in a serving and then choose to ignore the serving size indicated.

Daily Reference Values (DRV)
Values indicating precisely how much of each nutrient is required for a healthy person eating 2,000 calories in a day; established for nutrition information on food labels.

Nutrition information for labeling purposes is based on **Daily Reference Values** (DRV), values indicating precisely how much of each nutrient is required for a healthy

Nutrition Facts
Serving Size 1/2 cup (114g)
Servings Per Container 4

Amount Per Serving
Calories 260 Calories from Fat 120

	% Daily Value*
Total Fat 13g	**20%**
Saturated Fat 5g	**25%**
Cholesterol 30mg	**10%**
Sodium 660mg	**28%**
Total Carbohydrate 31g	**11%**
Sugars 5g	
Dietary Fiber 0g	**0%**
Protein 5g	

Vitamin A 4% • Vitamin C 2% • Calcium 15% • Iron 4%

* Percents (%) of a Daily Value are based on a 2,000 calorie diet. Your Daily Values may vary higher or lower depending on your calorie needs:

Nutrient		2,000 Calories	2,500 Calories
Total Fat	Less than	65g	80g
Sat Fat	Less than	20g	25g
Cholesterol	Less than	300mg	300mg
Sodium	Less than	2,400 mg	2,400mg
Total Carbohydrate		300g	375g
Fiber		25g	30g

1g Fat = 9 calories,
1g Carbohydrates = 4 calories
1g Protein = 4 calories

FIGURE 2.5 Example of the nutrition label required on food packages.

person eating 2,000 calories in a day. A fiber intake of 11.5 grams (g)/1,000 calories is recommended. DRVs for sources of calories each day are:

- Total fat: 30 percent
- Saturated fat: 10 percent
- Carbohydrate: 60 percent
- Protein: 10 percent

Nutritional information on a label is based on the amount of food designated as a serving. The number of calories provided by the defined serving is stated, with the calories from total fat (saturated, trans) being printed directly under the listing for calories. Other entries listed are cholesterol, sodium, potassium, total carbohydrate (dietary fiber, sugars), protein, vitamin A, vitamin C, calcium, and iron.

The weights (in grams or milligrams (mg)) of the nutrients are listed per serving, along with a listing of the % Daily Values. Calculations for the % Daily Values are based on a 2,000-calorie diet, using the DRVs, with the quantity of each nutrient being reported as the percentage of the day's DRV that a serving provided. Where space permits, labels may include a table showing the DRV for both a 2,000- and a 2,500-calorie diet.

Food packages may make nutrient content claims if products meet the required definitions. For example, foods can be labeled as "free" in terms of calories if they have less than 5 calories/labeled serving, "low" if 40 or less calories are in a reference amount, "reduced/less" if there are at least 25 percent fewer calories/reference amount than in an appropriate reference food, and "light" or "lite" if 50 percent or more of the calories are from fat and that fat is reduced at least 50 percent from the reference food.

Items can be labeled "free" in terms of fat if there is less than 0.5 g/reference amount and serving. "Low" in fat is defined as 3 g/serving; "reduced/less" can be used if the fat level is at least 25 percent less than the appropriate reference food. Terms for claims regarding saturated fat are "free" (<0.5 g saturated fat and <0.5 g trans-fatty acids/reference amount), "low" (1 g or less/reference amount and 15 percent or less of calories from saturated fat), and "reduced/less" (at least 25 percent less saturated fat/reference amount than in an appropriate reference food).

Foods may be labeled as sugar "free" (contain <0.5 g of sugar per labeled serving) or "reduced/less" (at least 25 percent less sugar per reference amount than an appropriate reference food). Definitions are also available for indicating modified levels of cholesterol and sodium.

Consumers can gain considerable insight into how well they are eating if they utilize all of the information that is available on food labels. The percentage of specific nutrients provided by the various food items eaten in a day can be added quickly to determine how close the total intake is to 100 percent of each of the nutrients. Persons who are trying to control their weight can add their total caloric intake each day and then identify some of the major sources of calories. After analyzing how well their diets are measuring up nutritionally, modifications can be implemented to improve them. The information on food labels not only helps draw attention to nutritional needs, but it also points the way to making wiser selections.

Health claims can be made on food products that meet the guidelines for their use. Among the claims that can be used at the present time on appropriate foods are messages drawing attention to the nutritional merits of the following:

- Calcium in relation to osteoporosis
- Fat and its potential role in cancer
- Saturated fat and cholesterol in relation to coronary heart disease (CHD)
- Fiber-containing grains and fruits and vegetables and their potential in protecting against cancer

- Possible relationships between sodium and hypertension
- Fruits and vegetables (particularly those high in vitamins A or C) and their possible role in protecting against cancer

These various claims are monitored carefully and can only be used when all requirements for their use are met. Health claims are useful to consumers who may not be aware of the potential merits of some of the foods that are able to carry these claims.

INTEGRATING NUTRITION INTO MENUS

Menus can be developed successfully using various approaches. Use of MyPyramid begins with finding the recommended intake of grains, vegetables, fruits, milk, and meat and beans for the consumer. Table 2.9 is the intake recommended for a 20-year-old woman who exercises between 30 and 60 minutes a day. Planning for this person's menus can begin with outlining the meals and snacks for the day and then allocating the recommended numbers of servings of each of the food groups in MyPyramid to the different meals and snacks (if any are to be eaten).

The equivalents of various foods in the different food groups are indicated in the details of MyPyramid. The basic information needed for menu planning includes:

Grains equivalent to 1 ounce:
1 slice bread
1 cup ready-to-eat cereal
1/2 cup cooked rice, cooked pasta, or cooked cereal

Vegetables equivalent to 1 cup:
1 cup raw or cooked vegetables or vegetable juice
2 cups raw leafy greens

Fruits equivalent to 1 cup:
1 cup fruit or 100% fruit juice
1/2 cup dried fruit

Milk equivalent to 1 cup:
1 cup milk or yogurt
1-1/2 ounces natural cheese
2 ounces processed cheese

Meat and beans equivalent to 1 ounce:
1 ounce meat, poultry, or fish
1/4 cup cooked dry beans
1 egg
1 tablespoon peanut butter
1/2 ounce nuts or seeds
An example of this basic distribution might be:

Break-fast	**Lunch**	**Dinner**	**Snacks**
1 cup fruit	1 cup vegetable	2 cups vegetables	1 cup fruit
2 ounces grains	2 ounces grains	3 ounces grains	
1 ounce meat/beans	2 ounces meat	3 ounces meat	
1 cup milk	1 cup milk	1 cup milk	

A quick check shows that this plan includes 7 ounces from the Grains Group, 3 cups from the Vegetable Group, 2 cups from the Fruit Group, 3 cups from the Milk Group; and 2 servings from the Meat and Beans Group. Obviously, other arrangements are possible too. However, this very rough outline of what is to be included in the

TABLE 2.9   MyPyramid daily dietary recommendations for female age 20

Food group	Amount
Grains	7 ounces
Vegetables	3 cups
Fruits	2 cups
Milk	3 cups
Meat and beans	6 ounces
Oils	6 teaspoons
Calories	2200

various meals provides assurance that the specific menus developed from this plan will contain the variety of foods and amounts of nutrients needed for good health if judicious choices are made and correct serving sizes are eaten.

The calorie content of menus based on these patterns will vary considerably, depending to a large extent on the amount of fat and the size of the servings. Specific recipe choices and quantities served need to be adapted to the people who will eat the food, but the goal of providing meals for good health requires that the planning incorporate ideas that assure appropriate nutrition each day.

The actual menus can be developed from this outline. Quick, simple menus might be similar to the ones shown here.

Breakfast	Lunch	Dinner	Snack
Orange juice (1 cup)	Tuna salad	Chicken and	Peach
Cornflakes (1 cup)	sandwich	vegetable stir-fry (3 ounces	
Toast (1 slice)	Carrot and celery	chicken, 1 cup mixed vegetables)	
Egg (1)	Sticks (1 cup)	Rice, cooked (1 cup) Dinner	
Fat-free milk (1 cup)	Fat-free milk (1 cup)	roll (1)	
		Green salad (1 cup)	
		Fat-free milk (1 cup)	

The serving sizes for these menus are planned to conform to the serving sizes specified in MyPyramid. This means that the sandwich consists of two slices of bread and the filling contains 2 ounces of tuna fish. Similarly, a serving of the stir-fry would include 3 ounces of chicken and 1 cup of assorted vegetables (perhaps summer squash, mushrooms, and bell peppers). The equivalent of 1 cup of carrot and celery sticks would be the lunch vegetable. Depending on the diner, there might be some sugar and milk (perhaps part of the cup of milk) added to the cereal at breakfast. The tuna salad sandwich probably would have some mayonnaise, lemon juice, and pickle relish in the filling, and a leaf of lettuce likely would be added for texture and color.

If these menus were calculated for comparison with the DRIs, all of these added ingredients would need to be calculated in addition to the items named in the menus to get a true picture of the actual nutrient intake for the day. Professionals responsible for planning menus for institutions, hospitals, or other large residential facilities need to check their plans with the accuracy afforded by using the DRIs.

Consumers can plan menus that are nutritionally appropriate by simply checking them against MyPyramid, monitoring serving sizes, and making wise choices to assure variety and an appropriate level of oils and fat. Table 2.10 presents sample menus for a week based on a 2,000-calorie food pattern. Table 2.11 presents the average intake of the various nutrients provided by the week's menus shown in Table 2.10.

TABLE 2.10 Sample Menus for a 2000 Calorie Food Pattern

DAY 1	DAY 2	DAY 3	DAY 4
Breakfast	**Breakfast**	**Breakfast**	**Breakfast**
Breakfast burrito	Hot cereal	Cold cereal	1 whole wheat English muffin
1 flour tortilla (7" diameter)	*1/2 cup cooked oatmeal*	*1 cup bran flakes*	*2 tsp soft margarine*
1 scrambled egg (in 1 tsp soft margarine)	*2 tbsp raisins*	*1 cup fat-free milk*	*1 tbsp jam or preserves*
1/3 cup black beans*	*1 tsp soft margarine*	*1 small banana*	*1 medium grapefruit*
2 tbsp salsa	*1/2 cup fat-free milk*	*1 slice whole wheat toast*	*1 hard-cooked egg*
1 cup orange juice	*1 cup orange juice*	*1 tsp soft margarine*	*1 unsweetened beverage*
1 cup fat-free milk		*1 cup prune juice*	
Lunch	**Lunch**	**Lunch**	**Lunch**
Roast beef sandwich	Taco salad	Tuna fish sandwich	White bean-vegetable soup
1 whole grain sandwich bun	*2 ounces tortilla chips*	*2 slices rye bread*	*1 1/4 cup chunky vegetable soup*
3 ounces lean roast beef	*2 ounces ground turkey,*	*3 ounces tuna (packed in water,*	*1/2 cup white beans**
2 slices tomato	*sauteed in*	*drained)*	*1 ounce breadstick*
1/4 cup shredded romaine lettuce	*2 tsp sunflower oil*	*2 tsp mayonnaise*	*8 baby carrots*
1/8 cup sauteed mushrooms	*1/2 cup black beans**	*1 tbsp diced celery*	*1 cup fat-free milk*
(in 1 tsp oil)	*1/2 cup iceberg lettuce*	*1/4 cup shredded*	
1/2 ounce part-skim mozzarella cheese	*2 slices tomato*	*romaine lettuce*	
1 tsp yellow mustard	*1 ounce low-fat cheddar cheese*	*2 slices tomato*	
3/4 cup baked potato wedges*	*2 tbsp salsa*	*1 medium pear*	
1 tbsp catsup	*1/2 cup avocado*	*1 cup fat-free milk*	
1 unsweetened beverage	*1 tsp lime juice*		
	1 unsweetened beverage		
Dinner	**Dinner**	**Dinner**	**Dinner**
Stuffed broiled salmon	Spinach lasagna	Roasted chicken breast	Rigatoni with meat sauce
5 ounce salmon filet	*1 cup lasagna noodles, cooked*	*3 ounces boneless skinless*	*1 cup rigatoni pasta (2 ounces*
1 ounce bread stuffing mix	*(2 oz dry)*	*chicken breast**	*dry)*
1 tbsp chopped onions	*2/3 cup cooked spinach*	*1 large baked sweet potato*	*1/2 cup tomato sauce tomato bits**
2 tsp canola oil	*1/2 cup ricotta cheese*	*1/2 cup peas and onions*	*2 ounces extra lean cooked ground*
1/2 cup saffron (white) rice	*1/2 cup tomato sauce tomato bits**	*1 tsp soft margarine*	*beef (sauteed in 2 tsp vegetable oil)*
1 ounce slivered almonds	*1 ounce part-skim mozzarella cheese*	*1 ounce whole wheat dinner roll*	*3 tbsp grated Parmesan cheese*
1/2 cup steamed broccoli	*1 ounce whole wheat dinner roll*	*1 tsp soft margarine*	Spinach salad
1 tsp soft margarine	*1 cup fat-free milk*	*1 cup leafy greens salad*	*1 cup baby spinach leaves*
1 cup fat-free milk		*1/2 ounce chopped walnuts*	*1/2 cup tangerine slices*
Snacks	**Snacks**	**Snacks**	**Snacks**
1 cup cantaloupe	*1/2 ounce dry-roasted almonds**	*1/4 cup dried apricots*	*1 cup low-fat fruited yogurt*
	1/4 cup pineapple	*1 cup low-fat fruited yogurt*	
	2 tbsp raisins		

DAY 5

Breakfast

Cold cereal
- 1 cup puffed wheat cereal
- 1 tbsp raisins
- 1 cup fat-free milk
- 1 small banana
- 1 slice whole wheat toast
- 1 tsp soft margarine
- 1 tsp jelly

Lunch

Smoked turkey sandwich
- 2 ounces whole wheat pita bread
- 1/4 cup romaine lettuce
- 2 slices tomato
- 3 ounces sliced smoked turkey breast*
- 1 tbsp mayo-type salad dressing
- 1 tsp yellow mustard
- 1/2 cup apple slices
- 1 cup tomato juice*

Dinner

Grilled top loin steak
- 5 ounces grilled top loin steak
- 3/4 cup mashed potatoes
- 2 tsp soft margarine
- 1/2 cup steamed carrots
- 1 tbsp honey
- 2 ounces whole wheat dinner roll
- 1 tsp soft margarine
- 1 cup fat-free milk

Snacks
- 1 cup low-fat fruited yogurt

DAY 6

Breakfast

French toast
- 2 slices whole wheat French toast
- 2 tsp soft margarine
- 2 tbsp maple syrup
- 1/2 medium grapefruit
- 1 cup fat-free milk

Lunch

Vegetarian chili on baked potato
- 1 cup kidney beans*
- 1/2 cup tomato sauce w/ tomato tidbits*
- 3 tbsp chopped onions
- 1 ounce lowfat cheddar cheese
- 1 tsp vegetable oil
- 1 medium baked potato
- 1/2 cup cantaloupe
- 3/4 cup lemonade

Dinner

Hawaiian pizza
- 2 slices cheese pizza
- 1 ounce canadian bacon
- 1/4 cup pineapple
- 2 tbsp mushrooms
- 2 tbsp chopped onions

Green salad
- 1 cup leafy greens
- 3 tsp sunflower oil and vinegar dressing
- 1 cup fat-free milk

Snacks
- 5 whole wheat crackers*
- 1/8 cup hummus
- 1/2 cup fruit cocktail (in water or juice)

DAY 7

Breakfast

Pancakes
- 3 buckwheat pancakes
- 2 tsp soft margarine
- 3 tbsp maple syrup
- 1/2 cup strawberries
- 3/4 cup honeydew melon
- 1/2 cup fat-free milk

Lunch

Manhattan clam chowder
- 3 ounces canned clams (drained)
- 3/4 cup mixed vegetables
- 1 cup canned tomatoes*
- 10 whole wheat crackers*
- 1 medium orange
- 1 cup fat-free milk

Dinner

Vegetable stir-fry
- 4 ounces tofu (firm)
- 1/4 cup green and red bell peppers
- 1/2 cup bok choy
- 2 tbsp vegetable oil
- 1 cup brown rice
- 1 cup lemon-flavored iced tea

Snacks
- 1 ounce sunflower seeds*
- 1 large banana
- 1 cup low-fat fruited yogurt

---

* Starred items are foods that are labeled as no-salt-added, low-sodium, or low-salt versions of the foods. They can also be prepared from scratch with little or no added salt. All other foods are regular commercial products which contain variable levels of sodium. Average sodium level of the 7 day menu assumes no-salt-added in cooking or at the table

TABLE 2.11 Nutrients Provided by Menus in Table 2.10.

Nutrient	Daily Average Over One Week
Calories	1994
Protein, g	98
Protein, % kcal	20
Carbohydrate, g	264
Carbohydrate, % kcal	53
Total fat, g	67
Total fat, % kcal	30
Saturated fat, g	16
Saturated fat, % kcal	7.0
Monounsaturated fat, g	23
Polyunsaturated fat, g	23
Linoleic Acid, g	21
Alpha-linolenic Acid, g	1.1
Cholesterol, mg	207
Total dietary fiber, g	31
Potassium, mg	4715
Sodium, mg*	1948
Calcium, mg	1389
Magnesium, mg	432
Copper, mg	1.9
Iron, mg	21
Phosphorus, mg	1830
Zinc, mg	14
Thiamin, mg	1.9
Riboflavin, mg	2.5
Niacin Equivalents, mg	24
Vitamin B6, mg	2.9
Vitamin B12, mcg	18.4
Vitamin C, mg	190
Vitamin E, mg (ΛT)	18.9
Vitamin A, mcg (RAE)	1430
Dietary Folate Equivalents, mcg	558

Starred items are foods that are labelled as no-salt-added, low-sodium, or low-salt versions of the foods. They can also be prepared from scratch with little or no added salt. All other foods are regular commercial products which contain variable levels of sodium. Average sodium level of the 7 day menu assumes no-salt-added in cooking or at the table.

Summary

Various tools are available to aid in planning nutritionally adequate menus. The *Dietary Guidelines for Americans* released in 2005 are designed to help consumers eat a diet that will promote growth for children and good health for people of all ages. It provides a food guide and many suggestions to aid in making appropriate choices for controlling weight and creating nourishing diets.

MyPyramid is an educational tool designed to aid consumers in choosing diets that provide appropriate amounts of all of the essential nutrients (proteins, fats, carbohydrates, vitamins, and minerals) needed for optimum growth and health. Information about serving sizes and some specifics within food groups is included.

The Dietary Reference Intakes (DRI) tables are used extensively by dietitians and other professionals responsible for planning menus that promote good health and provide the essential nutrients in appropriate amounts. Food labeling provides accurate information on ingredients and nutrient content in a standard, simple format. The nutrient values stated in labels are based on Daily Reference Values (DRVs).

Study Questions

1. How can you use the *Dietary Guidelines for Americans* when conducting a program to help consumers make wise food choices?
2. Based on MyPyramid, what are the recommended servings for each of the food groups that you should eat daily?
3. Are DRIs and DRVs used in the same way? If not, explain how and why each is used.
4. How can an overweight person use MyPyramid to achieve a healthy weight over a period of time?
5. How can MyPyramid be used when planning a day's menus for a person who is accustomed to eating foods typical of another culture?
6. Plan a day's menus that fit your cultural background and also conform to MyPyramid.
7. Compare the ingredient and nutrition labels on two different brands of a comparable product (e.g., macaroni and cheese). How would the information on these labels aid consumers in their choice between the two items?
8. Plan a lunch menu for a 22-year-old man who came from Taiwan to California two years ago. What factors did you consider in your plans?

Suggested Websites

http://www.usda.gov/cnpp/pyramid.html
Information on MyPyramid and historical perspective on the previous Food Guide Pyramid.

http://www.healthierus.gov/dietaryguidelines/
Dietary Guidelines for Americans 2005.

http://www.nal.usda.gov/fnic/foodcomp/search/
USDA nutrient database.

http://www.mypyramid.gov/
MyPyramid logo and guidelines for use.

http://www.mypyramidtracker.gov/
Program for monitoring personal dietary and physical behaviors.

http://fycs.ifas.ufl.edu/pyramid/index.htm
Supplemental MyPyramid materials developed by faculty at the University of Florida/IFAS Department of Family, Youth and Community Sciences.

http://www.cfsan.fda.gov/dms/flg-toc.html/
Federal guide to food labeling.

Bibliography

Barr, S. I., et al. 2002. Interpreting and using the Dietary Reference Intakes in dietary assessment of individuals and groups. *J. Am. Dietet. Assoc.* 102 (6): 780.

Chinese Nutrition Society. 2000. Dietary Guidelines and the Food Guide Pagoda. *J. Am. Dietet. Assoc.* 100 (8): 886.

Clemens, R., et al. 2005. MyPyramid adds new dimension to food guidance. *Food Technol.* 59 (6): 18.

Davis, T., and Reinhardt, W. 2005. Dietary Guidelines: Where food science and nutrition converge. *Food Technol.* 59 (3): 20.

Fiore, P. 2006. Consumers want clarity in labeling. *Food Technol.* 60 (6): 136.

Institute of Medicine. 1997. *Dietary Reference Intakes for Calcium, Phosphorus, Magnesium, Vitamin D, and Fluoride.* Food and Nutrition Board. National Academy Press. Washington, DC.

Institute of Medicine. 1998. *Dietary Reference Intakes for Thiamin, Riboflavin, Niacin, Vitamin B₆, Folate, Vitamin B₁₂, Pantothenic Acid, Biotin, and Choline.* Food and Nutrition Board. National Academy Press. Washington, DC.

Institute of Medicine. 2000. *Dietary Reference Intakes for Vitamin C, Vitamin E, Selenium, and Carotenoids.* Food and Nutrition Board. National Academy Press. Washington, DC.

Institute of Medicine. 2001. *Dietary Reference Intakes for Vitamin A, Vitamin K, Arsenic, Boron, Chromium, Copper, Iodine, Iron, Molybdenum, Nickel, Silicon, Vanadium, and Zinc.* Food and Nutrition Board. National Academy Press. Washington, DC.

Johnson, R. K., Frary, C., and Wang, M. Q. 2002. Nutritional consequences of flavored-milk consumption by school-aged children and adolescents in the United States. *J. Am. Dietet. Assoc.* 102 (6): 853.

McWilliams, M. 2007. *Food Around the World: A Cultural Perspective.* 2nd ed. Prentice Hall. Upper Saddle River, NJ.

Monsen, E. R. 2000. Dietary Reference Intakes for the antioxidant nutrients: Vitamin C, vitamin E, selenium, and carotenoids. *J. Am. Dietet. Assoc.* 100 (6): 637.

Painter, J., et al. 2002. Comparison of international food guide pictorial representations. *J. Am. Dietet. Assoc.* 102 (4): 483.

Pennington, J., et al. 2007. *Bowes and Church's Food Values of Portions Commonly Served.* Williams and Wilkins. Philadelphia.

Stables, G. J., et al. 2002. Changes in vegetable and fruit consumption and awareness among US adults: Results of 1991 and 1997, 5-A-Day for Better Health Program surveys. *J. Am. Dietet. Assoc.* 102 (6): 809.

Trumbo, P., et al. 2001. Dietary Reference Intakes: Vitamin A, vitamin K, arsenic, boron, chromium, copper, iodine, iron, manganese, molybdenum, nickel, silicon, vanadium, and zinc. *J. Am. Dietet. Assoc.* 101 (3): 294.

U.S. Department of Agriculture and U.S. Department of Health and Human Services. 2005. *Dietary Guidelines for Americans.* 6th ed. U.S. Government Printing Office. Washington, DC.

CHAPTER 3
Menu Planning

FACTORS

Menus are easy to read when they are finished, but the process of planning a menu requires consideration of several key factors. Even before starting the actual planning of a menu, some basic questions need to be answered. The answers then shape the rest of the planning process. Professionals planning menus for restaurants, hospitals, and other commercial situations have a challenging task, but menu planning for families and individuals may seem even more daunting because the process can appear never-ending.

The key factors to consider in menu planning include:

- Type of menu being planned
    Cycle
    Single use
    Static
- People being served
    Cultural or ethnic background
    Religious dietary considerations
    Ages
    Health conditions
- Resources available
    Economics
    Time
    Energy
    Equipment
- Nutritive value
- Food selection
    Color
    Flavor
    Aroma
    Texture
    Temperature
    Size and shape
    Availability
    Interest (variety and creativity)

The first three of these factors (type of menu, people being served, and resources available) are ones that need to be analyzed before beginning menu planning for commercial food service or in the home, but the specific characteristics identified for that particular setting usually do not change much from day to day. The other two factors (nutritive value and food selection) need to be considered each time a menu is being planned.

Creativity and aesthetic awareness are qualities that are real assets to menu planners. The items included in menus are influenced greatly by these characteristics. They help keep menus interesting and stimulating rather than dutiful and boring.

Type of Menu

Cycle Menu

Cycle Menu
Menu plan for a specified period of time and then followed repeatedly.

Cycle menus are daily menus that are written to span a designated number of days before being in the same sequence again and again, perhaps with minor adjustments to handle varying availability and the cost of foods at different times. Food services in schools, hospitals, or other institutions responsible for feeding groups of people continually use cycle menus. They also can be used as the basis for menu planning in the home.

The number of days planned in cycle menus may be determined by the person planning the menus or by the organization where they are to be used. Some institutions may wish to have a two-week cycle; others may prefer a longer cycle. Longer cycles are less repetitious because there is a long period between the reappearance of each menu (Table 3.1), but they require a greater initial effort to develop. Once a cycle menu has been planned and implemented, the time required for adjusting specific items to meet a particular problem is minimal.

In the long run, cycle menus are very useful and convenient management tools. The individual meal menus, each of the recipes required to prepare the meal, the market order for all of the ingredients, the nutritional analysis, time charts for preparation, and costs can all be compiled on a computer file for easy retrieval the next time the meal appears in the menu cycle. Few management decisions are needed when the specific meal is on the agenda.

Families may find it convenient to keep similar records of the meals that are served over a two-week period or a month. Where time is a major problem and food is not of critical significance to their feeling of well-being, a shorter cycle can be used, although some menus may become all too familiar. Other families may welcome the challenge of planning meals on a daily or weekly basis. Some keep records of the menus served each day, others may retain a record of menus and recipes served to guests, and others begin the menu planning afresh each time. There is more opportunity for individual approaches in family situations than when planning for an institution.

Single-Use Menus

Single-Use Menu
Menu planned for one specific occasion.

Single-use menus are planned for a specific circumstance and are not intended to become a part of a pattern of menus being served on a rotating basis. This type of menu often is used in planning for special events, such as a banquet or wedding. Families who are wishing to entertain friends with a lovely meal at home usually plan a single-use menu. If the menu produces a particularly pleasing event, families may wish to keep a record of the menu and recipes so the meal can be repeated at some future time, perhaps for other guests or as a special treat for themselves.

Thanksgiving dinner is an opportunity to plan a special menu that will illustrate a single-use menu. Many people have traditions they enjoy for this festive meal; others may enjoy creating a unique menu unencumbered by memories of holidays past. Regardless of the route to be followed in planning, the menu likely will be more elaborate than the usual dinner. Here is an example of a menu for this holiday meal:

THANKSGIVING DINNER
Cream of Pumpkin Soup
Roast Turkey and Holiday Stuffing
Candied Yams Flamed with Bourbon Sauce
Petite Peas and Boiling Onions
Grapefruit and Avocado Salad with Cranberry Dressing
Butterhorn Rolls Butter
Apple Pie Coffee

Static Menu

Static Menu
Type of restaurant menu offering some choices but not varied from day to day.

Some restaurants use a different type of menu, a **static menu**. The same menu choices are included each day, although special dishes may be added to attract diners who are interested in items beyond the regular set menu. A static menu is an efficient approach for restaurants. Menus can be printed for continuing use, and all of the subtleties of

TABLE 3.1 Cycle Menu for a Nursery School

Day	Week 1	Week 2	Week 3	Week 4
Monday	Cheese & Rice Casserole Green Beans Celery Stuffed with Peanut Butter Enriched Toast, Butter Apple Crisp Milk	Hamburger Stew (with Potato) Celery Sticks, Carrot Sticks Green Beans Whole-Wheat Toast Oatmeal Cookies Milk	Cheese & Ground Beef Pizza Buttered Corn Fresh Fruit Salad Ice Cream Milk	Frankfurters Stuffed with Cheese Buttered Rice Spinach Ice Cream & Bananas Milk
Tuesday	Porcupine Meat Balls Corn Fresh Fruit Enriched Toast, Butter Chocolate Pudding Milk	Spanish Rice with Bacon Chips Broccoli Deviled Egg Whole-Wheat Toast Angel Food Cake Milk	Swedish Meat Balls Mashed Potato, Milk Gravy Broccoli Garlic Bread Fresh Green Grapes Milk	Tuna Salad Vegetable Relish Plate, Lima Beans Cottage Cheese & Pineapple Salad Rolled-Wheat Muffins Butterscotch Pudding & Banana Milk
Wednesday	Spaghetti & Meat Sauce Buttered Broccoli Carrot Sticks Enriched Toast, Butter Pears Milk	Liver Strips Sauté Parsley Potatoes Buttered Carrots Fresh Fruit Rolled-Wheat Cookies Milk	Oven-Fried Chicken Creamed Rice, Green Beans Raw Cabbage Wedges Corn Bread Melon Milk	Roast Turkey Southern Spoon Bread Carrot Sticks, Brussels Sprouts Whole-Wheat Toast Sticks Watermelon Milk
Thursday	Beef Stew Noodles Sweet-Sour Green Beans Fresh Fruit Salad Oatmeal Cookies Milk	Ham Rice Pilaf Buttered Peas, Tomato Wedges Whole-Wheat Toast Fruit Gelatin Milk	Split-Pea Soup with Ham Fresh Fruit Salad Rolled-Wheat Muffins Baked Custard Brownies Milk	Beef Loaf Mashed Potato with Milk Gravy Buttered Peas Stuffed Celery Fresh Green Grapes Milk
Friday	Scrambled Eggs Oven-Browned Potatoes Brussels Sprouts, Stewed Apricots Whole-Wheat Toast Gingerbread Milk	Beef & Cheese Enchilada Spinach Tomato Wedges Whole-Wheat Toast Ice Cream, Ginger Cookies Milk	Fish Sticks Stir-Fried Cabbage Jellied Carrot & Pineapple Salad Toast Triangles Rolled-Wheat Spice Bars Milk	Baked Halibut Noodles au Gratin, Green Beans Carrot & Raisin Salad Whole-Wheat Toast Sticks Fresh Fruit Milk

preparation and service of the food can be controlled to achieve the optimum result. This approach is possible in restaurants because they serve a varied clientele rather than always serving the same population.

Such menu listings on a restaurant's static menu might include:

- New York steak (broiled to order), baked potato, and mixed baby vegetables
- Halibut steak (coated with macadamia nuts and panko Japanese-style coarse bread crumbs) and mixed baby vegetables
- Pacific salmon with dill sauce, saffron rice, and zucchini/mushroom medley

People Being Served

The cultural heritage of people for whom the menus are being planned needs to be considered so at least some familiar foods will be served. Although many people are willing to try new dishes, they still enjoy eating familiar foods too. Background information regarding the cultures represented in a dining facility can be obtained from simple observation or from records. Of course, families are well aware of their heritage when they are planning menus.

The increasing diversity in the United States has expanded the foods being served at home and throughout the food service industry. This has resulted in greater demand for relatively convenient access to the special ingredients that are essential to various Asian, Latin American, African, and Middle Eastern dishes (Figure 3.1). Asian markets stock the sauces (e.g., soy, teriyaki), spices (Chinese five-spice powder is one of the essential spices), as well as seaweed of various types, fish and fish products, and other ingredients needed to prepare ethnic dishes typical of that part of the world. Middle Eastern markets stock such items as bulgur, eggplant, couscous, lamb and ground lamb, chick peas, sesame oil, phyllo dough, pistachios, and garlic. Many regular markets stock

FIGURE 3.1   Some ingredients for cuisines of other cultures often can be found in local supermarkets.

TABLE 3.2   Possible Food Prohibitions Affecting Menu Planning

Food	Possible Religious Prohibition				
	Hinduism	**Buddhism**	**Judaism**	**Islam**	**Seventh-Day Adventist**
Beef	X				X
Pork	X	X	X	X	X
Alcohol				X	X
Nonkosher			X[a]		

[a]Prohibited if practicing the dietary requirements of kashruth.

fresh tortillas, taco and enchilada sauces, jicama, plantains, various types of dried beans, rice, cornmeal, greens, okra, black-eyed peas, pork products, and other ingredients needed to make Latin American and African recipes.

Whether planning menus for guests at home or in commercial food operations, any special dictates based on religion need to be considered (Table 3.2). Variations that might be necessary include vegetarian menus (some Hindus, Buddhists, and Seventh-Day Adventists) and avoidance of beef (Hindus) and pork (Jews and Muslims). When preparing meals for Orthodox Jews, kosher ingredients and special facilities, including separate sets of dishes for dairy foods and meats, are essential.

The ages of the diners may also influence menus. For example, menus for lunches at a nursery school are quite different in sophistication from those that might be served in a college dormitory or a corporate dining room. A menu planned for a dinner that will include as guests a family with preschool children, their parents, and a grandparent will need to include foods that are easy for the children to eat with minimum assistance and also at least one dish that will be especially pleasing to the adults.

Food allergies and special dietary needs of diners also influence menu planning. If these problems are known, menus can be planned to avoid problem foods. However, people with these problems need to assume some responsibility for avoiding the foods they know may trigger difficulties. People planning menus may not always be aware of individual problems. Dietitians are responsible for planning and supervising meal service for hospital patients on special diets.

Resources Available

Money

Economics clearly is an important factor in menu planning. In any commercial operation, food costs play a critical role in staying within the budget or making a profit rather than sustaining a loss. Similarly, family meals can vary widely in their cost, depending on the money available for food. Each month the USDA calculates the cost of food for individuals of various ages and for families of two or four who are eating at home (Table 3.3). Four expense levels are presented: thrifty, low cost, moderate, and liberal.

The estimated cost for the liberal plan is not quite twice as much as is stated for the thrifty plan. Families with limited resources who are trying to follow the thrifty plan can stretch their buying power through using food stamps and carefully planning menus that focus on relatively inexpensive ingredients. If more money is available, the possible choices for a menu are increased. Although some families can afford to plan menus without thinking about cost, the price of ingredients is something that usually needs to be considered, whether planning for commercial or family meals.

Control of food costs begins with the menu plan; marketing decisions also are a critical factor, and even food handling to minimize waste plays a role in keeping food expenses as low as possible. Menus based on less expensive cuts of meat can be as

TABLE 3.3   Official USDA Food Plans: Cost of Food at Home at Four Levels, U.S. Average, August 2006[1]

Age-Gender Groups	Weekly Cost[2]				Monthly Cost[2]			
	Thrifty plan	Low-cost plan	Moderate-cost plan	Liberal plan	Thrifty plan	Low-cost plan	Moderate-cost plan	Liberal plan
Individuals[3] Child:								
1 year	18.00	22.90	26.60	31.80	78.10	99.10	115.10	137.90
2 years	18.10	22.60	26.80	32.50	78.60	97.90	116.20	140.70
3–5 years	20.10	24.90	30.70	37.00	87.00	107.90	132.90	160.10
6–8 years	25.50	33.80	41.80	48.80	110.30	146.50	181.00	211.50
9–11 years	30.00	38.10	48.60	56.70	129.80	165.20	210.50	245.60
Male:								
12–14 years	31.10	43.10	53.20	62.90	134.90	186.90	230.40	272.70
15–19 years	32.40	44.60	55.20	64.30	140.30	193.40	239.30	278.50
20–50 years	34.50	44.20	54.90	67.20	149.40	191.50	237.90	291.10
51 years and over	31.10	41.80	51.60	62.20	134.80	181.30	223.60	269.50
Female:								
12–19 years	31.00	37.20	44.90	54.40	134.20	161.10	194.50	235.90
20–50 years	31.10	38.40	46.80	60.30	134.60	166.60	203.00	261.40
51 years and over	30.30	37.20	46.30	55.60	131.40	161.20	200.70	241.10
Families: Family of 2[4]								
20–50 years	72.10	90.80	111.90	140.20	312.40	393.50	485.00	607.70
51 years and over	67.60	86.90	107.70	129.60	292.90	376.70	466.70	561.60
Family of 4: Couple, 20–50 years and children—								
2 and 3–5 years	103.80	130.10	159.20	196.90	449.60	563.60	690.00	853.30
6–8 and 9–11 years	121.00	154.50	192.10	233.00	524.10	699.40	832.30	1009.50

[1] *Basic is that all meals and snacks are purchased at stores and prepared at home. For specific foods and quantities of foods in the Thrifty Food Plan, see family Economics and Nutrition Review, Vol. 13, No.1 (2001), pp. 50–64; for specific foods and quantities of foods in the Low-Cost, Moderate-Cost, and Liberal Plans, see The Low-Cost, Moderate-Cost, and Liberal Food Plans, 2003 Administrative Report (2003). All four Food Plans are based on 1989–91 data and are updated to current dollars using the Consumer Price Index for specific food items.*
[2] *All costs are rounded to nearest 10 cents.*
[3] *The costs given are for individuals in 4-person families. For individuals in other size families, the following adjustments are suggested: 1-person— add 20 percent; 2-person—add 10 percent; 3-person—add 5 percent; 4-person—no adjustment; 5- or 6-person—subtract 5 percent; 7- (or more) person—subtract 10 percent. To calculate overall household food costs, (1) adjust food costs for each person in household and then (2) sum these adjusted food costs.*
[4] *Ten percent added for family size adjustment.*
This file may be accessed on CNPP's home page at: http://www.cnpp.usda/gov

pleasing as premium cuts if they are prepared well. When possible, fruits and vegetables in season should be included in menus because their quality will be at the peak, and the cost will be relatively low. Unless time restrictions do not allow, preparation of recipes using basic ingredients can save money, improve quality, and be healthier because of the ability to reduce the salt and fat content.

Menu planning based on the thrifty food plan is particularly challenging. Careful attention to economies in the choice of all items is needed. Store brands and specials often save money. Quantities to buy are also part of the equation. Food waste needs to be minimized by buying only the quantity that will be used before it spoils. For example, leftovers planned from one meal need to be incorporated into another menu within a day or two, and prompt refrigeration must occur to assure food safety. Table 3.4 presents menus planned by the USDA to fit into its recommendations for the thrifty food plan. The shopping list for these menus for a family of four is shown in Table 3.5.

Time is a driving force in many people's lives today, so it consequently plays a significant role in determining menus, particularly for those during the work week. A

TABLE 3.4 Week I. Menus for a Family of Four

	Monday	Tuesday	Wednesday	Thursday	Friday	Saturday	Sunday
Breakfast	Orange juice (3 c) Ready-to-eat cereal (3 c flakes) Toasted English muffin (4) 1% lowfat milk (2 c)	Orange juice (3 c) Banana (4) Bagel (4) Margarine (4 tsp) 1% lowfat milk (2 c)	Orange juice (3 c) **Cooked rice cereal Bagel (4) Margarine (4 tsp)	Orange juice (3 c) Scrambled eggs (4) Hash brown potatoes (2 c) 1% lowfat milk (2 c)	Orange juice (3 c) Ready-to-eat cereal (3 c flakes) English muffin (4) Margarine (4 tsp) 1% lowfat milk (2 c)	Orange juice (3 c) *Baked French toast Cinnamon sugar topping (4 tsp) 1% lowfat milk (2 c)	Orange juice (3 c) *Baked potato cakes White toast (4 slices) 1% lowfat milk (2 c)
Lunch	*Turkey patties Hamburger bun (4) Orange juice (3 c) Coleslaw (2 c) 1% lowfat milk (2 c)	*Crispy chicken **Potato salad ***Orange gelatin salad Peaches, canned (1 c) **Rice pudding	**Turkey chili Macaroni (2 c) *Peach-apple crisp 1% lowfat milk (2 c) Orange juice (3 c)	Turkey ham (11 oz, 2 tbsp salad dressing) sandwiches (4) **Baked beans Banana, slices (2 c) **Oatmeal cookies Orange juice (3 c) 1% lowfat milk (2 c)	**Potato soup Snack crackers, low salt (5 each) *Tuna pasta salad Orange slices (2 c) **Oatmeal cookies 1% lowfat milk (2 c)	**Potato soup Snack crackers, low salt (5 each) Apple orange slices (2 apples, 2 oranges) (2 c) **Rice pudding 1% lowfat milk (2 c)	Baked fish (12 oz, 4 tbsp salad dressing) sandwiches (4) *Crispy potatoes **Macaroni salad Melon (1–1/3 c) Orange juice (3 c) 1% lowfat milk (2 c)
Dinner	**Beef-noodle casserole Lima beans (2 c) Banana orange salad (2 bananas, 2 oranges) (2 c) 1% lowfat milk (2 c)	*Turkey stir fry Steamed rice (3 c) White bread (4 slices) *Peach-apple crisp 1% lowfat milk (2 c)	**Baked cod w/cheese *Scalloped potatoes Spinach (1–1/3 c) Margarine (4 tsp) Chocolate pudding (2 c)	*Beef pot roast Egg noodles (4 c) Peas and carrots (1 c) Orange slices (2 c) Biscuits (8) Margarine (4 tsp) **Rice pudding 1% lowfat milk (2 c)	Beef pot roast (12 oz) Noodles (4 c) Green beans (1–1/3 c) Leaf lettuce (1–1/3 c) Salad dressing (4 tbsp) **Rice pudding 1% lowfat milk (2 c)	*Saucy beef pasta White bread (4) Canned pears (2 c) Orange juice (3 c) 1% lowfat milk (2 c)	*Turkey-cabbage casserole (8 c) Orange slices (2 c) White bread (2 slices) **Chickpea dip 1% lowfat milk (2 c)
Snack	White bread (4 slices) **Chickpea dip Lemonade (4 c)	Orange juice (3 c) *Crispy potatoes		Lemonade (4 c)	Biscuits (8) Margarine (4 tsp) Lemonade (4 c)	Lemonade (4 c)	

*Recipes were tested and sensory-evaluated in the food laboratory and by households.

**Recipes were tested and sensory-evaluated in the food laboratory.

Note: Daily menus are designed in no specific sequence. Amounts of foods that a family is expected to use are shown in parentheses for most foods. **Amounts of allowed margarine and milk can be combined or divided differently at meals.** Recipes are provided for foods shown with asterisks. Serving sizes are shown on the recipes.

48

TABLE 3.5   Week 1: Food for a Family of Four[1]

Fruits and Vegetables
Fresh[2]:

Apples	(6 small) 1 lb 8 oz
Bananas	(11 medium) 2 lb 12 oz
Melon	1 lb
Oranges	(26 small) 5 lb 7 oz
Cabbage	4 oz
Carrots	1 lb 4 oz
Celery	3 oz
Green pepper	3 oz
Lettuce, leaf	4 oz
Onions	2 lb 8 oz
Potatoes	11 lb 14 oz
Zucchini	7 oz

Canned:

Applesauce	2 oz
Peaches	1 lb 10 oz
Pears	13 oz
Green beans	12 oz
Spinach	10 oz
Tomato paste	6 oz
Tomato sauce	1 lb 1 oz
Tomato soup	10.5 oz

Frozen:

Orange juice, concentrate	8 12-oz cans
Green beans	5 oz
Peas	5 oz

Breads, Cereals, and Other Grain Products

Bagels, plain, enriched	(8) 1 lb
Bread crumbs	2 oz
Bread, white, enriched	2.2 lb
English muffins	8
French bread, enriched	8 oz
Hamburger buns, enriched	8
Crackers, snack, low salt	4 oz
Oatmeal, quick, rolled oats	3 oz
Ready-to-eat cereal (flakes)	6 oz
Barley, pearl	4 oz
Flour, enriched	1 lb 8 oz
Macaroni, enriched	1 lb 11 oz
Noodles, enriched	2 lb 3 oz
Rice, enriched	2 lb 5 oz

Milk and Cheese

Evaporated milk	16 fl oz
Milk, 1% lowfat	2 1/2 gal
Milk, whole	3 qt
Cheddar cheese	8 oz

Meat and Meat Alternates

Beef chuck roast	2.5 lb
Beef, ground, lean	2.4 lb
Chicken, fryer	1.5 lb

(continued)

TABLE 3.5 (continued)

Fish

Breaded portions, frozen	1 lb
Cod, frozen	1 lb
Tuna fish, chunk-style, water-pack	12 oz
Turkey breast	2 lb 4 oz
Turkey, ground	2 lb
Turkey ham (deli)	11 oz
Beans, kidney, canned	1 lb 11 oz
Beans, lima, dry	6 oz
Beans, northern, canned	9 oz
Beans, garbanzo (chickpeas), canned	10 oz
Eggs, large	16

Fats and Oils

Margarine, stick	7 oz
Shortening	2 oz
Salad dressing, mayonnaise-type	1 lb
Vegetable oil	9 fl oz

Sugars and Sweets

Sugar, brown	2 oz
Sugar, granulated	1 lb
Chocolate pudding, instant	3 oz
Lemonade (ready-to-drink)	1 gal

Other Food Items[3]

Baking powder
Baking soda
Beef bouillon cubes
Black pepper, red pepper
Catsup
Chicken bouillon cubes
Chili powder
Cinnamon
Cornstarch
Cumin
Dry mustard
Gelatin, unflavored
Lemon juice, bottled
Onion powder
Oregano
Paprika
Parsley flakes
Salt
Soy sauce
Sweet pickle relish
Vanilla
Vinegar

[1]*Provides food for a family of four. Amounts of food shown are for foods actually used during the week.*
[2]*Substitute other fruits or vegetables in season that contain similar nutrients if they are better buys.*
[3]*Small amounts used in preparing recipes and other foods in the menus and recipes; purchase as needed.*

time-saving strategy used by some is to plan menus in which some foods for the week can be prepared ahead on the weekend. Some may plan meals that require little preparation and cooking time. Others may rely heavily on frozen entrées or other items requiring only reheating. Food manufacturers are developing and marketing many packaged items that can be ready in a matter of minutes to meet the demand for foods that save time.

Energy, whether human or from power companies, is another aspect involved in menu planning. Foods prepared from basic ingredients require more energy to produce in the home than do items that are purchased ready-to-eat. However, the cost for many foods purchased in prepared form is higher, which works against keeping food costs as low as possible. Another disadvantage for some is the limit imposed on their creativity. If a menu includes a baked item, other foods might also be baked in the oven to save on power costs. An example is a meal featuring meat loaf, baked potatoes, and winter squash.

If special equipment is needed to prepare a particular recipe, that equipment needs to be available. Otherwise, a different preparation may need to be planned. For instance, a special menu featuring whole lobsters might require the purchase of a very large pot to cook the lobsters, or a brunch in which Belgian waffles are planned might trigger the purchase of the appropriate waffle iron. Unfortunately, such items may be used only rarely, but they still require storage space. Different menu choices can avoid such problems.

Nutritive Value

Optimal nutrition clearly needs to be a priority in planning menus. To achieve this objective, it may be convenient to start by structuring the day's overall servings of grains, vegetables, fruits, milk, and meats and beans according to MyPyramid. Specific menu items can then be identified for each of these servings, keeping in mind that variety helps provide a wider intake of nutrients to help ensure adequate levels of all of them. Attention should be given to including fish and poultry and to limiting red meats. Oils need to be included, but in small amounts for frying, in salad dressings, and perhaps in place of butter with bread. Whole-grain products are also recommended to enhance nutritive value.

Dietitians and other professionals responsible for planning meals in institutions, school food service, and other commercial sites evaluate nutritional aspects of menus using the DRI and guidelines required by funding agencies. The menus planned for each day should provide adequate amounts of all of the DRIs. However, excessive amounts of energy nutrients should be avoided. The suggested pattern of 10 percent of the calories from protein, 30 percent maximum from fat (10 percent maximum from saturated fats), and the remaining 60 percent from carbohydrates (minimal amounts from sugars) can serve as a useful tool in checking menus.

The burgeoning problem of overweight and obesity among people of all ages in the United States dictates that particular care be given to planning menus that satisfy appetites and provide eating pleasure without excessive calories. That is a tall order, but tempting, comparatively low-calorie menus can be created to help people modify their dietary patterns to gradually achieve a healthful weight.

Preparation techniques, such as poaching and steaming, can be planned for menu items to reduce the amount of fat added during cooking. Lemon zest, fresh herbs, and appropriate spices can add considerable interest to many menu items without adding calories and often can replace rich sauces that might otherwise be served. Using fat-free milk and reduced-fat dairy products can be another means of reducing calories. These are only some of the ways to help limit calorie content to healthful levels in meals.

BOX 3.1

Food Insights: Sweetening via Research

Xylitol is an alcohol that can be used as a sweetener but without the caloric price tag that sugars carry. Agricultural research chemist Badal Saha has genetically engineered a benign strain of *Escherichia coli* that can feast on the hemicellulose in corn stalks to make xylitol from the xylose and arabinose in the hemicellulose. Purification of the product results in a white crystalline powder suitable for sweetening such items as chewing gum and toothpaste. This beneficial action of a useful strain of *E. coli* presents quite a contrast to the lethal impact of *E. coli*.

Individuals need to assume responsibility for the quantities they eat at meals and also for their snacking habits if weight control is to be achieved.

Food Selection

Color

Food provides an excellent opportunity to create artistic effects. Color is an essential part of a beautiful meal. When making choices for a menu, visualize the actual appearance of the plates when the various items are served. Color changes that occur during cooking must be anticipated because the diner sees only the finished product, not the original colors of ingredients. The main concern for color choices involves foods that will be served at the same course in a meal. The colors of these foods should add visual excitement to each course, either as a result of the foods themselves or through a colorful garnish or other touch of color.

Fruits and vegetables are the foods providing the richest sources of color. Such a riot of color may be created with fruit or vegetable salads that a unifying focal point may be needed. For example, the shell of half a grapefruit (Figure 3.2) can be used to

FIGURE 3.2 The shells of citrus fruits make attractive and colorful holders for fruit salad.

hold a serving of mixed fresh fruit salad, or perhaps a thin ring of green pepper might serve as a unifying garnish atop a colorful carrot and cabbage salad.

More often, the problem may be a lack of color. Meats usually add only a limited amount of color. This becomes a particular problem if the plates are white, especially if the meat is white (sliced turkey, for instance). If such a menu also includes mashed potatoes or rice, and cooked cauliflower, the meal will be dull and unappealing because of the lack of color. Offering a choice of other items can be one way of adding color (e.g., perhaps sweet potatoes rather than white potatoes, or a colorful mixture of vegetables to replace the white cauliflower).

A colorful garnish such as a radish rose or carrot curls can be used to add color to a plate. These and other garnishes require preliminary preparation, but then they can be added quickly on the plate at the time the meal is being served. Other colorful vegetable garnishes are wedges of tomato, minced tops of green onions, or chopped chives, cilantro, or parsley.

Examples of fruit garnishes include candied kumquat (particularly pleasing with ham), spiced crabapples, and cinnamon apple rings. Thin slices of oranges or lemons can be cut from the center through the rind and then twisted to create a very colorful garnish that requires almost no time to prepare.

Hard-cooked eggs can be used as a garnish by slicing them crosswise and arranging them on potato salad (Figure 3.3) or other suitable dish, crumbling the yolk to brighten the top of a fresh spinach salad, or deviling them and serving as a garnish to a chilled vegetable salad. Still other color accents can be added by garnishing with such items as grated or crumbled cheeses, chopped pimiento, sliced stuffed or black olives, and bacon bits.

When planning menus, garnishes should be considered as ways of adding color to a meal. Touches such as these can elevate food from a subsistence level to a creative experience. The potential artistic contribution of garnishes should not be ignored.

Flavor

Good menu planning requires that a variety of flavors be included to excite the palate. A range of flavors from delicate to intense, with perhaps a suggestion of sweet to a sour and/or slightly salty taste, can add to the appeal of a meal. A dinner featuring a zesty barbecue sauce on the meat gains equilibrium in the mouth when accompanied by steamed rice.

Monotony in flavors comes from combining similar flavors or from lack of flavor highlights. A menu that includes two or more vegetables with common flavor tones (e.g., cabbage, cauliflower, broccoli, and Brussels sprouts) loses interest due to a lack of variety of flavors. Sometimes the addition of citrus zest or a little fresh basil or other herb can lift the flavor profile dramatically. The key to remember is that a variety of compatible flavors leads to an exciting dining experience.

Aroma

The aroma of foods is experienced first in the nasal passages, and then it combines with taste sensations in the mouth to result in the flavors that are experienced when a food is eaten. Aromas are released into the air while foods are being heated. Many aromas are tantalizing to diners, but certain strong odors may alienate some people. The aromas of a meal should mingle to stimulate appetites. The impact of aromas is part of the pleasure of a fine meal. Aroma is a factor that can be used to add interest to a meal. However, its impact may be less dramatic than that achieved by the effective choices of colors in a menu.

FIGURE 3.3 Sliced hard-cooked egg and paprika are easy and attractive ways to garnish potato salad.

Temperature

Temperature variations in a meal contribute interest in mouth feel (Figure 3.4). Some people like the variety of having some foods served hot and some cold in the same meal. A dessert of a fruit sorbet can be just the right antidote to a hot Thai entrée, for example. Weather may also influence the temperatures that are pleasing in a meal. Particularly on cold winter days, a hot meal can help chase away the chill, whereas a well-chilled salad may be the right choice on a sizzling summer day. Serve hot items on heated plates and cold ones on chilled dishes to achieve the maximum effect of temperature that foods can provide.

Temperature interest can be added through seasonings, as well as through heating or chilling foods. Very spicy, highly seasoned foods, particularly those containing irritants such as the ones found in hot chilies, give a sensation of heat in the mouth independent of the serving temperature of the food. A dollop of sour cream, some yogurt, or sherbet can help quench the burn in the mouth.

Texture

Texture is a term that includes a range of physical characteristics experienced when food is in the mouth. This quality of food is referred to as "mouth feel." Some of the adjectives appropriate to describing mouth feel include crisp, chewy, rubbery, smooth, grainy, viscous, brittle, fibrous, coarse, tender, and tough. Some of these convey positive attributes; others have negative connotations.

FIGURE 3.4   A chilled soup with a feathery garnish of dill weed provides a pleasing temperature contrast on a warm day.

When considering textures in menu planning, emphasize the positive aspects. The person preparing the food is responsible for maintaining the desired positive qualities. This is illustrated by the fact that boiled cabbage texture can range from very crisp to mushy, depending on how long it is cooked.

As is true with other sensory aspects of menu planning, creating a variety of texture is a useful means of adding to the interest of a meal. Methods used in preparing foods contribute to texture. A breaded, fried fish has a very different mouth feel than one that has been poached. Sliced almonds or other nuts can be added to heighten textural contrast. Raw fruits and vegetables or a bread with a crisp crust are other ways of adding a variety of textures within a meal.

Size and Shape

If all of the foods served in a meal are approximately the same size or shape, a meal has less visual appeal than if there is a bit of variety. Visualize a plate bearing a breast of chicken, an artichoke, and a baked potato to begin to appreciate the need for contrast in size and shape. At the other end of the spectrum from this plate of three very large units might be a plate with only small pieces (e.g., creamed chicken on rice, diced carrots, and buttered peas). Good menu planning provides a focal point on the plate and complements this feature with contrasting shapes and/or sizes. Food on the plate should present a unified, pleasing design rather than having items competing for attention.

Some foods can be prepared in a variety of shapes to suit the particular needs of a meal; others cannot be modified (Figure 3.5). A carrot is an example of a very versatile food that can be altered in size and shape. However, a T-bone steak demands its space. When a menu contains a large food with a fixed shape, the rest of the menu needs to be planned to enhance the appearance of the fixed piece. With T-bone steak, ranch beans or other small items can be served to help avoid adding to the massive feeling of the large steak. Another option is to serve the large piece with a small garnish on the main plate and serve the vegetables in side dishes.

FIGURE 3.5 Avocado slices arranged to create a rhythmic focal point in this salad demonstrate one of the artistic ways that avocados can be cut to add interest to foods.

Variety of shape is important for eye appeal. The choices when serving corn range from serving corn on the cob to kernels or scalloped corn in a casserole. Vegetables and fruits that are large enough to be cut in a variety of ways afford wonderful opportunities for varying size and shape in meals. Pineapple provides an outstanding example of the variety possible with large fresh produce items. For a fruit salad, pineapple can be cut in half or in quarters that can serve as boats for the salads after the interior fruit is removed and cut into pieces to be part of the fruit salad. Pineapple also can be sliced horizontally into rings, spears, chunks, tidbits, or even grated, depending on the requirements of the menu.

Availability

The food planned in a menu must be available. Fresh fruits and vegetables are sold at far more reasonable prices when they are in season than when they are out of season and only available as costly imports. Good and economical menu planning is based on prominent use of these crops when they are in season because they will be of high quality and at competitive prices.

Many foods are available throughout the year, so availability is not an issue. However, unique ingredients required for preparing some foreign recipes may be difficult to find in some markets. If such menus are being planned, the availability of ingredients needs to be checked early in the planning stage.

Variety and Creativity

Creative menu planning is the key to creating interesting, pleasing meals. Even outstanding menus, however, should be served only occasionally. Many different menus are needed to sustain high-quality meals, whether in commercial establishments or in the home. Different foods can be combined to expand the variety in menus. Foreign dishes can

FIGURE 3.6   Cookbooks and food magazines are valuable resources to use when planning menus.

be featured in some menus occasionally to broaden dining pleasures. Unique ways of preparing or of seasoning familiar ingredients can be incorporated in meal plans.

Fortunately, many sources of ideas for planning menus offer considerable variety and pleasure while also allowing people to eat for good health. The world seems to have an insatiable appetite for cookbooks, which means that new cookbooks are arriving in bookstores every week, and some of the old standards continue to be revised to fit the current tastes of consumers. If a selection of good cookbooks is at hand when you plan menus, ideas will seem to cascade from the pages as you thumb through them. Magazines featuring food and entertaining are other timely sources of ideas and recipes to help stimulate menu planning (Figure 3.6).

The Internet is another convenient source of menus and recipes. Various sites can be visited to acquire recipes, menus, and even shopping lists. Computer users can also build their own files of menus, recipes, and shopping lists as they create, prepare, and evaluate different meals over a period of time. These personal files can be reviewed quickly for successful plans, which may trigger some new ideas or may be used in their original form occasionally.

DEFINING THE SITUATION

Menu planning can be done effectively when the situation in which the meals are to become reality is known. The intended audience for the meals, the kitchen and dining facilities and personnel, and the resources available are all part of the parameters defining the success of the actual menus. Answers to the following questions can provide the context for menu planning.

BOX 3.2

Food Insights: Meals Out of This World

Consider the challenge of planning a meal to be eaten in the International Space Center. The basic problems of packaging for dining in a gravity-free environment and assuring food safety have been the subject of considerable research for many years, but the foods astronauts eat in space are not exactly what we might desire for a gourmet dinner. The French, who have long had the reputation of creating and appreciating fine food, have now turned their attention to improving dining in space. French chef Alain Ducasse created a menu of roasted quails in wine sauce, caponata (peppers, tomatoes, and zucchini with Sicilian seasonings), celery root puree seasoned with nutmeg, rice pudding, and fruit. Dining appears to be climbing to a new level in outer space. That menu would be a treat even for us earthlings.

AUDIENCE

Before actually starting to plan specific menus, be sure to identify some basics regarding the people who will be served. Answer each of the following questions:

1. How many people are to be served?
2. What are their approximate ages?
3. What cultures are represented?
4. Are there special needs (e.g., weight control, dietary restrictions or prohibitions)?

KITCHEN AND DINING FACILITIES

Kitchen equipment and layout need to be suitable so the food planned for a meal can actually be prepared effectively. Tableware needs to be available to meet the requirements of the menu. Consider:

1. What equipment limitations exist (e.g., ovens, refrigerators, counter space)?
2. What serving limitations exist (e.g., dishes, flatware, glassware)?

RESOURCES

Questions regarding cost of food, preparation, service, and cleanup include:

1. How much time is available for food preparation, service, and cleanup?
2. What budget is available for these meals?
3. What people are available to prepare the food?
4. What people will do the service and cleanup?

With the answers to these questions held firmly in mind, you can develop appropriate menu plans. These basic questions apply whether menus are being planned for families or for institutional food service. Obviously, the situations defined by the answers will differ widely for different menu planning assignments, and the resulting menus also will reflect these differences.

STRUCTURING THE PLAN

Now it is time to begin the actual planning process. The assignment may be to plan menus for a complete cycle menu (perhaps only a week, but probably two weeks or longer). Family menu plans can be made most efficiently by planning menus for a week and then shopping once a week, although some people prefer to plan a day or two at a

Meal	Sunday	Monday	Tuesday	Wednesday	Thursday	Friday	Saturday
Breakfast							
Fruit							
Grain							
Protein							
Beverage							
Lunch							
Entrée							
Veg/fruit							
Dessert							
Beverage							
Dinner							
Entrée							
Starch							
Vegetable							
Salad							
Bread							
Dessert							
Beverage							

FIGURE 3.7   Suggested format for planning menus for a week.

time. A chart showing each of the days and each of the meals to be planned on each day can serve as the overall planning tool (Figure 3.7).

Prior to actually selecting items for menus, it is helpful to check newspaper ads to spot food items that are being featured for the weekend sales. Specials usually can provide significant savings when they are incorporated into the week's menus. Other ideas can be triggered by a quick review of some cookbooks, the food section of the newspaper, food articles in magazines, or websites on menu planning.

An efficient way of planning is to start with the main meal of the day, which usually is dinner. The entrée is the focal point and also usually the most expensive item in that meal, so a decision on this item is the logical first step. The entrée can be planned for each dinner throughout the week and then reviewed to be sure there is variety in the preparation and kind of meat or meat substitute from day to day. Frequent use of poultry, fish, and legumes can help control food costs while promoting good health. The fat content of menus can be kept rather low by choosing recipes that minimize frying and limit the use of sauces and gravies that add fat to the entrée. Planning for portions that provide about 3 ounces of cooked meat or the equivalent is another useful way of limiting fat intake and also controlling cost.

If menus are being planned for lunch as well as dinner, the main course for lunch is the next item to be decided each day. Usually, this choice is less expensive than the one chosen for dinner. Hearty soups, perhaps a casserole that includes chunks of meat or fish, or a sandwich are some of the possibilities to provide a good source of protein at lunch.

The next item to be planned on each of the dinner and lunch menus is a complex carbohydrate or starch. Appropriate choices might include various potato preparations, sweet potatoes, pastas, rice, polenta, bulgur, and couscous. The choice for a specific menu should be based on its compatibility with the entrée. Bread items also need to be stated in the menu plan.

Vegetables can then be chosen for lunch and dinner menus. Variety in the choice and preparation of vegetables is important so meals afford color and flavor interest. Textures also can be varied by sometimes serving appropriate vegetables raw. Mixtures of vegetables can be used very effectively in meals that feature a simple entrée and starch choices. Some menus may be planned with more than one vegetable as part of the main course, but one vegetable may be sufficient if a salad is part of the menu.

Sometimes fruits may be served to accompany an entrée (e.g., applesauce with pork). Salads also may feature colorful fruits. The sweetness of most fruits makes them good choices for dessert, either alone or in combinations, such as in pies or other baked desserts.

Dessert is the last recipe item to be planned. In view of the immensity of the weight control problem confronting many people in the United States, this part of the menu could be eliminated for most meals. If this solution seems too spartan, a small serving of unsweetened fruit would be a suitable compromise.

Beverages may vary according to individual preferences. From the perspective of good nutrition, milk should be served at every meal regardless of the age or ethnicity of the diner. Children younger than two years should be given whole milk, but fat-free milk is an appropriate choice for most older children and adults. Lactose-free milk and yogurt are alternatives that some people may find helpful in meeting this recommendation. Other familiar beverages are tea and coffee. Although many Americans drink sodas, this is not a nutritious choice because they may take the place of milk without providing the key nutrients that are in milk.

The last meal to plan for the day is the first one eaten. Some people want the same basic breakfast each day; others are ready to start the day with an interesting menu. By planning breakfast last, it is possible to review the adequacy of the two major meals in meeting the recommendations of MyPyramid and then include appropriate breakfast items to round out the overall diet. For the person wanting a basic breakfast, the usual pattern can be fruit (probably citrus); cereal, toast or other bread item; and a glass of milk. Eggs in some form or some other protein food may be added to the usual pattern for those who need a more substantial breakfast. Regardless of the pattern selected for breakfast, it should complement the other meals to provide the quantity and variety of foods outlined in MyPyramid.

REFINING MENU PLANS

After the full menu cycle has been drafted, it is time to check each day's plans against the recommendations in MyPyramid. This comparison requires that the serving sizes of all items be defined according to the sizes specified. The total servings in each of the groups then must be compared with the recommendations to determine where servings need to be deleted or added. Such changes can be made in one or more of the day's menus to result in meals of appropriate amounts of food. Once each day has been adjusted to meet the recommendations, specific recipes can be identified so the menus can be prepared and served.

The dinner menu for the day is a good starting point. Final review of the recipe to use in preparing the entrée is the place to begin. Look for ways to keep the fat content low in preparing the entrée and any sauce or gravy that accompanies it. Similarly, check the recipes for vegetables.

Visualize the main course of the dinner as it will appear on the plate and be experienced by the diner. Consider the colors and shapes of the food on the plates. Anticipate the mouth feel of the various items and the aromas and flavors that will complete the diner's experience. Decide whether these sensory aspects are pleasing or

Quality	Comments
Color	
Flavor	
Aroma	
Texture	
Temperature	
Size/shape	
Availability	
Variety	
Creativity	

FIGURE 3.8   Check sheet for evaluating sensory qualities of a menu.

whether adjustments need to be made. Garnishes or other accompaniments can be added to the menu to enhance the sensory qualities of the dinner.

A similar review of the lunch and breakfast menus needs to be done, and appropriate adjustments should be made. These two menus should be reviewed in relation to the total day's food intake. For example, one of the meals might be a little high in the amount of protein and another might be slightly low to compensate. Usually, the intake of calories should be distributed fairly uniformly among the three meals. A suggested checklist to use in evaluating menus is presented in Figure 3.8.

An example of a menu plan for the day might be:

BREAKFAST
    Orange juice
    Toasted English muffin
    Fat-free milk or coffee

LUNCH
    Thai shrimp salad
    Baguette and butter
    Chilled honeydew melon
    Fat-free milk

DINNER
    Pork loin roast with chutney garnish
    Baked yam
    French-cut green beans
    Tomato and Maui onion salad
    Bran muffin
    Fresh mango slices with ice cream
    Fat-free milk or tea

These menus for a day could be altered easily to design meals that are tailored to the specific family or group for whom they are planned. Fresh produce could be modified according to the season of the year, which might significantly influence cost. Dessert can be deleted from the dinner menu to reduce calories. The portions usually should be the sizes stated in MyPyramid so diners will not consume excessive calories. If snacking is a part of the diner's lifestyle, the snack could be an item from one of the day's menus. The total consumption remains the same—only the time for eating the item would be changed. Minimal amounts of butter, salad dressing, and other condiments are assumed in planning these menus. The underlying philosophy in shaping these menus is to provide flavorful sources of calories in appropriate quantities of food to support a healthful lifestyle.

Summary

The overarching factors to consider when planning menus are (1) the type of menu (cycle, single use), (2) people being served (culture, religion, age, health), (3) resources available (fiscal, time, energy, equipment), (4) nutritive value, and (5) food selection (color, flavor, aroma, texture, temperature, size and shape, availability, interest). The specific audience to be served, the kitchen and dining facilities, and the human and nonhuman resources available need to be defined before actual menus are developed.

Plans for each day begin with dinner (or the main meal). The entrée for each dinner and the main dish for each lunch in the cycle are selected. The sequence for planning other selections on the lunch and dinner menus is complex carbohydrate or starch, vegetables, fruits (perhaps as accompaniment to the main course, as a salad, or dessert), dessert (optional), and beverages.

Evaluation of individual menus should be done in relation to the factors identified earlier. Nutritional merit of a day's menus can be evaluated by using MyPyramid recommendations. Dietitians and other nutrition professionals need the accuracy afforded by a computer analysis of each day's menus.

Study Questions

1. Describe the cultural/ethnic heritage and religious practices of the people dining where you usually eat dinner. Also identify approximate ages and any health conditions that influence menu planning.
2. Assess the availability of money, time, energy, and equipment for preparing meals in the dining situation described in the preceding question; identify any limitations these resources place on menu plans.
3. Using MyPyramid, create menus for a day for a person needing 2,500 calories daily. Analyze the levels of the nutrients. Write the results of your analysis, and suggest ways to correct any problems.
4. On the basis of color, flavor, aroma, texture, temperature, size and shape, availability, and interest, critique the lunch and dinner menus suggested for the 2,000-calorie diet presented in Table 2.8. What changes would you make to adapt the dinner menu to your food preferences?
5. How might the lunch menu need to be altered to fit into a low-cost food plan? A liberal plan?

Suggested Websites

http://www.cnpp.usda.gov/USDAFoodPlansCostofFood.htm
USDA Food Plans at four levels; cost by month.

www.foodtv.com
Menu and recipe suggestions.

www.meals.com
Menu and recipe ideas.

www.mealsforyou.com
Meal suggestions and recipes.

http://www.health.gov/dietaryguidelines/dga2005/report/HTML/D1_Tables.htm

Lists of good sources of various nutrients.

http://teamnutrition.usda.gov/Resources/menuplanner.html
Guide to planning school food service.

http://www.mhsqic.org/psam/nutrition/nutrition_cacfp.htm
Meal requirements to meet federal requirements for Child and Adult Care Food Program for feeding infants and children to age five.

Bibliography

Backas, N. 2006. Exploring Mediterranean cuisine. *Food Product Design*. 16 (2): 24.

Basaran, P. 1999. Traditional foods of the Middle East. *Food Technol*. 53 (6): 60.

Chinese Nutrition Society. 2000. Dietary Guidelines and the Food Guide Pagoda. *J. Am. Dietet. Assoc*. 992 (2): 886.

Clemens, R., et al. 2005. MyPyramid adds new dimension to food guidance. *Food Technol*. 59 (6): 18.

Clemens, R., and Pressman, P. 2005. Food craving: Signal of heart, head, or heritage. *Food Technol*. 59 (7): 21.

Curry, K. R. 2000. Multicultural competence in dietetics and nutrition. *J. Am. Dietet. Assoc*. 100 (10): 1142.

Decker, K. J. 2004. Crossing borders: Designing for the Hispanic demographic. *Food Product Design* 14 (6): 34.

Egbert, R., and Borders, C. 2006. Achieving success with meat analogs. *Food Techol*. 60 (1): 28.

Ge, K., and McNutt, K. 1999. Publication of the Chinese Guidelines and Pagoda: How it happened. *Nutr. Today*. 34 (3): 104.

Geiger, C. J. Communicating Dietary Guidelines for Americans. *J. Am. Dietet. Assoc*. 101 (7): 793.

Gordon, B. H. J., et al. 2000. Dietary habits and health beliefs of Korean-Americans in the San Francisco Bay Area. *J. Am. Dietet. Assoc*. 100 (10): 1198.

Green, J. H., et al. 2006. Translating nutrition innovation into practice. *Food Technol*. 60 (5): 26.

Gregoire, M.B., and Spears, M. 2007. *Foodservice Organizations: A Managerial and Systems Approach*. 6th ed. Prentice Hall. Upper Saddle River, NJ.

Harris-Davis, E., and Haughton, B. 2000. Model for multicultural nutrition counseling competencies. *J. Am. Dietet. Assoc*. 100 (10): 1178.

Keenan, D. P., and Abusabha, R. 2001. Fifth edition of the *Dietary Guidelines for Americans:* Lessons learned along the way. *J. Am. Dietet. Assoc*. 101 (6): 631.

MacPherson, A. E. 1998. Food Guide Pyramid for Puerto Rico. *Nutr. Today*. 33 (5): 198.

Matchuk J. 2005. Asian flavor invasions. *Food Product Design*. 15 (3): 78.

McWilliams, M., 2007. *Food Around the World: A Cultural Perspective*. 2nd ed. Prentice Hall. Upper Saddle River, NJ.

Packard, D., and McWilliams, M. 1993. Cultural foods heritage of Middle Eastern immigrants. *Nutr. Today*. 28 (3): 6.

Painter, J., Rah, J., and Lee, Y. 2002. Comparison of international food guide pictorial representations. *J. Am. Dietet. Assoc*. 102 (4): 483.

Raghavan, S. 2004. Taste of Cuba. *Food Product Design*. 14 (9): 69.

Raj, S., et al. 1999. Dietary habits of Asian Indians in relation to length of residence in the United States. *J. Am. Dietet. Assoc*. 99 (9): 1106.

Romero-Gwynn, E., et al. 1993. Dietary acculturation among Latinos of Mexican descent. *Nutr. Today*. 28 (4): 6.

Sloan, A. E. 2005. Demographic directions: Mixing of the market. *Food Technol*. 59 (7): 34.

Sloan, A. E. 2005. Fixated on fruit. *Food Technol*. 59 (11): 19.

Sloan, A. E. A. 2006. What, when, and where America eats. *Food Techol*. 60 (1): 18.

Stables, G. J., et al. 2002. Changes in vegetable and fruit consumption and awareness among US adults: Results of 1991 and 1997 5-A-Day for Better Health Program Surveys. *J. Am. Dietet. Assoc*. 102 (6): 809.

U.S. Department of Agriculture. 1999. *The Thrifty Food Plan, 1999 Administrative Report*. Center for Nutrition Policy and Promotion. USDA, 1120 20th St., NW, Suite 200 North Lobby. Washington, DC, 20036.

U.S. Department of Agriculture and U.S. Department of Health and Human Services. 2005. *Dietary Guidelines for Americans*. 6th ed. U.S. Government Printing Office. Washington, DC.

SECTION II

Food Buying

CHAPTER 4
Managing Marketing

OVERVIEW

Some people view food shopping as an interesting and entertaining mission, but many others see it as a necessary task to be endured. Regardless of the attitude of shoppers, food purchases represent an ongoing, significant expense. Smart shopping can help keep food costs reasonable while also providing food of excellent quality. Food-buying decisions are central to successful meal management because they influence not only finances but also time, energy, food quality, and health. Smart shopping can result in healthy meals that can be prepared without requiring excessive amounts of time and energy and yet contribute to dining pleasure.

THE MARKETPLACE

Wise food shopping begins with the selection of the market(s) to use. Urban settings have such an array of markets and types of markets that market selection may require several exploratory shopping trips to learn the advantages and disadvantages of possible stores. In rural settings, the appropriate market to use may be obvious. After surveying the possible markets, suitable market choices can be made.

Shoppers need to identify the features of a market that are important to them before deciding where to shop. These requirements may be somewhat different for various people; the important thing is that the market characteristics be compatible with the priorities of the shopper. Table 4.1 lists some of the factors that may influence choice of a market. These factors are discussed in the following sections.

Factors in Selecting a Market

Location

Time pressures are so great for many people today that a convenient location may be the most compelling reason for choosing a particular market. Ordinarily this would be quite close to home because driving time is kept to a minimum. Another advantage is that frozen foods and perishable foods such as meat will be at ambient temperature for only a short time before being placed in a refrigerator or freezer again. This is especially important in hot summer weather when risks of food spoilage and reduced quality are particularly great. If shopping needs to be done at a market located quite a distance from where the food will be stored and prepared, insulated carriers can be kept well chilled by packing them with blue ice and placing such perishables as meat and milk in them before driving away from the market.

TABLE 4.1 Some Factors Influencing the Choice of a Market

Factor	Importance		
	Low	**Medium**	**High**
Location			
Cleanliness			
Physical factors			
Services/personnel			
Overall food quality			
Fresh produce			
Meat and dairy			
Deli/bakery			
Breadth of inventory			
Food prices			

FIGURE 4.1 A level parking lot with adequate space is an important factor in selecting a market.

Adequate parking is important in selecting a market because it saves time and frustration (Figure 4.1). A level parking lot is helpful in avoiding damage from shopping carts. Security may need to be considered in some areas, particularly if shopping is being done after dark. A well-lighted parking lot increases safety for shoppers.

Some people find another solution to obtaining groceries rather than going to the market themselves. People who can afford the added cost sometimes use personal shoppers and/or home delivery. Another option in some locations is to shop via the Internet. Although these approaches to procuring groceries can be relatively expensive, people with physical limitations or severe time pressures may find such services are appropriate ways to solve their food shopping problems.

Cleanliness

The interior of a grocery store must also meet consumer expectations if the choice of a market is to be totally satisfactory. Clean floors free of litter and spills are indicative of a quality market. Refrigerated and frozen food units need to be maintained well and monitored for correct temperature control. These aspects of store maintenance are important for optimizing food quality and safety, as well as creating a pleasant environment for shopping.

Physical Features

The physical features that contribute to consumer satisfaction when shopping at a store include lighting, temperature control, aisle width, height of shelves, and size and maintenance of shopping carts. Although personal preferences differ on these features, consumers can evaluate them according to their own needs. However, good lighting is important not only for the positive feeling it creates for shoppers, but also because it facilitates label reading (Figure 4.2). It may inspire store managers to strive for high levels of cleanliness throughout the store to avoid having shoppers seeing dirty floors.

FIGURE 4.2 Wide aisles and good lighting are some of the attributes that attract shoppers to this market.

Although it may have a subtle influence, the temperature of a store is important. A great deal of label reading may need to be done in the store so wise shopping decisions can be made. However, some markets are so cold that the principal motivation is to select items as quickly as possible and retreat to the warmer world outside. For optimal shopping, select a store that is maintained at a comfortable temperature, or else dress warmly enough to be able to shop without needing to rush through the store.

The width of aisles can make a significant difference in wheeling carts around a store. Aisles wide enough for passing another cart or for steering around displays or other obstacles reduce frustration and save time. Crowded aisles draw attention to navigating through traffic and distract attention from making purchasing decisions.

The height of the shelves may influence the choice of a market. Very high shelves make it impossible for short people to reach the items on top. They also make it difficult to see signs telling the items located in each aisle. An added potential problem with high shelves is lack of security for shoppers.

Shopping carts need to be an appropriate size for the width of the store aisles, and they need to be maintained so that are easy to push and steer. Carts that are too big to move past one another in a store aisle require too much negotiation between shoppers. Anybody who has wrestled with a cart that refuses to proceed in the desired direction appreciates the importance of having carts that are maintained well.

Services and Personnel

The services provided by a market may be particularly important for people on tight schedules who have little time for errands and marketing. Check cashing and credit card charges are services that may be of great importance. In-store banking not only is convenient, but it also may be safer than withdrawing money from an ATM located in a spot that is less secure. Film developing and dry cleaning are other examples of services that some people may want to handle at a market. If these various services are desired, they may influence the selection of a market.

Courteous and helpful personnel can make a big difference to shoppers. Time can be wasted hunting through a store for items that are purchased only occasionally. If employees in the store are knowledgeable about the location of various items and are helpful in locating them, shopping is less frustrating.

The attitudes and accuracy of checkers can also make a big difference. Even when checkers do their best, mistakes can be made; it is the consumer's ultimate responsibility to check register tapes and request a correction if errors do occur. Careful bagging of groceries can make a difference in the condition of groceries by the time they are unloaded at home. Careless people bagging groceries can cause broken eggs and bruised produce, which can be both frustrating and costly.

The design of the check stand may be important to shoppers. Some stores are designed so that shoppers have to unload all of their groceries from the cart or basket to the counter; others are designed so the cart is driven into position for checking directly by the cashier. This latter design saves one more handling of the groceries, a feature that benefits thin-walled cans, eggs, and fresh produce.

Overall Food Quality

Stores vary on the quality of foods they stock. Some cater to fussy shoppers who place emphasis on quality over price; other stores are stocked to attract people who are focused on economy. Some chain stores feature their own brand of products throughout the store. These products are manufactured to meet the specifications defined by the chain's procurement people. Store brands are intended to provide acceptable quality at very competitive prices, and the quality is usually acceptable to people shopping for low prices.

Open dating
Date on food packages so that consumers can be able to buy the freshest packages within the time period deemed to be safe for purchase.

The care with which a market checks dates and removes outdated merchandise is important to food quality. **Open dating** makes it convenient for shoppers to check on the freshness of items themselves, but stores should maintain shelves and displays with current dates only. Discriminating customers check dates wherever possible; this is particularly important when buying milk, cheeses, and other perishable refrigerated items.

Fresh Produce

The quality and variety of fresh produce available varies considerably from one market to another. With the emphasis today on consuming five or more servings of fruits and vegetables each day, the caliber of the produce section may be one of the key factors in choosing a market. Attractive displays of unblemished fruits and vegetables are the hallmark in some stores (Figure 4.3).

Produce should appear fresh and show no signs of wilting. Gourmet markets usually feature rare fruits and vegetables, as well as extra-large fruits and baby vegetables, all of which are chosen to attract shoppers who are willing to overlook price. Fortunately, less exclusive markets are likely to have less dramatic produce but at a far more reasonable price. The market where consumers decide to shop for produce can have a significant impact on grocery bills. Careful selection of fresh fruits and vegetables can result in high quality at reasonable prices.

Meat and Dairy

Most markets sell meat in packages, which may suit the needs of many consumers. Often it is possible to ask a butcher to cut meat according to specific requirements, but customers may have to wait a few minutes for this service. Meat cases are filled with several packages of the same cut of meat; similarly, other cuts of meat are displayed so customers can pick the specific package that most closely meets their needs. Some shoppers appreciate the convenience of simply selecting a package of meat. No time is wasted waiting for a butcher to help them individually.

FIGURE 4.3 Beautiful displays and unusual fruits and vegetables always await shoppers in this gourmet market.

A good fish counter is important to many consumers today as they strive to eat a healthy diet (Figure 4.4). Careful sanitation is particularly critical to maintaining a safe, attractive display that is free of fishy odors. Shoppers who frequently buy fish usually place a high priority on selecting a market with an excellent fish counter. Others may simply opt to buy frozen fish.

Dairy products require adequate refrigeration throughout the marketing process. Thermometers should be mounted in the dairy cases and the storage temperature monitored frequently. The cleanliness of the dairy cases also needs to be checked

FIGURE 4.4 Well-iced fresh fish invite shoppers to include fish in their diets.

because leaking cartons make puddles of milk on the floor of the cases, where bacteria can multiply. Consumers should be sure to check the pull date on containers when selecting all dairy products.

Delicatessen and Bakery

Many large markets feature excellent delicatessen counters where customers can select a wide range of products freshly prepared for serving as quick meals at home. This market feature may be compelling to customers who are interested in these convenience foods. Not only are they time-savers for busy people, but they also may be more tempting than might be prepared at home by people who are not interested in cooking. Sanitation is important to help assure the safety of delicatessen items. People who expect to rely heavily on food from the delicatessen counter will want to choose a market with very pleasing and varied menu items.

An in-store bakery is a welcome part of some of the large markets. The appetizing aroma of freshly baked bread can draw many eager customers to buy special breads and other baked goods in this department. Some stores may team this section with a coffee and beverage bar so shoppers can relax and enjoy a snack as a part of the shopping experience.

Breadth of Inventory

The time required for grocery shopping can be kept to a minimum by purchasing all items on the list at one store. For shoppers whose time is a top priority, the market selected should stock everything that is needed.

If foreign ingredients or other specific specialty items are essential to prepare the menus that are planned, the market selected should be one that is known to stock these items. Adventurous eaters may seek a store that carries some interesting, unique ingredients to broaden their dining experiences. Other shoppers may require only typically American ingredients that can be found in any large market. Clearly, not all people have identical shopping needs, but suitable market choices are available to fit most shoppers' requirements.

Food Prices

The prices charged for various items in the grocery store may ultimately be the deciding factor in determining where to shop. The factors listed previously are important for efficiency and pleasure, but a tight budget may require that economy supersede these other considerations. The difference of a cent or two consistently on comparable items will influence the total cost of groceries significantly over a period of time. Choice of a store based on the lowest prices for items frequently purchased can help keep the food budget as low as possible.

Determination of price differences needs to be done on the basis of the items that are usually bought when doing the week's shopping. Comparison of the cost of items not ordinarily purchased may give a false impression of the best store to choose. A typical shopping list can be taken to the stores being considered and the actual prices determined. If this study is done periodically, it will verify that the best choice is being made.

Another useful means of determining relative pricing in different stores is to study newspaper ads of the possible markets. Large supermarkets usually run large newspaper ads once a week to draw shoppers into their stores. These ads often feature a **loss leader** that is intended to attract shoppers that weekend. Although the featured item may be sold below cost, stores gamble on shoppers buying many other items at full price so the store actually makes money. Although these ads do not list everything

Loss leader
Item sold at a very low price (often below cost) to draw shoppers into the store.

that may need to be purchased, they do provide a reasonable comparison without actually going to the markets. If the choice between two markets is about equal in most of the other factors identified previously, the ads may be useful in deciding which market to patronize for that particular week's shopping. Other weeks the advertised special might make the other market a more economical choice.

The cost of the same food item in various stores often differs. Discount stores, such as Wal-Mart and Costco, may be less expensive than supermarkets on standard items, but the quantity bundled together as a single unit may be too great for small families to use. Specialty stores, such as Whole Foods Markets, may price items slightly higher than a supermarket would. The variation in pricing practices makes it necessary for individual shoppers to determine the most cost-effective place to shop.

Store prices are influenced by a large number of factors. Very large chains often are able to make favorable purchases, which may allow them to sell at a slightly lower price than a smaller market can. Services made available to customers influence prices. For example, stores with a large number of personnel in relation to the number of customers have higher labor costs than stores with lower staffing and longer lines. Such costs ultimately are reflected in the prices charged. In some areas, the cost of doing business is very high because of crime and the high insurance rates associated with such problems. These costs have to be covered by charging higher prices if the store is to remain open and serve its community.

When considering economy, the question of the number of stores to patronize is pertinent. Often one item may be less expensive at one store, but another item at that store may be more expensive than at the first store. If the bargain is something that can be kept a long time, it may occasionally be worth shopping at more than one store, but regularly shopping at two or more stores each week can be costly both in time and gasoline.

Ultimately, decisions need to be made regarding the place(s) where marketing usually is done. Prospective markets can be evaluated on the basis of the priorities identified using Table 4.1. This can be done for each prospective store by using a format (Table 4.2) in which these priorities are listed and the unimportant items are minimized. Comparison of the ratings for the various stores can be done to make the decision best suited to the individual shopper.

TABLE 4.2   Market Evaluation Check Sheet   Market_____

Factor	Evaluation Comments	Rating[a]
Location		
Cleanliness		
Physical factors		
Services/personnel		
Overall food quality		
Fresh produce		
Meat and dairy		
Deli/bakery		
Breadth of inventory		
Food prices		
Other:		

[a] 5 = excellent, 1 = unacceptable.

Types of Markets

Costs of food are a concern of grocers and consumers alike. Numerous factors influence the final cost of items. These include farmers' costs, the cost of processing (including costs stemming from such regulations as nutrition labeling), distributors' costs, and retailers' costs. At all points along this sequence from farm to table, there are labor costs, and these costs account for a substantial part of retail food prices.

Before pricing a product, retailers have to add the various costs of doing business, plus a small profit. The actual markup varies with the type of item: Dried foods and packages with good shelf life and relatively rapid sale usually are marked up between 10 and 17 percent; slow-moving items with good shelf life, such as spices, may be marked up as much as 35 percent because of the extended time on expensive shelf space; meats, because of the potential loss due to short shelf life, are marked up 20 to 25 percent; produce is marked up about 30 percent because of losses from trimming and spoiling; and nonfood items may be marked up more than 30 percent to help offset inadequate markups on food items.

Although retailers' expenses for different parts of their operation vary from one retailer to another, usually labor and its associated costs for benefits represent more than half of the operating budget exclusive of inventory costs. Other costs include rent, utilities, advertising, taxes, and a profit of usually 2 percent or less. Retailers have been able to minimize the number of employees by the effective use of computers and scanners.

Retailers plan the physical layout very carefully to promote traffic flow within the store, with particular attention being directed toward assuring that customers come in contact with items they wish to promote. The need for electricity for frozen and refrigerated food cases and for water for fresh produce may define where these special displays should be placed. By stretching refrigerated cases for dairy, meat, and delicatessen items along the back and/or side walls, retailers achieve two objectives: easy access to electricity and direction of customers throughout the store.

Because about 95 percent of shoppers make purchases in the meat section, most shoppers have to walk some path through the store to reach that section if it is along the back wall, and they may pick up other items they see en route. Slightly fewer people (90 to 93 percent) buy dairy items, so placement of dairy cases along a side wall is a practical location to help spread shoppers a bit and avoid congestion at the meat counter.

Supermarkets

Today's supermarkets usually present an efficient opportunity for one-stop shopping. The array of products available is far greater than many shoppers need and may provide more temptations and decisions than they desire. Nevertheless, supermarkets capture about 75 percent of the market for groceries. Most supermarkets are units in a chain owned by a large corporation (Figure 4.5). The huge quantities purchased by these chains make it possible for them to buy items for their inventories comparatively inexpensively. Such economies enable them to mark their retail prices competitively to attract many shoppers.

Some supermarkets are owned independently, which immediately spawns the problem of purchasing goods at low enough prices to be able to retail them competitively against chain market prices. Independent markets can organize themselves into retailer-owned cooperatives, which are large enough to be able to purchase in very large quantities at prices competitive with those obtained by chains. Certified Grocers is an example of this type of cooperative.

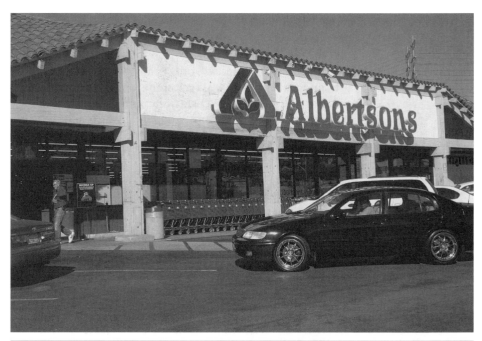

FIGURE 4.5   This supermarket in Southern California, part of a large chain, is typical of the chains where many shoppers choose to buy their groceries because of competitive prices and a broad selection of products.

Supermarkets have a wide assortment of food, including fresh meats, produce, dairy products, canned and frozen goods, breads and many other packaged items, as well as often boasting a delicatessen counter and an array of foreign ingredients (depending on the clientele in the area). In addition, such nonfood items as detergents, paper products, over-the-counter drugs and other personal care items, and even some clothing are stocked in supermarkets. This aggregation of merchandise makes it efficient for shoppers to park their cars conveniently and purchase most items on a shopping list with just one stop.

Because of the high volume of business done in successful supermarkets, the turnover of merchandise is rather fast, which is particularly pertinent to the quality of perishable foods. The combination of competitive prices and high-quality fresh produce and other perishables provides a continuing appeal to consumers and promotes their return visits, which gradually develops store loyalty.

Niche Markets

Some chains featuring markets a bit smaller than supermarkets have been achieving success by shaping stores and their inventories to meet the grocery needs of the niche market each has defined. Perhaps the largest and best known of these chains is Whole Foods Markets, which features stores designed for shoppers who want their food to be healthy and pleasurable (Figure 4.6). "Organic" and "natural" are key words they use to describe their foods. This chain, based originally on the concept of so-called health foods, now has 135 stores across the nation and is gearing toward attracting upscale, health-conscious shoppers. Shoppers in Whole Foods Markets can do most of a week's grocery shopping in one visit, but the cost will probably be higher than at a neighboring chain supermarket.

FIGURE 4.6   Whole Foods Markets are designed to appeal to shoppers seeking organic and natural products.

Other upscale markets are available in wealthy communities around the nation; high-quality produce and other ingredients are featured in them but at a definitely higher cost than at a chain supermarket. Examples of such stores in California are small chains, such as Bristol Farms and Gelson's. Trader Joe's is a niche market chain that attracts customers because of unique, somewhat gourmet items at a moderate price but with a rather unpredictable inventory.

Discount Stores

Discount stores provide a different shopping opportunity. These very large stores are so immense that they may be too challenging physically for some shoppers. They offer as many as 60,000 items throughout their entire store, which is about 20 percent more than the approximately 50,000 items in a large supermarket. These stores also have enormous parking lots because of the large numbers of people shopping there.

Crowds of shoppers can mean slow checkout lines. The combination of the vast area to be covered in shopping and parking plus the potentially slow checkout system means that shoppers using these stores need to plan more time for shopping than they would in a supermarket. On the positive side is the prospect of very competitive prices. Examples of discount stores include Target, Wal-Mart, and Kmart.

Warehouse Clubs

Warehouse clubs afford yet another shopping option. These clubs (e.g., Costco and Sam's Club) usually require an annual membership fee for shopping privileges. The inventory in this type of facility usually includes about 4,000 to 5,000 products, which is much more limited than the number carried by either supermarkets or discount stores. Another unique characteristic is that warehouse clubs usually market items in large packages (e.g., several packages of paper towels bundled into one large single unit for purchase).

The strong advantage of warehouse clubs is that the prices usually are extremely low. Counterbalancing this benefit are: lack of service, limited selection, items available only in large quantities, and no guarantee that desired items will be in stock. For these reasons, warehouse clubs generally do not serve shoppers' needs for weekly shopping, but they are suitable for an occasional trip.

These stores can be particularly useful for shoppers who are preparing for a large event (perhaps a banquet or party) or who cook regularly for several people. In fact, some of the platters of prepared foods and other catering items now available in warehouse clubs may save shoppers both time and money when they are entertaining.

Warehouse stores are an economical destination for an occasional shopping trip for people who have storage space for the inventory of goods resulting from shopping in bulk. Only items that can be used during the viable shelf life of a product should be purchased. Certainly storage of frozen foods should not extend beyond approximately six months, and canned and other nonperishables should be bought only in quantities that will be used in a year or less. Shoppers need to remember that the money spent to acquire these stored products is no longer available for buying items that are currently needed.

Convenience Stores

Convenience stores are small stores located conveniently close to residential areas so small items can be picked up quickly if needed between weekly shopping trips. The cost of these items usually is higher than at a supermarket, and the inventory is quite limited. Also, the turnover may be slow, so items may not be fresh. However, they often have extended hours and are not usually crowded, making them convenient stops for busy people.

Farmers' Markets

In some localities, farmers' markets (Figure 4.7) are held at a regular time and place each week. At these approved sites, farmers can sell their produce directly to consumers,

FIGURE 4.7   Farmers' markets usually are the source of excellent fruits and vegetables at very competitive prices.

thus eliminating the costs of shipping and retailing. This arrangement makes it possible to harvest crops when they are mature, rather than needing to ship them while they are still green enough to resist damage during shipping. These outdoor markets also foster a degree of camaraderie between farmers and consumers seldom found in the market-place today. The produce available varies from season to season and even from week to week, but the items available are of excellent quality and at very reasonable prices. Although farmers' markets cannot be used as the place to do the entire week's shopping, they are interesting and economical places to get produce if they are open when a person can go there.

THE SHOPPING LIST

A well-prepared shopping list greatly simplifies shopping even though some specific choices may need to be made at the store. When all food purchases are listed, it is possible to obtain everything needed for the intended period (preferably a week) so interim trips are not needed. Both time and energy, including fuel costs, are saved if extra trips are avoided. Impulse buying opportunities are limited, too, which can mean additional savings. Another advantage of buying all items needed for the week in one trip is that it avoids the temptation to buy forgotten items at a convenience store where prices may be higher.

A complete weekly shopping list includes not only the specific foods needed that week, but also any staples that may need replenishing. Staples in most kitchens include flour, sugar, salt, spices and seasonings, shortening, baking powder, and salad oil; depending on the cook, there may be other items that always need to be available too. For economical buying, it is practical to buy these items only in the amount that probably will be used within a reasonable period of time while their quality is still optimal.

A shopping list structured according to the market's floor plan, but with produce and frozen foods at the end, provides an efficient guide to avoid detours while getting all of the items in the cart. Table 4.3 presents an example of a shopping list format designed to fit a typical store layout. Canned goods and other heavy items are at the top of the list, followed by refrigerated items, including meats and milk. Fresh produce can be selected just prior to frozen foods. This sequence prevents bruising of delicate fruits, keeps refrigerated foods quite cool, and minimizes the thawing of frozen foods.

After doing the week's shopping, post next week's shopping list in a convenient spot in the kitchen so items needing to be replenished can be added to the list immediately. This avoids such problems as discovering there is insufficient flour to finish making biscuits that might already be in progress.

In view of the increasing problem with weight that many Americans are experiencing, decisions on how much food to buy can be very important. Portion sizes need to be planned keeping in mind the (1) people to be fed (ages, amount of physical activity, and appropriateness of weight) and (2) total menu for a meal. Even though a recipe may indicate it serves four people, the actual size of the product may be far more than is suggested as being a serving size in the Daily Food Guide (see Chapter 2).

It is fine to plan to prepare the full recipe if the excess can be refrigerated or frozen for later use, but the portion served to each person should be appropriate for that person's nutritional needs. The habit of preparing recipes that are a bit too large for the intended number of diners can lead to overweight because of the tendency many people have to keep eating until the item has all been eaten.

The quantity of any single dish that will be eaten at a meal is related to the complete menu. For example, an accompanying dinner salad requires a much smaller portion

TABLE 4.3 Suggested Format for a Week's Shopping List at a Supermarket

Canned, bottled, and packaged items[a]

    Beverages
    Vinegar, pickles, salad dressings
    Dried beans, rice, pastas
    Coffee, tea, cocoa
    Syrups, jams, peanut butter
    Canned vegetables
    Canned fruits, juices
    Dried fruits
    Cereals
    Baking supplies
    Shortenings, salad oils
    Spices
    Mixes
    Soups (canned and concentrates)
    Canned and powdered milks
    Crackers, cookies
    Household supplies
Bakery goods
Refrigerated items
    Eggs
    Meat, poultry, fish
    Dairy (milk, butter, cheeses)
    Delicatessen
Frozen foods
    Fruits, vegetables
    Juices
    Ice cream
    Convenience foods
Fresh produce

[a] *Sequence may differ from store to store; delete categories not usually needed.*

than if the salad is the main item on the menu. This should be considered when deciding the quantity of the various ingredients that actually will be required.

Before finishing the shopping list, the existing inventory in the refrigerator, freezer, and cupboards should be checked to see if items on the list are already available in an adequate amount. Be sure to check the amounts of staples such as flour, rice, or other food left in opened packages. The list should be adjusted appropriately.

Converting Measures to Package Units

Recipes are written in measures that do not automatically convert to the package units available at the market. Conversions are easiest to do when the shopping list is being finalized. Table 4.4 includes some of the conversions needed to convert recipes into units needed. For example, many recipes require grated cheese, but some shoppers prefer to grate the cheese themselves and save a bit of money. If the shopper knows that a pound of cheese converts to about $4\frac{1}{2}$ cups of grated cheese, the necessary weight of the cheese can be put on the shopping list, thus avoiding indecision at the time of purchase. Similarly, knowing that a pound of onions will yield about $2\frac{2}{3}$ cups of chopped onions makes it easy to estimate the weight of onions to buy.

TABLE 4.4   Approximate Volume and Weight Equivalents of Selected Foods[a]

Food	Approximate cups/pound	Food	Approximate cups/pound
Apples, raw, unpeeled	4	Macaroni, elbow, uncooked	$3\frac{1}{2}$
Avocado, fresh	2	Margarine or butter	2
Banana, mashed	2	Mushrooms, raw, sliced	$4\frac{3}{4}$
Barley, uncooked	$2\frac{3}{4}$	Onions, raw, chopped	$2\frac{2}{3}$
Beans, dry Great Northern		Pecans, chopped	$4\frac{1}{4}$
uncooked	$2\frac{1}{2}$	Peppers, green, raw, chopped	3
cooked	$3\frac{1}{3}$	Potatoes, raw, sliced	3
Cabbage, raw, shredded	$6\frac{1}{3}$	Rice, brown, uncooked	$2\frac{1}{2}$
Carrots, raw, shredded	4	Rice, minute, dry	$4\frac{1}{2}$
Celery, raw, diced	$3\frac{3}{4}$	Rice, white, uncooked	$2\frac{1}{3}$
Cheese, cheddar or Swiss, grated	$4\frac{1}{2}$	Sugar	
Flour, wheat		brown	2
all purpose, sifted	4	confectioner's, sifted	$4\frac{3}{4}$
cake, sifted	$4\frac{1}{2}$	granulated	$2\frac{1}{3}$
self-rising, sifted	$4\frac{1}{4}$	Walnuts, chopped	$3\frac{3}{4}$
whole wheat, sifted	$3\frac{3}{4}$		

[a]*Adapted from* Average Weight of a Measured Cup of Various Foods. *Home Economics Research Report No. 41. Agricultural Research Service. USDA. Washington, DC. 1977.*

Can Sizes

If canned foods are on the list, it is helpful to know the volume measures of various can sizes. This information is useful in translating the measured amounts listed in recipes into the appropriate can sizes and the number of cans needed. For example, for a chili recipe that requires 2 cups of stewed tomatoes, either two 8-ounce cans or one No. 303 can will provide the necessary quantity. Table 4.5 provides a guide to the can sizes commonly used in the food industry.

TABLE 4.5   A Guide to Can Sizes

Can size	Volume	Foods for Which Used
6 oz	~$\frac{3}{4}$ cups (6 fl oz)	Frozen concentrated and single-strength juices
8 oz	~1 cup (8 oz); ($7\frac{3}{4}$ fl oz)	Fruits, vegetables, and specialty items
No. 1 (Picnic)	~$1\frac{1}{4}$ cups ($10\frac{1}{2}$ oz); ($9\frac{1}{2}$ fl oz)	Condensed soups, some fruits, vegetables, meats, and fish products
No. 300	~$1\frac{3}{4}$ cups ($15\frac{1}{2}$ oz); ($13\frac{1}{2}$ fl oz)	Beans with pork, spaghetti, macaroni, chili, date and nut bread, variety of fruits, cranberry sauce
No. 303	~2 cups ($15\frac{1}{2}$ oz); (15 fl oz)	Vegetables, fruits (e.g., cherries), fruit cocktail
No. 2	~$2\frac{1}{2}$ cups (1 lb, 4 oz); (1 pt, 2 fl oz)	Vegetables, many fruits and juices
No. $2\frac{1}{2}$	~$3\frac{1}{2}$ cups (1 lb, 13 oz); (26 fl oz)	Fruits (e.g., peaches, pears, plums), fruit cocktail
46-oz	~$5\frac{3}{4}$ cups (46 oz)	Juices, whole chicken
No. 10 (Institutional)	~12 cups (6 lb, 9 oz) (3 qt)	Most fruits and vegetables (not in retail stores)

PREPARING FOR SHOPPING

Before shopping, it is wise to clean the refrigerator and remove any leftovers that may not be used promptly. This makes it easy to refrigerate the new groceries after shopping.

If shoppers are planning to use coupons, these should be reviewed and organized before going to the market. Coupons have the potential for saving money when used wisely, but they also may be rather time consuming. They infiltrate homes from a wide array of newspapers and advertising promotions as well as from those stuffed into grocery bags or given to consumers with their sales slips. If coupons are used to buy items that are needed, they will be a means of saving money. However, if extraneous or more costly items are selected because of the coupons, they can represent a false economy.

MAXIMIZING SHOPPING

Timing

Weekends are the most economical time to shop for groceries because these are the days when markets usually feature specials to attract more shoppers into the store than their usual clientele. Another advantage of weekend shopping is that shelves are well stocked, and the produce quality is usually optimal. This situation is particularly true early in the weekend.

Weekend shoppers face the problem of a crowded store late Friday afternoon and from midmorning to late afternoon on Saturdays. Often the best times for shopping are Friday morning (if the store's specials are in effect on Friday) or early Saturday morning. The crowds are usually minimal at these times, and the shelves are fully stocked. By noon on Sunday, the effects of numerous shoppers are evident—shelves may begin to be low on stock and produce may begin to wilt.

Monday mornings are devoted to restocking shelves in most markets, which means shoppers may have to dodge around stacks of merchandise still in boxes. Items on the shopping list may still be in those boxes rather than being available on the shelves. Fresh produce may not have arrived yet to replenish the bins ravaged by the weekend shoppers. The final frustration is that the weekend sale prices are no longer in effect.

Shopping ideally is done alone, soon after a meal (to avoid the impulse shopping triggered by hunger pangs), and with adequate time to read labels and make informed choices. Unfortunately, this ideal situation may differ significantly from reality. Today's two-income families and single people often are very short on time and must race through the store without stopping to analyze products and prices. Parents distracted by small children while they are trying to shop also have a challenging situation that may result in uneconomical choices, due both to too little time and to children clamoring for foods (often expensive) they have seen advertised on television.

Factors in Shopping Decisions

Even people who usually have to shop with little children or have too little time may be able to find an opportunity to do one in-depth shopping trip alone to obtain basic information about items that are bought frequently. This trip can be used productively to compare the cost of (1) different brands of a product, (2) different forms of a food (canned, frozen, or fresh), (3) an ounce (or other measure) of the same item in packages of different sizes, and (4) prepared, semi-prepared, or basic ingredients for such items as salad greens and pies. Conclusions from these comparisons should be recorded so the information is available when making subsequent trips, thus making it possible to make smart decisions quickly.

Supermarkets often carry more than one brand of common items, such as catsup, canned peaches, canned tuna, and many others. By trying different brands and noting the quality of each, it is possible to decide which brand is preferred. If the preferred brand is more costly than the other brands, a decision will need to be made whether or not the higher quality fits within the budget and is worth the difference. Such decisions are personal ones to be made by the shopper.

Often large-chain supermarkets carry their own brand as one of the choices, and these products usually are less expensive (but not always). When making the decision to buy the store brand, it is wise to check it against competitors if the item is something that will be bought frequently. As a shopper acquires experience with some of the items carrying the store brand, an expectation of the probable quality will develop and influence future decisions on buying store brands.

Economical decisions regarding the quality to buy need to be based, in part, on the role of the ingredient in the menu. For example, a pie crust of top quality requires an excellent flour; cheaper flours result in a pastry. Another example is using kidney beans in chili versus in a salad. The other ingredients in chili combine with the kidney beans to produce an overall appearance and texture, whereas kidney beans in a salad are highly visible and preferably top quality. If economy is an important objective, a less-expensive brand of kidney beans can be used effectively in chili.

Sometimes choices are available in the way a food has been processed. For example, green beans may be purchased canned, frozen, or fresh. Selection of the type may be dictated by the desired outcome in a recipe. Canned green beans are an olive drab that may detract from a vegetable dish that is expected to be the lively green provided by either fresh or frozen green beans, but canned green beans are an acceptable color when used in a mixed bean salad.

Orange juice is another example of a food available in different forms. Fresh oranges can be purchased for squeezing in the kitchen. Some markets sell freshly squeezed juice, as well as juice that has been prepared from fresh concentrate, often with calcium added to it. This latter product is an excellent choice because the calcium in it is absorbed well in the body and contributes meaningfully toward the day's requirement for calcium. These ready-to-drink juices from fresh oranges or fresh orange concentrate usually are more expensive than frozen orange concentrate. In essence, shoppers have the choice of paying others a bit more to cover the costs of shipping more water, requiring more shelf space, and limiting storage life. To avoid these costs, consumers can buy the frozen concentrate and reconstitute it themselves. Shoppers also need to be aware that orange drinks are not as high in vitamin C as 100 percent orange juice. Careful label reading needs to be done when selecting juices.

Decisions regarding the form of a food to buy may be critical to the success of a meal. An example might be whether to buy fresh, frozen, or canned pineapple. If it is to be used in a gelatin product, canned fruit is needed because bromelain, an enzyme in fresh pineapple, prevents gelation. However, a fresh fruit salad featuring pineapple is more dramatic and flavorful if fresh pineapple is used. If a recipe requires fruits or vegetables that are out of season, economy might dictate buying them in either the frozen or canned form. When making such a decision, the effect of the choice on the finished quality also should be considered.

Some products are packaged in more than one size, and often the larger size is more economical. Thanks to unit pricing, which must be maintained in an obvious place on grocery shelves, shoppers can quite easily compare the unit price for each of the package sizes to determine which size actually is least expensive. Surprisingly, a special on a smaller size sometimes happens to make that size the most economical choice. Blind belief that the biggest is the cheapest is not warranted because of occasional sales promotions.

Before deciding to buy a very large package of an item, it is wise to be sure there is a large enough storage space available for it. To illustrate, if storage is extremely limited underneath the sink and near the dishwasher, a giant package of dishwasher detergent could prove to be a very inconvenient purchase despite the savings it may represent. The other aspect to consider before buying a perishable food in a large quantity is whether or not it will be consumed while it is still of good quality. If some of the food needs to be discarded, the apparent economy of the good buy is lost.

One of the big dilemmas in food shopping is how much convenience is appropriate to include in shopping decisions. A frozen pie can be baked in a preheated oven and then served for dessert, a process requiring time for baking, but almost no time from the person opening the package and baking the preprepared pie. Even a skilled baker probably requires about 30 minutes or more to create the pastry, make the filling, and assemble the pie for baking (and many less-skilled workers may require an hour or more because of the time required for measuring, mixing, rolling the dough, fitting the pastry into the pie pan, and finally adding the filling and finishing the edge of the pastry). The questions then become how much the cook's time is worth, and is that time available? For people who find baking a relaxing and rewarding task, the decision to make the pie using basic ingredients may be suitable, but for a busy executive, preparation of the pie from the beginning is not economical and may not be a satisfying choice. The higher cost of the frozen pie (or one already baked) actually is cheaper if the value of the executive's time is added to the cost of the basic ingredients.

Satisfaction with the finished product is another dimension to consider. If the pie baker can be counted on to make a very high-quality pie from the ingredients, the pleasure that pie brings to its diners probably far outweighs any economic considerations. However, not all people are good at baking, and the frozen pie baked at home may be a palatable dessert that outshines what would have been the result if an unskilled cook transformed the ingredients into a pie.

Other examples of buying convenience are illustrated by the choices in bread and potato products. Bread can be bought in various forms, such as commercial loaves or rolls on the grocer's shelf; freshly baked from a supermarket's bakery section; frozen bread dough; refrigerated cans of biscuit dough (Figure 4.8); dry mixes; or the basic ingredients (flour of various types, yeast or baking powder, eggs, milk, sugar, and/or optional items).

FIGURE 4.8   Bread can be obtained in a variety of forms to meet the individual shopper's preference for quality and price.

Obviously, there are basic choices to be made regarding the preferred form, followed by specific decisions regarding the types or flavors desired. It is clear that simply listing "bread" on a shopping list is just the beginning of making the actual selection.

The range of potato products designed to save preparation time presents additional options to supermarket shoppers. Frozen hash browns and french fries save cooks time and energy because they are pared and either sliced or grated prior to being packaged and frozen. They have the additional advantage of being convenient to store in the freezer until needed for either their planned use or to meet unexpected meal emergencies. Dehydrated potatoes are featured in such products as instant mashed potatoes and scalloped or au gratin potatoes that are processed and packaged for storage at room temperature. These require little of a person's time to prepare (although baking time is necessary for the scalloped and au gratin products), and they can be stored at room temperature for planned or emergency use. These various convenience products also compete with fresh potatoes of different varieties in the produce section.

Many other examples of products that allow shoppers to buy convenience are available throughout supermarkets (Figure 4.9). Packaged ready-to-use salad greens are available in an array of mixtures to suit individual preferences for simple or more exotic ingredients . Sometimes all of the components for a salad (suitable greens, a packet of croutons, and a pouch of appropriate dressing) may be included in the package. The time required for washing and tearing the greens, plus the convenience of not buying a variety of greens, seems to be appreciated by shoppers, for the sales of these products have been remarkable.

FIGURE 4.9   Brussels sprouts and other fresh vegetables require more time to prepare than do their frozen counterparts, but the quality may be more pleasing.

BOX 4.1

Food Insights: Sous Vide

Sous vide (pronounced "soo veed") is a cooking technique refined in France in the 1970s Basically, the food ingredients are vacuum-packed in plastic and heated slowly in a water bath maintained at simmering temperatures for an extended period until the food reaches the desired degree of doneness. Then the food is either served or stored in a refrigerator or freezer until it is reheated and served. This low-temperature cooking permits slow, rather uniform heat penetration throughout the food, and it pasteurizes but does not sterilize the product. To avoid the risk of food-borne illness from protein foods prepared by sous vide, immediate chilling and refrigerator or freezer storage are essential from the end of heating until the food is reheated and served.

Sous vide
French cooking technique in which food is vacuum-packed in plastic and simmered for a long time until the food is done as desired.

The range of menu items available in this style is increasing significantly. Sous vide entrées are available for food service, in some retail markets, and on the Internet. The items available often are designed to add a gourmet touch to a meal while requiring virtually nothing in the way of preparation other than reheating in an oven or a microwave.

Some restaurants are preparing sous vide products and serving them to customers, sometimes immediately after they have been cooked and sometimes after refrigerated storage for varying lengths of time. Meats, fish, poultry, and egg dishes prepared in vacuum-sealed plastic bags using this low-temperature, slow-cooking technique are very tender and have a pleasing mouth feel. However, city health departments are concerned because of potential risks associated with viable pathogenic microorganisms or their toxins if foods prepared by sous vide techniques are not stored safely. Microorganisms that may possibly be a risk with foods prepared by sous vide include *Listeria inocula, Clostridium botulinum, Salmonella* spp., *Campylobacter* spp., *Vibrio parahaemolyticus, and Bacillus cereus.*

Ready-to-eat salads, main dishes, and desserts are available at the delicatessen counters in many supermarkets. These offer shoppers convenience but usually at a price far above the cost of the ingredients. Nevertheless, such tempting foods of excellent quality may be appropriate choices to save time for busy people with enough income to afford the cost.

Less costly, but convenient entrées and side dishes are available as frozen or shelf-stable items. Frozen entrées require only heating, which usually can be done satisfactorily in a microwave oven when time is limited. Frozen dinners are designed to meet the needs of people living or eating alone. These dinners not only are convenient time-savers, but they also avoid the need to handle leftovers that would result if the same meal was prepared to serve only one person. Special frozen baked products, such as waffles, make it convenient to serve items without acquiring the special equipment needed to make the item.

SHOPPING AIDS

Ingredient Labeling

Ingredient labeling is required by federal mandate on all packaged food products. All ingredients must be listed, beginning with the one that is present in the largest quantity by weight and continuing sequentially in descending order. People who must avoid certain ingredients are able to identify products they should avoid if they take the time to examine the ingredient label.

In addition, ingredient labeling provides information to help consumers make wise choices between competing products. For example, two brands of beef stew can be compared to see the order of key ingredients. If beef is listed first on one and potatoes are the first ingredient on a competing brand and they are priced about the same, the first product would be the better buy because beef is more costly than potatoes. Although it takes time to read ingredient labels, they can be excellent guides to buying the maximum food values.

Unit Pricing

Unit pricing
Price of an ounce or other measure of a product to facilitate price comparisons by shoppers.

Shoppers need price information where they are making their selections. Labels stating the price of the item and also **unit pricing** are positioned on the shelf edge in front of each type and size of food item so consumers can know and compare prices between brands and between sizes of the same product.

Open Dating

Open dating
Date printed clearly on a container, usually to indicate the pull date.

Open dating gives consumers important information about the remaining shelf life that can be expected. Ideally, the date carries an explanation of what the date signifies. The usual practice is to print the date when the product should be pulled from the shelf and no longer sold. However, a date can mean the date it was manufactured or, as in the case of some cheeses, the date when optimum quality will develop.

Despite minor ambiguities in meaning, open dating is a valuable tool for consumers to aid them in selecting items that are fresh and wholesome so they can reduce the possibility of food spoiling after purchase and before it is consumed. Shoppers should check the dates on packaged items to be sure they are still within the date printed on them. Sometimes containers in a display carry different dates. If this is the case, consumers are wise to look for the container(s) carrying the date that extends furthest into the future.

Bar Codes

Bar code
Digital numeric code printed on packages that permits scanning products for identity and price at check-stands.

Scanners at check stands and **bar codes** on merchandise are useful to consumers because they speed the checking of groceries and produce a printed record of everything that is purchased and the price paid. Market owners also find them useful in helping maintain store inventories. Sometimes errors occur when bar codes are scanned because price changes may not be posted promptly. Careful scrutiny of register tapes is wise to be able to have any such problem corrected. Although stores can face penalties for errors in the prices posted, it ultimately falls on consumers to find problems and receive appropriate compensation for the error.

Bar codes have the potential for helping trace food items during a product recall and sometimes tracing a specific item through the route from farm to market. Information on date of manufacturing, lot, or other data can help identify specific items.

Because of the potential for detailed tracing of foods using bar codes, interest has grown in developing a system that allows bar codes to be placed directly on foods. An example of a useful application would be placing bar codes on each beef carcass so it can be traced all the way from the farmer to retail markets. This degree of identity would be potentially valuable in tracing the route of possible cases of bovine spongiform encephalopathy (BSE), an arena where tight controls are being imposed to prevent the spread of a disease with great potential threat to the cattle industry nationally and internationally. Work on applying bar codes directly on foods is in rather early stages of development, but it can be expected to increase in significance as threats to food safety continue to be a public issue.

Summary

One of the particularly important decisions consumers make is the store where they will shop, for this decision significantly influences the range and quality of food available, the time and energy required for shopping, and the actual cost of the food. Location, cleanliness, physical factors, services/personnel, overall food quality, fresh produce, meat and dairy, deli/bakery, breadth of inventory, and food prices are factors to consider when making that choice.

Retailers base their pricing on such factors as viable shelf life (short for meats, dairy, and produce), anticipated time in inventory, wholesale cost of food, and operating costs. Labor costs account for more than half of a retailer's operating budget. Market layouts are planned so utilities are available for the refrigerated and frozen cases and the produce section. These areas also are located to direct shoppers past as many items as possible on their way to the meat and dairy sections, thus promoting the sale of goods and easing congestion.

Shoppers have their choice of several different types of stores. Supermarkets are dominant, but other choices include niche markets, discount stores, warehouse clubs, convenience stores, and farmers' markets.

Management of marketing begins with a well-prepared shopping list so the required items can be purchased without costly extra visits. This list should be in a sequence that conforms to the floor plan of the market selected. Planning should be based on the quantities of food appropriate to maintaining healthy weight and stated in package sizes that are in the market. Before shopping, a quick inventory of household items and foods in the refrigerator, freezer, and pantry is needed to avoid gaps and overlaps; the refrigerator also should be cleaned in preparation for the new supplies.

Weekend shopping is recommended because of the specials and the excellent inventory available then. Shopping alone soon after a meal usually is most effective because there are few distractions when considering such choices as brands, forms of foods, prices of various quantities, and convenience in relation to cost. Also, hunger does not influence purchases. Unit pricing on store-shelf labels helps consumers compare prices. Open dating and ingredient labeling on food packages are other useful aids to shoppers.

Study Questions

1. What factors are important to you when you are deciding where to shop for groceries? Describe why each factor is significant.
2. Prepare a shopping list for a week's groceries. Visit two different supermarkets and compare the total cost if you were to buy the items at each store. Then compare the costs of individual items. Was there a difference in the total cost? Were certain items priced quite differently in the two stores? What conclusions can you draw regarding the economics of shopping at these stores?
3. After identifying the factors that are important to you in selecting a supermarket for weekly shopping, evaluate two supermarkets in your neighborhood. Which of these is the better choice for you? Why?
4. Use the shopping list developed in question 2 in a visit to a discount store. How do the prices compare with those found in the supermarkets? Compare the experience of shopping for this list at the discount store with that at the supermarket. Which store would you select for doing weekly food shopping?
5. What steps do you need to take to develop a shopping list that will include the items required for preparation of the week's menus and general kitchen operation?
6. Plan a menu for a lunch that includes a main dish. Copy the recipe for the main dish and write the shopping list for preparing it to serve six people. Describe the six people to be fed, and rationalize the decision on the quantities of ingredients ordered for preparing the main dish.

7. Briefly observe five different customers in a super-market. Write a description of the shopping practices of each customer. What suggestions could be made to help each person shop more effectively?

8. Compare the cost of buying (1) a frozen apple pie, (2) a frozen pie crust and apple pie filling, (3) the basic ingredients to make the pastry and filling for an apple pie, and (4) an apple pie from the bakery. Estimate the time required to make each of these pies. Discuss the merits and disadvantages of each option.

9. In a market, make a list of all of the forms in which milk is available; indicate (1) where each is located in the store, (2) the sizes available, (3) the cost of each size and product, and (4) storage requirements and estimated shelf life. Discuss the advantages and disadvantages of each type of milk.

Suggested Websites

http://www.pigglywiggly.com
Site for Piggly Wiggly Stores.

http://www.safeway.com
Site for Safeway Stores.

http://www.traderjoes.com
Trader Joe's site.

http://www.wholefoods.com/
Site for Whole Foods.

http://www.mygrocerychecklist.com
Site for aids in making grocery list.

http://www.Albertsons.com
Albertsons site.

http://www.heb.com/mealtime/groceryList.jsp
Online grocer.

http://www.cfsan.fda.gov/~dms/fc01-a6.html
FDA regulations on reduced oxygen packaging, including discussion of microbiological hazards and storage requirements.

Bibliography

Anonymous. 2002. *Consumer Reports Buying Guide.* Consumers Union. Yonkers, NY.

Anonymous. 2002. Kitchen works. *Consumer Reports.* 67 (8): 14.

Anonymous. 2002. Where to buy. *Consumer Reports* 67 (7): 11.

Anonymous. 2002. Quick, cheap, and healthy: Three words every parent wants to hear around dinnertime. *J. Am. Dietet. Assoc.* 102 (5): 656.

Berry, D. 2004. Keeping foods fresh. *Food Product Design.* 13 (10): 86.

Brecher, S. J., et al. 2000. Status of nutrition labeling, health claims, and nutrient content claims for processed foods: 1997 Food Label and Package Survey. *J. Am. Dietet. Assoc.* 100 (9): 1057.

Fiore, P. 2006. Consumers want clarity in labeling. *Food Technol.* 60 (6): 136.

Fonda, D. 2002. Organic growth. Inside Business Bonus Section. *Time.* 160 (7): Y1.

Fulmer, M. 2002. Lettuce grows into a processed food. *Los Angeles Times.* August 19, C1.

Harding, T. B., Jr., and Davis, L. R. 2005. Organic foods marketing and labeling. *Food Technol.* 59 (1): 41.

Heffernan, J. W., and Hillers, V. N. 2002. Attitudes of consumers living in Washington regarding food biotechnology. *J. Am. Dietet. Assoc.* 102 (1): 85.

Kennedy, E. T., et al. 2001. Popular diets: Correlation to health, nutrition, and obesity. *J. Am. Dietet. Assoc.* 101 (4): 411.

Nightingale, S. D., and Christens-Barry, W. 2005. Placing bar codes directly onto food. *Food Technol.* 59 (2): 36.

Pszczola, D. E. 2001. Convenience foods: They've come a long, long way. *Food Technol.* 55 (9): 85.

Sloan, A. E. 2005. Cruising the center-store aisles. *Food Technol.* 59 (10): 28.

CHAPTER 5

Buying Dairy Products and Substitutes

Dairy products are available in various forms, including pasteurized milks with varying levels of fat, alterations in lactose, and various bacterial cultures. Similarly, soy and rice drinks also are available as alternative beverages. In addition, the traditional cheeses of years past may be found as low-fat cheeses, and they are competing with soy-based "cheeses." All of these products are found in refrigerated cases in markets.

Other milk products are located on market shelves. They have been processed using heating, canning, and/or drying so they do not require refrigeration until opened. Among these forms of milk are ultra-heat-treated (UHT) milk, evaporated milk of various fat levels, sweetened condensed milk, and dried milk. This chapter reviews many of the options confronting consumers when their shopping lists say milk and cheese.

MILK CHOICES

Fluid Milks

Heat Treatment

Pasteurized milk
Milk that has been heat treated to kill disease-causing microorganisms.

Certified raw milk
Unheated milk that may contain viable disease-causing microorganisms.

UHT (ultra-heat-treated) milk
Sterilized milk that can be stored at room temperature until opened.

Fortunately **pasteurized milk** is the type of milk sold in all markets in the United States, and raw (unpasteurized) milk is rarely available. Pasteurized milk has been subjected to a heat treatment (holding at 71°C for 15 seconds or 63°C for 30 minutes) that is sufficient to kill harmful microorganisms. Raw milk, including **certified raw milk**, has not been heat treated, which means any microorganisms in the milk are still viable and capable of causing illness in humans.

UHT (ultra-heat-treated) milk is another choice found on supermarket shelves. It has been heated to 138°C and held at least two seconds. UHT milk, in contrast to pasteurized milk that must be stored in refrigerated display cases, is stocked on shelves without refrigeration. It is presently available in a 1-quart container and also in a three-pack of 8-ounce boxes suitable for inclusion in a lunch box. Room temperature storage of UHT milk is possible because this milk has been sterilized to kill all of the bacteria that might have been in the milk originally. Until the package is opened, UHT milk does not require refrigeration. However, once it has been opened, microorganisms may enter the milk, and refrigerator storage is essential to retard their growth. In other words, pasteurized or certified milk always needs to be refrigerated, and UHT milk requires refrigeration after the container is open.

Fat Level

Fluid milks can be purchased at four levels of fat—whole (possibly as high as 3.8 percent fat), reduced fat (2 percent fat), low-fat or light milk (1 percent fat), and nonfat or fat-free milk (<0.1 percent fat). Whole milk has 160 calories per cup, reduced fat has 125 calories, low fat has 102 calories, and nonfat has 90 calories per cup (Table 5.1). The high calorie contribution of fat in milk makes the choice of fat level of interest to dieters.

From the perspective of optimum nutrition, the best choice for most people older than two years is nonfat milk, both for drinking and cooking. Some people prefer the flavor of a richer type of milk. A reasonable compromise for them is reduced or, preferably, low-fat milk. For building and maintaining a healthy body throughout life, milk (especially nonfat) is the recommended beverage at meals regardless of a person's age or race.

Flavored Milks

Chocolate is the flavored milk most commonly available. Its acceptability, particularly among children, enables this form of milk to be an active competitor with soft

TABLE 5.1   Types of Milk, Their Fat Content, and Price/Unit[a]

Type	Fat Content	Calories/8 oz	$/Quart	$/Half Gallon	$/Gallon
Whole	3.5% (8.6 g)	160	$1.35	$2.39	$3.79
Reduced fat	2% (4.9 g)	125	1.19	2.19	3.79
Low fat	1% (2.7 g)	102	1.19	2.19	3.69
Nonfat	<0.1% (0.4 g)	90	1.14	2.091	3.49
Lactose free					
Whole	3.5% (8.6 g)	160	2.19	3.79	
Reduced fat	2% (4.9 g)	125	2.19	3.79	
Buttermilk					
Whole	2.4 g	100	1.49	2.49	
Nonfat	0.2 g	88	1.49	2.49	
Chocolate					
Whole	3.5% (8 g)		2.59	2.99	3.79
Reduced fat	2% (3 g)		1.79	3.79	3.79
Soy	4 g	100	2.28	3.47	6.49
Rice	2 g	130		3.99	

[a] *Prices in a Los Angeles, California, supermarket in November 2006.*

drinks as the beverage served at meals. Johnson et al. (2002) found that children drinking flavored milk (including chocolate) had a higher calcium intake than those who did not drink flavored milk, but their caloric intake from fat and added sugars was about the same. These researchers found that those who drank flavored milk had a reduced intake of fruit drinks and soft drinks in comparison with the children who did not drink flavored milk. Consumption of fruit juices by the two groups was similar. Clearly, flavored milk can be purchased as a beverage option for children and adults to promote milk consumption. The nutritional merits of flavored milk, although not quite as great as nonfat milk, are vastly superior to fruit drinks and soft drinks.

Lactase-Treated Milk

Lactaid

Milk in which lactase has digested much of the lactose.

Lactose, the sugar in milk, is digested by lactase to form glucose and galactose in enzyme-treated milk, such as **Lactaid**. The formation of glucose and galactose from lactose results in a slightly sweeter taste, but this type of milk is preferred by some people who experience discomfort when they drink milk containing lactose. The nutritional merits of milk are comparable for either type of milk.

Although Lactaid and other brands of lactase-treated milk are readily available in supermarkets, most consumers also have the option of buying milk that contains lactose. Many people with lactose intolerance may be able to drink regular milk if they drink one glass to accompany each meal or snack throughout the day and on an ongoing basis. Pribila et al. (2000) found that African American adolescent girls consuming a diet that contained about 1,100 mg of calcium each day for 21 days were able to tolerate the diet very well at the end of the study. In fact, the improving tolerance resulted in the calcium sources being shifted from a considerable content of yogurt at the beginning to primarily milk by the end of the study.

Buttermilk

Cultured buttermilk is yet another option among the fluid milks. This milk is made from skim milk that has been heated to 85°C for 30 minutes and then fermented with lactic-acid-producing bacteria at 22°C to produce a somewhat thickened, slightly acidic milk. Despite its creamy consistency, the only fat content is a very small amount of butter flecks. Essentially, the fat content is negligible. Many people enjoy **cultured buttermilk** as a beverage, and it also is useful as an ingredient in quick breads. The increased acidity promotes lightness and tenderness in baked products.

Cultured buttermilk
Skim milk thickened somewhat by the action of lactic-acid-producing bacteria.

Goat's Milk

Goat's milk is another fluid milk option that is available in the refrigerated dairy case in some supermarkets. This type of milk, which has a somewhat stronger odor and flavor than cow's milk, appeals to some consumers. Some people who are allergic to cow's milk are able to drink goat's milk without having an allergic response. They may opt to use goat's milk as their regular beverage and source of calcium.

Canned Milks

Canned milks are processed at high temperatures for an extended period of time in airtight cans. The combination of a tight seal on the cans and a very high processing temperature kills all of the microorganisms that are present prior to processing and prevents the entry of new sources of contamination until the cans are opened. These milks are useful because they can be stored at room temperature until they are opened, which makes them convenient for emergency use.

Evaporated Milk

Evaporated milk is a form of canned milk in which about half of the water has been evaporated from the milk before canning. Removal of half of the water reduces the volume and weight of the remaining milk. This means that shipping costs also are reduced. Canned evaporated milk is available with varying fat content (whole, low fat, and nonfat). Table 5.2 compares the nutrient content and cost of various canned milks. Any of these evaporated milks have a cooked taste because of the extensive heat treatment required for sterile canning. They also will have a rather creamy color due to the browning (Maillard) reaction that occurs between lactose and milk proteins during the sterilizing process.

When evaporated milk is used as a beverage, it should be diluted with an equal amount of water to approximate the concentration of other fluid milks. Some recipes that include evaporated milk as an ingredient do not intend for the milk to be diluted and will not give the expected results if diluted evaporated milk is used. Any recipe in which evaporated milk is an ingredient must be read carefully to determine the need for diluting the canned milk.

Sweetened Condensed Milk

Sweetened condensed milk is another canned milk product that has had approximately half of its water removed prior to canning. However, this form of canned milk is very different because it has a large amount of sugar added to it, making its caloric content very high. As a result, sweetened condensed milk is not suitable for use as a beverage or to feed infants even if diluted.

The viscosity of sweetened condensed milk is much greater than that of evaporated milk, which causes it to appear to pile slightly as it is poured from the can. Obviously, the large amount of added sugar makes it an extremely sweet milk, one that is suited for use in making some desserts and candies. Sweetened condensed milk is not diluted when it is used in recipes. In fact, it is even possible to heat it in the can in a

TABLE 5.2   Content of Selected Nutrients in Canned Milks and Comparative Cost[a]

Type of Canned Milk	Calcium (mg)	Fat (g)	Calories	Cost
Evaporated				
Whole	252/half cup[b]	7.9/half cup[b]	160[b]	$1.19/can
Low fat			100[b]	1.19/can
Nonfat			100[b]	1.19/can
Sweetened condensed	262/half cup[c]	8.7/half cup[c]	321[c]	3.24/can
UHT[d]	291/cup	8.1/cup	160[d]	2.69/qt
Dry nonfat[e]	303/cup	0.4/cup	90[e]	1.16/qt
Dry cultured buttermilk				1.12/qt

[a] Data collected from can labels and shelf prices in a supermarket in the greater Los Angeles area, November 2006.
[b] Evaporated milk is reported here undiluted, but another half cup of water would be added if it is to be consumed as a beverage (= 8 fl oz).
[c] Sweetened condensed milk should not be used as a beverage; figures are reported for undiluted sweetened condensed milk as it is used in desserts.
[d] UHT is used directly from the container without dilution. It also is available in a pack of three single servings.
[e] Nonfat dry milk solids are comparable to nonfat milk when reconstituted according to package directions. Each envelope makes 1 quart reconstituted.

scalding water bath for an hour or more to create a caramel dessert with the consistency of a pudding. Other desserts (e.g., lemon pie filling) can be made with sweetened condensed milk by stirring in some juice from a lemon or lime, which thickens the milk without even heating it.

Dried Milk

Milk can be dehydrated to a dry powder that can be stored without refrigeration for a reasonably long time as long as its packaging remains sealed. Once the dried milk solids are reconstituted, this type of milk must be kept refrigerated (just like other fluid milks). Nonfat dried milk solids are useful when food budgets are very tight, as emergency rations, and on camping trips, especially for backpacking where weight is a problem and potable water will be available. The shelf life of dried milk is limited by the possible development of rancidity in the fat. For this reason, nonfat dried milk solids have the longest shelf life.

Usually dried milks are reconstituted and used in cooking in place of fluid milks or as a beverage. Reconstituted dried milks have a detectable, slightly cooked flavor, which is objectionable to some people. Diluting reconstituted dried milk with an equal amount of fluid milk reduces this problem. The advantages of dried milk are the relatively low cost and long shelf life of unopened packages.

Milk Substitutes

People who are allergic to milk proteins may need to find another dietary source of calcium. This allergy problem is totally different from having a deficiency of lactase. Soymilk and rice drinks are available in markets today to offer a possible solution to avoiding milk proteins while still obtaining useful amounts of calcium (Table 5.3). Various flavoring and texturizing agents are included in these beverages to enhance their acceptability to consumers. Neither soymilk nor rice drinks can be substituted for milk in most cooking applications.

TABLE 5.3 Calcium and Protein Content of Milk and Milk Substitutes[a]

Beverage	Calcium/8 fl oz	Protein	
		Protein/8 fl oz	Type
Whole cow milk	291	8.0 g	Casein
Soymilk	55	8.9 g	Soy
Rice beverage	130	1.0 g	Rice

[a]Data from nutrition and ingredient labels found in the market in November 2006.

CREAMS

Whipping Cream

Whipping creams have a fat content between 30 and 36 percent. When chilled, they can be whipped into a foam that is stabilized by the large amount of fat in them. Heavy whipping cream with 36 percent fat whips readily to a more stable foam than regular whipping cream, which has less fat present to stabilize the foam. A convenient form is available in aerosol cans. These can be shaken vigorously before spraying out a garnish of whipped cream. Another form of whipped cream is available frozen in a plastic container in the freezer section of the store. Neither the aerosol nor frozen product is suitable if a recipe requires whipping cream as a liquid rather than as a whipped foam. Care needs to be exercised in reading recipes to determine whether the ingredient specified is whipping cream (a liquid) or whipped cream (a foam). Whipping cream can be whipped to make whipped cream, but the reverse operation is impossible.

Half-and-Half

Half-and-half is a very light cream that usually contains between 10.5 and 18 percent fat. This type of cream still has a rich flavor, which makes it acceptable as a cereal topping and coffee whitener to people who want a creamy flavor without as much fat as is contained in light whipping cream. Half-and-half cannot be whipped into a stable foam because there is too little fat in it to provide stability. Consequently, it cannot be used if whipped cream is required. As is true for any cream available in markets, half-and-half is pasteurized to kill harmful microorganisms that might be present, which makes it safe to use. However, all creams need to be refrigerated for safety.

Sour Cream

Sour cream is a clabbered form of cream with a fat content of 18 percent. Clabbering is accomplished by introducing lactic-acid-forming bacteria, which are allowed to ferment the cream until enough lactic acid is produced to precipitate the casein (principal protein in milk) to form a soft curd. Sometimes sour cream is used as an acid ingredient that interacts with baking soda to produce carbon dioxide and leaven a baked product. Frequently it is used as a topping for baked potatoes or a garnish for soups and salads. It also is an ingredient in a variety of recipes, especially in casseroles. Sour cream, with its comparatively low fat content, contributes a fourth of the calories that would be provided by the same measure of butter (Table 5.4).

TABLE 5.4   Fat Content and Calories in Various Cream Products[a]

Type of Cream	Fat content	Calories	Cost
Heavy whipping cream	5 g/Tb	60/Tb	$3.49/pt
Whipping	4.5 g/Tb	45/Tb	2.59/pt
Whipping (aerosol)	1 g/2 Tb	15/Tb	2.99/7 oz
Whipped, frozen	1 g/Tb	13/Tb	2.39/qt
Half-and-half	1.5 g/Tb	20/Tb	1.89/pt
Nondairy creamer	1.5 g/2 Tb	10/Tb	1.20/pt
Sour cream	3 g/Tb	30/Tb	1.89/cup
Light sour cream	1 g/Tb	20/Tb	1.89/cup
Fat free sour cream	0.25 g/Tb	15/Tb	1.89/cup

[a] *Information from nutrition labels on packages and shelf prices in Los Angeles, November 2006.*

YOGURT

Placamo-bacterium yoghourti, Lactobacillus bulgaricus, and *Streptococcus thermophilus* are added to either whole or nonfat milk and allowed to ferment to make yogurt. The lactic acid produced by this culture causes the milk to clabber, forming a smooth and soft curd. This texture usually prevents yogurt from being used as a beverage, but it is very popular when eaten with fruit or other complementary foods, or when simply eaten plain. Some people like to use yogurt rather than milk with cold cereals. It also can serve as a recipe ingredient. Frozen yogurt competes with ice cream as a dessert choice for many consumers.

Yogurt drinks, often with probiotics intended to lower cholesterol and promote desirable intestinal microflora, are gaining a foothold in the marketplace. The fact that they are a beverage makes yogurt drinks a particularly healthy and convenient choice for people who eat on the run during hectic days on the job. The content of these drinks varies, but some even have omega-3 fatty acids added to enhance the health claims.

ICE CREAM

Several different ice creams are available in the market (Figure 5.1). One of the variables in ice cream is the fat content. Rich vanilla ice cream may contain approximately 16 percent fat; regular vanilla ice cream may contain only 10 percent fat. Fat content

---

BOX 5.1

Food Insights: Microorganisms Counterattack

Food safety is a constant concern, and various approaches to preventing foodborne illnesses are being used. French researchers have been investigating the possibility of finding lactic acid bacteria capable of blocking the growth of harmful microorganisms in milk and milk products. They found certain *Enterococcus faecium, Lactococcus garvieae,* *Vagococcus carniphilus,* and *Enterococcus* spp. exerted an antagonistic effect against some pathogenic bacteria and served as some protection against spoilage. Early efforts suggest that continued research may result in using appropriate microorganisms as biopreservatives.

FIGURE 5.1   Ice cream is consumed frequently by itself and also used as an ingredient in strawberry shakes and other recipes.

influences texture and flavor. Of course, the higher fat content means more calories than in the lower fat ice cream, the former being about 520 calories per cup versus about 290 calories in a cup of regular vanilla ice cream (Table 5.5).

During the freezing process in manufacturing, ice cream is stirred to incorporate air and create a lighter feeling on the tongue than is true of still-frozen ice cream (frozen without agitation). Agitation also constantly disrupts the ice crystals that are forming during freezing to promote a smoother texture. This agitation results in an increased volume in the frozen product, termed **overrun**. Excessive overrun creates an almost frothy texture, but too little overrun produces a texture that is almost too compact in the mouth. The amount of overrun can be determined by weighing comparable volumes of ice creams.

Ingredients added to commercial ice creams include stabilizers and flavoring agents. Stabilizers help control the rate of melting when ice cream is served. They not

Overrun
Increase in the volume of ice cream because of air incorporated during the freezing process.

TABLE 5.5   Fat Content and Calories of Selected Frozen Dessert Products[a]

Frozen Product	Fat	Calories
Premium ice cream	36 g/cup	520
Regular ice cream	18 g/cup	290
Yogurt	9 g/cup	230
Ice milk	8 g/cup	136
Sherbet	6 g/cup	300
Sorbet	0 g/cup	280

[a]*Data from nutrition and ingredient labels on packages in November 2006.*

only make the ice cream easier to serve, but they also promote a smoother texture. Flavoring agents may be artificial flavoring agents or they may be added ingredients. If the flavor is achieved by simply adding an artificial flavoring agent, the ice cream cannot be called the name of the flavoring agent (e.g., an ice cream flavored with an artificial strawberry flavoring must be called strawberry-flavored ice cream, not strawberry ice cream). However, the name of strawberry ice cream can be used when the product is flavored with strawberries.

Ice milks are products related to ice creams, but they contain more water and less fat (in the vicinity of 4 percent fat). The flavor of these ice milks is less full than the flavor of ice creams, but the calorie content is only about two thirds that of an ice cream with 10 percent fat. Dieters may have the added bonus of discovering that large servings of ice milks are less tempting than a rich ice cream, which also helps curb calories. In addition, the price of ice milks is ordinarily lower than the price of a premium ice cream.

Fruit sherbets are fruit and/or frozen desserts containing fruit juice. The fat content is between 1 and 2 percent, but the sugar content may be higher than in many ice creams. The net result is that the calorie content of sherbets is similar to ice creams with 10 percent fat but significantly higher than ice milks. Ices also are available, but these are made without milk or milk products. Some frozen desserts are made using sugar substitutes and/or fat substitutes. The calorie content on these is quite variable, which makes it particularly important to read nutrition labels when making selections.

CHEESES

Natural Cheeses

Cheeses are classified on the basis of their manufacturing procedures and ingredients, usually milk from cows, sheep, or goats. Pasteurized milk should be used to avoid such bacterial hazards as *Listeria monocytogenes* and *Campylobacter*. Fatal outbreaks of listeriosis among people who had eaten some locally manufactured soft Mexican cheese made using raw milk in Los Angeles several years ago reinforced the importance of making cheese only from pasteurized milk.

Sometimes Brie and other soft or semisoft cheeses with a relatively high moisture content are made using raw milk, but these cheeses need to be aged a minimum of 60 days as a means of helping to ensure safety. This length of storage reduces potential populations of *E. coli* and *Salmonella* but allows an increase in *Listeria monocytogenes* if present. Because of this potential problem, emphasis is being placed on sanitation measures and control of the manufacturing environment in the production of these cheeses if raw milk is the starting product. Ingredient labels on cheeses indicate if pasteurized milk was used to make them.

Manufacturing of cheese begins with clotting pasteurized milk with acid or rennin (an enzyme from the stomach of calves). The resulting curd is cut, and the whey (soluble proteins, lactose, and water) is drained until the desired moisture level is achieved in the curd, which now contains a concentration of insoluble proteins and fat. The cheese may be marketed as a natural, unaged cheese, or it may be stored under carefully controlled conditions for an extended period of time (Figure 5.2).

Special cultures may be added so that desirable textural and flavor changes occur as the cheeses age. Aged cheeses are designated as "ripened" cheese. Particularly noteworthy examples of ripened cheeses are Camembert, Brie, and Liederkranz. The labyrinth of holes that characterizes a high-quality Swiss cheese is the result of gas formation by microorganisms in the cheese during the aging process. Stilton, gorgonzola, and blue are

FIGURE 5.2   Many imported and domestic ripened and unripened cheeses are marketed in refrigerated cases in supermarkets and niche grocery stores.

aged with a special mold that contributes the somewhat marbled, veined appearance of these aged cheeses.

Cheddar cheese not only develops a more interesting flavor profile during aging, but it also becomes more crumbly and blends more readily with other ingredients because it is aged to the point where it is identified as "sharp" or "extra sharp." The longer the ripening period for cheddar or any other ripened cheese, the higher the price is likely to be because storage costs are increased.

Natural cheeses with moderately high water content cannot be aged without spoiling. Instead, soft cheeses such as cottage cheese, ricotta, and mascarpone are marketed as soon as they are manufactured. These require careful refrigeration to maintain their safety, whereas firmer cheeses with low water content can be held safely for short periods at room temperature. Some soft cheeses have cream added to the cheese curd during manufacturing, for example, cream cheese and creamed cottage cheese.

Processed Cheeses

Processed cheeses are made by heating shredded natural cheeses and an emulsifier to produce a product that is usually rather bland in flavor but easy to use in cooking. The emulsifier is effective in binding the fat to prevent separation when processed cheeses are heated during food preparation. If a distinctive cheese flavor is desired in a product, an appropriate natural cheese is preferable to use. However, natural cheeses should be heated as briefly and at as low a temperature as is compatible with the dish being prepared.

Several types of processed cheese products are available. These include pasteurized processed cheese, pasteurized processed cheese food, and pasteurized processed cheese spreads. The consistency of these various products differs because of the amount of water and fat (Table 5.6). Another processed cheese product is coldpack cheese, also called club or crock cheese. The difference between this type of processed

TABLE 5.6   Fat Content, Calories, and Prices of Selected Cheeses[a]

Cheese	Fat	Calories	Price>
Cheddar	9 g/oz	110/oz	$4.49/lb
Sharp cheddar	9 g/oz	110/oz	4.99/lb
Very sharp cheddar	9 g/oz	110/oz	5.74/lb
Grated cheddar	9 g/oz	110/oz	4.94/lb
Swiss	8 g/oz	110/oz	5.99/lb
Sliced Swiss	8 g/oz	110/oz	3.45/10 oz
Mozzarella	4.5 g/oz	80/oz	2.69/8 oz
Grated mozzarella	4.5 g/oz	80/oz	3.29/8 oz
Brie	7.8 g/oz	94/oz	4.50/8 oz
Cream cheese	4.5 g/Tb	50/Tb	3.59
Low-fat cream cheese	22 g/Tb	35/Tb	3.59
Creamed cottage cheese	4.2 g/cup	239/cup	3.59/12 oz
Cottage cheese	10 g/cup	226/cup	1.99/12 oz
Light cottage cheese	5 g/Tb	200/cup	2.99/12 oz

[a] *Data from nutrition labels and shelf prices in Los Angeles, November 2006.*

cheese and others is the lack of a heat treatment during production. However, only pasteurized milk is used to make coldpack cheese.

Summary

All milk should be pasteurized to assure safety from harmful microorganisms. Ultra-heat-treated milk (UHT) is sterilized during processing and can be stored at room temperature until the package is opened, but then it needs to be refrigerated, just like pasteurized milk. Milk is available as whole milk (as much as 3.8 percent fat), reduced fat (2 percent fat), low fat (1 percent fat), and fat free <0.1 percent fat). Flavored milks, lactose-reduced milks, and buttermilk are other forms of cow's milk found in the market.

Evaporated milk is available in varying fat levels. Half of the water is evaporated from the milk before the milk is canned. When used as a beverage, water is added to dilute evaporated milk to its original volume. Sweetened condensed milk also is evaporated before being canned, but sugar is added. The very sweet, viscous product is usually used undiluted as an ingredient in desserts. It is not suitable for use as a beverage.

Heavy whipping cream whips readily to a rather stable foam when it is chilled, and regular whipping cream can also be whipped to a less stable foam. Half-and-half cannot be used to make a stable foam; its use is on cereal, in cooking, and as a coffee whitener. Sour cream is used in various applications in cooking and is a popular topping on baked potatoes and other dishes.

Yogurt is a clabbered milk product, which often is combined with fruit. Ice creams are quite varied in their fat content and their flavoring ingredients. They often are high in fat and sugar, both of which make them high in calories. Because of the wide variation in characteristics and price, consumers need to read nutrition labels if they wish to make a selection that is moderate in calories. Sherbets, sorbets, and ices are also available. Again, label reading is important because some of these have rather high calorie counts due to the quantity of sugar in them.

Natural cheeses often have rather distinctive flavors that make them useful in food preparation. Aging of some of the natural cheeses develops the desired flavor in cheeses such as Brie and cheddar. Soft natural cheeses with moderate moisture content cannot be aged because undesirable microorganisms may develop in them, causing spoilage. Processed cheeses are made by adding an emulsifier to a mixture of natural cheeses before the final pasteurization. Processed cheeses are easy to use in cooking, but they lack distinctive flavors.

Study Questions

1. What type of milk would be the best choice for a family of four (two adults and two children in elementary school)? Explain the rationale for this recommendation.
2. Describe a safe way for a child to carry milk to school to serve as the beverage at lunch.
3. During a trip to a local supermarket, make a chart that presents the prices of all of the competing milk products. Select the one that best fits your requirements, and write a justification for the choice.
4. Mary Sue says she cannot drink milk because it makes her uncomfortable due to gas. What can you suggest to help her be well nourished?
5. Identify at least 10 recipes that include milk as a major ingredient. Why is it important to be familiar with a variety of ways to incorporate milk in menu planning?
6. What cheese would be a good choice when making each of the following: (a) cheesecake, (b) macaroni and cheese, (c) cheese platter, (d) grilled cheese sandwich, and (e) fondue? Explain why each is suitable to use in preparing the dish.

Suggested Websites

www.dairycouncilofca.org
Website of the Dairy Council of California.

www.nationaldairycouncil.org
National Dairy Council website.

www.milk.co.uk
Dairy Council of the United Kingdom website.

www.oregondairycouncil.org
Website of Oregon Dairy Council.

www.wdairycouncil.com
Western Dairy Council website.

http://www.cheese.com/
Information about various cheeses and recipes for their use.

http://www.aboutyogurt.com/
Site of the National Yogurt Association.

http://homecooking.about.com/od/milkproducts/a/canmilk history.htm
Background and history of canned milks.

http://www.foodsci.uoguelph.ca/dairyedu/concprod.html
Information on concentrated and dried milk.

Bibliography

Ammor, S., et al. 2006. Antibacterial activity of lactic acid bacteria against spoilage and pathogenic bacteria isolated from the same meat small-scale facility. *Food Control.* 17 (6): 454.

Barr, S. I., et al. 2000. Effects of increased consumption of fluid milk on energy and nutrient intake, body weight, and cardiovascular risk factors in healthy older adults. *J. Am. Dietet. Assoc.* 100 (7): 810.

Bell, R. A., et al. 2002. Dietary calcium intake and supplement use among older African-American, white, and Native American women in a rural southeastern community. *J. Am. Dietet. Assoc.* 102 (8): 844.

Bowman, S. A. 2002. Beverage choices of young females: Changes and impact on nutrient intakes. *J. Am. Dietet. Assoc.* 102 (9): 1234.

Donelly, C. W. 2006. Raw-milk cheeses can be produced safely. *Food Technol.* 60 (4): 100.

Hazen, C. 2004. Cultured dairy products. *Food Product Design.* 13 (12): 73.

Huth, P. 2005. Dairy's fit for health. *Food Product Design.* 15 (7): 87.

Johnson, R. K., et al. 2002. Nutritional consequences of flavored-milk consumption by school-aged children and adolescents in the United States. *J. Am. Dietet. Assoc.* 102 (8): 853.

Peregrin, T. 2002. Expanding vitamin D fortification: A balance between deficiency and toxicity. *J. Am. Dietet. Assoc.* 102 (9): 1214.

Pribila, B. A., et al. 2000. Improved lactose digestion and intolerance among African-American adolescent girls fed a dairy-rich diet. *J. Am. Dietet. Assoc.* 100 (5): 524.

Shanklin, C. W., and Wie, S. 2001. Nutrient contributions per 100 kcal and per penny for the 5 meal components in school lunch: Entrée, milk, vegetable/fruit, bread/grain, and miscellaneous. *J. Am. Dietet. Assoc.* 101 (11): 1358.

Vierhile, T. 2006. Functional 'add-ins' boost yogurt consumption. *Food Technol.* 60 (7): 44.

Wosje, K. S., et al. 2001. No differences in growth or body composition from age 12 to 24 months between toddlers consuming 2% milk and toddlers consuming whole milk. *J. Am. Dietet. Assoc.* 101 (1): 53.

CHAPTER 6

Buying Protein-Rich Foods

Usually the most expensive item in a meal is meat or an alternative protein source. Not only is it the most expensive, but it also may be the focal point of the menu. This significance makes it very important to make selections with knowledge of the various factors influencing quality. This chapter discusses the selection of various meats, poultry, fish, and legume products.

RATIONALE FOR VARIETY OF SELECTIONS

Planning menus that contribute toward optimal health is a goal that interfaces with the choice of entrées and their ingredients. Red meats are appropriate two or three times a week, but their content of saturated fat makes it wise to limit their frequency and portion sizes when planning menus. This guideline directs attention to other options for the remaining meals in the week. Fish, with their omega-3 fatty acid content, are recommended at least twice each week. Poultry is another wise choice nutritionally (and economically as well). Cheese and eggs have a slightly limited role to play: cheese because of its rather high fat content and eggs (perhaps an average of about one daily) because of their cholesterol content. Soybean-based alternatives and other legumes are yet other possibilities.

FACTORS IN CHOOSING MEATS AND ALTERNATIVES

The choices among meats and meat alternatives afford wide opportunity for creativity in menu planning and cost control as well. The actual costs within this category vary considerably, depending on a number of marketing factors. However, many meat cuts and some of the highly prized fish are usually more expensive than poultry, cheese, eggs, and legumes.

Particularly when watching costs, the first choice in planning becomes which of these categories to choose. Then the specific choice can be made within the selected category of meat, poultry, fish, or legumes. Careful shopping is the final step in procuring the best possible cut.

CONTROLLING SAFETY

Expanded polystyrene (EPS)
Synthetic material used in making trays for retail packaging of meats.

Polyvinyl chloride (PVC)
Synthetic material that can be extruded to make films suitable to enclose meats and their trays for the retail market.

Centralized packaging
Large plant that prepackages meats and poultry in specialized safe packaging for distribution to many different stores.

Control of microorganisms is a primary concern in the marketing of all types of meat, poultry, and fish. The safety of the large quantities of packaged meats and poultry that are marketed (e.g., almost 9 billion packages of beef each year) is a daunting challenge. Poultry often is packaged as specific parts placed on trays made of **expanded polystyrene (EPS)**, which then are wrapped in a **polyvinyl chloride (PVC)** film. Many of these packages (in preparation for distributing to markets) are wrapped in large bags that can maintain a modified internal atmosphere. Pork currently is being distributed to markets in a similar fashion.

Preparation of the retail-sized packages of beef still often is done at supermarkets, which receive primal cuts and chubs of coarsely ground beef in barrier bags that maintain a reduced level of oxygen. Butchers then package the cuts they have prepared from the primal cuts, using EPS trays and PVC wrapping. The beef trays displayed in some supermarkets are prepared in the store in this fashion.

However, there is a growing trend to centralize the packaging of beef, just as was done successfully for poultry for many years. The advantage of **centralized packaging** rather than in-store preparation is that temperature and sanitation of the packaging area can be controlled more effectively to produce a safer package of beef than can be assured in some supermarkets. Beef that has been packaged in a centralized packaging facility has a shelf life of several days. This benefits retailers because centralized packaging helps reduce the losses that are incurred from the shorter shelf life of meats packaged in the store.

Packaging materials and technology are an important focus now. The fact that meats are so susceptible to spoilage from such microorganisms as *E. coli* impacts both cost and safety. Obviously, meats that are altered in quality by microorganisms during the marketing process may lose visual and olfactory appeal to consumers buying meats, and there are clear repercussions if a food poisoning outbreak is traced to meat and to the outlet selling it. The goal of packaging of meats is to extend shelf life, thus gaining a somewhat longer time when packaged meat can be available for purchase.

Gas-barrier trays
Packaging that traps gases in the package and also prevents other gases from entering.

Packaging experts have developed several technologies to meet the demands of packaging meats for ultimate retail purchase. Wal-Mart, because of its high demand for prepackaged meat, has had a strong influence in this area. Its specification is that primary packaging use **gas-barrier trays**, which are sealed (with a gas-barrier heat-sealed lidding closure) in 80 percent (high) oxygen. Many beef cuts and almost half of the ground beef marketed today are packaged using this technology (high-oxygen packaging, barrier trays, and barrier heat-sealing lid). The added costs of the specialized materials and equipment used in this type of packaging are no more than, and may be less than, the costs of doing packaging in retail stores.

CHOOSING BEEF CUTS

Many supermarkets offer a choice of two federal grades of beef: USDA Choice and USDA Select. A few gourmet markets offer Prime, the top grade for beef. USDA Prime is characterized by its excellent flavor, juiciness, and tenderness (characteristics enhanced by its comparatively high fat content). USDA Choice has somewhat less fat than Prime but more than the next lower grade, USDA Select.

Table 6.1 provides a comparison of the effect of this difference in fat content between some beef cuts graded Choice and Select. The recommendation to limit the intake of fat, particularly saturated fatty acids, supports the choice of Select beef despite the fact that the same cut of Choice grade scores higher for palatability.

BOX 6.1

Food Insights: Cattle Versus Corn

Much of the beef available in American grocery stores is grass-fed, but some USDA Prime and Choice cuts can be found, depending on the market. Some people prefer the flavor of corn-fed beef; other diners may opt for grass fed because its flavor is satisfactory and the fat content may be lower. The choice is personal, but economics may be the deciding factor. Grass-fed beef usually is less costly than corn-fed beef.

Surprisingly, the high cost of gasoline may be adding another dimension to the discussion regarding cattle feed. Ethanol is becoming a fuel of interest as alternatives to gasoline are being sought. Corn that previously has been used to feed some cattle and many hogs is now a competitor in the market for alternative fuels because ethanol can be produced from corn. This competition is driving up the price of corn, which then adds to the cost of producing beef, pork, and poultry that are fed corn to bring them to market weight. Dairy cows being fed corn require about 10 pounds of corn daily for milk production.

Prior to the surge in interest in ethanol as a fuel, the food industry mainly had to worry about the bounty of the corn crop. Suddenly, it is competing for corn against fuel producers. In 2006, 106 ethanol plants were operating and another 48 were being built. Livestock production has a new concern that may influence the cost of meat and poultry.

TABLE 6.1 Content of Fat, Saturated Fatty Acids, Cholesterol, and Calories in Beef Cuts[a]

Cut (3 oz cooked)	Total Fat (g)	Saturated Fatty Acids (g)	Cholesterol (mg)	Calories
Eye of Round, Roasted				
($\frac{1}{4}$" trim)				
Lean Only				
USDA Select	3	1	59	136
USDA Choice	5	2	59	149
Lean and Fat				
USDA Select	10	4	61	184
USDA Choice	12	5	62	205
Rib Eye, Broiled				
(0" trim)				
Lean Only				
USDA Select	7	3	68	168
USDA Choice	10	4	68	191
Lean and Fat				
USDA Select	17	7	70	242
USDA Choice	19	8	70	265
Ground Beef Patty				
(cooked)				
Extra Lean	14	5	71	215
Regular	17	7	76	245

[a]*Adapted from "How to Buy Meat." Home and Garden Bulletin #265. Agricultural Marketing Service. U.S. Department of Agriculture. Washington, DC. 1995.*

Consumers can resolve this problem by electing to eat a slightly smaller portion of Choice beef or having a little larger portion of Select beef.

Occasionally, consumers may decide while shopping to substitute one cut for a different (but suitable) one that happens to be on sale in the market at a special price. If the cut will work equally well in the recipe, or if another preparation will fit the menu, such a substitution can be a smart buy. Knowledge of the tenderness and textural characteristics of the various beef cuts is necessary for making informed on-site decisions while shopping.

Primal cuts
First cuts made on meat carcasses; cuts from which retail cuts are made.

Figure 6.1 shows the **primal cuts** of beef and identifies whether they usually are classified as yielding tender or less tender retail cuts. In beef the tender cuts are from the rib, short loin, and sirloin; dry heat cookery methods (roasting, broiling, and frying) are appropriate to prepare them. Cuts from the other primal cuts are suited for moist heat cookery methods (stewing or braising).

Labels that identify the primal cut as well as the retail name of the cut contained in the package help shoppers determine whether it is classified as a tender or less tender cut. A very visible clue to determining its original location on the carcass is the shape of the bone in the cut. Figure 6.2 contains sketches of the various bones and indicates where they are located. A general guideline using bone to categorize cuts is that cuts with back, rib, pin, flat, or wedge bones are classified as tender. Bones signifying less tender cuts are arm, blade, leg (round), and breast. The T-shaped backbone easily identifies steaks cut from the loin. Sirloin steaks have part of the pin bone if they are from near the short loin, a flat bone if a center cut, or a wedge bone if cut from close to the round. These variations in sirloin are the result of their origins from three different parts of the hipbone. At the opposite end is the brisket, which is a less tender cut containing the breast and adjoining rib bones.

Flavor, an important quality in beef, is enhanced as the animal matures. The color of the meat darkens, the fat looks less pink, and the bones ossify with increasing age. These characteristics can be seen in the various packages of beef displayed at a

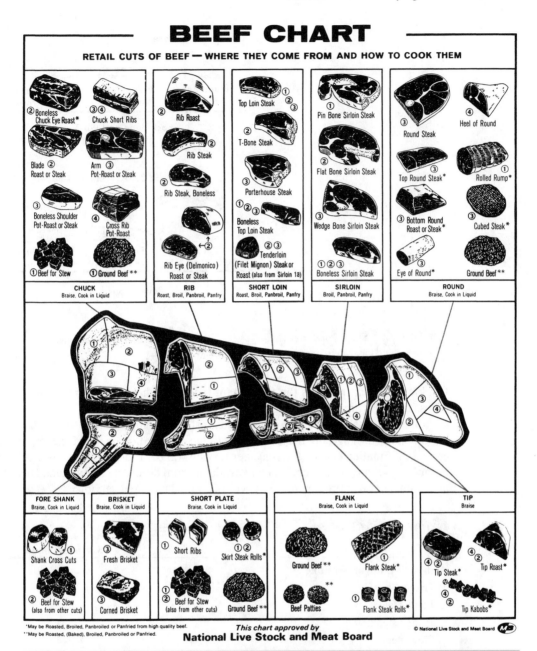

FIGURE 6.1 Beef chart showing primal and retail cuts, as well as suggestions for appropriate cooking methods. (Provided by the National Live Stock and Meat Board.)

supermarket, and they can serve as a guide to selecting beef mature enough to have developed a pleasing flavor.

Ground beef selection presents a dilemma because of the varying levels of fat and the difference in cost. At least 15 percent fat provides the flavor and juiciness that consumers desire, although people on very low-fat diets may wish to select ground meat with a fat content below 15 percent. Ground beef with a fat level of 15 percent has only a few detectable flecks of fat showing. As the fat level in ground beef increases, the fat flecks are more obvious; the color of the ground beef becomes a moderately light red.

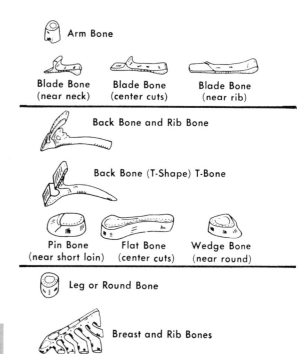

Arm Bone

Blade Bone
(near neck)   Blade Bone
(center cuts)   Blade Bone
(near rib)

Back Bone and Rib Bone

Back Bone (T-Shape) T-Bone

Pin Bone
(near short loin)   Flat Bone
(center cuts)   Wedge Bone
(near round)

Leg or Round Bone

Breast and Rib Bones

FIGURE 6.2 Shapes of various beef bones and location in the carcass.

Cooking losses increase as the fat content increases; the caloric content also increases unless the fat is drained thoroughly from the cooked meat.

One key to selecting which cut to buy is cost. It is a simple matter to read the price per pound on the package, but this is only part of the information needed for comparison. The critical information is what the price per serving will be. Table 6.2 provides a guide to the number of servings per pound that are available from different cuts of meat. These figures are estimated on approximately 3 ounces of cooked meat per serving.

TABLE 6.2 Estimated Servings Per Pound of Selected Beef Cuts

Beef Cut	Servings/Pound
Cuts with Little or No Bone	
Ground beef	4
Flank steak	4
Round steak	3–4
Stew meat	3–4
Boned roast	3–4
Liver	4
Cuts with Medium Bone	
Rib roast	$2\frac{1}{2}$
Brisket	$2\frac{1}{2}$–3
Porterhouse steak	$2\frac{1}{2}$–3
Much Bone, Gristle, Fat	
Spareribs	$1\frac{1}{2}$–2
Shank	$1\frac{1}{2}$–2
T-bone steak	2

VEAL

Veal is well suited to such dishes as veal scallopini, where the delicate flavor of this meat from cattle younger than 3 months adds a subtle quality to the dish. Cuts of veal comparable to beef cuts from the same carcass location are smaller, less juicy (due to little fat), and finer in texture than their beef counterparts. Although many markets carry veal, the inventory of veal usually is far more limited than the beef selections.

Demand for veal generally is far less than for beef. Probably one of the main reasons for this difference in demand is the higher cost of veal compared with beef. Table 6.3 provides some price comparisons between beef and veal, as well as lamb and pork. When selecting veal, priority is given to choosing light-colored veal because delicacy of flavor is usually preferred. Primal and retail cuts of veal are shown in Figure 6.3.

LAMB

Rack
Rib section of lamb.

As shown in Table 6.4, lamb commands a premium price among the red meats. The small amount of meat in relation to bone adds still more to the cost in relation to the actual edible portion. However, the distinctive flavor is valued greatly by people who savor lamb. Blade and arm chops come from the shoulder (Figure 6.4); the **rack** is the source of rib chops and roast, loin chops are from the loin, and leg of lamb is from the leg. To compensate for their small area, chops are cut to a thickness of 1 to 2 inches. Thinner chops will become too dry during their preparation. When selecting a package of lamb chops, it is important to have chops that are of an even thickness so they can be cooked uniformly.

PORK

Cured
Pork or beef that has been processed using heat, salt, and sodium nitrate.

Pork may be purchased fresh or **cured** (process combining heat, salt, and sodium nitrate). Curing alters the flavor and color of the meat, so the meat retains its reddish color during cooking. When buying and preparing cured pork products, it is important to read the label carefully to determine whether or not the item has been precooked. If it has, the cooking time will be shorter because it is only necessary to reheat the meat. In contrast, cured pork that has not been precooked needs to be heated until the interior temperature reaches 160°F to avoid the possibility of viable *Trichinella spiralis* in the meat.

Cured hams with the bone in may be purchased at the meat display, and they also are available canned but are still marketed in refrigerated display cases.

TABLE 6.3   Costs of Comparable Cuts of Beef, Veal, Lamb, and Pork[a]

Cut	Beef $/lb	Veal $/lb	Lamb $/lb	Pork $/lb
Rib roast	$6.99		$9.99	$3.99
T-bone steak or chop	9.49	$7.99	9.89	3.99
Tenderloin	12.79			3.99
Stew meat	3.10			
Ground meat	2.50	3.99	4.39	3.49

[a]*Data obtained in a supermarket in the Los Angeles area, November 2006.*

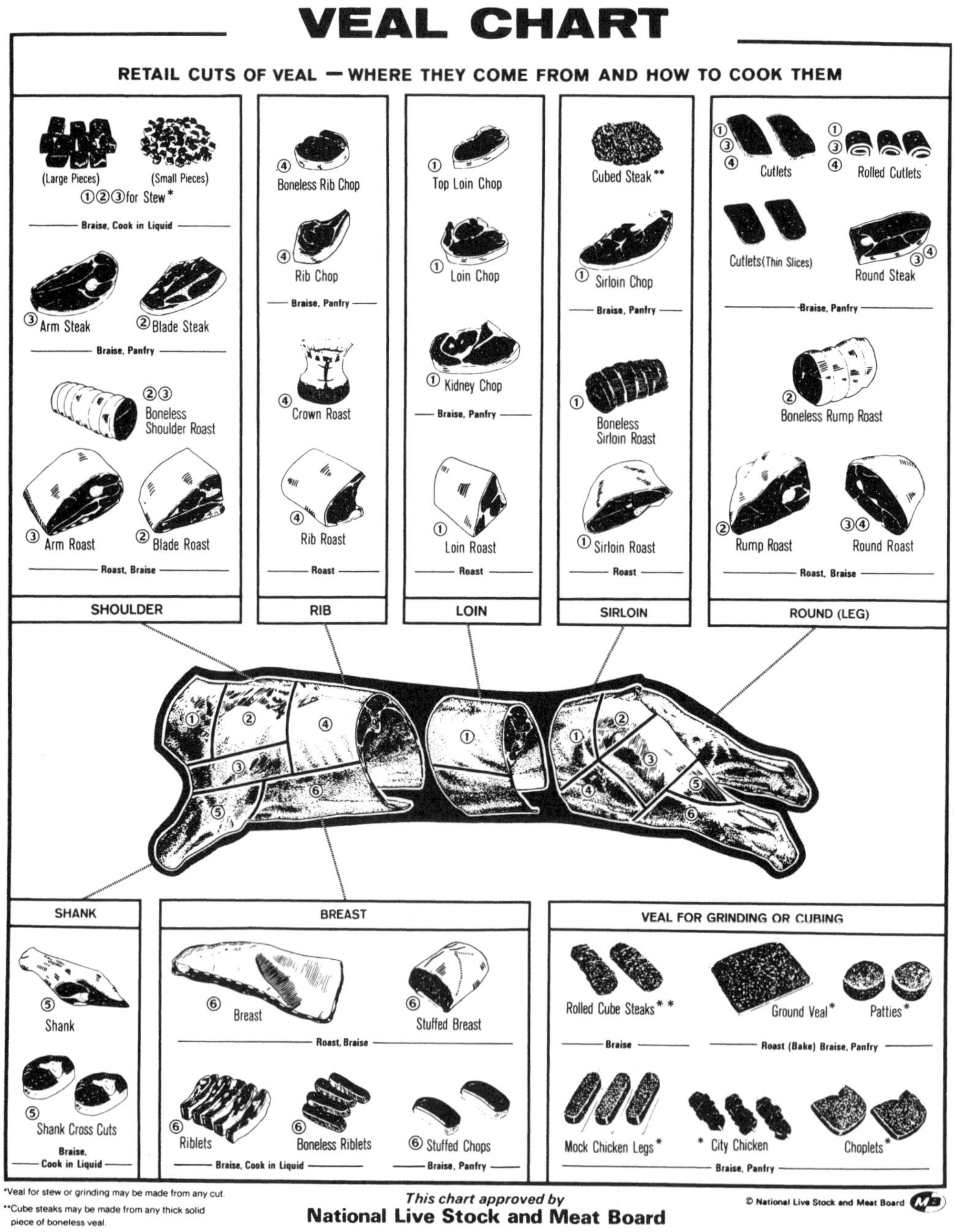

FIGURE 6.3 Veal chart showing primal and retail cuts, as well as suggestions for appropriate cooking methods. (Provided by the National Live Stock and Meat Board.)

Canned hams commonly require refrigeration because they have not been heated to a high enough temperature during canning to ensure safe storage at room temperature. An advantage of canned ham is that the bone has been removed to save space in the can, and the boneless ham is easy to carve into attractive slices when it is served.

TABLE 6.4   Fat Content and Comparative Costs of Selected Meats[a]

Type of Meat	Fat (%)	Cost/lb
Emu[b]	0	$7.50
Ostrich[c]	2.7	14.95
Duck[d]	11.2	1.19
Chicken[e]	9.7	0.79
Beef[f]	9.6	6.79
Pork[g]	9.8	4.69

[a]*Adapted from Daniel, D. R., Thompson, L. D., and Hoover, L. C. 2000. Nutrition composition of emu compares favorably with that of other lean meats. J. Am. Dietet. Assoc. 100 (7): 836.*
[b]*Average of inside drum and full rump; cost based on premium fillet.*
[c]*Broiled; cost based on premium fillet, July 1999.*
[d]*Domesticated, cooked, flesh only; cost based on whole duck.*
[e]*Dark meat without skin, roasted; cost based on thigh, July 1999.*
[f]*Loin, separable lean, broiled; cost based on whole tenderloin, July 1999.*
[g]*Choice short loin trimmed to 0" fat, cost based on T-bone steak, July 1999.*

Fresh pork often is marketed today in packages bundled at a centralized packaging operation. Such packaging makes it easy to see the chops or other cuts in their packages, but individual requests to the butcher regarding the thickness or quantity may not be possible. Fortunately, some supermarkets have butchers available to help consumers get what they actually wish to buy. Figure 6.5 shows the various primal and retail cuts of pork.

Pork products are quite varied and can be used occasionally to add variety to meals. A wide variety of sausages can be found, particularly in some markets with a clientele desiring a range of flavorings and sizes. Bratwurst is but one example of sausages intended for use as an entrée; pepperoni and salami illustrate sausages that are used as an ingredient for adding flavor excitement to a recipe.

Sausages may be processed for marketing as fresh, fresh smoked, cooked, cooked smoked, or dry (either dry or semidry). Although pork frequently is the principal ingredient in sausages, they also often are fabricated using beef, poultry (chicken or turkey), and even soy protein. They are stuffed into a casing of various dimensions, depending on the specific type of sausage and its traditional size. Refrigerated storage is important for sausages, although a dry sausage, such as pepperoni, can be held at room temperature for a few days. Some link or breakfast sausages are marketed in the frozen food case.

Bacon and Canadian bacon are cured pork products that are popular, particularly on breakfast menus or in sandwiches. The choice between thin and thick slices of bacon is a matter of individual preference. Shoppers need to note the weight of bacon packages when comparing prices between brands. Some weigh less than a pound, which used to be the standard weight for a package of bacon. The lighter package may be preferred if bacon is served infrequently.

The high fat content of bacon, even when fried crisp (13.5 g/3 strips), means that people who are watching their weight and limiting fat in the diet do not choose bacon often. Canadian bacon, which is cured pork tenderloin, contains only about a third of the fat in bacon after each is fried. The flavor may make Canadian bacon a suitable substitute for bacon, but it does not become crisp enough to crumble into bits for salads.

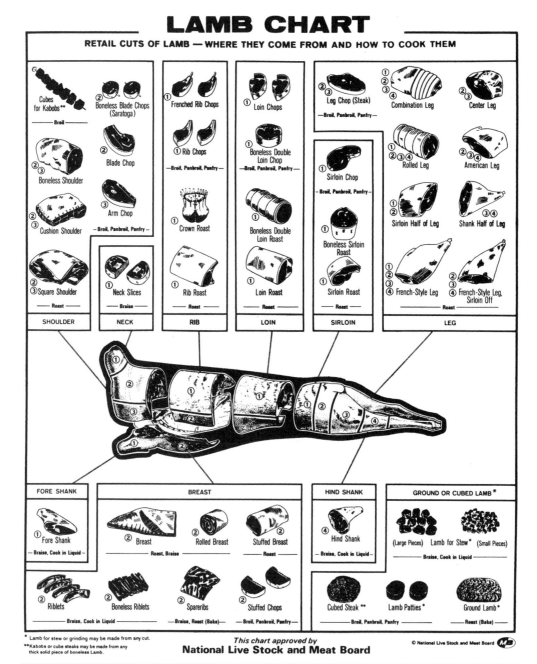

FIGURE 6.4 Lamb chart showing primal and retail cuts, as well as suggestions for appropriate cooking methods. (Provided by the National Live Stock and Meat Board.)

POULTRY

Production of poultry, particularly chickens and turkeys, often involves large commercial businesses that raise the fowl and others that ultimately prepare them for market at centralized packaging plants. Packages of cutup parts placed on EPS trays and wrapped with plastic film are bundled in master bags (usually barrier bags that can maintain an altered atmosphere). The individual packages may consist of only one type of part or may comprise the entire chicken cut into serving pieces.

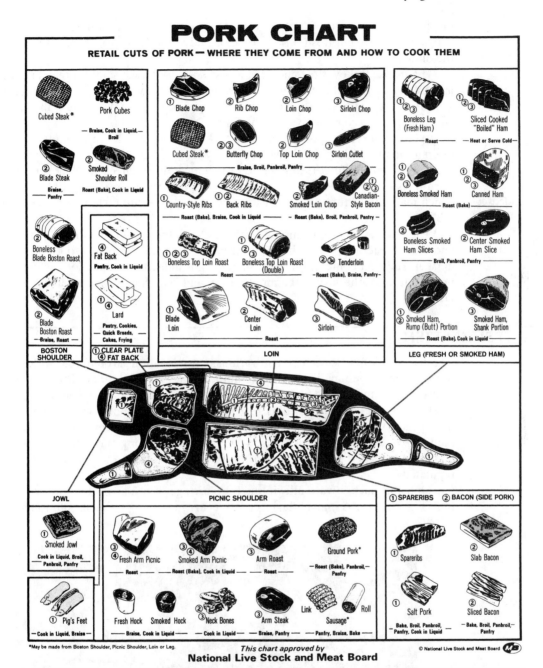

FIGURE 6.5 Pork chart showing primal and retail cuts, as well as suggestions for appropriate cooking methods. (Provided by the National Live Stock and Meat Board.)

Options for shoppers to consider are bone in or boneless and with or without the skin. Such choices make it easy to tailor the purchasing decision to fit the preferences of the diners or to conform to the specific ingredient required in a recipe. Small households may find that a half breast of turkey is a convenient choice to add variety from the seemingly ubiquitous chicken.

Poultry usually is available frozen or fresh. If chicken will not be prepared for several days after purchase, the choice well may be between buying the chicken already frozen or freezing the unopened fresh chicken package as soon as possible. Turkeys are particular favorites for Thanksgiving and Christmas holiday dinners. A convenient choice is to reserve a fresh turkey to be picked up at the supermarket the day before the dinner.

If a frozen turkey is the choice, it is necessary to thaw it safely. It may take as long as four days to thaw it in the refrigerator, and it is occupying valuable space that entire time. A quicker option is to thaw it in its unopened bag by immersing it in cold water, which is changed completely every half hour.

Whole chickens, capons, ducks, and turkeys are desirable for roasting in the oven or on a rotisserie. They should be free of any feathers and the skin free of any tears or breaks. If a frozen fowl is purchased, it is important to check the bag for any tears. Torn bags cause the exposed skin to become desiccated, resulting in **freezer burn**, which mars the beauty of the roasted fowl if it is presented whole for carving at the table.

Freezer burn
Dehydrated surface of frozen skin or meat due to direct exposure during frozen storage as a result of torn packaging.

The emphasis on reducing fat in the diet has fostered a small market for ostrich and emu. Generally these birds are raised on very small ranches to meet this niche market. Their fat content, shown in Table 6.4, is indeed especially low, actually to the point that it is rather dry in the mouth. Emu and ostrich may be available as steaks or ground.

FISH AND SHELLFISH

Because overfishing is occurring in various ocean locations around the world, the supplies of some popular fish are being depleted at alarming rates. Now international efforts are being directed toward controlling the quantities of endangered species that can be caught. Publicity regarding these problems has prompted cries urging that certain species, such as Chilean sea bass and orange roughy, be removed from restaurant menus. Abalone harvesting has long been banned along the California seacoast, and salmon fishing in the waters of the Pacific Northwest and Alaska also is tightly regulated.

One approach toward alleviating the shortage of fish is production by fish farming (Figure 6.6). A particularly creative arrangement to farm salmon in Chile

FIGURE 6.6   Abalone and mussel farms along the Pacific Coast are important sources of these types of seafood.

involves hatching the salmon in a large freshwater lake near the coast and then trucking the young salmon to the Pacific Ocean a short distance away when they are large enough to survive the trip. They are then released into saltwater enclosures just offshore where they are allowed to remain until mature enough to be harvested.

Fish farming is a very large industry in Chile. It also is becoming important in various locations in the United States. Abalone and mussels are examples of the fish farming on the coast of California, and salmon farming is an illustration from the Pacific Northwest. Some controversy has risen regarding the merits of farmed salmon versus wild salmon. Regardless of the source, salmon are recommended for a place on menus because of their very useful content of omega-3 fatty acids. Freshwater fish farming is the source of trout and catfish, as well as some other species produced in the United States. An advantage of the fish from farms is that they come from water monitored to minimize contamination of the fish, thus helping promote food safety.

The short shelf life of fish presents a particular challenge at all points along the way from the water to the dinner table. Fresh fish need to be kept well iced from the time they are caught and cleaned until they are cooked for the diner (Figure 6.7). Even when iced promptly, it is important to transport fish rapidly to the market so they can be purchased, cooked, and consumed within a day or two.

Time and temperature control are essential components of getting safe, high-quality fish to consumers. Airfreight is the mode of transport that has been particularly important in making fish of excellent quality and variety available in markets across the nation. Supermarkets have been quite effective in installing and maintaining clean, well-stocked fish counters to meet consumer demand for fish.

FIGURE 6.7   Halibut are transferred from a ship in Alaska to containers packed with ice in preparation for shipment to markets in the lower 48 states.

TABLE 6.5 Total Fat, Cholesterol, and Omega-3 Fatty Acids in Selected Fish[a]

Fish or Seafood	Total Fat (g)	Cholesterol (mg)	18:3[b] (g)	20:5[c] (g)	22:6[d] (g)
Catfish, channel	4.3	58	Trace (Tr)	0.1	0.2
Cod, Pacific	0.6	37	Tr	0.1	0.1
Flounder, yellowtail	1.2	—	Tr	0.1	0.1
Haddock	0.7	63	Tr	0.1	0.1
Halibut, Pacific	2.3	32	0.1	0.1	0.3
Ocean perch	1.6	42	Tr	0.1	0.1
Pike, walleye	1.2	86	Tr	0.1	0.2
Salmon, Atlantic	5.4	—	0.2	0.3	0.9
Salmon, coho	6.0	—	0.2	0.3	0.5
Snapper, red	1.2	—	Tr	Tr	0.2
Swordfish	2.1	39	—	0.1	0.1
Trout, brook	2.7	68	0.2	0.2	0.2
Tuna, albacore	4.9	54	0.2	0.3	0.1
Crab, Alaska king	0.8	—	Tr	0.2	0.1
Lobster, northern	0.9	95	—	0.1	0.1
Shrimp, northern	1.25	125	Tr	0.3	0.2
Scallop, Atlantic	0.8	37	Tr	0.1	0.1

[a]*Adapted from Provisional Table on the Content of Omega-3 Fatty Acids and Other Fat Components in Selected Foods. U.S. Dept. of Agriculture. Human Nutrition Information Service. Nutrient Data Research Branch. Nutrition Monitoring Division. Washington, DC. 1988.*
[b]*Linolenic acid.*
[c]*Eicosapentanoic acid (EPA).*
[d]*Docosahexanoic acid (DHA).*

Most supermarkets have a tempting counter where customers can select the actual fish they wish to buy. Some consumers may appreciate this personalized service because it also provides the opportunity to ask questions about the fish and how to prepare it. Of particular interest is the amount of fat and cholesterol in various fish (see Table 6.5).

Fish may be purchased fresh, frozen, and canned, but the types available in each of these forms may be rather restricted. The kinds of fresh fish available at a supermarket probably will vary from one shopping trip to the next, which makes it difficult to plan precisely until standing in front of the counter. However, fish farming has made the stocks slightly more predictable. Depending on the size of the market and the geographic location, shoppers will soon gain a reasonable idea of which fish generally are available where they do most of their shopping. Coastal cities have the advantage of being very close to where fishing boats bring in local catches from the sea to help stock the fish markets and some supermarket fish counters.

Among the fish and seafood that frequently are available fresh at fish counters are trout, catfish, halibut, salmon, sea bass, orange roughy, shrimp, and scallops. Various other choices probably will be offered at various times too. Fresh fish should have flesh that looks fresh and slightly moist, and the odor should be very mild. Fresh fish counters should not have a fishy smell. If they do, the market may not be keeping the fish iced and chilled adequately, and they may not be keeping the area clean enough to assure the fish are of high quality. Frozen or canned fish may be a better selection if shopping must be done at that supermarket.

Cod, ocean perch, lobster tails, fish sticks, and breaded fish fillets are among the fish options in the freezer section. Frozen fish can be a very suitable alternative to fresh fish in many fish entrées and other recipes. They have the added advantage of being able to be stored in the freezer until they are needed, whereas fresh fish is best if it is prepared the same day it is purchased. Canned tuna, crab, clams, lobster, and shrimp are other choices in the canned meat section of supermarkets. They can be used very satisfactorily in salads and some casseroles or other recipes where they are mixed with other ingredients, but they are not well suited to being served alone as the entrée.

EGGS

The quality of eggs printed on egg cartons ordinarily is the federal grade that was determined at the time they were being evaluated against federal standards. The grades found most commonly in markets are Grade AA (the highest) and Grade A. As eggs age, they slowly lose moisture and gas through the shell, which can mean that the eggs in the carton are not as high a quality as printed on the carton. The flavor and performance of Grade AA eggs are better than those of Grade A quality, but they do cost a bit more. Consumers need to weigh the importance of economy versus quality and choose accordingly.

Conditions during marketing and storage are of paramount importance in maintaining the quality in eggs during storage until they actually are used (Figure 6.8). Consumers need to notice the quality of eggs when they are broken from the shell and used in food preparation. If eggs from a store generally are of low quality

FIGURE 6.8   Eggs in markets must always be refrigerated to maintain quality and safety.

TABLE 6.6   Sizes, Weight per Dozen, and Approximate Volume per Dozen Eggs

Size of Eggs	Weight/Dozen	Approximate Volume/Dozen
Jumbo	30 oz	3 cups
Extra large	27 oz	~3 cups
Large	24 oz	2½ cups
Medium	21 oz	2⅓ cups
Small	18 oz	2 cups

(indicated by yolks breaking easily and whites spreading over a large area), shopping in another store might help assure procuring eggs of a satisfactory quality. Stores that do not display eggs in refrigerated cases are certainly not the best place to buy eggs.

The price of eggs is determined by size (Table 6.6) as well as by the quality of eggs. Recipes generally assume that large eggs will be used in preparation, but extra large eggs may be substituted. Usually there are at least two different sizes available in supermarkets. Jumbo is the largest size, followed by extra large, large, medium, and small; extra large and large are two commonly available sizes. Size does not determine if eggs are better. A jumbo egg of Grade B quality is simply a large amount of a low-quality egg. If eggs are usually being used in baking or in other food mixtures, large is an appropriate size to buy; extra large may be preferred for other applications such as fried or poached eggs. Some recipes require a specified volume of egg; Table 6.7 lists the equivalent number of eggs of various sizes required to equal 1 cup.

Some markets feature eggs that are touted to have special nutritional benefits—at elevated prices. The benefits of brown-shelled eggs or of so-called natural eggs have not been demonstrated. The freshness (as demonstrated by the quality when broken out of the shell) is extremely important when buying eggs, but eggs marketed with sales appeals implying unique health benefits may not merit a higher price tag.

Egg substitutes are available for people who need to be particularly watchful of their cholesterol intake. These are made by combining whites with a blend of ingredients that simulate the qualities of the yolk. Scrambled eggs or other recipes requiring whole eggs can be prepared using egg substitutes. However, the substitutes cannot be used when recipes use yolks and whites separately.

Egg substitutes
Liquid or frozen egg products in which the yolk has been removed from the whites and replaced with ingredients that simulate the character of the yolk.

TABLE 6.7   Number of Eggs of Different Sizes to make 1 Cup of Egg (Whole, Whites, Yolks)

Stet	To Make 1 Cup		
	Whole	Whites	Yolks
Jumbo	4	5	11
Extra Large	4	6	12
Large	5	7	14
Medium	5	8	16
Small	6	9	18

STORAGE OF HIGH-PROTEIN FOODS

Refrigeration and high levels of sanitation are essential in handling beef, veal, pork, lamb, poultry, fish, and eggs. All high-protein foods can provide a rich environment in which microorganisms can flourish. Two keys are critical to keeping these foods safe: (1) keeping microorganism populations to an absolute minimum by avoiding contamination from food handlers or unclean surfaces and (2) maintaining temperatures no higher than 40°F throughout commercial handling and marketing.

Consumers are responsible for continuing safe storage and handling from the point of sale until high-protein foods are eaten. Meats need to be refrigerated as quickly as possible. They can be placed in the coldest part of the refrigerator in their original packaging. The temperature in the refrigerator must be no higher than 40°F, and preferably may be just above freezing. If fresh meats are being placed in the freezer for delayed use, pieces can be wrapped in heavy aluminum foil or in freezer bags that seal tightly. Layers can be separated within a package by a sheet of foil so they can be separated when they are being thawed. Freezer packages need clear labels that indicate their contents and the date they were placed in the freezer. Table 6.8 provides guidelines for storing high-protein foods in the refrigerator and freezer.

TABLE 6.8   Guidelines for Storing Selected High-Protein Foods[a]

	Storage Period	
Type	**Refrigerator**[b]	**Freezer**[c]
Beef, Pork, Lamb		
Steaks	3–5 days	6–12 months
Roasts	3–5 days	6–12 months
Ground	1–2 days	3–4 months
Stew meat	1–2 days	3–4 months
Variety meats	1–2 days	3–4 months
Corned beef	7 days	2 weeks
Ham, half, fully cooked	3–5 days	1–2 months
Frankfurters	7 days	1–2 months
Sausage, smoked	7 days	1–2 months
Sausage, dry or semidry	2–3 weeks	1–2 months
Luncheon meats	3–5 days	1–2 months
Cooked leftovers	3–4 days	2–3 months
Gravy, broth	1–2 days	2–3 months
Poultry		
Chicken, turkey, duck	1–2 days	6 months
Giblets	1–2 days	3 months
Cooked, with broth	1–2 days	6 months
Cooked, no broth	1–2 days	1 month
Cooked casseroles	1–2 days	4–6 months
Fried chicken	1–2 days	4 months
Fish	1–2 days	1 month

[a]*Adapted from A Quick Consumer Guide to Safe Food. Home and Garden Bulletin No. 248. USDA, Food Safety and Inspection Service. Washington, DC. Revised 1995.*
[b]*40°F or cooler.*
[c]*0°F or below.*

Summary

Meats, poultry, and fish are important, but expensive, protein sources in the diet; eggs and legumes are less costly sources. Microorganisms can multiply rapidly if they are present on meats or other high-protein foods. To reduce the possibility of foodborne illness and to extend the shelf life of these foods, sanitary handling conditions and cold storage temperatures (<40°F) are imperative. Centralized packaging of meats and poultry is one way the industry is implementing increasingly to help assure that meats are safe when consumers buy them.

Most beef in retail markets is graded either USDA Choice or Select, the former being a higher quality in terms of expected flavor, juiciness, and tenderness. Beef cuts from the rib, short loin, and sirloin are more tender than cuts from the other parts of the carcass. Veal cuts are similar to those from beef, but they are less juicy and flavorful because of immaturity.

Lamb is a particularly flavorful meat, but the cuts are much smaller than comparable ones from beef. They also are more costly per pound. Pork cuts are distinctly larger than lamb, and they are less expensive. Pork may be sold either fresh or cured. Bacon, sausages, Canadian bacon, frankfurters, and luncheon meats are popular meat products that often feature pork.

Poultry and fish are healthful high-protein options. Chickens and turkeys often are raised in large commercial facilities. Some fish (both saltwater and freshwater types) are being farmed today to help meet the increasing demand for fish, particularly for certain species. Freshness of fish is a key factor to note when selecting fish.

The expected safe shelf life of refrigerated meats, poultry, and fish varies depending on the precise handling conditions and storage temperature, but it is quite limited and needs to be respected. Poultry spoils more quickly than meats when not refrigerated adequately or handled under sanitary conditions.

Study Questions

1. In a supermarket near you, what types of packaging are used for (1) beef, (2) pork, (3) lamb, and (4) poultry? What are the advantages and disadvantages of each different type of packaging? Is it possible to have the butcher prepare specific cuts of each type of meat?

2. At the same supermarket, what grades of beef are available? What levels of fat in ground beef are displayed? Discuss how well this supermarket's meat counter meets your shopping requirements.

3. What are the ingredients listed on five different brands of frankfurters? Do the ingredients appear to influence price? If so, explain your answer. Identify which would be your choice, and explain why.

4. Describe the choices (parts and numbers of pieces and any other options) of packaged chicken displayed in this market. Compare the prices of the various parts with and without skin; rank them in order according to price per pound. Which would you choose? Why?

5. At the fish counter, note the types available and the price per pound of each. Compare this information with the frozen fish that are available.

6. You are cooking Thanksgiving dinner for your family and plan to serve roast turkey. Describe the meat you plan to serve, including what and how much you will buy. Also explain how you will store it and cook it.

Suggested Websites

http://www.beef.org/
Website for National Cattlemen's Beef
Association.

http://www.nppc.org/
National Pork Producers Council.

http://www.americanlambboard.org/
American Lamb Board.

http://www.poultryegg.org/
U.S. Poultry and Egg Association.

http://www.aeb.org/
American Egg Board website.

http://beef.unl.edu/stories/200609290.shtml
Report on research testing consumer preferences
for corn-fed and grass-fed beef.

Bibliography

Anonymous. *How to Buy Meat*. 1995. Home and Garden Bulletin No. 265. Agricultural Marketing Service. U.S. Department of Agriculture. Washington, DC.

Brody, A. L. 2002. Case-ready fresh red meat: Is it here or not? *Food Technol.* 56 (1): 77.

Brody, A. L. 2004. Case for case-ready meat. *Food Technol.* 58 (6): 84.

Daniel, D. R., et al. 2000. Nutrition composition of emu compares favorably with that of other lean meats. *J. Am. Dietet. Assoc.* 100 (7): 836.

Dubberley, M. 2002. Fowl play: Creating delicious chicken dishes. *Food Product Design.* 12 (5): 78.

Egbert, R. & Borders, C. 2006. Achieving success with meat analogs. *Food Technol.* 60 (1): 28.

Flick, G. J. 2002. U.S. aquaculture is fighting an upstream battle. *Food Technol.* 56 (9): 124.

Santerre, C. R. 2004. Farmed salmon: Caught in a numbers game. *Food Technol.* 58 (2): 108.

Walsh, D. 2002. Sausage: The international indulgence. *Food Product Design.* 12 (1): 76.

Walter, J. M., et al. 2000. Ground ostrich: A comparison with ground beef. *J. Am. Dietet. Assoc.* 100 (2): 244.

Zino, D. 2005. Taking a closer look at beef. *Food Product Design.* 15 (9): 62.

CHAPTER 7
Buying Fruits and Vegetables

The array of fresh fruits and vegetables available to consumers today is truly exciting. Developments in transportation and marketing have been responsible for stocking produce departments with fresh produce of excellent quality and considerable variety throughout the year. Imports from Chile and other countries south of the equator bring summer fruits and vegetables to supermarkets in the middle of winter, usually at an affordable price. The variety of fruits and vegetables that consumers need for a healthy diet is available. The challenge to consumers is to select wisely to obtain produce that is not only of high quality but also includes considerable variety.

ORGANIC PRODUCE

Organic
Legally defined as being produced without using growth hormones, antibiotics, or petroleum-based or sewage sludge–based fertilizers.

Despite the lack of convincing scientific evidence that the nutritive value of fresh produce is affected significantly either negatively or positively by agricultural methods, standards are now in place regulating use of the term **organic** in reference to marketing produce (Figure 7.1). The National Organic Program went into effect late in 2002. Animal and plant foods meeting the requirements may be marked with the USDA Organic seal and also may be identified as "organic."

Animal products (including milk, meat, eggs, and poultry) bearing labels stating "organic" or "95% organic" must have been produced without growth hormones or antibiotics. Fruits and vegetables designated as "organic" or "95% organic" cannot have undergone any of the following treatments: petroleum-based or sewage sludge–based fertilizers, conventional pesticides, ionizing radiation, or bioengineering. The stipulation for both the animal and the plant foods carrying these designations is that at least 95 percent of the weight of the product (except for water and salt content) meets the requirements.

FIGURE 7.1   Apples and other fresh produce that meet the standards of the National Organic Program can now be marketed as "organic."

BOX 7.1

Food Insights: Breeding in the Fast Lane

Selective breeding is an accepted way of improving farm crops, but improvements come slowly because of the time required to grow each new generation as research moves toward the desired goals. Gene splicing is a faster technique, but there has been resistance from some consumers because of their concern over the safety of genetically modified crops. A high-tech approach toward selective breeding is a possible way of achieving desired results in a rather short time.

Decoded genetic blueprints of seeds are now available to help pinpoint plants with high levels of the desired trait. Plant tissues are scanned to find DNA fragments or markers associated with that trait. The time required for this high-tech approach is about half as long as traditional selective breeding projects because the DNA fragments can be analyzed when the plant is young rather than having to wait until the plant has matured.

The increased interest in selective breeding has also fostered interest in searching very old crops in an attempt to find earlier characteristics that may promote stronger or more disease-resistant plants. Some of these characteristics have been bred out of contemporary crops, but examples are still available to researchers wishing to breed a specific characteristic into today's crops. Research is done on traditional field crops, such as corn and wheat, but the ease of finding genetic markers with the use of modern techniques and computer analysis has reduced costs enough to stimulate interest in selective breeding of fruits and vegetables, too.

On food mixtures in which at least 70 percent of the ingredients (by weight) meet the requirements for being identified as "organic," the package display panel may include the statement "made with organic ingredients" and list a maximum of three qualified organic ingredients. If less than 70 percent of the ingredients (by weight) are "organic," the main display label may not use "organic." Any ingredient label indicating "organic" must identify each organic ingredient and provide the name and address of the agent who certified its "organic" status.

Although many consumers use the words "organic" and "natural" as though they were synonymous, legally they clearly are not. "Natural" is not defined at all legally, and, as previously noted, "organic" in terms of food labeling is described very precisely in legal terms. However, many consumers doubtless will continue to imbue foods they choose to call "natural" and/or "organic" with healthful qualities that may or may not be merited. In realistic terms, the freshness of produce is evident in the marketplace and provides the key to buying nutritious fruits and vegetables. If "organic" produce looks tired, it clearly is not a better buy for health than is fresh produce of high quality that is not "organic."

PHYTOCHEMICALS

The federal focus on promoting the consumption of at least five servings of fruits and vegetables daily began in 1991 and continues today. Among the anticipated benefits to consumers is possible protection against cancer, heart disease, and stroke. Assessment of the effectiveness of the "5-a-Day" program continues as the educational program proceeds. By 1997, increased consumption was noted, particularly among Hispanics and nonsmokers.

Research efforts have been directed toward attempting to identify compounds in plant foods that may play a role in helping protect against cancer, coronary heart disease, and stroke. Although the evidence is not as strong for the protective role of compounds in fruits and vegetables, these plant foods may be involved in reducing the likelihood of cataracts, chronic obstructive pulmonary disease, diverticulosis, and hypertension.

Phytochemicals
Compounds that may have protective action in the body.

Among the **phytochemicals** (plant compounds exhibiting possible protective action in the body) that have been identified in various fruits and vegetables are sulfides (diallyl sulfide, allyl methyl trisulfide, and dithiolethione), carotenoids (α-carotene, ß-carotene, lutein, and lycopene), flavonoids (quercetin, kaempferol, tangeretin, nobiletin, and rutin), glucosinolate/indoles (glucobrassicin and indoles), phytoestrogens (genistein, biochanin A, and lignans), isothiocyanates (sulphorophane and D-limonene), phytosterols, protease inhibitors, saponins, phenols (chlorogenic acid, ellagic acid, caffeic acid, coumarin, and catechin), capsaicin, resveratrol, anthocyanins, tannins, terpenes, dietary fibers, vitamins C and E, folic acid, potassium, and selenium. All of these compounds except three of the flavonoids (tangeretin, nobiletin, and rutin) are contained in one or more vegetables. Various fruits contain all of these with the exception of sulfides, α-carotene, glucosinolates/indoles, genistein, biochanin A, sulphorophane, phytosterols, protease inhibitors, and saponins.

Vegetable sources of sulfides are primarily the allium vegetables: onion, garlic, green onion, leek, and chives. Carotenoids are available in greens, yellow/orange vegetables, and various yellow or reddish fruits. Flavonoids are found in many fruits and vegetables. Cruciferous vegetables (broccoli, bok choy, cauliflower, green cabbage, and kale) are sources of indoles. Among the special contributions of legumes are phytoestrogens, isothiocyanates, phenols, saponins, and phytosterols. Phenols also are widely available in other vegetables and fruits. The message at this time is that a diet containing at least five servings of a variety of fruits and vegetables (Figure 7.2) may be important to health because of the various phytochemicals contained in the different types.

FIGURE 7.2   Fruits and vegetables are important sources of phytochemicals that may help protect against some serious illnesses.

GRADES

Grading standards for such characteristics as shape, color, defects, and texture have been established by the U.S. Department of Agriculture and are administered by its Agricultural Marketing Service, under the authority of the Agricultural Marketing Act of 1946. These are the grade designations:

U.S. Fancy: premium produce
U.S. No. 1: chief trading grade
U.S. No. 2: intermediate quality range
U.S. No. 3: lowest commercially useful grade

Standards have been developed for 82 fruits and vegetable products according to this nomenclature, although not all four levels are defined for each product. Grade designations are of major importance for the wholesale market so that buyers can specify the quality standard their retail customers require. However, grades are not generally identified by name in retail markets.

Fresh produce ideally has a brief trip from farm to table so loss of quality is kept to a minimum. Chemical changes continue to occur in fruits and vegetables after harvest, which leads to changes in flavor and texture. Fortunately, chilling and/or prompt refrigeration retard deteriorative changes and loss of water from cells.

FRESH FRUITS

Quantity to Buy

The amount of fresh fruit to buy is determined by the amount of waste associated with the preparation to be done and the anticipated shelf life of the fruit after purchase. Approximately three to four servings are available from a pound of apples, bananas, figs, peaches, nectarines, pears, or plums. Grapes, cherries, and apricots yield about four to five servings per pound. Berries are usually sold in pint or quart containers; a pint yields two to four servings. Table 7.1 provides a guide to the approximate quantities of selected fruits that equal 1 pound.

TABLE 7.1 Approximate Quantities Provided by 1 Pound of Various Fruits

Fruit	Approximate Volume/Unit Per Pound
Apples, whole	3 medium
Apples, peeled and sliced	2¾ cups
Apricots, whole	8–12
Apricots, sliced	2½ cups
Avocado, sliced	2 cups
Banana, whole	3–4
Banana, mashed	4½ cups
Cherries, pitted	2⅓ cups
Cranberries	4 cups
Grapes	2 cups
Peaches, whole	4 medium
Peaches, sliced	1 cup
Pineapple, cubed	1½ cups
Rhubarb	4–8 stalks
Rhubarb, cooked	2 cups

FIGURE 7.3   This market is displaying five different varieties of apples to meet consumer needs.

Selection

Variety

Apples (Figure 7.3), pears, and plums are examples of fruits that may be available in more than one variety. Because each variety has different characteristics, consumers need to select the variety that has the specific characteristics they are seeking. For example, Bartlett pears are excellent for eating, but comice pears are better for cooking. Apples often are available in at least two or three varieties. Table 7.2 indicates some apple varieties that are well suited to different uses. However, individual preferences may play a key role in deciding between varieties.

Condition

Because of their rather fragile character, fruits tend to bruise easily during harvesting and marketing (Figure 7.4). Damaged tissue begins to soften and spoil fairly rapidly, making it wise to examine fruits for bruises or soft spots when selecting them. Berries and grapes need to be checked for any mold, for this quickly spoils adjacent berries and grapes even when they are stored in the refrigerator. Melons showing evidence of mold starting around the stem area will not keep well. Clearly, selecting fruit requires that buyers be alert to possible damage that can accelerate deterioration before the fruit is eaten.

TABLE 7.2   Apple Varieties Recommended for Various Uses

Eating	Pies and Sauce	Baking
Cortland	Gravenstein	Jonathan
Delicious	Grimes Golden	McIntosh
Golden Delicious	Jonathan	Northern Spy
Jonathan	Newtown Pippin	Rhode Island Greening
McIntosh	Stayman	Rome Beauty
Stayman	Wealthy	Winesap
Winesap	York Imperial	York Imperial

FIGURE 7.4 Pineapples, bananas, and Maui onions are of optimum quality when they are purchased at a roadside stand on Maui. (Courtesy of John Peterson.)

Climacteric
Fruit that continues to ripen after harvesting.

Some fruits (classified as **climacteric**) continue to ripen after they are harvested, which means they can be harvested and marketed before they are fully ripe. Apples, apricots, bananas, some tropical fruits, and other climacteric fruits can be purchased when they are still a bit green because they continue to ripen at room temperature (Table 7.3). However, nonclimacteric fruits, such as citrus and berries, need to be ripe when picked because they will not ripen any more once they are harvested. For optimal flavor and quality of nonclimacteric fruits, it is important to select only those that were ripe when picked.

TABLE 7.3 Some Climacteric and Nonclimacteric Fruits

Climacteric Fruit	Nonclimacteric Fruit
Apple	Cherry
Apricot	Citrus
Avocado	Fig
Banana	Grapes
Peach	Melons
Pear	Pineapple
Plum	Strawberries
Tomato	
Tropical (papaya, mango)	

BOX 7.2

Food Insights: What's in a Name?

Creativity is apparent in the vegetable section these days. The standard list of vegetables—green beans, peas, carrots, celery, and other traditional vegetables—is being broadened, particularly in upscale markets where retailers are eager to pique the interest of consumers. Broccolini, sometimes called Asparation, is a vegetable created by crossing broccoli with gai lan, an Asian broccoli. The result is a vegetable with very thin stalks and delicate flowerets that is more delicate than broccoli. Some people prefer it because of its novelty. Another vegetable variation that may turn up at your market is baby bok choy; its small size (due to early harvesting) suits it well to steaming or braising. A dash of soy sauce can be used to relate this attractive vegetable to its origins.

FRESH VEGETABLES

Quantity to Buy

The quantity of a fresh vegetable to buy depends on the amount of trimming required and the length of time it will retain its quality. Table 7.4 indicates the servings that can be expected from 1 pound of various fresh vegetables. These yields are based on moderate trimming and normal serving size.

TABLE 7.4 Servings per Pound of Selected Fresh Vegetables[a]

Vegetable	Servings Per Pound
Lima beans in pods	2
Peas in pods	2
Winter squash	2 or 3
Cauliflower	3
Asparagus	3 or 4
Beets without tops	3 or 4
Broccoli	3 or 4
Onions	3 or 4
Summer squash	3 or 4
Sweet potatoes	3 or 4
Carrots (when cooked)	4
Celery (when cooked)	4
Parsnips (without tops)	4
Potatoes	4
Spinach	4
Brussels sprouts	4 or 5
Cabbage (when cooked)	4 or 5
Okra	4 or 5
Tomatoes	5
Snap beans	5 or 6
Carrots (raw)	5 or 6
Celery (raw)	5 or 6
Kale (untrimmed)	5 or 6
Cabbage (raw)	9 or 10

[a]*Adapted from Your Money's Worth in Foods by B. Peterkin and C. Cromwell. Home and Garden Bulletin No. 183. Agricultural Service. USDA. Washington, DC. 1977.*

TABLE 7.5 Storage of Fresh Vegetables

Vegetable	Storage Conditions	Maximum Time
Asparagus	Unwashed, refrigerator crisper	2–3 days
Beans (green, wax)	Refrigerator crisper	7 days
Beets	Refrigerated	14 days
Broccoli	Refrigerator crisper	3–5 days
Brussels sprouts	Refrigerator crisper	3–5 days
Cabbage	Refrigerator crisper	7–14 days
Carrots	No tops; refrigerator	14 days
Cauliflower	Refrigerator crisper	7 days
Celery	Refrigerator crisper	7 days
Cucumbers	Refrigerator crisper	7 days
Eggplant	Plastic bag; cool room temperature	1–2 days
Greens; spinach	Wash, drain; refrigerator crisper	3–5 days
Lettuce	Wash, drain; refrigerator crisper	7 days
Lima beans	In pods; refrigerator crisper	3–5 days
Mushrooms	Refrigerator crisper	1–2 days
Okra	Refrigerator crisper	3–5 days
Onions, green	Refrigerator crisper	3–5 days
Onions, mature	Mesh bag; cool room temperature	Several months
Parsnips	Refrigerator crisper	14 days
Peas, green	In pods; refrigerator crisper	3–5 days
Peppers, green	Wash, dry; refrigerator crisper	7 days
Potatoes, sweet	Mesh bag; cool room temperature	Several months
Potatoes, white	Dark, dry, 45–50°F, well ventilated	Several months
Radishes	No tops; refrigerator crisper	14 days
Rutabagas	Mesh bag; cool room temperature	Several months
Squash, summer	Refrigerator crisper	3–5 days
Squash, winter	Mesh bag; cool room temperature	Several months
Sweet corn	Unhusked; refrigerator	1 day or less
Tomatoes	Refrigerate ripe; green at room temperature	7 days
Turnips	No tops; refrigerator crisper	14 days

Storage

Table 7.5 lists the storage time that may be expected for vegetables of good quality when they are purchased. Storage conditions needed for various vegetables are also included in Table 7.5.

Condition

Loss of turgor in fresh greens, the result of loss of moisture from the cells, is obvious if wilted greens are on display in the produce section. Shriveled mushrooms are easy to spot and can be avoided. Somewhat limp bunches of celery also are easy to detect. In other words, consumers should observe the overall freshness and also avoid blemishes when selecting fresh vegetables.

FROZEN AND CANNED VEGETABLES AND FRUITS

Canned and frozen fruits and vegetables are convenient because they can be stored on the shelf or in the freezer, respectively, until needed. They save time because necessary trimming and cutting have been done during processing. Canned vegetables and fruits can be used without further cooking, or they can be incorporated into recipes according to directions.

Frozen fruits and vegetables need to be thawed, but microwave ovens make this a very quick process. In fact, frozen fruits (especially strawberries and melon balls) retain texture better if they are served when only partially thawed so their cells are still slightly rigid, not flabby. Frozen vegetables can be thawed and cooked far more quickly than their fresh counterparts.

Juices

Many different choices of fruit beverages are available. They may be in the form of fresh pasteurized juices, such as the orange juice in the refrigerated case, frozen concentrates, and canned or bottled beverages (some of which are prepared from concentrates). Many of these are ready to drink, but frozen concentrates need to be reconstituted when they are being served as a beverage. In contrast to ready-to-drink orange juice, frozen concentrates are lighter and comparatively inexpensive to ship from the processor to the market because they have had more than 70 percent of their water removed, saving both weight and volume. They are less convenient to serve than ready-to-drink beverages. Preparation requires opening a lid that sometimes is stubborn, then diluting the concentrate with the proper amount of water, and finally stirring to disperse the concentrate uniformly.

Fruit juice
Beverage that is 100 percent juice.

Juice drink
Drink that is at least 50 percent juice.

Nectar
Drink that is at least 30 percent juice.

Ade
Drink that is at least 25 percent juice.

Fruit drink
Drink containing at least 10 percent juice.

Wise consumers read beverage labels carefully to determine just how nourishing the drink is. The wording identifying the product needs to be noted precisely. If the beverage is identified as a type of **fruit juice**, the beverage is 100 percent juice. A **juice drink** has to contain at least 50 percent juice. Fruit **nectar** has to contain at least 30 percent juice. A juice **ade** must be at least 25 percent juice. A beverage containing no less than 10 percent juice is labeled a **fruit drink**.

Consumers have been shifting from widespread use of orange juice concentrate to ready-to-drink pasteurized orange juice. This shift has been accompanied by a drop in the percentage of adults with an adequate serum vitamin C concentration. This prompted Johnston and Bowling (2002) to study the actual vitamin C content in ready-to-drink orange juices in screw-top and in nonresealable containers and reconstituted frozen concentrates. Initially, the reconstituted frozen concentrate juice was significantly higher in reduced vitamin C than the ready-to-drink juices, and that relationship continued throughout the 4-week period of storage and testing (at weekly intervals) after the containers were initially opened. From this study, it is clear that using frozen orange concentrate from a container size that will be consumed in a week or less provides a much richer source of vitamin C than provided by using the ready-to-drink pasteurized juices.

If ready-to-drink juices (Figure 7.5) are the choice, they need to be bought at least 3 (and preferably 4) weeks before the expiration date on the container and consumed promptly so the content of vitamin C will be as high as possible. They should be consumed within a week or less after they are opened. These findings endorse the idea of buying a quantity that can be consumed in a week to ensure that vitamin C intake is optimal even though this may be more expensive than buying larger sizes.

Some beverages, notably orange juice and a few others, have calcium added, which is an important improvement; this addition can significantly improve calcium intake in the diets of many people who drink little milk. Unfortunately, many fruit beverages have a considerable amount of sugar or other sweetener added to them, which raises the calorie content considerably without any corresponding nutritional benefit (Table 7.6). Vitamin D deficiency is a growing cause of concern in the United States. This has led to the possible fortification of commercially processed orange juice with vitamin D as a means of improving nutritional status. The level of vitamin D fortification in a quart of

FIGURE 7.5   Many orange juice products are displayed in different sizes; optimal vitamin C content lasts only about three weeks on the shelf and one week after being opened.

milk was established with the assumption that people would drink enough milk to meet their vitamin D requirement. However, reduced consumption of milk concomitantly means inadequate vitamin D intake. The efficiency with which vitamin D is absorbed when it is added to orange juice makes this vitamin D–fortified juice a very efficient vehicle for improving vitamin D intake.

TABLE 7.6   Some Fruit Juice Options[a]

Juice Source	Form	% Juice	Vitamin C[b]	Other[c]	Cost $\frac{1}{2}$ Gallon
Orange	Frozen concentrate	100	120%	30% Ca	$2.29
	RTD from concentrate[d]	100	120%	30% Ca	4.29
	RTD fresh[e]	100	120%	20% Ca	4.29
Apple	RTD	100	120%	0%	3.39
Cranberry juice cocktail	RTD	100	130%	10%	4.59
Grape	RTD, bottled	100	120%	0%	4.29

[a]Prices in Los Angeles area supermarket, November 2006.
[b]Label information in percentage of RDI.
[c]Added calcium in percentage of RDI.
[d]Ready-to-drink (RTD), prepared from concentrate.
[e]Ready-to-drink (RTD), fresh juice.

Summary

The National Organic Program was implemented in 2002, defining requirements to be met if a food product is to be labeled "organic" or "95% organic." Some people willingly pay higher prices for "organic" produce even though the benefits of food produced following these requirements have not been proven scientifically. "Natural" often is considered synonymous with "organic," but its definition has not been legally established.

Fruits and vegetables are excellent sources of several phytochemicals that may exhibit protective roles against such health problems as coronary heart disease, cancer, and stroke. Phytochemicals occurring in different fruits and vegetables include sulfides, carotenoids, flavonoids, glucosinolate/indoles, isothiocyanates, phytosterols, phenols, anthocyanins, vitamins C and E, folic acid, potassium, and selenium.

Grading of produce according to federal standards is important in the wholesale market but is not generally shown in retail markets. Estimated yield of fresh fruits and vegetables after preparation vary with the specific type of produce. Quantity to buy and the importance of variety and condition of fruits and vegetables in the market are aspects of selection that were discussed in this chapter. Climacteric fruits continue to ripen after harvest, but nonclimacteric fruits need to be picked when they are ripe.

Canned and frozen fruits and vegetables are other options available for use in certain recipes. They require less preparation time because they are already trimmed and either canned or frozen ready for use with very little effort or cooking required. Fruit juices often are purchased as ready to drink (pasteurized and refrigerated), bottled for room temperature storage, or as frozen concentrates that require dilution to the correct concentration before serving. Beverages labeled as fruit juice must be 100 percent juice; juice drink has at least 50 percent juice, nectar has at least 30 percent juice, ade has at least 25 percent juice, and fruit drink must have at least 10 percent juice. Reconstituted frozen orange concentrate has a higher vitamin C content and retains it better than does either pasteurized fresh ready-to-drink orange juice or ready-to-drink orange concentrate.

Study Questions

1. Is it important for a shopper on a very tight budget to buy organic vegetables? Explain your answer.
2. Identify at least three fruits and/or vegetables that are sources of sulfides. Similarly, name three plant sources for each of these other phytochemicals: flavonoids, carotenoids, and indoles.
3. Visit a supermarket in your area and identify all varieties of apples and of any other fruits having more than one variety on display. Describe the most suitable way(s) of using each variety.
4. Compare the cost of 2 cups of cooked string beans from each of the following sources: fresh, frozen, and canned. Also discuss the advantages and disadvantages of each source.
5. What vegetable juices are available in a supermarket in your area? Describe the packaging used for each, and compare the cost per ounce of the different sizes. Identify the circumstances that might make each size an appropriate choice.
6. Buy five vegetables or fruits you have never eaten before. How should each be prepared and served? How does the cost compare with familiar vegetables? Are there additional ways you can prepare them?

Suggested Websites

http://www.texasproduceassociation.com/availability/
Background information on many fruits and vegetables from Texas

http://www.thefruitpages.com/citrus.shtml
Information on a wide array of citrus fruits.

http://www.oregon-berries.com/
Background on the various berries grown in Oregon.

http://www.proscitech.com.au/trop/link.htm
Information and images of many tropical fruits.

http://www.crfg.org/pubs/frtfacts.html
Background information and images of rare tropical fruits from California.

http://commhum.mccneb.edu/fstdatabase/HTM_files/veggie/vegtables.htm
Broad range of information on vegetables.

http://www.uga.edu/vegetable/
Information on vegetables grown in Georgia.

http://www.rain.org/greennet/docs/exoticveggies/html/index.html
Information on many unusual vegetables.

http://www.friedas.com/
Information on unusual fruits and vegetables plus many recipes using them.

Bibliography

Bowman, S. A. 2002. Beverage choices of young females: Changes and impact on nutrient intake. *J. Am. Dietet. Assoc.* 102 (9): 1234.

Clemens, R. A. 2001. Redefining fiber. *Food Technol.* 55 (2): 100.

Fonda, D. 2002. Inside business: Organic growth. *Time.* 160 (7): Y1.

Foster, R. J. 2004. Fruit's plentiful phytochemicals. *Food Product Design Supplement (September):* 75.

Haard, N. F. 1984. Postharvest physiology and biochemistry of fruits and vegetables. *J. Chem. Educ.* 61 (4): 277.

Harding, T.B., Jr., & Davis, L. R. 2005. Organic foods marketing and labeling. *Food Technol.* 59 (1): 41.

Johnston, C. S., and Bowling, D. L. 2002. Stability of ascorbic acid in commercially available orange juices. *J. Am. Dietet. Assoc.* 102 (4): 525.

McCullum, C. 2000. Food biotechnology in the new millennium: Promises, realities, and challenges. *J. Am. Dietet. Assoc.* 100 (11): 1311.

Montecalvo, J. 2001. The National Organic Program: An opportunity for industry. *J. Food Technol.* 55 (6): 26.

Newman, V., et al. 2002. Amount of raw vegetables and fruits needed to yield 1 c juice. *J. Am. Dietet. Assoc.* 102 (7): 975.

Peregrin, T. 2002. Expanding vitamin D fortification: A balance between deficiency and toxicity. *J. Am. Dietet. Assoc.* 102 (9): 1214.

Stables, G. J., et al. 2002. Changes in vegetable and fruit consumption and awareness among US adults: Results of the 1991 and 1997 5-a-Day for Better Health Program surveys. *J. Am. Dietet. Assoc.* 102 (6): 809.

Turner, R. Elaine. 2002. Organic standards. *Food Technol.* 56 (6): 24.

Van Duyn, M. A. S., and Pivonka, E. 2000. Overview of the health benefits of fruit and vegetable consumption for the dietetics professional: Selected literature. *J. Am. Dietet. Assoc.* 100 (12): 1511.

Winter, C. K. 2006. Organic foods. *Food Technol.* 60 (10): 44.

CHAPTER
8
Buying Grains and Grain Products

OVERVIEW

Consumer interest in natural foods and educational programs emphasizing the importance of whole-grain breads and cereals in the diet have triggered development and marketing of a wide range of products. The food industry has worked vigorously to generate choices in breads, cereals, pastas, and snack foods. The result is a vast range of choices for consumers shopping for good nutrition in the breads and cereals sections of supermarkets.

Supermarkets carry a variety of flours for consumers who are choosing to make their breads and other baked products at home by hand or using appliances such as a bread machine. Shoppers also have many choices of ready-to-eat and basic cereal products, ranging from cornmeals to several types of rice and various pastas (fresh or dried). Decisions influence the amount of time and effort needed for preparation, as well as the cost.

Berry (2002) summarized the many different challenges faced by food technologists in developing bread and cereal products that meet consumer desires for the nutritional benefits potentially available from these foods while also providing considerable eating pleasure. For example, the uneven heating of foods in microwave ovens is a problem that has to be recognized when manufacturers are developing new food products that will ultimately be heated by consumers in their microwave ovens.

The speed of heating in a microwave oven may provide consumer appeal, but the better textural characteristics resulting from heating in a toaster, toaster oven, or conventional oven may counterbalance the appeal of speed when the final choice is made to buy a particular item. Products that can be heated in toaster ovens include chemically leavened doughs (e.g., biscuits), pizza crust, flaky doughs (frozen pastry shells), filled tarts, waffles, and even breakfast entrée items in flaky pastry.

FLOUR

Refined wheat flour
Wheat flour made with the bran and embryo removed from the grain.

Wheat flour is required for good structural properties in baked goods. No other grain contains proteins with the structural and cohesive qualities contributed by wheat gluten (protein complex formed from gliadin and glutenin during dough formation). **Refined wheat flour** provides baked products with optimal texture. Even whole-wheat flour needs to be augmented with refined flour because the bran in it interferes somewhat with gluten development; bread made with only whole-wheat flour has a very heavy, dense structure in comparison with bread made with refined flour.

Supermarkets usually stock refined all-purpose flour and cake flour, both of which are made from the milling of wheat. The quality of all-purpose flours varies somewhat among brands. Consumers who use all-purpose flour for baking may wish to test the store brand against a premium all-purpose flour to determine whether the added cost of the premium flour is justified for their purposes. Once this decision has been made, it is not necessary to continue to debate which to buy. The quality of a particular brand of flour usually remains consistent.

Upscale grocery stores and markets featuring so-called natural foods often carry a large variety of flours to meet the needs of their customers. Rye, quinoa, triticale, buckwheat, oat, and rice are just some of the specialty flours that might be found on their shelves. These flours can sometimes add desirable color and/or flavors to baked products, but wheat flour must be included in the recipes if reasonably desirable texture is the expected result. If baked goods are being prepared for people with an allergy to wheat gluten, wheat flour cannot be used; a crumbly, often heavy product can be expected.

ENRICHMENT

Enrichment of *refined flour* and bread made with refined flour with thiamin, riboflavin, niacin, and iron was initiated in 1941 to help eliminate beriberi, ariboflavinosis, pellagra, and anemia in the United States. Subsequently, calcium and vitamin D were identified as nutrients that could be added but were not mandatory. In 1996, the Food and Drug Administration (FDA) passed a requirement for enrichment with folic acid. Under this decision, folic acid was added to the list of nutrients that must be added to flour, corn-meal and grits, farina, rice, macaroni and noodle products, and breads, rolls, and buns (Figure 8.1). The FDA also defined the addition of folic acid to breakfast cereals and baby foods at the same time. Enrichment standards are presented in Table 8.1.

BREADS

Breads vary widely in price and in ingredients, making selection rather difficult (Figure 8.2). Choices need to be made to meet price limitations as well as taste preferences. The best possible buys are found at bakery outlets where returned goods are sold at greatly reduced prices. If a large quantity of bread and related products will be consumed in a reasonable length of time and adequate freezer space is available, consumers can save enough to more than pay for the time and effort of going to the outlet occasionally. Bread freezes well and thaws rapidly for almost immediate use, making thawing in advance unnecessary. If frozen storage space is adequate, several kinds of breads, rolls, and muffins can be held in the freezer to add variety to menus.

FIGURE 8.1   Breads, flour, rice, cornmeal, pasta, and other cereal products are enriched with thiamine, riboflavin, niacin, folic acid, and iron if they are made with refined cereals.

TABLE 8.1   Enrichment Standards

Product	Thiamin (mg/lb)	Riboflavin (mg/lb)	Niacin (mg/lb)	Folic Acid (mg/lb)	Iron (mg/lb)
Wheat					
Bread	1.8	1.1	15.0	0.43	8–12.5
Flour	2.9	1.8	24.0	0.7	13–16.5
Durum wheat					
Pastas	4.0–5.0	1.7–2.2	27–34	0.9–1.2	13–16.5
Corn					
Self-rising cornmeal	2.0–3.0	1.2–1.8	16–24	0.7–1.0	13–26
Rice					
Enriched rice and related foods	2.0–4.0	1.2–2.4	16–32	0.7–1.4	13–26

Breads can be purchased with or without mold inhibitors and other additives. Preservatives may be important to consumers who require a few days to finish a loaf of bread. However, breads can be stored in the freezer or refrigerator to help extend the shelf life if consumers wish to avoid additives.

Usually the least expensive bread is the store brand of white bread. Although this is a nourishing choice, selection of a loaf of bread using significant amounts of whole-grain flours provides more nutrients and also fiber. The prices of various whole-grain breads vary widely, depending on the bakery and the ingredients added to enhance the flavor and character of the loaf. The importance of economy needs to be considered before opting for a tempting loaf featuring exotic seeds, black olives, macadamia nuts, or other expensive ingredients. Such creative bread formulas can be very tempting, but their prices can wreck a tight budget. Highly nourishing breads can be found at a reasonable price.

Comparative shopping for bread needs to be based on weight rather than volume. A very large loaf may weigh less than a more compact loaf. If they sell at the same

FIGURE 8.2   Molasses, wheat germ, and bran are ingredients that add nutrients and interest to this bread.

TABLE 8.2   Comparison of Bread Loaves on the Shelf in a Supermarket[a]

Bread	Calories/Slice	Weight. of loaf	Cost/loaf	Cost/oz	Special Ingredients
White	110	24 oz	$3.79	$0.16	All-purpose flour
Mixed grain	110	24 oz	3.79	0.16	Brown sugar, honey
Whole wheat	90	24 oz	3.79	0.16	Molasses
Raisin	60	16 oz	3.79	0.24	Raisins, cinnamon
Rye	110	16 oz	3.49	0.22	Rye, barley malt, wheat bran, molasses
Pita	140		1.99/10	0.17	All-purpose flour
Corn tortilla	110		2.49/12	0.07	Limed corn
Flour tortilla	150		2.35/10	0.08	Refined wheat flour

[a] Los Angeles area, November 2006.

price, the compact loaf is a better buy even though the light loaf is larger. This is one case where the "eyes" do *not* have it. A careful shopper reads ingredient labels and nutritional information as well as weight. Table 8.2 presents examples of comparative shopping information about bread loaves available on store shelves.

Assorted breads are found not only on the shelves and in the bakery section in a supermarket but also in the refrigerator and freezer cases (Table 8.3). Tubes of ready-to-bake biscuits and similar bread items are displayed in refrigerated cases, and fresh tortillas sometimes are found there. Freezer cases are where frozen bread dough, heat-and-eat cinnamon and other rolls, pizza dough, waffles, and other bread items are displayed. The convenience, cost, and quality of these items need to be weighed against the same foods prepared at home using the basic ingredients. Time saved and the variety provided by these foods may counterbalance the higher cost for many consumers. In addition, not all consumers are excellent bakers.

TABLE 8.3   Comparison of Assorted Breads in a Supermarket[a]

Bread	Yield	Time Needed	Cost/Package
Shelf Display			
Brown-and-serve rolls	12	8 min.	$1.98
Dinner rolls	8	0 min.	2.99
Refrigerator Case			
Biscuits	10	~17 min.	1.39
Buttermilk biscuits	8	~17 min.	2.89
Cinnamon rolls	8	~25 min.	3.49
Crescents	8	~17 min.	2.39
Freezer Case			
Bread dough	3 loaves	2 hr. 30 min.	4.29
Dinner rolls	18	10 min.	3.39
Pizza	2	20 min.	5.29
Phyllo dough	40 sheets	1 hr. 0 min.	4.39
Waffles	10	2 min.	3.39
Pancakes	12	1 min.	3.69
Garlic bread	1 loaf	10 min.	4.21
Puff pastry	6	25 min.	3.99

[a] Los Angeles area, November 2006.

Food Insights: Cultural Contributions

Wheat bread traditionally has been the predominant form of bread in the United States, but supermarkets are now reflecting the culturally diverse nation we are becoming. Mexican and other Latin American immigrants brought tortillas to dinner tables in the United States. Corn and flour tortillas have become so popular that stacks of fresh tortillas in plastic bags are available in markets for making many delectable dishes.

Corn tortillas may be made from either white or yellow corn, which has been subjected to a lime treatment to remove the pericarp (outer layer) of the corn kernel. Skilled tortilla makers transform this soaked corn into a soft dough by grinding with a stone or pestle on a *metate* while slowly adding just the right amount of water. Then they are shaped into flat circles of dough and baked briefly on both sides on a *comal* (griddle). Flour tortillas are made from a dough comprised of wheat flour mixed with baking powder, salt, a liquid, and a small amount of fat or oil. Then they are shaped and baked in the same way as corn tortillas. Flour tortillas typically are larger in diameter than corn tortillas, although both types may be made into the desired size. Flour tortillas are favored for burritos and other applications requiring some flexibility to avoid breaking while wrapping ingredients inside. The distinctive flavor and crispness of corn tortillas may be preferred for tacos and enchiladas.

Pita or pocket bread is another relatively recent addition to bread choices in the United States. These are convenient as holders for such fillings as beef and yogurt or grilled vegetables and feta cheese. The United States is indebted to its Middle Eastern and Greek immigrants for this unique bread.

BREAKFAST CEREALS

Hot breakfast cereals are excellent sources of nutrients at a comparatively inexpensive price (Figure 8.3). The amount of preparation and convenience varies with the product. Some require several minutes to cook; some are precooked and require only the addition of boiling water or milk. Packaging also impacts the cost of hot cereals. Individual packets are convenient to prepare but are more costly. The size of packages may be another factor influencing price. Table 8.4 provides examples of hot cereal options, their features, and their cost.

Ready-to-eat cereals present a vast array of choices to consumers. Their cost and nutritional merits vary greatly, from such simple traditional cereals as corn flakes to highly fortified competitors (e.g., Total). All of these products save the same amount of time to prepare (just the time to pour them in a bowl and add milk and perhaps sugar). A bit more time may be required to chew and swallow such cereals as Grape Nuts, but that usually is not a critical factor in selecting a cereal for breakfast.

Nutritional content is of great importance to many consumers despite the fact that many of the highly fortified cereals are quite costly. The sugar level in highly fortified cereals often is high because of the need to mask the flavors of some of the added vitamins (Hazen, 2002). Some consumers studiously avoid cereals with high sugar content.

Textural properties, especially after milk has been added, are of considerable importance to some people. Flavor may be a key characteristic some consumers consider when selecting a breakfast cereal. Table 8.5 presents comparisons of some familiar ready-to-eat cereals.

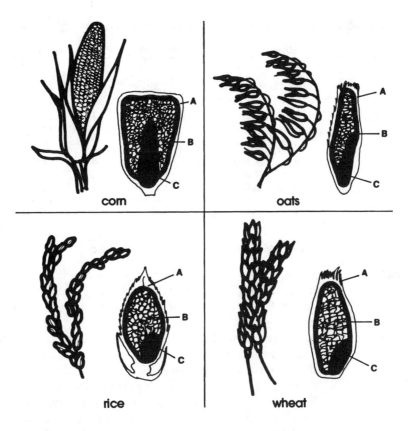

A *BRAN consists of several thin outer layers of the grain kernel and is its protective coat.*

B *ENDOSPERM is the stored food supply for the new plant which develops as the kernel germinates. It comprises about 85% of the kernel.*

C *EMBRYO or GERM is the miniature plant which enlarges and develops after the kernel germinates.*

FIGURE 8.3   Grains used to make hot and cold breakfast cereals include corn, oats, rice, and wheat.

TABLE 8.4   Comparison of Hot Cereals in Markets[a]

Cereal	Preparation Time (min.)	Package Weight	Price	Price/oz	Ingredients; Packaging
Cream of wheat	1 min.	28 oz	$4.49	$0.16	Added calcium & iron
Oatmeal, regular	7 min.	18 oz	3.29	0.18	
Oatmeal, quick	2 min.	18 oz	3.29	0.18	
Oatmeal, instant	1 min.	13.8 oz	2.91	0.21	Several flavors
Grits, quick	8 min.	20 oz	3.29	0.16	

[a] *Los Angeles area, November 2006.*

RICE

Pszczola (2001) highlighted the growing trend in rice consumption in the United States (doubling in a decade to more than 21 pounds per person annually). Although this amount is paltry compared with the estimate of about 300 pounds per person in Asian countries, clearly rice is being served quite frequently on

TABLE 8.5 Comparison of Selected Ready-to-Eat Cereals in a Supermarket[a]

Cereal	Cost/oz	Grain	Calories/cup	Fiber	Sugar	Fat	Iron[b]	B vitamins[c]
				(g/cup)	(g/cup)	(g/cup)	(%)	(%/cup)
Cocoa Puffs	$0.27	Corn	120	0	14	1	25	25
Golden Grahams	0.31	Corn, wheat	120	1	10	1	25	25
Cocoa Rice Krispies	0.31	Rice	120	1	14	1	25	25
Frosted Flakes	0.29	Corn	126	1	12	0	25	25
Corn Flakes	0.29	Corn	100	1	2	0	45	25
100% Bran Flakes	0.17	Wheat	80	8	7	0.5	45	25
Shredded Wheat	0.31	Wheat	160	6	0	1	6	<15
Cranberry Almond Crunch	0.36	Wheat	210	3	14	3	10	25
Total	$0.29	Wheat	170	5	20	1	100	100

[a] Los Angeles area, November 2002.
[b] Percent of Daily Value.
[c] Percent of Daily Value for thiamin, riboflavin, niacin, vitamin B_6, folic acid, and vitamin B_{12}.

Brown (unpolished) rice
Rice that has not been polished to remove the bran.

American tables (Table 8.6). Rice Krispies have been seen on breakfast tables for decades, but rice flour, rice starch, and many varieties of rice have been added to the larder today.

Brown (unpolished) rice is popular among some diners for its fiber content, nutty flavor, and slightly crunchy texture. Polished rice and parboiled rice choices have traditionally included short- and long-grain rices. The former is a sticky rice and the latter a fluffy product. When the diner is using chopsticks, sticky rice is usually the preferred type.

Basmati and jasmine (classified as aromatic) rice varieties have now entered the market. Their unique flavor profile is highlighted by elevated levels of acetylpyrroline, a natural flavor component of all varieties of rice. Della rice, a variety that represents a cross between basmati and regular long-grain rice, sometimes is identified as Popcorn, Texmati, or similar names. It incorporates the aromatic quality of basmati with the fluffiness of long-grain rice. Other varieties that may be seen on supermarket shelves are arborio (medium grain from Italy) and *koshihikari* (a Japanese short-grain rice), both of which work well in risotto and paella.

Consumers have the choice of several different rice products that include packets of flavorings; serving ideas on the packages help stimulate sales while also adding an international aura. Although expensive compared with buying plain rice, the convenience and quality of the various flavors have made these popular choices for preparing risottos and/or pilafs. Risotto is made using medium- or short-grain rice because of the high content of amylopectin, the branched starch molecule that contributes the desired

TABLE 8.6 Selected Rice Products in a Supermarket[a]

Product	Rice Type	Cost/oz	Characteristics
Brown	Long grain	$0.19	Light brown; nutty flavor
Instant brown	Long grain	0.14	Light brown; nutty flavor
Polished	Extra long	0.07	Fluffy
Polished	Medium	0.03	Somewhat fluffy
Parboiled	Long grain	0.09	Fluffy
Jasmine	Medium	0.27	Aromatic; from Thailand
Arborio	Medium	0.21	For risotto; from Italy
Basmati	Long	0.19	Flavorful

[a] Los Angeles area, November 2006.

sticky, creamy texture after it is gelatinized. Long-grain rice is preferred for making pilaf because its relatively high content of amylose results in the desired fluffy grains of rice after gelatinization.

SEMOLINA PRODUCTS

Couscous
Semolina product rolled into fine pellets and steamed.

Couscous is a unique pasta product that competes with pilaf and risotto for a place on many menus. It usually is produced using semolina (purified middlings that include bran and germ) from durum wheat, but similar versions are made using millet, *fonio* (North African grain), barley, or corn. Packages of couscous combined with flavoring ingredients (e.g., roasted garlic and olives, broccoli and cheese, or Parmesan cheese) are available on store shelves to provide convenience and variety in menus.

Production requires that freshly ground whole grains be combed with fingers while drops of water are sprinkled in until many tiny balls (between 1 and 3 mm) form. These minuscule balls are dried in the air until they are extremely hard. This laborious process coats the balls with starch, which greatly extends their shelf life by blocking oxidation of the fat molecules in the germ. The preferred way of cooking couscous is by steaming to gelatinize the starch. Bulgur (parched cracked wheat) and kasha (buckwheat groats) are related grain products that sometimes are used in place of couscous or pilaf.

Pastas can be purchased fresh (in the refrigerated case) or dried. Either form is made from a dough prepared by mixing semolina (coarsely ground durum wheat, a strain of hard wheat that is very high in protein) with water. This dough can be rolled, extruded, or molded into a wide variety of shapes designed for specific dishes. These range in shape and size from very thin strands of angel hair to thick lasagne noodles or tubes of manicotti suitable for stuffing. Some consumers elect to buy special dried pastas imported from Italy because they feel the slightly rough surface texture aids in retaining sauces on the individual pieces. To others, price may be more important than this subtle difference.

Summary

Flours and cereals are enriched (under federal requirements) by the addition of thiamin, riboflavin, niacin, folic acid, and iron. Breads are displayed on store and bakery shelves, in refrigerator cases, and in the freezer sections of supermarkets. Careful reading of labels enables consumers to make choices suited to their priorities (e.g., economy, variety, nutrition, or flavors). Hot cereals are limited in choice compared with the wide variety in ready-to-eat cereals, but they are much less expensive. Wheat flours (from either hard or soft varieties) are needed in baked products because of the structural contribution made by gluten. However, various flours from other grains are available to add variety when making batter and dough products from basic ingredients.

Rice is often marketed according to the length of its grain: short (sticky because of its high amylopectin content), medium (intermediate textural properties), and long (fluffy due to its high amylose content). Flavorful basmati and jasmine rices, as well as arborio (for risotto), della, and other varieties are now found in many markets in addition to the traditional choices.

Semolina products (made from milled durum wheat) include couscous and pastas. Pastas may be available fresh in refrigerated cases; dried pastas in a multitude of shapes are on store shelves to meet the requirements of various recipes. Imported Italian pastas may bring a premium price.

Study Questions

1. How do ingredient and nutrition labels on bread and cereal products help consumers make decisions regarding specific bread and cereal purchases?
2. What are the benefits and disadvantages of commercially baked products versus those prepared by consumers?
3. Identify a specific choice you would make when buying (a) bread and (b) biscuits. Explain how your values and goals impacted each choice.
4. Identify a specific breakfast cereal you would buy. Rationalize this choice in preference to others available in the supermarket.
5. In a store convenient to you, identify at least three of the rice products available. For each, indicate the conditions under which the product is a good choice to buy.
6. Prepare the following and sample them: buckwheat, arborio rice, basmati rice, sweet glutinous rice, couscous, and wild rice. Describe your impression of each of these cereals and suggest menus in which they might be used effectively.

Suggested Websites

www.foodsubs.com/Grainoth.html
Pictures and brief descriptions of various grains.

http://breadnet.net/
Many bread recipes.

http://www.cs.cmu.edu/~mjw/recipes/bread/index.html
Collection of bread recipes hosted by Carnegie Mellon University.

http://www.usarice.com/consumer/guide.html
U.S. Rice Federation's guide to various types of rice and other information about rice.

http://www.cuisinenet.com/digest/breakfast/cereal.shtml
Background on the history of breakfast cereals.

http://www.thecaloriecounter.com/Foods/800/Food.aspx
Site for calorie and other nutrition information about many breakfast cereals.

www.ilovepasta.org
Information about pastas.

Bibliography

Backas, N. 2006. Exploring Mediterranean cuisine. *Food Product Design.* 16 (2): 24.

Berry, D. 2002. Toast of the town. *Food Product Design.* (September): 33.

Caudle, A. G., and Bell, L. 2000. Caffeine and theobromine contents of ready-to-eat chocolate cereals. *J. Am. Dietet. Assoc.* 100 (6): 690.

Decker, K. J. 2002. Risottos and pilafs. *Food Product Design.* (September): 87.

Decker, K. J. 2005. Looking at the whole-grain picture. *Food Product Design.* 15 (9): 49.

Hazen, C. 2002. Breakfast cereal—the original functional food. *Food Product Design.* (September): 47.

Keegan, C. W. 2004. Latin cuisine. *Food Product Design.* 14 (7): 82.

Kuntz, L. A. 2002. Fortification (r)evolution. *Food Product Design.* (September): 33.

Marquart, L., and Cohen, E. A. 2005. Increasing whole grain consumption. *Food Technol.* 59 (12): 24.

McEligot, A. J., et al. 2002. High dietary fiber consumption is not associated with gastrointestinal discomfort in a diet intervention trial. *J. Am. Dietet. Assoc.* 102 (4): 549.

Pszczola, D. E. 2001. Rice: Not just for throwing. *Food Technol.* 55 (2): 53.

Screier, A. 2005. Refreshing ideas from south of the border. *Food Product Design.* 15 (7): 76.

Slavin, J., and Kritchevsky, D. 2002. Pass the whole-grain snack food, please. *Food Technol.* 56 (5): 216.

Van Horn, L., et al. 2001. Oats and soy in lipid-lowering diets for women with hypercholesterolemia: Is there synergy? *J. Am. Dietet. Assoc.* 101 (11): 1319.

CHAPTER 9
Buying Other Foods

FATS AND OILS

Fats and oils are frequently in the news because of health concerns and the potential influence they can exert on health—from such conditions as cancer and coronary heart disease to obesity. Much remains to be discovered about how specific choices of fats and oils may contribute to these problems; however, the one incontestable fact is that excessive consumption of fats and oils can lead to obesity. This chapter discusses the options available to consumers when selecting fats and oils for cooking, baking, frying, and making salads.

Table Spreads

Butter essentially serves as the hallmark when choosing fats and oils for table use. Ordinarily, spreads are chosen for table use—the options being between butter and margarine. Margarines have been crafted to mimic the excellent qualities of butter (notably its color and flavor) but also with improved spreadability over a wide temperature range. Olive oil (perhaps garnished with a generous splash of balsamic vinegar) sometimes is served at a meal so that diners can dip bread in this healthful, flavorful oil rather than spreading a solid fat on it.

Consumers buying a table spread need to decide first whether to buy butter or margarine. If the choice is margarine, the next decision is which source of oil to select. An examination of ingredients to find one that lists that oil as the first ingredient likely will provide a choice that is high in polyunsaturated fatty acids. Table 9.1 compares various table spreads in the market today.

Margarines may contain hydrogenated fats from the oils of soybeans, cottonseed, corn, rapeseed (marketed as canola oil), sunflower, or other sources. The actual fatty acid content depends on the source of the oil. By reading the label on the various margarines, consumers can make a decision to buy based on the relative amounts of saturated,

---

BOX 9.1

Food Insights: Seeking 0 *Trans*

Trans fats have been the subject of numerous news stories because these fatty acids are potential health hazards. The food industry has been working on ways to reduce the level of *trans* fatty acids in products. In 2006, Kentucky Fried Chicken took a major step by shifting to a special soybean oil for frying many of its products. They are just one of the fast-food chains attempting to reduce the levels of *trans* fatty acids to help promote health of customers. Although this is a helpful step, an even greater benefit would be to reduce the amount of fat in products.

Research to develop oils with reduced *trans* fatty acids have been conducted in several laboratories. Efforts at Iowa State University centered on breeding a strain of soybeans containing oil with low levels of linolenic acid. Regular linolenic acid, a polyunsaturated fatty acid, has a rather short shelf life because of oxidative rancidity. To promote shelf life, soybean oil can be partially hydrogenated; this change not only extends shelf life but also creates undesirable *trans* fatty acids. Soybean oil with levels ranging between 1 and 3 percent linolenic acid (compared with the usual 7 percent) is now available as a result of selective breeding for low levels of linolenic acid over several generations of soybeans. Low linolenic acid soybean oils are quite well suited for use in deep-fat frying. Asoyia and Vistive are two of the commercial low-linolenic-acid soybean oils that are helping to reduce *trans* fatty acids in foods.

TABLE 9.1   Comparison of Some Table Spreads in Supermarkets[a]

Spread	Type of Fat	$/oz	Ingredient Listing
Butter	Milk	0.343	Cream, salt, annatto
Margarine	Corn	0.137	Corn oil, partially hydrogenated soybean oil, water
Margarine	Soybean	0.093	Soybean oil, partially hydrogenated soy oil, water, whey
Soft margarine	Soybean	0.099	Soybean oil, whey, water, hydrogenated soybean oil
Soft margarine	Corn	0.074	Corn oil, whey, partially hydrogenated soybean oil
Smart Balance	Plant oils	0.174	Palm, soy, canola, and olive oils
Promise	Plant oils	0.173	Soy, canola, sunflower, palm, and palm kernel oils
Benecol	Canola	0.749	Canola oil, water, partially hydrogenated canola oil, plant stanol esters

[a]*Southern California, November 2006.*

Trans fatty acid
Fatty acids that have had hydrogen atoms added to double bonds in the *trans* configuration (opposite sides of the longitudinal axis of a double bond).

monounsaturated, and polyunsaturated fatty acids. Ingredient labels that list an oil first have a higher content of polyunsaturated fatty acids than one that begins with a hydrogenated fat. The content of **trans fatty acids** is a concern when hydrogenated fats are in food products, and they clearly are present in margarines. Stick margarines usually have a *trans* fatty acid content between 19 and 49 percent; soft margarines range between 11 and 28 percent.

Because of the concern that *trans* fatty acids may be unhealthful, there is increasing interest in including the actual content of *trans* fatty acids on nutrition labels. When this labeling is available, consumers will be able to select margarines with low levels of *trans* fatty acids.

Biotechnologists are conducting research to modify the fatty acid content of various seed oils by modifying the genetic makeup of the plants. Another approach toward lowering the levels of *trans* fatty acids is to modify the hydrogenation process so the addition of hydrogen at double bonds occurs less frequently in the trans configuration. One way this can be accomplished is by using carbon dioxide in hydrogenation. Other techniques being explored are interesterification and enzymes.

Consumers who are battling high cholesterol levels sometimes select special spreads rather than using either butter or margarine. The spreads currently on the market are made with either a stanol or a sterol ester. Benecol contains sitostanol fatty acyl ester. Take Control is made with ß-sitosterol fatty acyl ester. Both of these are available in markets now, but their price is quite high in comparison with either butter or margarine. Studies have demonstrated that both stanol and sterol esters are effective in helping lower serum cholesterol levels, which may motivate consumers with very high cholesterol levels to use these costly spreads. Research is ongoing to bring competitors to the market. Phytrol, a complicated compound incorporating sitosterol, campesterol, and sitostanol, is not yet available on the market to compete with these other two expensive spreads.

Fats for Baking

Butter and margarines may be used for baking, but shortening and lard often are preferred because of their contributions to texture and flavor. Table 9.2 compares shortenings and lard in the marketplace today. Shortening is produced by the hydrogenation of vegetable oil, a process that creates some *trans* fatty acids. Presently, the level of *trans* fatty acids in shortenings is between 14 and 18 percent, down significantly from 25 percent levels in the past.

TABLE 9.2 Comparison of Shortenings and Lard in Supermarkets[a]

Fat	Packaging	$/oz	Color	Ingredients
Shortening	Can	0.19	White	Partially hydrogenated cottonseed and soybean oil
Shortening	Can	0.19	Yellow	Partially hydrogenated cottonseed and soybean oil, mono- and diglycerides
Shortening	Stick	0.21	Yellow	Partially hydrogenated soybean and cottonseed oil, mono- and diglycerides, artificial butter flavor, beta-carotene
Smart Balance	Can	0.22	White	Oil blend (soybean, palm, canola), monoglycerides
Enova	Can	0.28	White	Canola and soybean oils with added diglycerides

[a]*Southern California, November 2006.*

Shortening is made with added monoglycerides to promote its emulsifying ability in cake batters. This attribute is of importance in cakes but has little impact in pastry dough. The value of shortening in pastries is its contribution to texture; it can be cut into small pieces that remain during mixing and melt during baking to create the desired flaky texture. The two sensory disadvantages of shortening, white color and little flavor, have been overcome by the addition of yellow color and butter flavor to some shortenings.

Lard can be used effectively in some types of baking and some people prefer it, especially for making pastry. Although its properties are slightly different from shortening, it can be used effectively in pastries. However, its use in cakes results in a somewhat greasy crumb and a heavy texture. The very mild flavor of lard contributes to the flavor profile of pastry but is difficult to detect in cakes because of the other ingredients. No coloring or flavoring agents are added to lard.

Oils

Extra-virgin olive oil
First pressing (cold) of olives to extract the oil; best quality.

Olive oil is a particularly suitable choice for vinegar and oil salad dressings (Figure 9.1). Its delicate flavor and its health benefits make this an important ingredient for preparing stir-fry dishes, sauces for pastas, and other recipes. Olive oil can be purchased at various prices, depending on its processing and source. **Extra-virgin olive oil** is the most expensive because it is obtained by cold pressing and without the use of solvents, a process that produces a flavorful yellowish green oil. These qualities can be appreciated best in salad dressings because the oil is used at room temperature. Some of the flavor components are lost when olive oil is heated because of their volatility.

Many other oils also can be found on market shelves today. Macadamia nut, walnut, and some other nut oils with distinctive flavors are sometimes available but often quite expensive. These flavors may be of merit in preparing dishes with other flavors delicate enough to permit the nut oil flavor to be detected. Peanut oil (derived from the legume and not a true nut) is very well suited for frying foods. Its flavor is a pleasing addition, and its high smoke point minimizes smoking and formation of acrolein during frying.

The most common oils are extracted from cottonseed, corn, soybean, and canola (rapeseed). These are suitable for use in frying, salad dressings, and other recipes that include oil. The smoke point of these oils is high enough to permit them to be used effectively in frying foods. Their moderate cost makes them more economical

FIGURE 9.1   Olive oil is the oil used in the vinegar and oil dressing served with this Italian salad of assorted greens.

but less flavorful than peanut oil for this purpose. Table 9.3 compares the various oils on market shelves today.

All fats are susceptible to the development of rancidity during storage, which means they should be purchased in quantities small enough to be used in a reasonable length of time. Butter and margarine can be stored in the refrigerator to extend shelf life, but oils solidify and are inconvenient to use if they are stored there. Shortening does not require refrigerated storage because it has added antioxidants to aid in blocking rancidity. Nevertheless, fats in opened cans of shortening gradually undergo oxidative rancidity that reduces shelf life. If only a little baking is done, a small can or sticks of shortening are the preferred choice when buying shortening.

TABLE 9.3   Comparison of Oils in Markets[a]

Type	Appearance	Package. Size	$/fl oz
Extra-virgin olive	Greenish	17 fl oz	0.53
Virgin olive	Yellow	17 fl oz	0.44
Extra-light virgin olive	Very light yellow	17 fl oz	0.41
Corn	Yellow	32 fl oz	0.09
Soybean	Light yellow	32 fl oz	0.14
Safflower	Medium yellow	32 fl oz	0.13
Canola (rapeseed)	Yellow	24 fl oz	0.15
Peanut	Medium yellow	24 fl oz	0.18
Grape seed	Yellow	32 fl oz	0.24

[a]*Southern California, November 2006.*

The amount of oil to buy is determined by how much will be used. A small bottle is a wise choice for individuals or even families if the oil is to be used primarily to make salad dressing. The choice to buy small bottles may mean that it is appropriate to stock more than one type of oil, making it possible to add more variety to different dishes. If food is being prepared in large quantities, large sizes are appropriate when buying oils.

SWEETENERS

The inventory of sweeteners needed is related very directly to the types of foods that ordinarily are prepared. Baked goods require sugar in many of the recipes, with large amounts used for desserts and small amounts used for various quick and yeast breads. Because of their long shelf life, it is practical to maintain an inventory of the various sweeteners that are used somewhat regularly.

Sugars

Granulated sugar, whether made from sugar cane or sugar beets, is simply sucrose. This disaccharide is the most common sweetener used by consumers in food preparation, typically in granulated form (Figure 9.2). Although the source of granulated sugar may be highlighted in advertising, there is no significant difference between the various granulated sugars displayed on market shelves (Table 9.4). The least expensive granulated sugar for the quantity being purchased is the wisest buy. Despite the fact that the cost per pound is reduced significantly by buying a 10-pound bag (Table 9.4), this could prove to be a false economy unless this large amount will be used in a reasonable period of time. Superfine sugar is more costly than regular granulated sugar, but its fine texture is sufficiently advantageous in making meringues to warrant the cost if meringues are prepared frequently.

Brown sugars vary in color, depending on the amount of molasses added to the sugar syrup during processing. The added flavor is valued in some applications, but its nutritive value is essentially the same as that of refined sugar. As can be seen in Table 9.4, organic sugar is available at an elevated cost, but the nutritional merits are no greater than the other forms of sugar. This added cost is a good example of "Let the buyer beware!"

BOX 9.2

Food Insights: Food-Safe Utilitarian Spray

Cooking sprays are convenient for coating baking and frying pans with a minimum amount of fat without getting it on hands or other equipment. Various cooking sprays are available in the consumer market, including some made with olive oil, canola oil, butter flavoring, or flour. Other special sprays are designed to withstand the high temperatures of grilling. The two-year shelf life of cooking sprays makes it feasible to have more than one cooking spray available in the kitchen.

These sprays can be used to help solve other kitchen complaints. Because cooking spray contains oil, it is useful in forming a thin coating on plastic containers to block contact of water-based sauces with the plastic. This keeps leftovers containing tomato, curry, or other colored ingredients from staining them. It also can be used on ice cube trays and gelatin molds to make it easier to release the frozen cubes or molded gelatin.

FIGURE 9.2   Confectioners' sugar adds sweetness as the finishing touch to bastilla, a Moroccan dish.

Turbinado
Tan-colored sugar due to impurities remaining in partially refined sugar.

Turbinado is an off-white sugar with some impurities (but no significant nutritional benefits). This sugar is produced by centrifuging and steaming raw sugar. Similarly, the product that is in the markets as "raw sugar" has been refined a bit to make it safe but it is not higher in nutrients. The benefits are in the mind of the beholder.

Sugar Substitutes and Sweeteners

Saccharin has been serving as an artificial sweetener or sugar substitute since before the beginning of the 20th century. Sweet 'N' Low is a familiar saccharin tabletop sweetener in markets today. Cyclamates entered the market and competed very effectively until 1970 when they were banned in the United States. Recently, efforts have been renewed to get them back into U.S. markets, but that still has not happened. However, cyclamates have enjoyed wide popularity in Canada, Europe, and most of South America all of the time that cyclamates have been restricted here.

Aspartame
Sweetener comprised of phenylalanine and aspartic acid.

Aspartame (acid dipeptide of phenylalanine and aspartic acid) is a sweetener that was approved by the Food and Drug Administration in 1981. Although it has to carry a warning label for people with phenylketonuria, it has been widely accepted as a sugar substitute. It gained favor because it was very sweet and did not carry the bitter aftertaste associated with saccharin. Equal, NutraSweet, and NutraTaste are trade names under which aspartame is marketed. Another sweetener is acesulfame-K, which is marketed as Sunett. Recently, sucralose was approved. It is popular because of its sweetness and lack of even the small amount of bitterness associated with acesulfame-K. Sucralose is marketed under the trade name Splenda.

TABLE 9.4 Comparison of Various Sugars and Sweeteners in Supermarkets[a]

Description	Source	Package Weight	Cost/oz
Granulated Sugar			
National brand	Cane	10 lb	$0.041
National brand	Cane	5 lb	0.042
National brand	Cane	4 lb	0.051
National brand	Cane	1 lb	0.068
Store brand	Beet	5 lb	0.037
Store brand	Beet	2 lb	0.053
Superfine bakers	Cane	4 lb	0.058
Cubes	Cane	1 lb	0.090
Other Sugars			
Golden brown[b]	Cane	1 lb	0.062
Light brown[c]	Beet	1 lb	0.068
Dark brown[b]	Cane	1 lb	0.051
Dark brown[c]	Beet	1 lb	0.062
Organic brown	Cane	1 lb	0.137
Turbinado	Cane	1 lb	0.112
Raw cane	Beet	1 lb	0.109
Confectioners	Beet	1 lb	0.081
Sugar Substitutes[d]			
Sugar Twin	Saccharin		0.053/g
Splenda	Sucralose		$5.49/2 cups
Sweet 'N' Low	Saccharin		0.064/g
NatraTaste	Aspartame		0.259/g
NutraSweet	Aspartame		0.259/g
Equal	Aspartame		0.086/g

[a]Southern California, November 2006.
[b]National brand.
[c]Store brand.
[d]Trademarked brands.

In 2002, neotame became the newest artificial sweetener to be approved by the Food and Drug Administration. It is produced by reacting aspartame with 3,3-dimethylbutyraldehyde. Although it bears some relationship to aspartame, neotame does not break down in the body to yield phenylalanine. Amazingly, it is 8,000 times sweeter than sucrose. In comparison, aspartame is only 200 times sweeter and sucralose is 600 times sweeter than sucrose. Alitame is another sweetener related to aspartame, but it is still in the developmental stage.

Liquid Sweeteners

Molasses is a flavorful sweetener that is used in some products for its color and flavor. It provides some iron; a tablespoon of light-colored molasses contains 0.8 milligrams of iron; medium and blackstrap contain 1.4 and 3 milligrams, respectively. The strong flavor of blackstrap molasses is objectionable to some people.

Corn syrup is used in some recipes for icings and various baked products, such as pecan pie. In crystalline candies, it is used to promote a fine texture by introducing a mixture of sugars. Dark corn syrup also may be used as pancake syrup.

Honey often is served in place of jams and jellies for use on bread and rolls. It also is an ingredient in some baked products. Up to a third of the sugar may be replaced by honey when making crisp cookies. Conventional and chiffon cakes may be made while substituting up to 40 percent of the sugar with honey. However, honey results in products that brown much more quickly than those made only with sugar, and they need to be watched carefully to avoid burning them when they are baking.

SEASONINGS

Spices

Many different spices may be used in preparing various dishes to bring a wonderful array of flavors to food (Figure 9.3). Fortunately, they have a relatively good shelf life. However, the flavors gradually begin to dissipate, and the spices cease to be effective as exciting flavoring agents. This means that spices need to be replaced from time to time. Fortunately, they do not all have to be replaced at the same time because some of them are fairly expensive. Most spices remain fresh for a year or longer.if they are stored in closed containers in a dark, cool cabinet.

The inventory of spices considered essential varies from kitchen to kitchen, depending on the types of foods that are prepared frequently. Adventurous cooks will probably stock many different spices; others may have salt, pepper, and little else. A wide array of spices in the kitchen helps liberate most cooks to begin to experiment with seasonings. Table 9.5 lists some of the most widely used spices in the United States.

Herbs and Seeds

Herbs, the leaves of certain nonpoisonous plants, can be added to augment and highlight foods. Basil, rosemary, tarragon, sage, and dill (Figure 9.4) are some examples of

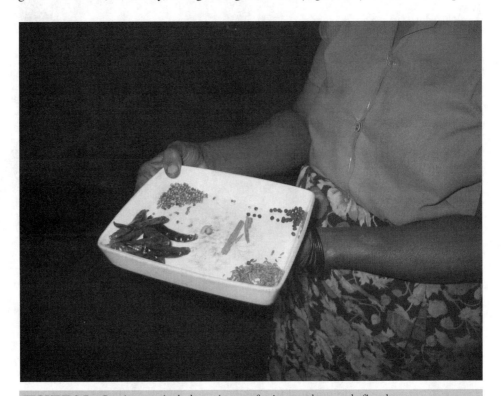

FIGURE 9.3   Curries may include a mixture of spices to please a chef's palate.

TABLE 9.5 Selected Spices and Some Suggested Uses

Spice	Some Suggested Uses
Allspice	Whole—pickling, meats, gravies
	Ground—Baked products, puddings, relishes, and preserves
Cayenne	Meats, sauces, fish, eggs
Cinnamon	Sticks—Pickling, preserving, fruits
	Ground—Baked products, mashed sweet potatoes
Cloves	Whole—Ham, stews, pickled fruit
	Ground—Baked products, puddings, vegetables
Ginger	Whole—Conserves, chutney, pickling, dried fruits, applesauce
	Ground—Baked products, pot roast, fruits, puddings
Mace	Whole—Pickling, fish sauces
	Ground—Chocolate, cakes, and puddings
Mustard	Whole—Seeds for salad garnish, pickled meats, fish
	Dry—Meats, sauces, gravies
Nutmeg	Whole—Grated for seasonings
	Ground—Baked products, eggnog, puddings, custard, fruits, cauliflower
Paprika	Garnish on vegetables, poultry, and fish, in salad dressings, and gravy
Pepper	Whole—Pickling, meats, soups
	Ground (black and white)—Meats, sauces, vegetables, soups, salads and dressings, eggs
Saffron	Baked products, rice, chicken
Turmeric	Pickling, meats, dressings, salads, relishes

FIGURE 9.4 Fresh dill weed adds flavor while also serving as a delicate garnish.

the fresh herbs that often are available in supermarkets. Unfortunately, they do not retain their freshness very long and must be used within a few days of purchase to be of optimum quality. Dried herbs, available in the spice section, can be kept for a year or more (Table 9.6). The strong flavors of dried herbs make it possible to use smaller amounts than are required when cooking using fresh herbs.

TABLE 9.6 Herbs, Seeds, and Blends of Seasonings

Seasoning	Suggested Uses
Herbs	
Basil	Tomato dishes, peas, squash, string beans, lamb
Bay leaf	Stews, soups, beef, fish, sauces, pickles
Chervil	Soups, salads, eggs, fish, chicken
Marjoram	Stews, soups, poultry, fish, lamb
Mint	Beverages, sauces, lamb, stews, soups
Oregano	Stews, meats, omelets, chili, gravies
Parsley	Soups, vegetables, sauces, fish, poultry, meats
Rosemary	Soups, stews, meats, fish
Sage	Dressing for poultry, pork, fish, salads
Savory	Meats, sauces, poultry, eggs
Tarragon	Chicken, meats, eggs, tomatoes, gravies
Thyme	Dressing for poultry, soups, stews, tomatoes, gravies
Seeds	
Anise	Cookies and some breads
Caraway	Baked products (particularly breads), cabbage, noodles, cheeses
Cardamom	Mixed pickling spice, cookies, biscuits, stuffing for poultry, vegetables
Celery	Potato salad, pickling, fish, vegetables
Coriander	Mixed pickling spice, cookies, biscuits, stuffing for poultry, vegetables
Cumin	Curry and chili recipes, soups, eggs
Dill	Pickling, sauerkraut, gravies, salads
Fennel	Pickles, pastries
Poppy	Bread, rolls, cookies, cakes, noodles
Blends	
Chili powder	Mexican recipes, eggs, meats
Curry powder	Fish, poultry, rice, vegetables
Fines herbes	Vegetables, meats
Mixed pickling spice	Pickling, preserving, relishes, gravies
Poultry seasoning	Stuffings for poultry and fish, rice
Salad herbs	Salad dressings
Sausage seasoning	Meat loaf, veal dishes, sausage

Seeds are another part of plants that find their way into a number of recipes. Poppy seeds, sesame seeds, and caraway seeds are added on the surface of some rolls and breads. Poppy seed cakes are also popular. Various stir-fries include seeds.

SALAD DRESSINGS

The key components for making salad dressings are a pleasing vinegar and an oil of high quality and flavor. Olive oil is an excellent choice to have available for making salad dressings, but other suitable oils to bring flavor to a dressing also can be found. Walnut or other nut oils are all good possibilities. Rice vinegar or other special vinegar can add a distinctive flavor accent to a salad dressing.

Consumers who make their own salad dressings may wish to keep small bottles of vinegars and/or oils to broaden the range of flavors in their vinegar and oil dressings. Packets of seasonings appropriate to flavor various salad dressings can be purchased as another way of adding variety to salad dressings.

Commercial salad dressings are convenient and generally of pleasing quality, but they are more expensive than those prepared in the kitchen using basic ingredients.

SPREADS

Jams, Jellies, and Preserves

When buying jams, jellies, marmalade, and preserves, the color of the product is a very helpful guide to quality (Figure 9.5). A bright, reasonably light color is a good indication that the fruit flavor should be relatively prominent because the mixture has been boiled a comparatively short time to achieve the desired sugar concentration. A darker color results when fruit mixtures have to be boiled quite a long time to reach the appropriate concentration of sugar. Prolonged boiling evaporates some of the volatile fruit flavors and also causes some chemical breakdown of sucrose. These changes have a detrimental effect on flavor.

Peanut Butter

Hydrogenation
Addition of hydrogen to oil to alter its melting point and improve spreading characteristics.

Peanut butters are available with varying sizes of chopped peanuts, ranging from very chunky to a smooth texture. The choice is strictly a matter of personal preference. Another choice to be made is whether to buy hydrogenated or regular peanut butter with its oil layer at the top of the jar. **Hydrogenation** has the advantage of altering the melting point of the fatty acids so the fat no longer flows at room temperature and rises to the top of the jar. This saves the tedious task of stirring the oil into the peanut butter mass until it is blended very thoroughly. Unfortunately, it creates some *trans* fatty acids. The choices are in the hands of individual consumers.

Summary

Consumer choices for table spreads include butter and margarines made with different hydrogenated or partially hydrogenated oils in different formulations. Safflower, canola (rapeseed), corn, cottonseed, soybean, and sunflower seeds are sources usually used for

FIGURE 9.5 Jams and jellies typically have a bright color when they are of excellent quality.

making margarines. The hydrogenation process produces some *trans* fatty acids, which is triggering research efforts to reduce the amount of these fatty acids in margarines.

Spreads incorporating stanol or sterol esters are being used by some consumers who have very high blood cholesterol levels. Benecol contains sitostanol fatty acyl ester, and Take Control contains β-sitosterol fatty acyl ester. These are quite expensive compared with other margarines.

Choices for baking are butter, margarine, shortening, or lard. Shortenings may be purchased in sticks for easy measuring, but they cost more than the shortenings in cans. Lard has a distinctive flavor and creates a slightly greasy crumb.

Extra-virgin olive oil is a favorite oil for salads and other applications where little or no heat is applied. Peanut oil is especially well suited to frying, but cottonseed, corn, soybean, and canola oils also are excellent for that purpose, as well as in salad dressings.

When buying oils and shortening, buy amounts that will be used in a reasonable length of time. This strategy avoids having them become rancid before being used.

Sugars have a very long shelf life so they can be purchased in quantities that are convenient to store. Sometimes superfine is a bit more expensive than regular granulated sugar and is only needed when making meringues. Light brown sugar has a milder flavor than dark brown sugar. No sugar is a significant source of vitamins or minerals.

Spices and herbs are convenient to store and are useful in adding variety to foods. However, they are expensive and do need to be replaced occasionally because of some loss of volatile flavors.

Salad dressings made using basic ingredients are less costly than buying ready-to-use dressings. Various oils and vinegars, as well as seasonings, can add pleasing variety.

Study Questions

1. Compare the ingredient listing on two different margarines. Which would you buy? Explain your answer.
2. What specific fats and/or oils would you plan to stock as staples for use in baking? Explain the reason for keeping each one in stock.
3. What sugar(s) would be wise buys for making chocolate chip cookies? Are there specific options you would avoid? Explain your answer to each of these questions.
4. What spices, herbs, and seeds do you want to stock regularly? In what products will each be used?
5. Compare the ingredient labels on three different peanut butters. Which would you choose? Why?
6. Can olive oil be substituted for butter when making chocolate chip cookies? Explain your answer.

Suggested Websites

www.caloriecontrol.org/lowcal.html
Information on several low-calorie sweeteners.

www.dietitian.com/sugar.html
Answers to some questions about sweeteners.

www.eatright.org
Website of the American Dietetic Association.

http://www.culinarycafe.com/Spices_Herbs/index.html
Dictionary of spices and herbs, plus many recipe and food suggestions.

http://www.americanheart.org/presenter.jhtml?identifier=1200009
Healthy lifestyle information by the American Heart Association.

http://www.foodsubs.com/Oils.html
Comments on a variety of salad and cooking oils.

http://www.zerotranssoy.com/sol_lowlin_main.html
Information on low-linolenic-acid oils.

http://www.enovaoil.com/kitchen/library.asp
Information about Enova.

Bibliography

Adair, M., et al. 2001. Acceptability of peanut butter cookies prepared using mungbean paste as a fat ingredient substitute. *J. Am. Dietet. Assoc.* 101 (4): 467.

Berry, D. 2004. Fresh advice on herbs and spices. *Food Product Design.* 14 (2): 61.

Campbell, A. D., and Bell, L. N. 2001. Acceptability of low-fat, sugar-free cakes: Effect of providing compositional information during testing. *J. Am. Dietet. Assoc.* 101 (3): 354.

Clark, J. P. 2005. Fats and oils processors adapt to changing needs. *Food Technol.* 59 (5): 74.

Coulston, A. M., and Johnson, R. K. 2002. Sugar and sugars: Myths and realities. *J. Am. Dietet. Assoc.* 102 (3): 351.

Deis, R. C. 2005. How sweet it is—using polyols and high-potency sweeteners. *Food Product Design.* 15 (7): 57.

Elias, S. L., and Innis, S. M. 2002. Bakery foods are the major dietary source of *trans*-fatty acids among pregnant women with diets providing 30% energy from fat. *J. Am Dietet. Assoc.* 102 (1): 46.

Furth, P., and Cox, D. 2004. Spice market expands. *Food Technol.* 58 (6): 30.

Guthrie, J. F., and Morton, J. F. 2000. Food sources of added sweeteners in the diets of Americans. *J. Am. Dietet. Assoc.* 100 (1): 43.

Hicks, K. B., and Moreau, R. A. 2001. Phytosterols and phytostanols: Functional food cholesterol busters. *Food Technol.* 59 (1): 63.

Hollingsworth, F. 2001. Margarine: Over-the-top functional food. *Food Technol.* 55 (1): 59.

Hollingsworth, P. 2002. Artificial sweeteners face sweet 'n' sour consumer market. *Food Technol.* 56 (7): 24.

Kuntz, L. A. 2001. Fatty acid basics. *Food Product Design.* 11 (8): 93.

McNutt, K. 2000. What clients need to know about sugar replacers. J. *Am. Dietet. Assoc.* 100 (4): 466.

Nabors, L. O. 2002. Sweet choices: Sugar replacements for foods and beverages. *Food Technol.* 56 (7): 28.

Ohr, L. M. 2006. Functional fats. *Food Technol.* 60 (3): 81.

Prakash, I., et al. 2002. Neotame: Next generation sweetener. *Food Technol.* 56 (7): 36.

Pszczola, D. E. 2005. Spice companies take advantage of new opportunities. *Food Technol.* 59 (11): 43.

Rodriguez, L. M., and Castellanos, V. H. 2000. Use of low-fat foods by people with diabetes decreases fat, saturated fat, and cholesterol intakes. *J. Am. Dietet. Assoc.* 100 (5): 531.

Sloan, A. E. 2005. Time to change the oil? *Food Technol.* 59 (5): 17.

Figure C1 Avocadoes hang heavily from this tree in Ecuador.

Figure C2 Ripe grapefruit are ready for harvest at the same time that some blossoms signal the next crop.

Figure C3 Baskets of grape vines cradle eggplant, squash of various types, peppers, and tomatoes on steps on the Greek island of Santorini.

Figure C4 Broccoli free of pesticides shows evidence of the voracious appetite of pests roaming on the leaves.

Figure C5 Poblano pepper is a fairly mild variety of peppers.

Figure C6 Jalapeño peppers add plenty of fire to Mexican dishes.

Figure C7   Farmers' markets are a pleasant venue for buying locally-grown fresh produce.

Figure C8   Potato salad made with potatoes and onions from the farmers' market gains added nutrition and interest with plenty of hard-cooked eggs, some of which add a colorful garnish.

Figure C9   Uniform slices of hard-cooked egg can be cut using this egg slicer.

Figure C10   Organic produce is identified clearly in this market.

Figure C11 Mango, persimmons, kiwi fruit, and malua melon (rear) add exciting flavors and colors to salads.

Figure C12 Zucchini form below the base of the blossom; both the squash and the blossom can be eaten.

Figure C13 Salmon filet topped with couscous and chopped parsley makes a colorful and very nourishing entrée that can be baked in a few minutes.

Figure C14 Chicken breast that has been marinated in garlic-flavored olive oil marinade briefly is grilled to perfection on an outdoor grill.

Figure C15 Grilled chicken breast, rice with sautéed mushrooms, steamed broccoli, and hot French bread combine to make a perfect patio feast.

Figure C16 Turkey is lowered very carefully into a vertical deep fat fryer containing enough oil to just cover the turkey. Frying must be done outdoors away from flammable materials.

Figure C17 When done, the turkey is raised from the oil and transported to the kitchen for carving. The skin is too dark to be pleasing to eat, but the meat is delicious and very juicy and, surprisingly, is not at all greasy.

Figure C18 Fresh mango, some leftover turkey (Fig. C17), and colorful peppers mingle with cheese to top this tasty pizza.

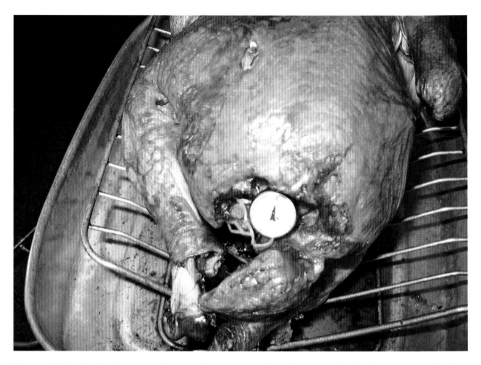

Figure C19 Turkey is roasted breast down in a V-shaped rack until the thermometer in the stuffing reaches 165°F.

Figure C20 When done, the turkey is removed from the oven and allowed to rest at room temperature for a few minutes before it is placed on a platter to be carved at the table or is carved in the kitchen.

Figure C21   Turkey soup with plenty of vegetables is a delicious way of eating some of the leftovers.

Figure C22   Greek-style pizza features artichoke hearts, Greek olives, feta cheese, and chopped tomatoes. (Courtesy of Fleischmann's and ACH Food Companies, Inc.)

Figure C23   Greek onion, custard, and broccoli pie features phyllo dough.

Figure C24   Pork teriyaki with pineapple is served on a bed of rice; the bamboo place mat accents the Japanese overtone of the meal.

Figure C25 The rice seen in Figure C24 could have come from rice paddies such as these that are being planted by many villagers in Sri Lanka.

Figure C26 Papadam is a crisp fried dough that accompanies curry for lunch and dinner in Sri Lanka.

Figure C27   Cashews are an important export from Southeast Asia. (Courtesy of Bill Malcolm.)

Figure C28   Loukoumades are made from a soft yeast-leavened dough that is fried and then topped with a drizzle of honey and chopped pistachios.

Figure C29 Pods from the *Theobroma cacao* tree contain the nibs that are ultimately processed into chocolate to help satisfy candy lovers around the world.

Figure C30 Butterhorn rolls are made from a yeast dough that is fairly high in butter and eggs. (Courtesy of Fleischmann's and ACH Food Companies, Inc.)

Figure C31 Old world rye bread makes a hearty lunch when served with pickled onions, radishes, cucumbers, a variety of cheeses, and beer. (Courtesy of Fleischmann's and ACH Food Companies, Inc.)

Figure C32 Challah is a rather sweet bread traditionally served on the Jewish Shabbat and holidays. (Courtesy of Fleischmann's and ACH Food Companies, Inc.)

Figure C33 Table set for the Seder, the important dinner at the beginning of Passover.

Figure C34 Pumpkin pie garnished with pecan halves is a simple, yet very tasty pie.

Figure C35 Balsamic vinegar in the center of the cruet is surrounded by olive oil. The two necks in the cruet make it convenient to pour a little balsamic and olive oil onto a bread plate so the diner can dip French bread in them. Grape seed oil, garlic-infused oil, and oil with some herbs are other flavorful oils.

Figure C36 Tea from the mountains of Sri Lanka will be a welcome beverage with pumpkin pie, as well as with many other foods.

Figure C37   Kitchen before remodeling had a tile counter, walnut-stained cabinets, and a dark floor.

Figure C38   Cherry cabinets, a polished Caesarstone counter, and a light tan tile floor in the remodeled kitchen give the feeling of space and light.

Figure C39 Pull-out shelves in the cabinet under the counter provide easy access to pans that will be used on the range to the left.

Figure C40 Electrical appliances stored in this cabinet with a door that folds back for full access are located conveniently.

Figure C41   Kitchen with a long marble island containing the sink; the range against the wall has counter space on both sides and lighting under the upper cabinets.

Figure C42   The tungsten filament in this halogen burner can be seen in the middle of the element when the unit is heating.

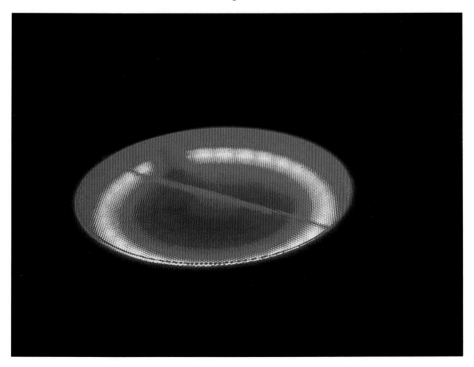

Figure C43   This design is attractive without food, but also frames food arranged on it.

Figure C44   Place setting for a dinner that includes a salad plate above the forks and a bread plate to the right of the salad.

Figure C45   Place setting for a less formal dinner than is the setting in Figure C44.

Figure C46   Place setting set for dessert.

Figure C47 A runner serves as the place mat for this informal breakfast setting.

Figure C48 Pasta prima vera, a tossed salad, and garlic bread are the main course of this casual dinner.

CHAPTER 10

Food Safety

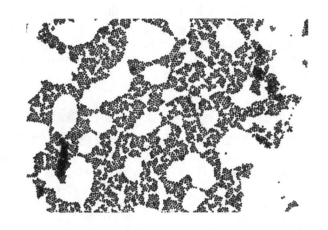

OVERVIEW

Food safety is an aspect of meal management that cannot be overemphasized. Proper handling of food, from the time it is purchased at the store or received at a restaurant or other food service facility, is the responsibility of the food manager. Temperature control and carefully supervised sanitation are key factors in assuring optimal quality and safe food for diners. Bacteria that can multiply and cause food losses due to spoilage are responsible for some food losses that occur during marketing and storage (Table 10.1).

Pathogenic microorganisms can lead to food-borne illnesses if ingested. Prompt refrigeration and cooking to a safe final temperature, followed by a safe holding temperature (if necessary), are essential to helping prevent food-borne illnesses. In addition, all food handlers must practice good hygiene, and all kitchen surfaces and storage areas need to be maintained at a high level of sanitation.

FOOD-BORNE INFECTIONS

Food-borne illnesses are caused by such microorganisms as:

- Bacteria
- Molds
- Viruses
- Parasites
- Algae

Bacterial Infections

Bacteria, the cause of several food-borne illnesses, are very tiny (commonly 0.5 to 3 μm and occasionally up to 10 μm) single-celled organisms, which usually are shaped in the form of a sphere (cocci) or a rod (bacilli). They are able to reproduce by binary fission and can grow into very large populations because the generation time may be as short as 20 minutes under favorable growing conditions.

Spore
Primitive form capable of surviving difficult environmental conditions and then reproducing to form new and viable bacterial cells.

Spore-producing bacteria, such as *Clostridium botulinum*, are able to survive under very negative conditions because they can form *spores*. Although bacteria normally may be killed by heating or some other aggressive treatments, **spores** are remarkably resistant to extremes in temperature, drying, chemicals, or abrasives, and they allow production of toxin if storage conditions are favorable.

TABLE 10.1   Some Bacteria Causing Food Spoilage

Bacterium	Type of Food Affected
Xanthomonas	Fruits and vegetables
Acetobacter	Fruit juices, alcoholic beverages
Gluconobacter	Pineapple, pears, apples
Shewanella putrefaciens[a]	Fish, meat
Flavobacterium	Milk, meat
Alcaligenes	Protein-rich foods
Psychrobacter	Poultry, meat, fish
Erwinia	Fruits and vegetables

[a]Formerly classified as *Pseudomonas putrefaciens*.

Cryophilic
Bacteria flourishing below 15°C.

Mesophilic
Bacteria growing well between 15 and 45°C.

Thermophilic
Bacteria growing well between 45 and 95°C.

Enterotoxin
Toxin affecting the gastrointestinal tract.

Neurotoxin
Toxin affecting the nervous system.

Endotoxin
Toxin released from cell wall.

Exotoxin
Toxin formed during the replication and growth phase.

Salmonella
Bacteria that are often the cause of food-borne illness.

Salmonellosis
Bacterial infection caused by eating Salmonella-tainted food.

Salmonella enteritidis
Form of *Salmonella* sometimes occurring in eggs from hens that are infected with this kind of bacteria.

Salmonella typhi
Bacteria that cause typhoid fever.

Listeriosis
Bacterial infection caused by eating food such as soft cheeses from raw milk tainted with *Listeria*.

Listeria monocytogenes
Pathogenic bacteria causing listeriosis.

Various factors affecting the growth of different bacteria include temperature and the presence of air. **Cryophilic** bacteria flourish in cold temperatures (below 15°C or 59°F). Bacteria growing best at temperatures between 15 and 45°C (59 and 113°F) are classified as **mesophilic**, and those thriving between 45 and 95°C (113 and 203°F) are termed **thermophilic**. The type of bacteria present in a food dictates the temperature control measures required in handling, cooking, and storing that food to protect against food-borne illnesses.

Some bacteria produce toxins that can cause illness and even death when they are ingested. If the toxin affects the gastrointestinal system, it is classified as an **enterotoxin**. A **neurotoxin** acts on the nervous system. Among those capable of causing food-borne illnesses are certain strains of *Escherichia coli, Salmonella, Campylobacter, Shigella, Listeria, Clostridium,* and *Vibrio*.

Toxins classified as **endotoxins** are released from the cell wall of bacteria by enzymes and cause vomiting, diarrhea, or other physiological effects in the person who has ingested them. **Exotoxins** are formed during the reproduction and growth of *Clostridium botulinum* and some other bacteria.

Salmonella

Of the food-borne illnesses, one of the most common is **salmonellosis**. Its symptoms include diarrhea, vomiting, chills, fever, and headache. Very severe infections can result in death. Various forms of *Salmonella* (Table 10.2) can cause this infection.

Salmonella enteritidis is a strain occasionally found in eggs. Eggs contaminated with *Salmonella enteritidis* during formation in the hen are the source of this type of salmonellosis (Table 10.3). Inspection of eggs does not detect the presence of *S. enteritidis,* so it is possible that infected eggs may be sold. Fortunately, pasteurizing or heating eggs to at least 71°C (160°F) kills this type of bacteria if it is present and prevents infection. For this reason, all egg products need to be heated to at least this temperature before being eaten.

Another type of salmonellosis (typhoid) is caused by ingestion of ***Salmonella typhi***. Infection may come from ingesting contaminated water, meat, milk, or other food. Pasteurization of milk, chlorination of water, and other sanitation measures have been quite effective in reducing the incidence of this form of salmonellosis in the United States, although it still is a potential problem in some developing countries. Prompt treatment with antibiotics is extremely important to help recovery from the infection, which usually takes at least two to three weeks.

Listeria monocytogenes

Although **listeriosis** (the infection resulting from ingestion of ***Listeria monocytogenes***) had been diagnosed occasionally, it emerged as a more frequent and serious health problem at the end of the 20th century. *Listeriosis* is particularly a problem among the very young, the elderly, and those with a compromised immune system. Among deaths in the United States due to food-borne infections, listeriosis is second only to those attributed to salmonellosis.

Listeria monocytogenes is widely found in the food supply, including fresh produce that often is consumed without cooking. Soft cheeses made from unpasteurized (raw) milk have been a source of this infection among pregnant women and the elderly. Unfortunately, this type of bacteria grows at refrigerator temperatures, which underlies the importance of good personal hygiene and very sanitary environments during the processing and handling of food to keep the population of *Listeria monocytogenes* in food to a minimum.

TABLE 10.2 Some Microorganisms Associated with Food-Borne Illnesses

Microorganisms	Favorable Growth Factors	Food Hosts	Onset	Symptoms
Salmonella	35–37°C max; 5–46°C range	Animal foods, sewage-contaminated plants	8–42 hours	Cramps, diarrhea, vomiting, fever, chills
Listeria monocytogenes	35–37°C max; 1–44°C range	Wide range of foods	1–7 days	Begins with above symptoms; then enters organs
Escherichia coli[a]	Below pasteurizing temperature	Fecal matter from handlers, unpasteurized cheeses	Lasts 7–12 days.	Severe diarrhea, fever, headache, chills
Escherichia coli[b]	30–42°C max; 10–45°C range	Animal foods, sewage-contaminated plants	3–9 days	Bloody diarrhea, colitis
Shigella[c]	37°C optimal; 7–46°C range	Fecal-contaminated foods	12 hours–7 days	Headache, diarrhea, mucus, fever, chills, abdominal pain
Campylobacter[d]	42°C optimal; 32–45°C range	Fecal-contaminated foods	2–5 days	Severe diarrhea, vomiting, fever, headache and stomachache, chills
Yersinia enterocolitica	25–29°C max; 0–44°C range	Raw milk, meat	24–30 hours	Diarrhea, vomiting, fever, lower abdominal pain
Vibrio[e]	30–37°C max; 5–42°C range	Fish and seafood	10–24 hours	Headache, vomiting
Streptococcus pyrogenes	Below pasteurizing temperature	Raw milk, salads		Sore throat, weakness, maybe vomiting, cramps, fever, chills
Staphylococcus aureus	20–37°C max; 7–48°C range; can grow at low pH and water and high salt	Meats, eggs, salads, poultry	1–3 days	Salivation, vomiting, diarrhea, cramps, chills, headache
Clostridium botulinum	Anaerobic, pH >4.6 or salt level <5.5%, 3–48°C	Fruits, vegetables, fish from contaminated soil or water	2–36 hours	Gastrointestinal followed by neurological symptoms leading to death
Aspergillus flavus, A. parasiticus	Can grow in refrigerator and pH 3.5; warm and damp promotes growth	Grains, peanuts, breads, cheese, spices, dry sausages, legumes	Unknown	May cause cancer
Hepatitis A virus	Doesn't grow in foods	Fecal-contaminated foods	2–7 weeks	Inflamed liver, fever, malaise, vomiting
Norwalk-like viruses	Doesn't grow in foods	Fecal-contaminated foods	12–24 hours	Vomiting, diarrhea

[a] *Enteroinvasive E. coli (e.g., shigellosis).*
[b] *Enterohemorrhagic E. coli (e.g., E. coli 0157:H7).*
[c] *Very similar to a strain of enteroinvasive E. coli.*
[d] *Campylobacter jejuni and Campylobacter coli are most common.*
[e] *Includes Vibrio cholerae, Vibrio parahaemolyticus, Vibrio vulnificus, and Vibrio mimicus.*

Escherichia coli

Escherichia coli
Type of bacteria that has caused some serious outbreaks of food-borne illness.

Although the estimated cases of illness caused by ***Escherichia coli*** are far fewer than from *Salmonella* (more than 55,000 versus more than 1,340,000 in the United States), this is still a significant cause of food-borne illness that requires a great effort if it is to be brought under control. Fecal contamination of food and water is the cause of outbreaks from this type of bacteria. If food and/or equipment are washed with contaminated water or food handlers are careless about frequently washing their hands in warm, soapy water, *E. coli* likely will contaminate the food and set the stage for an outbreak of gastroenteritis.

TABLE 10.3   Overview of Food-Borne Illnesses Caused by Microorganisms

Microorganism	Prevention/Control Measures	Illness Caused	Prominence
Salmonella	Heating to >72°C, chill to 3–4°C if not eaten in 2 hours, careful personal hygiene, clean cutting boards, sanitary kitchen	Salmonellosis	Leading cause
Listeria	Controls in processing foods, adequate reheating of leftovers and ready-to-eat foods, avoiding soft cheeses made from raw milk	Listeriosis	Sporadic
Escherichia coli	Pasteurization, prompt refrigeration, adequate heat treatment, good sanitation practices, food irradiation	Gastroenteritis	Sporadic
Shigella	Good sanitation by food handlers, chlorinated water, adequate refrigeration, no cross-contamination	Shigellosis	Warmer months are frequent cause
Campylobacter	Adequate heat treatment, no raw meats eaten, water free of fecal contaminants, good personal hygiene	Campylobacteriosis	Increasing
Yersinia	Adequate heat treatment, avoid recontamination (grows in refrigerator storage), good personal hygiene	Yersiniosis	Occasional
Vibrio	Eat no raw seafood, adequate heat treatment, prompt refrigerated storage, short storage time, avoid cross-contamination	Gastroenteritis	Occasional
Streptococcus	Pasteurization, proper sanitation, proper refrigeration	Streptococcal infection	Occasional
Staphylococcus aureus[a]	Healthy, sanitary food handlers and conditions, prompt refrigeration (chill fast to <5°C)	Staphylococcal intoxication	Decreasing
Clostridium botulinum[a]	Pressure canning low-acid food, proper time and temperature control	Botulism	Occasional
Aspergillus flavus, A. parasiticus	Anaerobic packaging, freezing, preservatives	Mycotoxicosis	Rare
Hepatitis A virus	Pasteurization or other heat treatment, hypochlorite in wash water, good personal hygiene, no infected food handlers, vaccination	Hepatitis A	Increasing
Norwalk-like viruses	Avoiding infected food handlers, hypochlorite in wash water, good personal hygiene	Gastroenteritis	Increasing

[a] *Intoxication due to ingestion of preformed toxin (not the microorganism itself).*

Dairy and meat animals apparently often have *E. coli* in their intestines, which ultimately may contaminate raw milk or meat, particularly ground meat. Pasteurization is effective in killing any *E. coli* that might be in milk. Cheeses should be made using pasteurized milk.

Irradiation is a very effective way of killing any bacteria that might be present, thus eliminating the risk of illness from meats. Deaths that occurred when people ate under-cooked hamburger contaminated with *E. coli* 0157:H7 have focused attention on the need to cook meats adequately or to irradiate them before marketing them.

Shigella

Fecal contamination is the ultimate source of **Shigella** in food, whether it comes from food handlers, sewage-polluted water, or poor sanitation standards. Infections from this type of bacteria are a greater problem during the warmer months than during the colder period from late fall to early spring. Chlorinated water is very important in controlling this type of bacteria. In developing countries lacking chlorination for drinking water, **shigellosis** can be a health problem for residents and tourists alike. Poor sanitation facilities and practices add to the likelihood of this food-borne illness in these countries. Only a small population of *Shigella* can cause

Shigella
Disease-causing bacteria sometimes contaminating water that has not been chlorinated.

Shigellosis
Bacterial infection caused by ingesting water infected with *Shigella*.

BOX 10.1

Food Insights: The Three Ws

When outbreaks of food-borne illness impact many people, food sleuths are busy trying to trace the source of the infection. Their detective work traces from the point of purchase back through the entire marketing and production chain and may ultimately end at the farm if the infection site has not been found. This describes the efforts that were put into play in 2006 when spinach tainted with *E. coli* O157: H7 caused a few deaths and many serious cases of food-borne illness. Ultimately, the problem was traced to four farms in the Salinas Valley of California where matching samples of the bacteria were found.

When the problem originates in the fields, its cause needs to be controlled. There are three Ws—workers, water, and wildlife—that may be infecting the field. To control the possibility of fecal contamination from workers, portable latrines are placed in fields and workers are instructed in safe handwashing procedures. If water (either irrigation or natural) is the source, the bacteria need to be eliminated. This may mean creating adequate distance between fields for crops and areas where livestock are raised. The third W, wildlife, may be from the feces of wandering animals or birds flying over the field. In the case of the tainted spinach, feral pigs were found to be at least part of the source of contamination.

---

illness, which means that prevention of contamination is the primary means of avoiding shigellosis.

Campylobacter

Campylobacter
Bacteria sometimes found in chicken and raw milk and capable of causing illness in humans.

Illness due to **Campylobacter** is estimated to number almost 2 million cases a year in the United States. Fortunately, only about 100 people among this number die. Infected chicken and raw milk are the common sources of *Campylobacter*. Careful handling of food during processing, preparation, and service help keep the population of this type of bacteria fairly low. Because animal feces may be contaminated with *Campylobacter*, it is wise to avoid using it as fertilizer for growing vegetables and fruits. Very careful washing of all foods that are to be consumed raw also helps avoid infections.

Yersinia

Yersinia
Bacteria that can be in raw milk and cause yersiniosis, a potentially fatal food-borne illness.

This microorganism can survive and even grow at 0°C (32°F), which means that refrigerator storage is not effective in controlling it. However, pasteurization and other heat treatments kill it. *Yersinia* provides yet another reason for choosing pasteurized milk and cheeses made from pasteurized milk, rather than selecting raw milk or its products. Estimates are for two deaths and almost 87,000 cases of yersiniosis annually in the United States (Ray, 2001).

Vibrio

Vibrio parahaemolyticus
Bacteria sometimes fond in seafood and capable of causing food-borne illness.

Infection from **Vibrio parahaemolyticus** is a greater problem in Japan than in the United States because of the frequent consumption of raw fish there. Seafood from estuaries is a common source of this form of bacteria, and the problem is increased in warm months. Control requires prompt refrigeration and adequate heating. Unsafe handling temperatures can result in a rapid increase in the bacterial population, and reheating does not correct the problem.

Vibrio vulnificus
Bacteria that may be in raw oysters and cause serious illness if the oysters are eaten raw.

Raw oysters may contain **Vibrio vulnificus**. If contaminated raw oysters are eaten, people can develop a fulminating septicemia that results in death in some cases. Those most susceptible to this food-borne illness are people with a compromised immune system or diseases of the liver and stomach. Such problems can be minimized by careful handling, including prompt refrigeration and care in avoiding cross-contamination. Obviously, oysters should be cooked before eating to assure safety.

Streptococcus

This type of bacteria is most likely to be a problem when infected food handlers work with salads or other foods that are eaten without additional cooking. Undercooked dressing in a turkey or roast chicken can lead to a streptococcal infection. To assure destruction of ***Streptococcus***, as well as *Staphylococci* and *Salmonellae* (which might also be present), a thermometer should be used to determine that the dressing has reached a temperature of 74°C (165°F).

Control measures include being certain that all food handlers practice such sanitary measures as frequently washing their hands in warm water with soap and prompt refrigeration of foods. Standing time at room temperature should be limited to two hours (preferably a much shorter time).

Staphylococcus aureus

Enterotoxins leading to gastroenteritis are produced by several strains of ***Staphylococcus aureus*** and also may be present in streptococcal infections. Staphylococcal contamination in food can come from food handlers with active cases of acne, respiratory infections, skin rashes, or cuts. Infected foods should be cooked quickly to a temperature high enough to kill live bacteria.

It is important to refrigerate and/or cook meat, poultry, and eggs before *Staphylococci* have time to produce much toxin because heat does not reduce the potency of toxins after they are formed in foods. Prompt and thorough chilling of protein-rich foods, followed by refrigeration, can be very effective in reducing the likelihood of food-borne staphylococcal infections. Food handlers need to practice good hygiene and avoid the cross-contamination that can occur if work surfaces are not kept clean.

Clostridium botulinum

The toxins produced by four strains (A, B, E, and F) of ***Clostridium botulinum*** under anaerobic conditions can cause **botulism** and often can be lethal. They can enter the bloodstream to block some crucial nerve impulses, such as those required for breathing and swallowing. Death can follow rather quickly unless an appropriate antitoxin can be administered in time.

Canned (particularly home-canned) low-acid vegetables, meat, or fish are the most common causes of botulism. To eliminate this risk, heat processing must be done at the recommended pressure for the stated length of time. By canning under pressure, the canned food can be heated to a high enough temperature to inactivate any spores that might be present in the food. Unless this is done, toxin will be formed from the spores easily because the anaerobic conditions provide the preferred environment for toxin formation.

Before even tasting home-canned low-acid vegetables (e.g., corn or beans), they should be heated to a rolling boil and then maintained at a full boil for 5 minutes. These procedures are recommended as a way of being sure such products are safe to eat. Another heat treatment considered to assure safety is to heat the food and maintain a temperature of at least 90°C for 15 minutes or more throughout. However, absolute safety can be assured by not eating potentially dangerous foods.

Molds

Molds and their spores can cause food spoilage, and some produce **mycotoxins** that may cause people to develop **mycotoxicosis**, which may result in death following ingestion. A warm, moist environment promotes growth of these anaerobic microorganisms, but

---

Streptococcus
Common bacteria transmitted on poultry and other food by unsanitary food handling.

Staphylococcus aureus
Enterotoxin-producing bacteria spread in foods by unsanitary food handling.

Clostridium botulinum
Several strains of spore-forming bacteria capable of producing a lethal toxin in foods.

Botulism
Sometimes fatal condition caused by eating a toxin formed by *Clostridium botulinum* spores.

Mycotoxin
Toxin produced by molds or other fungi.

Mycotoxicosis
Infection from toxins of molds and their spores.

slow growth can occur at refrigerator temperatures. An acidic medium slows growth to as low as pH 3.5. Vacuum packaging prevents growth because of the lack of air.

Although some molds are introduced deliberately in the manufacturing of various foods (e.g., Stilton cheese), some molds cause serious economic and health risks. An example of the potentially serious risks from mycotoxins produced by molds were the deaths in medieval Europe from **ergotism** caused by rye bread made from rye flour infected with the mycotoxin-producing mold *Claviceps purpurea*. In the 20th century, some deaths occurred in Africa from **aflatoxin**, the mycotoxin made by *Aspergillus flavus* that was present in moldy peanuts.

Preventive measures to avoid formation of mycotoxins in grains include being sure that rye, wheat, and other grains are dry enough when they are put into storage after being harvested. Too much moisture promotes the growth of molds and spore formation, which ultimately means that more mycotoxins will form during storage. Cold storage temperatures are another aid in retarding growth of molds and their spores if they are present in foods.

Aspergillus flavus and Aspergillus parasiticus

Both *Aspergillus flavus* **and** *Aspergillus parasiticus* produce aflatoxins. *A. flavus* forms aflatoxin at a maximum rate in moist conditions at pH 5 and 33°C (91°F). Fortunately, molds are visible, which makes it possible to know when a food may be contaminated and perhaps contain aflatoxins. Identification of various types of aflatoxins can be done by various means. However, removal of aflatoxins from foods is not practical at this time.

Molds are unfortunately widespread in various types of foods. Cereal grains (including corn, wheat, barley, rice, and rye) and their breads and flours are favorite hosts to molds if they are not stored in dry, cool conditions. Cheeses and dry sausages also may be hosts to molds and their spores. The acidity of apple cider makes cider another food where molds may be found. Even spices may be contaminated with molds.

Irradiation is an approved method of eliminating mold contamination in spices. Molds and spores can be killed by heat, but aflatoxins can retain their toxicity if they are present in a food. Vacuum-packed cheeses are protected from mold growth by the anaerobic packaging, but molds and spores can grow and produce mycotoxins after the package is opened. Refrigerator storage slows but does not eliminate formation of mycotoxin in the cheese. Although mold can be removed from infected cheese or other foods, it is not possible to be sure the invisible mycotoxins are removed. Therefore it is prudent to discard the food without risking ingestion of some of the mycotoxin.

Viruses

Hepatitis A and Norwalk-Like Viruses

Enteric viruses are becoming a major cause of food-borne illness. **Norwalk-like and hepatitis A viruses** are the two enteric viruses responsible for the greatest numbers of diagnosed infections. Unfortunately, the long incubation period before such symptoms as fever, vomiting, and nausea present means that infected food handlers or tainted water might continue to infect many other people before the problem is recognized and traced to the source.

These viruses can spread through fecal contamination by people who are already infected with an enteral virus. Another source of infection is fish or shellfish from waters polluted with raw sewage. Once the live virus is ingested, the human body serves as its host, and the virus begins to reproduce until eventually the host evidences

---

Ergotism
Infection caused by ingesting mycotoxin formed by *Claviceps purpurea*, a mold.

Claviceps purpurea
Mold causing ergotism.

Aflatoxin
Toxin produced by *Aspergillus flavus* and *Aspergillus parasiticus*, which are molds.

Aspergillus flavus
Mold capable of producing a fatal aflatoxin.

Aspergillus flavus **and** ***Aspergillus parasiticus***
Molds that produce aflatoxin in moist foods at room temperature.

Hepatitis A and Norwalk-like viruses
Enteric viruses sometimes found in food; capable of causing food-borne illness.

the symptoms of the infection. Food does not support the growth of these viruses; they require a human host to allow them to flourish and achieve a toxic level.

To avoid spreading either of these viruses, food handlers need to be very careful regarding their personal habits, particularly thoroughly washing their hands frequently in warm, soapy water while working with food and after using bathroom facilities. Kitchen equipment that comes in contact with foods that may be contaminated with viruses should be kept meticulously clean by using such cleansing agents as sodium hypochlorite. Seafood and fish should be cooked to assure that any live virus that might be in the food is killed. Eating raw shellfish and other fish and seafood is an invitation to a possible viral infection.

Parasites

The most widely known parasite is probably *Trichinella spiralis*, the roundworm that used to be fairly common in pork before people learned that uncooked garbage should not be fed to hogs. It only occurs occasionally today. However, other parasites are beginning to be familiar problems. These include *Giardia lamblia*, *Toxoplasma gondii*, *Cryptosporidium parvum*, *Taenia* spp., *Anisakis simplex*, and *Cyclospora cayetanensis*. These various parasites may be classified as roundworms, flatworms, tapeworms (collectively called **helminths**), and protozoa.

Trichinosis

Undercooked or raw pork or wild game infected with larvae of **Trichinella spiralis** can be the source of trichinosis. The encysted larvae in the ingested pork or other meat can be freed from the cyst to subsequently invade the epithelial lining of the gastrointestinal tract to mate with other *Trichinae* and perpetuate the life cycle. The host then begins to show the symptoms of trichinosis: diarrhea, vomiting, muscle pains, difficulty breathing, and swollen eyes.

Cooking pork or wild game to at least 60°C (140°F) kills viable *Trichinella spiralis* and prevents trichinosis. Microwave heating of pork is not recommended because the uneven distribution of heat can mean that some parts may not be heated adequately. Frozen storage at −20°C (−4°F) for a minimum of 20 days is another excellent way of assuring that no viable encysted larvae are contained in pork or wild game.

Giardiasis

Giardia lamblia is the intestinal parasite responsible for causing **giardiasis**. Streams contaminated with fecal matter from wild animals infected with this parasite can be the source of this infection for some hikers, backpackers, and campers who drink from these seemingly pure waters in the mountainous back country. Untreated water in some of the developing countries also is a source of this infection for people living or traveling there. Filtration affords a means of removing *Giardia* if a water supply may be contaminated. Good personal hygiene helps prevent the spread of giardiasis. Its symptoms are severe to chronic diarrhea and stomach pains.

Toxoplasmosis

Although many people are not susceptible to infection from **Toxoplasma gondii**, **toxoplasmosis** can develop in people with compromised immune systems if they ingest this type of protozoa. Cat feces are the likely source, with the protozoa actually being carried via undercooked meat or raw milk. If meat is frozen at a temperature of −20°C (−4°F) or heated above 70°C (158°F), the temperature extremes kill the protozoa in the food.

Helminths
Roundworms, flatworms, and tapeworms.

Trichinella spiralis
Parasitic worm that can occur in pork from pigs fed raw garbage and cause trichinosis in humans.

Trichinosis
Condition characterized by diarrhea, vomiting, muscle pain, and other symptoms; caused by eating pork infected with *Trichinella spiralis*.

Giardia lamblia
Intestinal parasite sometimes found in streams contaminated with fecal matter.

Giardiasis
Illness caused by drinking water contaminated with *Giardia lamblia*, an intestinal parasite.

Toxoplasma gondii
Protozoa from fecal matter that can cause toxoplasmosis.

Toxoplasmosis
Infection from eating meat or other food contaminated with *Toxoplasma gondii*.

Cryptosporidium parvum
Intestinal protozoan causing cryptosporidiosis.

Cryptosporidiosis

Cryptosporidium parvum, another intestinal protozoan, is the cause of **cryptosporidiosis**. Fecal contamination in food and water is the source of this protozoan. The condition includes fever, aching muscles, and diarrhea accompanied by dehydration. Good sanitation is the most effective means of avoiding this parasite.

Taeniasis

Taenia solium is a tapeworm that can be found in pork. Its counterpart in beef is ***Taenia saginata***. The larvae from these two tapeworms can sometimes even invade an organ. Depending on the sites that are attacked, **taeniasis** can be a mild to very severe digestive problem. Adequate cooking of these meats is the way of avoiding infection with these tapeworms.

Anisakiasis

Fish infected with ***Anisakis simplex*** can cause **anisakiasis** if they are eaten raw. Although fish can be brined (placed in a very salty solution) or smoked, these techniques may not kill the protozoa in the fish if too little salt is used or the smoking is inadequate. People eating inadequately smoked, brined, or cooked fish are at some risk of consuming viable *Anisakis simplex*, and they may experience the irritation of both the throat and the gastrointestinal tract that characterize anisakiasis. Adequately cooked fish can be eaten with no concern for this infection.

Cyclosporiasis

Cyclospora cayetanensis is a type of protozoa beginning to cause **cyclosporiasis** in the United States. Raspberries, lettuce, and basil tainted with *C. cayetanensis* have been determined to be sources of the infection. Fecal contamination introduced by polluted water, field workers, or food handlers is the likely cause of the problem. As cases of cyclosporiasis have been increasing recently, the need for better hygiene practices at all points from the field to the consumer is becoming apparent.

Algae

Ciguatoxin

If ***Gambierdiscus toxicus***, a toxic algae, is present in mud and reefs along the seacoast, fish eating in that area may ingest the algae in sufficient quantities that **ciguatoxin** accumulates in the roe, intestines, and liver, with smaller amounts in the flesh. Sea bass, grouper, and snapper are three of the popular ocean fish that may eat in infected areas, but the problem is not widespread.

Symptoms of ciguatera poisoning include vomiting, diarrhea, and nausea, plus such neurological involvement as tingling and numbness of the mouth and tongue and blurred vision. Unless the amount of toxin ingested is extremely high, patients usually recover quickly.

Gonyaulax catanella

When ocean conditions favor growth of ***Gonyaulax catanella***, levels of the toxin accumulate in scallops, mussels, and clams in the area. Warning of the abundance of this type of algae is visible as "red tide," which tints the ocean water a reddish hue and gives a luminescence at night. At such times, these shellfish are not harvested because they accumulate levels of **saxitoxin** that can cause **paralytic shellfish poisoning**. Neurological symptoms develop very quickly and involve most of the body. Severe cases result in death from respiratory failure, but people with mild cases recover.

Cryptosporidiosis
Condition with fever and aching muscles due to ingesting *Cryptosporidium parvum*.

Taenia solium
Tapeworm sometimes found in pork.

Taenia saginata
Tapeworm sometimes found in beef.

Taeniasis
Severe digestive problems due to tapeworm.

Anisakis simplex
Protozoa sometimes found in fish.

Anisakiasis
Irritation of the throat and gastrointestinal tract due to ingesting *Anisakis simplex*, a protozoa.

Cyclosporiasis
Food-borne illness caused by ingesting viable *Cyclospora cayetanensis*.

Cyclospora cayetanensis
Protozoa sometimes found in unsanitary food handling of berries and other field crops; cause of cyclosporiasis if contaminated food is eaten raw.

Gambierdiscus toxicus
Type of algae that produces a toxin that causes human illness.

Ciguatoxin
Poison produced by *Gambierdiscus toxicus*, algae sometimes found in fish.

Gonyaulax catanella
Algae that produce saxitoxin and cause paralytic shellfish poisoning.

Ptychodiscus brevis and Dinophysis fortii

Saxitoxin
Toxin produced by algae that causes paralytic shellfish poisoning.

Red tide can also warn of the presence of ***Ptychodiscus brevis***, another toxic algae that can build up in shellfish in affected coastal waters. This type of algae causes neurological problems, but the symptoms are fairly mild. ***Dinophysis fortii*** is yet another type of toxic algae capable of causing gastrointestinal upsets, but this form of shellfish poisoning has not been diagnosed in the United States.

CONTROLLING FOOD SAFETY

Foods Associated with Food-Borne Illnesses

Paralytic shellfish poisoning
Neurological symptoms caused by toxin from large algae populations.

Although microorganisms can present health hazards in most foods if subjected to sufficiently poor environments, certain foods are particularly problematic because of the favorable medium they provide for growth. Table 10.4 identifies some of the bacteria that are potential causes of food-borne illnesses in selected foods.

Ptychodiscus brevis* and *Dinophysis fortii
Algae that can cause paralytic shellfish poisoning.

Protein-rich foods require very careful attention to temperature control and sanitary conditions to keep contamination and growth to an absolute minimum (Figure 10.1). Failure to control the growth of microorganisms in these foods can lead to serious outbreaks of various food-borne illnesses (Table 10.5). However, other foods may also cause illnesses if proper safety measures are not taken in handling foods.

Hazard Analysis and Critical Check Point (HACCP)
Plan to monitor the safety of food to prevent food-borne infections.

Food Industry HACCP

The food industry and the government have made extensive efforts in the past decade to improve food safety for consumers. A system that has been implemented throughout the food industry is **Hazard Analysis and Critical Check Points (HACCP)**. Under this system, each company develops its own HACCP plan and implements it. In food processing and manufacturing companies and in food service operations, these plans are reviewed to continue to match them with the current procedures and practices. Constant monitoring and enforcement of the plan must be done to help avoid contamination and health hazards in the products being prepared for consumers.

Fight BAC
FDA educational program on safe food handling practices.

Thermy ™
FDA educational program promoting proper use of cooking thermometers.

Consumer Education Programs

Industry efforts to produce and maintain a safe food supply are key to keeping microbiological contamination and growth very low. However, consumers need to assume this responsibility as soon as they buy food. To help educate consumers on safe food handling, the U.S. Department of Agriculture/Food and Drug Administration have developed **Fight BAC** and **Thermy™**, educational programs about food safety in the home. The Food Safety and Inspection Service (FSIS) in the USDA has a widespread program to get food safety information to the public via radio, television, and the Internet.

Fight BAC is a program emphasizing the importance of cleaning, separating, cooking, and chilling foods properly. Thermy™ teaches the proper use of cooking thermometers to assure adequate heating and chilling of foods to promote food safety. These messages are quite simple and are repeated frequently to help consumers develop awareness of food safety and instill safe food handling practices.

HACCP for Consumers

Recently, the FSIS launched a more complicated and thorough educational program to aid consumers in developing and implementing a HACCP plan for their own living situation. Six points comprise the HACCP plans: purchasing, home storage, pre-preparation, cooking, serving, and handling leftovers.

TABLE 10.4   Bacteria Causing Illnesses in Various Foods

Kind of Food	Potential Pathogens
Dairy foods	*Salmonella, Listeria, Pseudomonas, Leuconostoc*
Eggs	*Salmonella*
Meats	*Escherichia coli, Salmonella, Staphylococcus aureus*
Fish	*Vibrio, Clostridium*, Norwalk-like viruses, algae
Fruits, vegetables	*Clostridium, Cyclospora, E. coli, Bacillus, Leuconostoc*
Salads	*Salmonella, S. aureus, Shigella* spp.

These points cover the spectrum of opportunities for food contamination and spoilage that can lead to food-borne illnesses. Emphasis is placed on appropriate temperature control at all times, personal hygiene, and avoidance of cross-contamination. Each of the specific instructions under these critical points is important in being sure that a personal HACCP plan results in food safety for consumers in their homes. These points, as stated by FSIS, are as follows:

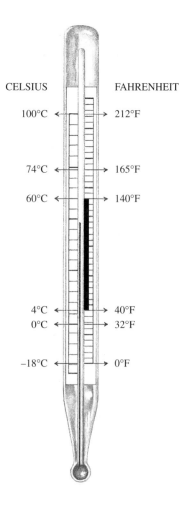

FIGURE 10.1   Food safety is protected by keeping protein-containing foods out of the temperature range of 40 to 140°F.

CELSIUS   FAHRENHEIT

100°C ←——→ 212°F

74°C ←——→ 165°F

60°C ←——→ 140°F

4°C ←——→ 40°F
0°C ←——→ 32°F

−18°C ←——→ 0°F

TABLE 10.5   Recommended Interior Temperatures for Cooking Protein-Containing Foods[a]

Food	°F
Ground Meat & Meat Mixtures	
Beef, pork, veal, lamb	160
Turkey, chicken	165
Fresh Beef, Veal, & Lamb	
Medium rare	145
Medium	160
Well done	170
Poultry	
Chicken & turkey, whole	165
Poultry breasts, roasted	165
Poultry thighs, wings	165
Duck & goose	165
Stuffing (cooked alone or in bird)	165
Fresh Pork	
Medium	160
Well done	170
Ham	
Fresh (raw)	160
Precooked (to reheat)	140
Eggs & Egg Dishes	
Eggs	Cook until yolk & white are firm
Egg dishes	160
Leftovers & Casseroles	165

[a] *USDA Food Safety and Inspection Service.*

Critical Point 1. Purchasing

- Purchase meat and poultry products last and keep packages of raw meat and poultry separate from other foods, particularly foods that will be eaten without further cooking. Consider using plastic bags to enclose individual packages of raw meat and poultry.
- Make sure meat and poultry products—whether raw, prepackaged, or from the deli—are refrigerated when purchased.
- USDA strongly advises against purchasing fresh, pre-stuffed whole birds.
- Canned goods should be free of dents, cracks, or bulging lids.
- Plan to drive directly home from the grocery store. You may want to take a cooler with ice for perishables. Always refrigerate perishable food within two hours. Refrigerate within one hour when the ambient temperature is above 33°C (90°F).

Critical Point 2. Home Storage

- Verify the temperature of your refrigerator and freezer with an appliance thermometer—refrigerators should run at 4°C (40°F) or below; freezers at –18°C (0°F). Most food-borne bacteria grow slowly at 4°C (40°F), a safe refrigerator temperature. Freezer temperatures of –18°C (0°F) stop bacterial growth.
- At home, refrigerate or freeze meat and poultry immediately.
- To prevent raw juices from dripping on other foods in the refrigerator, use plastic bags or place meat and poultry on a plate.
- Wash hands with soap and water for 20 seconds before and after handling any raw meat, poultry, or seafood products.

- Store canned goods in a cool, clean dry place. Avoid extreme heat or cold, which can be harmful to canned goods.
- Never store any foods directly under a sink, and always keep foods off the floor and separate from cleaning supplies.

Critical Point 3. Pre-Preparation

- The importance of handwashing cannot be overemphasized. This simple practice is the most economical, yet often forgotten, way to prevent contamination or cross-contamination.
- Wash hands (gloved or not) with soap and water for 20 seconds before beginning preparation; after handling raw meat, poultry, seafood, or eggs; after touching animals; after using the bathroom; after changing diapers; or after blowing the nose.
- Don't let juices from raw meat, poultry, or seafood come in contact with cooked foods or foods that will be eaten raw, such as fruits or salad ingredients.
- Wash hands, counters, equipment, utensils, and cutting boards with soap and water immediately after use. Counters, equipment, utensils, and cutting boards can be sanitized with a chlorine solution of 1 teaspoon liquid household bleach per quart of water. Let the solution stand on the counter after washing, or follow the instructions on sanitizing products.
- Thaw in the refrigerator, *never on the counter*. It is also safe to thaw in cold water in an airtight plastic wrapper or bag, changing the water every 30 minutes until thawed. You may also thaw in the microwave and cook the products immediately.
- Marinate foods in the refrigerator, *never on the counter*.
- USDA recommends that if you choose to stuff whole poultry, it is critical that you use a meat thermometer to check the internal temperature of the stuffing. The internal temperature in the center of the stuffing should reach 74°C (165°F) before removing it from the oven. Lacking a meat thermometer, cook the stuffing outside the bird.

Critical Point 4. Cooking

- Always cook thoroughly. If harmful bacteria are present, only thorough cooking will destroy them; freezing or rinsing the foods in cold water is not sufficient to destroy bacteria.
- Use a meat thermometer to determine if your meat, poultry, or casserole has reached a safe internal temperature. Check the product in several spots to assure that a safe temperature has been reached and that harmful bacteria like *Salmonella* and certain *E. coli* have been destroyed. Recommended internal temperatures are at least 145°F (63°C) for beef, lamb, and veal; 160°F (71°C) for pork and ground beef; 180°F (82°C) for whole poultry and thighs; 170°F (77°C) in poultry breasts; and 165°F (74°C) for ground chicken, stuffing, or turkey. Eggs should be cooked until the white and the yolk are firm. Avoid foods containing raw eggs, such as homemade ice cream, mayonnaise, eggnog, cookie dough and cake batter, because they carry a *Salmonella* risk. Cooking the egg-containing product to an internal temperature of at least 160°F (71°C) kills the bacteria.
- Avoid interrupted cooking. Never refrigerate partially cooked products to finish cooking later on the grill or in the oven. Meat and poultry products must be cooked thoroughly the first time, and then they may be refrigerated and safely reheated later.
- When microwaving foods, carefully follow the manufacturer's instructions. Use microwave-safe containers and covers, rotate, and allow for standing time, which contributes to thorough cooking.

Critical Point 5. Serving

- Wash hands with soap and water before serving or eating food.
- Serve cooked products on clean plates with clean utensils and clean hands. Never put cooked foods on a dish that has held raw products unless the dish is washed with soap and water.

- Hold hot foods above 60°C (140°F) and cold foods below 4°C (40°F).
- Never leave foods (raw or cooked) at room temperature longer than two hours. On a hot day with temperatures over 90°F, this decreases to one hour.

Critical Point 6. Handling Leftovers

- Wash hands before and after handling leftovers. Use clean utensils and surfaces.
- Divide leftovers into small units and store in shallow containers for quick cooling. Refrigerate within two hours of cooking.
- Discard anything left out too long.
- Never taste a food to determine if it is safe.
- When reheating leftovers, reheat thoroughly to a temperature of 74°C (165°F) or until hot and steamy. Bring soups, sauces, and gravies to a rolling boil.
- If in doubt, throw it out.

If consumers concentrate on putting this HACCP plan into action in their kitchens, most food-borne illnesses will be eliminated. The impediment to achieving this level of safety is that habits have to be broken and new habits developed so safe practices become almost automatic. Handwashing and temperature control are two key areas where habits are likely in need of a change. If frequent washing of hands and checking of safe temperatures using the correct thermometer and time limits can be achieved, much of the HACCP plan for consumers will be in place and effective.

BIOTERRORISM AND FOOD SAFETY

One of the responses to terrorism following the infamous attacks of September 11, 2001, was the Public Health Security and Bioterrorism Response Act of 2002. This act has many facets to it, but of particular interest here are the changes in the powers of the FDA and USDA's Food Safety and Inspection Service. This act gives FDA the power to take these actions:

- Detain food believed to "present a threat of serious adverse health consequences or death to humans or animals" with the approval of the Secretary of Health and Human Services or a designee for up to 30 days.
- Inspect and copy records (up to two years previously) of "each person (excluding farms and restaurants) who manufactures, processes, packs, distributes, receives, holds, or imports" food articles if there is a reasonable belief that a food may be adulterated.
- Register all domestic and foreign food manufacturing, processing, packing, and holding facilities.
- Bar food importers who commit serious and/or repeated import violations.
- Fund inspection and enforcement by state agencies to assist the FDA.
- Require importers of food additives and color additives that will be incorporated into export items to maintain identification of all who will be in possession of these additives in the United States.
- Require importers to give prior notice of food importation.

These new powers are of particular merit in relation to food imports. Prior to enactment of this law, only about 1 percent of imported food was inspected. Obviously, such minimal inspection provided a serious gap in food safety within the United States. The challenge remains to implement effective enforcement.

Summary

Food-borne infections are caused by contamination with various microorganisms including bacteria, molds, viruses, parasites, and algae that are capable of causing illness in humans if foods are not handled under sanitary conditions and with proper temperature controls.

Among the bacteria of concern are *Salmonella, Listeria, Escherichia coli, Shigella, Campylobacter, Yersinia, Vibrio, Streptococcus, Staphylococcus aureus*, and *Clostridium botulinum. Aspergillus flavus* and *Aspergillus parasiticus* are molds that can form aflatoxin (a mycotoxin) in warm, moist storage conditions. Hepatitis A and Norwalk-like viruses can infect human hosts, where they can thrive and cause illness. Parasites that may be in food and/or water include *Trichinella spiralis, Giardia lamblia, Toxoplasma gondii, Cryptosporidium parvum, Taenia solium, Taenia saginata, Anisakis simplex*, and *Cyclospora cayetanensis*. Toxic algae include *Gambierdiscus toxicus, Gonyaulax catanella, Ptychodiscus brevis*, and *Dinophysis fortii*.

Food safety requires careful attention to personal hygiene, sanitation, and temperature control, particularly when handling protein-rich foods. Federal programs targeted at improving safe food handling in the home include Fight BAC, Thermy™, and a new HACCP program for application in the home. The HACCP program pinpoints the critical points as purchasing, home storage, pre-preparation, cooking, serving, and handling leftovers.

Bioterrorism has resulted in passage of a new law, the Public Health Security and Bioterrorism Response Act of 2002. This law greatly strengthens the powers of the FDA and the FSIS.

Study Questions

1. Provide information about: (1) causative microorganism, (2) possible food sources, (3) symptoms, and (4) measures to help prevent each of the following food-borne illnesses:

   Trichinosis
   Salmonellosis
   Paralytic shellfish poisoning
   Botulism

2. What temperatures encompass the danger zone for safe food handling of protein-rich foods? What is the maximum time considered safe for such foods to be held in the danger zone?

3. What sanitation measures are needed to avoid listeriosis? Explain why each measure is effective in helping to reduce the likelihood of infection.

4. Is a food that has mold growing on it safe to eat after the visible mold has been removed? Explain your answer.

5. Review how to handle food safely from the market to the table in your home. Develop a personal HACCP plan that will help you assure your food is safe to eat.

6. Find at least four episodes of food-borne illness that have been reported and traced by public health authorities. Describe how each was traced, what the causative agent was, and the avenues used to curb each outbreak.

Suggested Websites

www.fsis.usda.gov
Food Safety and Inspection Service website.

www.fsis.usda.gov/thermy
Website for Thermy.

www.foodsafety.gov
Extensive federal government information on food safety.

http://riley.nal.usda.gov/nal_display/index.php?
info_center=16&tax_level=1
Food safety information home page.

http://www.cdc.gov/foodsafety/
Centers for Disease Control and Prevention website on food safety.

http://www.fsis.usda.gov/Food_Safety_Education/Ask_
Karen/index.asp#Question
Questions and answers on food safety sponsored by the Food Safety and Information Service.

http://www.ers.usda.gov/AmberWaves/November06/Features/FoodSafety.htm
Article highlighting efforts to improve food safety of foods in China for domestic use and export.

http://www.fsis.usda.gov/Fact_Sheets/Keep_Food_Safe_Food_Safety_Basics/index.asp
Brief statements about food safety issues.

Bibliography

Arthur, M. H. 2002. Emerging microbiological food safety issues. *Food Technol.* 56 (2): 48.

Cliver, D. O. 2006. Cutting boards in *Salmonella* cross-contamination. *JAOAC International.* 89 (2): 538.

Daniels, R. W. 2001. Increasing food safety awareness. *Food Technol.* 55 (4): 132.

Giese, J. 2002. Food biosensors. *Food Technol. 56 (7):* 72.

Greenberg, E. F. 2002. Bioterrorism law gives FDA new food powers. *Food Technol.* 56 (8): 20.

Looney, J. W., et al. 2001. The matrix of food safety regulations. *Food Technol.* 55 (4): 60.

McWilliams, M. 2005. *Foods: Experimental Perspectives.* 5th ed. Prentice Hall. Upper Saddle River, NJ.

Medeiros, L. C., et al. 2001. Identification and classification of consumer food-handling behaviors for food safety education. *J. Am. Dietet. Assoc.* 101 (11): 1326.

Messick, J. 2002. Perspectives: Irradiating the future. *Food Product Design.* 12 (2): 109.

Muranom, P. S. 2003. *Understanding Food Science and Technology.* Wadsworth. Belmont, CA.

Pszczola, D. E. 2002. Antimicrobials: Setting up additional hurdles to ensure food safety. *Food Technol.* 56 (6): 99.

Ray, B. 2001. *Fundamental Food Microbiology.* CRC Press. Boca Raton, FL.

Sachs, S., and Hulebak, K. 2002. A dialogue on pathogen reduction. *Food Technol.* 56 (9): 55.

Taylor, M. R. 2002. Reforming food safety: A model for the future. *Food Technol.* 56 (5): 190.

Vela, G. R. 1997. *Applied Food Microbiology.* Star Publishing. Belmont, CA.

Zottola, E. A. 2001. Reflections on Salmonella and other "wee beasties" in foods. *Food Technol.* 55 (9): 60.

CHAPTER 11

Organizing the Kitchen

A LOOK AT KITCHENS

Most people cook in kitchens that were designed by others, whether the plan was efficient or not. Even with the many convenience foods available, people usually spend a considerable amount of time in the kitchen. The pleasure experienced when working there is influenced by the convenience and appearance of this room. The arrangement of equipment and the location of all items used in preparing and serving meals are essential to saving time and energy. Whether cooking in an existing kitchen or planning a remodeled or new kitchen, the basics are the same. The location of the sink, range, and refrigerator may be fixed by the existing floor plan, but the storage layout can be adjusted to promote efficiency in preparation, service, and cleanup in any kitchen. The principles involved in planning storage of equipment and work flow presented in this chapter can be applied to an existng home or institutional kitchen.

Whether designing the entire floor plan or simply organizing the contents of cupboards in a kitchen, the decisions made have a tremendous effect on the pleasure and efficiency of all who work in it. If the plan is done well, work proceeds smoothly in the kitchen from the assembly of ingredients through preparation, cooking, and service. Ideally, work progresses from the preparation area toward the final service with little, if any, backward movement or shifting of supplies and/or equipment.

FLOOR PLANS

Before starting to develop a floor plan for a kitchen, it is important to conceptualize how the kitchen will function. A kitchen that is intended to be strictly utilitarian and used for only simple meals can be quite small and very basic. However, a kitchen intended for family gatherings or frequent informal parties may need to be more expansive so several people can work at the same time while others may be supervising from chairs or stools adjoining the cooking area. People who view food preparation as a favorite outlet for creativity may want a far more elaborate, well-equipped kitchen.

There is no specific design that meets these various visions for a kitchen. The crucial step is to define the use and characteristics that are important before beginning the planning. If a kitchen is to be remodeled, plans may have to be adapted to the existing dimensions of the kitchen. However, remodeling may also involve some major changes in walls, doors, and windows.

Basic dimensions have to be determined before designing the floor plan. Within the confines of the basic dimensions, a configuration of the sink, refrigerator, and cooking area must be established to define the anticipated traffic patterns that will result when meals are being prepared (Figure 11.1). These three fixtures mark a triangular pattern of activity. Ideally, the combined length of the three sides of this triangle is between 12 and 26 feet. If the measured outside length is less than 12 feet, the space will be too crowded for more than one person to work, whereas a perimeter of more than 26 feet requires an unduly large amount of energy during meal preparation.

Galley Kitchen

Galley kitchen
Kitchen arranged lengthwise along two walls.

Sometimes the dimensions and the placement of door(s) and window(s) define the basic layout plan for a kitchen. For example, a long, narrow room dictates a *galley* design, that is, one in which the two parallel long walls are the sites for the refrigerator, sink, cooktop, oven, and counters (Figure 11.2). A good arrangement in a **galley kitchen** is to have the sink and refrigerator on one wall, with the cooking area along the parallel wall.

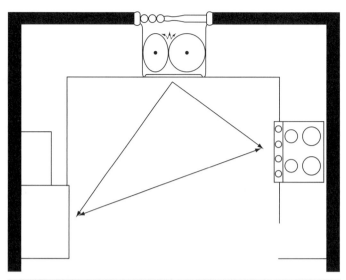

FIGURE 11.1 The traffic patterns in this U-shaped kitchen are unobstructed from the sink to the refrigerator (left) and the range (right).

Ideally, the distance between the opposing counters is at least 6 feet, although it is possible to function with an aisle as narrow as 4 feet. One benefit of a galley kitchen is that it is easy to shift from working at one side of the kitchen to the other with a minimum of steps. Unfortunately, this convenience can quickly become congestion if anybody else is walking through the kitchen or trying to help with meal preparation.

FIGURE 11.2 The dimensions of the room dictated placement of the ovens and refrigerator (disguised by the wood paneling) near the right end of the long wall. The cooktop and sink are along the other side of this galley floor plan. (Photo courtesy of John Peterson.)

FIGURE 11.3 This L-shaped kitchen has the sink below the window and the range and refrigerator on the long side, with an island for additional counter and storage space.

Single-Wall kitchen

Single-wall kitchen
Kitchen with the refrigerator, sink, and cooking area all on one wall.

The least convenient kitchen arrangement is one that allots only a single wall to locate the sink, refrigerator, and cooking area. This **single-wall kitchen** usually has the refrigerator at one end and the cooking area at the other, with the sink somewhere in between. The single-wall kitchen creates a single traffic lane paralleling the wall, resulting in a situation that requires a relatively large amount of walking. It is essential to have counter space on both sides of the sink and adjacent to the refrigerator and cooking area so food can be placed easily when using either appliance.

L-Shaped kitchen

L-shaped kitchen
Kitchen with the sink, refrigerator, and cooking area creating a triangle on two walls at right angles (forming the letter L).

An **L-shaped kitchen** is generally more efficient and pleasant to work in than either the galley or single-wall kitchen (Figure 11.3). The somewhat more open feel of the kitchen space and the convenience of the work triangle that can be arranged within the L are advantages that meal managers appreciate. The right angle created by the two arms of the L makes it practical to position the sink and refrigerator on one wall and the cooking area on the other. This arrangement (or a variation of it) allows easy movement between the sink, refrigerator, and cooking area. Traffic generated by meal preparation is primarily within the triangle defined by these key kitchen components. People who are in the area but not involved in meal preparation probably will be out of the way of the meal manager and any helpers.

U-Shaped Kitchen

U-shaped kitchen
Kitchen with the sink, refrigerator, and cooking center arranged on different walls, forming a U.

The easiest kitchen to work in is the **U-shaped kitchen** (Figure 11.4). The space for food preparation is defined by the arms of the U, and traffic from others wandering through is restricted. In this layout, the sink can be on one wall, the refrigerator on another, and the cooking area on the third. The most efficient configuration is to position the refrigerator on the wall farthest from the dining area. The sink can be on the

FIGURE 11.4   This U-shaped kitchen has the sink on the left, the range on the far wall, and the refrigerator on the right.

wall forming the bottom of the U, and the cooking area should be closest to the dining area. This floor plan creates a logical flow of work during meal preparation.

To accommodate a U-shaped kitchen, the wall at the bottom of the U needs to be at least 8 feet long because the counters on each of the two arms will be 2 feet deep. When these are installed, there will only be 4 feet remaining for the sink on that wall, and the floor space between the two arms will also be only 4 feet. Ideally, the room will be somewhat larger than this so a more spacious kitchen can be created. Depending on the size of the kitchen, there should be a minimum of 13 feet of base cabinets and preferably 16 feet or more. This length of cabinets provides reasonable counter space, and storage will be adequate when corresponding wall cabinets also are in place.

If a U-shaped kitchen is being created as a part of a much larger space, one arm of the U can be defined by a counter rather than by a solid wall. This design creates an open feeling that makes cooking a part of the activities taking place in that area of the house without having extra people in the kitchen.

In the corner formed by this arm and the bottom of the U, the corner cabinet under the counter can open into the adjacent room. This takes advantage of a space that otherwise is difficult to fully utilize.

WORK CENTERS

Positioning Work Centers

Meals need to be prepared regardless of whether or not the kitchen is ideal. The management challenge is to arrange the work centers for maximum efficiency while also creating a pleasant work environment. Regardless of the kitchen and its limitations, thoughtful attention to space utilization can contribute significantly to work efficiency. Physical convenience in performing preparation tasks helps save human energy and promotes psychological satisfaction in meal preparation. There is no single "right" way to plan and organize a kitchen because each person brings unique expectations and needs to the planning process. These unique requirements, work flow, and traffic patterns should be the basis on which plans are made for positioning the work centers.

The various stages of meal preparation define the work centers for a kitchen. These are the kitchen work centers:

1. Food storage
2. Preparation
3. Cooking
4. Serving
5. Clean-up
6. Planning

The position of these centers and the area required for each center are determined by such factors as the typical kind of food preparation, the type and frequency of entertaining anticipated, the equipment available, the usual number of people to be served, the method of food service ordinarily used, and the number of people regularly doing the preparation. The responses to these factors are important in planning the work centers.

Space requirements for the various centers influence their possible locations. Food storage space requirements increase as the number of people to be served increases. Large economy-size packages occupy more shelf space, whether in refrigerators and freezers or in a cupboard. Large amounts of fresh produce require more preparation space than will be needed if frozen foods are chosen. If baking is to be done in the kitchen, more preparation and cooking space will be needed than if baked items are purchased. Storage space required for dishes and glasses is directly related to the number of people being served regularly and the frequency of entertaining.

Ideally, the work centers can be arranged so the refrigerator and freezer can be placed on the wall farthest from the dining area, with a pantry or appropriate food storage cupboards located nearby. The sink, which serves as a key part of the preparation center, preferably is placed on the wall that is at right angles to the refrigerator. Useful counter space is needed adjacent to the refrigerator and on both sides of the sink so preparation and cleanup can be done efficiently (Figure 11.5). The cooking center, which includes the cooktop and oven(s), also needs counter space with a surface suited to handling very hot pans. Having enough space for serving adjacent to these appliances and close to the dining area adds to the efficiency in a kitchen.

When possible, the kitchen sink should be placed under a window so there will be an interesting view available for the person working there. That window should be a generous size to contribute to the light and airy feeling desired in a kitchen. However, a big window automatically signals the need for additional cupboard space to compensate for the storage space lost above the counter where the window is located. In some kitchens, it may be possible to create a window that serves as a passthrough to a patio located against the outer wall of the kitchen. Similarly, a passthrough can be created between the serving center of the kitchen and the dining room.

Particularly key decisions involved in creating a functional kitchen are the materials chosen for the countertops and the designs of cabinets for the various centers in the kitchen. Kitchen counters may be made of the same material throughout, or there may be different materials used in the preparation and cooking centers. The usual choices are laminate, ceramic tile, solid-surface material, butcher block, stone, and stainless

FIGURE 11.5 The refrigerator is at the left and shares counter space with the gas range. Counter space also is available to the right of the range and on both sides of the sink.

steel. The least expensive counter material is a laminate, such as Formica brand. Laminates are available in many designs to create the ambience desired in a kitchen. They are made by bonding plywood or particleboard and a rather thin polymer sheet. When treated with respect, laminates can last for many years, but they can be damaged by placing extremely hot pans on them or by accidentally cutting into them with a sharp knife.

Ceramic tile can be obtained in many colors and designs. Additional variety is afforded by the choice of grouting color. Light-colored grouting requires some maintenance to keep it looking fresh. The depressions created between the tiles by the grouting may harbor microorganisms unless careful maintenance is done regularly. This type of counter is very durable, although it can be chipped if struck hard with a heavy pan or other object. In addition, dishes are more likely to break than the tile if they are accidentally dropped or bumped on a tile counter. Knives will be dulled if they are used to cut or chop directly on a tile counter, but the tile will not be harmed. Tiles also are quite resistant to hot pans.

Solid-surface materials Composite materials that are the same throughout and with suitable characteristics for kitchen counters (e.g., Corian).

Several types of **solid-surface materials** are available for countertops. Corian is an example of this type of counter material. Unlike the thin layer of laminate on a supporting surface of particleboard or plywood, solid-surface counters are composed of a single layer that is the thickness of the counter. This type of counter is resistant to stains and can be wiped clean easily. Unfortunately, very hot pans and sharp knives can cause visible difficulties. Although such damage can often be repaired, the repair may be expensive.

Granite counters are pleasing because of their appearance and their ability to withstand some heat abuse. Highly polished granite counters are quite easy to maintain. Their biggest disadvantage is their expense.

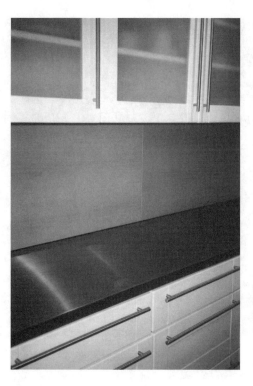

FIGURE 11.6 Stainless steel countertops give a cold appearance, but they are very functional, making them especially useful in institutional kitchens.

Some kitchens feature butcher block as the countertop in a section of the preparation counter or the island. Butcher block provides a knife-friendly surface for cutting and chopping. However, it tends to absorb liquids and juices, often creating stains that are difficult to eliminate. The cost is about half that of a solid-surface material.

Professional kitchens usually have counters of stainless steel. These are easy to maintain, and as a result are very sanitary. Stainless steel counters (Figure 11.6) can be used without worrying about placing hot pans on them or damaging them in other ways. For these reasons, stainless steel often is the choice of cooking professionals. However, it lacks the warm ambience that can be achieved by using other colorful countertop materials.

Cabinets afford opportunities for creating storage consistent with the items that need to be stored in a kitchen. Individual situations are so varied that it is impractical to discuss them in detail here. One of the realities of kitchens is that they rarely have enough storage space, so the first thing to consider is how efficiently the existing space is laid out. If the distance between shelves is too high, installing adjustable shelves or simply placing portable racks of a useful height in cabinets may add a significant amount of space. In cabinets under the counter, increased storage area may be gained by installing shelves that pull out (Figure 11.7). This change makes it possible to access pans and equipment at the back of a shelf, effectively increasing the useful space. Access to corner cabinets can be improved significantly by installing a lazy Susan (Figure 11.8). Various designs of corner cabinets are available for installation.

Implementing Work Centers

Food storage center

Food storage encompasses storage of frozen, refrigerated, and nonrefrigerated food items. A refrigerator, preferably one with a freezer compartment large enough to store at least a week's worth of frozen foods, is an essential component of the food storage

FIGURE 11.7   Pull out-shelves in under-the-counter cabinets make it easy to access any item stored there.

center. The refrigerator door should be hinged to allow the food to be transferred directly to the adjacent counter without needing to reach around the door or walk to another part of the kitchen. Convenient, fast removal of food from the refrigerator and freezer compartments saves human energy and electricity.

For families with access to inexpensive fresh produce in season, and particularly to economical quantity meat purchases, a freezer may represent a significant asset in

FIGURE 11.8   This lazy Susan in a corner cabinet is particularly easy to access because of the hinged door design.

managing food costs. Of course, locating the freezer in the kitchen theoretically provides the greatest convenience. However, the garage, basement, or a laundry/utility room may be the expedient location.

Room temperature storage may be done in a separate pantry or in cupboards convenient to the preparation area (Figures 11.9a and 11.9b). The ideal temperature for this type of storage is cool. Fruit cellars or basements that used to be available for storage in most homes rarely are a storage option in today's homes and apartments. Most commonly, kitchen cabinets are the place to store canned goods, cereals, pastas, dried foods, potatoes and other vegetables and fruits not needing refrigeration, packaged ready-to-eat items, and mixes suitable for storing at room temperature. When possible, such storage should be located beneath the counter and away from the cooking center and the refrigerator because it will be the coolest area in the kitchen. By locating the cabinet(s) used for room temperature storage close to the preparation area, some steps are saved.

If storage must be done in cupboards above the counter, paper products and similar items should be placed on a high shelf. The lower (and consequently cooler) shelves then can be used for storing canned goods, mixes and other packaged products, and potatoes and other fruits and vegetables that need to be held at room temperature.

Preparation Center

The washing of foods, cutting and chopping, and baking are all tasks performed in various parts of the preparation center. For work to flow smoothly, the sink needs to be part of the preparation area. A divided sink with a disposer in one side adds to the efficiency of this center. Fresh produce can be washed on one side while dirty dishes can be soaking in the other part of the sink. A drain board adjacent to the sink is a desirable option.

Because cutting and chopping of fresh produce often need to be done after scrubbing, efficiency is enhanced if a chopping board and/or food processor is located next to the drain board. The cutlery needed for vegetable and fruit preparation should be stored in this area, either in a drawer equipped with a suitable cutlery holder or in a knife rack designed for storage on the counter or wall directly in back of the chopping board (Table 11.1). If a food processor is part of the preparation center equipment, its blades and accessories should be stored in this area. Adequate counter space is required in this part of the preparation center. Preparation of salads, casseroles, and other recipes for the main part of the meal is done most efficiently when all ingredients can be gathered together and then combined without shifting items to make space for mixing bowls and other equipment that may be required.

The height of counters traditionally is 36 inches. This height may not be comfortable for people who are either considerably taller or shorter than average. Unfortunately, adjustment to the best counter height for a person can be a very costly alteration in a kitchen. If the kitchen is being remodeled or installed in a home under construction, counters can be installed at the desired height. Otherwise, it may not be feasible to alter the counter height in the preparation center.

The other part of the preparation center is the baking area (Figure 11.10). Spices and other ingredients used in baking need to be stored here for easy access and visibility. Spices displayed alphabetically in a spice rack located in a cupboard, on the counter, or mounted on the wall are convenient to use. Canister sets arranged on the counter in the baking area provide an attractive and handy place to store flour, sugar, and other ingredients.

Mixing bowls, baking pans, and an electric mixer are among the items usually stored in the baking center. These can be stored in cupboards under the counter.

(a)

(b)

FIGURE 11.9   (a) The vertical storage cabinet to the left of the microwave and conventional oven is a deep cabinet. (b) Racks attached to the doors and vertical shelves that open outward afford easy access to the rear shelves and provide maximum storage space.

TABLE 11.1   Recommended Items Needed in Work Centers[a]

Work Center	Equipment to Be Stored	Appliances[b]
Preparation Center		
Sink area	Colander, strainers, salad spinner	Food processor[c]
	Chopping board	Blender[c]
Baking area	Cutlery	Electric mixer[c]
	Mixing bowls	
	Canisters (flour, sugar, other)	
	Spice rack	
	Assorted baking pans	
	Measuring cups and spoons	
	Whisks, eggbeater	
	Spatulas	
	Pastry blender, cookie cutters	
Cooking Center		
	Assorted pans and lids	Range/cooktop/oven
	Frying pans	Microwave oven[c]
	Assorted spoons (slotted, solid)	Toaster[c]
	Spatulas	Toaster/oven[c]
	Cooking forks	Coffee maker[c]
	Cooking thermometer	Rice cooker[c]
	Hot pads	Electric wok[c], etc.
	Can opener, bottle/jar opener	
Serving Center		
	Plates, bowls, cups, saucers	
	Serving bowls and platters	
	Glasses	
	Flatware	
Cleanup Center		
	Detergents, etc.	Dishwasher
	Dish towels	Disposer
	Waste container	Trash compactor[c]
	Plastic containers, foil, wraps, bags	
Planning Center		
	Cookbooks	Laptop computer[c]
	Warranties, etc.	
	Pens, pencils, paper, scissors	

[a]Basic items. Specific choices vary according to cooking practices.
[b]Suggested locations for major and small appliances.
[c]Optional items, depending on space available and individual preferences.

Access to equipment is facilitated if the shelves are designed to pull out. Vertical storage compartments are useful for storing cookie sheets, pizza pans, jelly roll pans, and trays (Figure 11.11). The mixer may be stored at the back of the counter or in a cupboard in the area, depending on how frequently it is used. An electric outlet is essential in the baking center so the mixer can be operated there.

Drawer space is needed in the baking center to store measuring spoons, an eggbeater, a whisk, spatulas, mixing spoons, a pastry blender, cookie cutters, and other tools needed for baking. Graduated and glass measuring cups and spoons need to be stored conveniently in a drawer or cupboard, depending on where they fit best.

FIGURE 11.10 The baking center in this kitchen has easy access to spices above and equipment below the counter; additional counter space is available on the island.

FIGURE 11.11 Vertical storage in the cabinet above the microwave oven (see Figure 11.9a) makes it easy to pull out the baking sheet or tray needed for baking foods such as cookies and pizza.

Cooking Center

The cooking center contains all of the appliances used to cook food. The minimum equipment needed will be either a range (surface units and at least one oven) or a cooktop (Figure 11.12) and built-in oven. The range or cooktop and oven should be located close to the preparation center to permit easy transfer of the prepared food to the surface units or oven. Similarly, a microwave oven needs to be located close by if it

FIGURE 11.12   The sleek design of this cooktop and the smooth marble surface behind and around it make cleaning this area easy.

is to be one of the kitchen appliances. This location also is convenient for stirring or checking foods while they are cooking.

A warming drawer (Figure 11.13) is a useful addition in the cooking center if space permits. Plates can be heated there before dinner is served, which helps keep food warm during meals. It also is useful for holding hot foods safely until the meal is served.

FIGURE 11.13   A warming drawer offers controlled low temperatures for warming plates or holding food at serving temperature.

Additional items used in this area might include such portable appliances as a toaster, toaster oven, wok, coffee maker, and rice cooker. Countertop storage of small appliances used at least a few times each week may be very convenient. However, countertop storage of appliances that are rarely used causes unnecessary clutter in the kitchen. These can be stored in any available cupboard under the counter. If a sturdy stool is available in the kitchen, the top shelf or other available space may be a suitable storage location for these appliances.

Pans, frying pans, and small utensils used in cooking can be kept conveniently in a cupboard under the counter. The storage drawer of a range is a convenient place to store pan lids. Small utensils, such as spatulas, cooking forks, slotted spoons, and wooden spoons, should be stored very close to the surface units. They might be kept in a drawer just below the counter, or perhaps some might be placed in a suitable container on the counter to add to the kitchen décor while awaiting use. The important thing is that these utensils are within easy reach. Hot pads are a vital part of safety in the kitchen. They should be stored where they are readily accessible for use whenever using the oven and/or surface units. Adjacent drawers or hooks can be the answer to storing hot pads.

Serving Center

The serving center requires storage for dishes, glasses, silverware, and serving dishes. It also needs a counter large enough to spread out several dishes or bowls at one time. This is the area where foods are served, either into serving dishes or directly onto individual plates for diners. Dishes and glasses usually are stored most conveniently above the counter.

Cupboards with adjustable shelves permit maximum utilization of these important cupboards. Sometimes portable storage racks may be used in cupboards to store two types of dishes, one above the other, between fixed shelves. This arrangement can significantly increase effective storage space.

Another means of ensuring safe storage while also increasing efficiency is the use of cup racks. Vertical stacking in portable vertical racks designed for storing cups helps reduce breakage while saving shelf space. Another possible solution to storing cups is to install hooks on the bottom of the shelf above the area where the cups are to be stored. If this is done, it is essential to screw the hooks in a pattern that allows easy access and removal of individual cups without the possibility of bumping other cups from their hooks.

A variation of this type of cup storage is an overhead cup rack with hooks, designed for installation on the bottom of an upper shelf. This type of rack is convenient because the rack can be pulled out on its track to permit easy replacement and removal of cups. Although storing cups by suspending them from hooks uses space that might not otherwise be used, the hanging cups do limit the height of stacks of dishes on the shelf below them.

Silverware is stored efficiently either in a silverware chest or a compartmentalized storage tray designed especially for holding flatware. This arrangement permits the separation of each type of flatware (knives, forks, spoons, salad forks, soupspoons, butter spreaders, and other pieces). Table setting can then be done by quickly counting out the required number of forks and other flatware before proceeding to arrange individual place settings at the dining table. Replacement of flatware in the correct compartment after being washed and dried can be done very quickly. A silverware chest can be kept in a cupboard for easy access; a compartmentalized tray usually is stored most conveniently in a drawer in the serving center.

In homes in which two or more sets of flatware, glasses, and/or dishes need to be stored, it may be more convenient to store those used less frequently in the dining room or other convenient storage area outside the main kitchen preparation area. This permits a compact arrangement of kitchen space for the items needed daily while providing access to the special items important when entertaining.

Cleanup center

The cleanup center overlaps with the portion of the preparation center devoted to preparing fresh produce. The sink must be arranged for preparing dishes for washing and then either convenient placement in the dishwasher or washing, rinsing, and drying in the sink area. Maximum efficiency is achieved by arranging this center so the disposer is always accessible. A faucet that can be turned on by a foot pedal, as well as traditionally, is convenient because this avoids having to touch the handle when washing after kneading dough or doing other messy cooking and baking operations (Figure 11.14).

Many kitchens are equipped with dishwashers. A dishwasher has the advantage of providing a place for holding soiled dishes and preparation utensils after they are rinsed. When used in this manner, a dishwasher makes it possible to leave a kitchen in good order when the meal is served. It will be ready to receive dishes as they come from the dining area.

A dishwasher is usually plumbed into a position adjacent to the sink. This location makes it easy to scrape plates into the sink containing the disposer, rinse them, and then place them directly into the dishwasher. If the kitchen floor plan has enough space, the dishwasher should be positioned so the cupboard doors under the sink can be opened when the dishwasher door is open. If the dishwasher is a portable model, a storage space will be needed, preferably fairly close to the sink.

Dishes need to be washed by hand if a kitchen is not equipped with a dishwasher. If only one sink is available, all items to be washed need to be scraped and rinsed

FIGURE 11.14   A foot switch is convenient to turn on water when hands are dirty.

before that sink can be used to hold the wash water. A large container placed adjacent to the sink and filled with very hot water can serve for rinsing. A rack and drain board next to the rinse unit completes this arrangement for washing dishes.

A double sink makes washing dishes by hand a fairly efficient task, especially if it is possible to arrange the area so the procedure moves from left to right (for those who are right handed). The first sink is used for washing, and the second is for rinsing. If the dish rack fits the second sink, dishes can be placed directly in the rack for rinsing and drying. Otherwise, dishes need to be rinsed in the second sink and then placed in the dish rack, which is positioned on a drain board. For efficiency, the dish and glass storage should be within easy reach of the rack where the dishes are dried.

Storage for all items needed for washing dishes should be under the sink. That is also the area where scouring pads, cleanser, detergent, and other cleaning supplies are most conveniently located. If the cupboards under the sink are ventilated, dish towels can be hung on racks installed there. However, there needs to be enough ventilation to dry them and avoid mildew.

For added convenience in the cleanup area, space is needed for storing garbage bags, plastic storage containers, aluminum foil, plastic wrap, and a wastebasket. This is also the most convenient place for a trash compactor.

Planning Center

Many people find it convenient to include a planning center in the kitchen. Basic needs in this center revolve around a desk designed to meet individual requirements (Figure 11.15). It may be as simple as a shelf of adequate width and depth to permit simple menu planning and preparation of shopping lists. Space probably is needed for a telephone. A drawer to hold pens, pencils, paper, coupons, and scissors is helpful.

Good planning centers may contain a bulletin board so menus and reminders can be placed in a convenient, conspicuous spot. A file drawer for storing appliance warranties,

FIGURE 11.15 A planning center with a desk, chair, and space for cookbooks is convenient and efficient.

instruction books, and other household documents also is useful in this location. A shelf for cookbooks puts useful information right where it is needed for planning. Today's meal manager may find this planning center is the right place for a desktop or laptop computer.

SELECTING EQUIPMENT

Major Appliances

Ranges

When buying a range, the first decision is whether to buy a gas or an electric model (Table 11.2). This decision may be dictated by the existing availability of gas or 220-volt wiring. In other situations, consumers may be able to make this decision. Gas has the advantage of providing maximum heat that can be adjusted to infinite settings as soon as it is turned on. It is less expensive than an electric range to operate. The advantage of an electric range is that kitchen walls and surfaces stay cleaner than they do with a gas range. Electric ranges require a little time to heat to the intended temperature, and they hold the heat for some time after they are turned off, which requires that the operator think a bit ahead of the timeline. However, this adjustment is not difficult to make and soon becomes a habit.

Ranges can vary in width (24 to 36 inches), with the price increasing with the width. Usually, there are four heating elements, but an extra unit may be available on the wide models. For large families and those who entertain frequently, a fifth element may be used enough to justify the added space required and the greater expense of a 36-inch range.

Ranges are designed as free-standing, slide-in, or drop-in models. As the name implies, a free-standing range is installed by either plugging into a 220-volt outlet or attaching to the gas outlet, depending on the type of energy selected. Finished panels

TABLE 11.2   Checklist for Selecting Ranges, Ovens, and Countertops

Feature	Options	Desirable	Unimportant	Choice[a]
Power	Gas, electric			
Energy[b]	Varies with model & maker			
Size	24, 30, or 36 inches wide			
Oven	Conventional			
	Convection			
	Self-cleaning, standard			
	Window, solid door			
	Shelf design			
	Capacity			
Broiler	In or below oven			
Storage	Drawer below oven			
Surface units	4 or 5			
	Ease of cleaning			
Electric	Radiant			
	Halogen			
Gas	Sealed			
Price	Budgeted amount			

[a]Consumer's personal decision.
[b]Check manufacturer's information on models being considered.

are included, allowing this type of range to be installed wherever there is an opening wide enough for it or at any suitable location in the kitchen. Drop-in and slide-in ranges lack the side panels and are usually designed to fit into an opening 30 inches wide.

Several different designs and features are offered in the ovens of various ranges (Figure 11.16). **Conventional ovens** are designed for circulating the air naturally as hot air rises and the cooler air falls. **Convection ovens** feature a fan that circulates air effectively throughout the oven and its contents to shorten baking time a bit. Some ovens combine microwave and convection capability in a single unit.

A recent technological development in ovens is General Electric's **Advantium**, which integrates halogen bulbs (two 1,500-watt on the top and one 1,500-watt on the bottom of the oven) with microwaves to reduce cooking time to about a quarter of traditional baking times for many foods. A turntable operates to promote uniform cooking throughout the food. The oven size is smaller than conventional and convection ovens. The unusual nature of the Advantium oven requires learning how to program the cooking operations and experimenting if information is not available on cooking specific dishes.

Broilers are a function of ranges that may be important to some users and of almost no interest for others. If broiling is an expected part of food preparation, consumers selecting a range need to note its ease of access and use. Most commonly, broiling is simply a cooking process requiring that the food be placed very close to the top of the oven directly below the heat source. The design of shelves in the oven compartment influences broiling as well as baking and should be checked for ease of adjusting positions, stability, and locations for broiling and baking.

In addition to actual heating features, consumers may select other options. Some people want to have an oven with a window in the door so they can check on their food without opening the door and releasing some of the heat. The drawer below the oven in some range models provides storage that some people value highly. Other features that may be available include programming for the oven and a timer. The significance of programming is discussed in Chapter 12 as a potential tool for effective time management.

Conventional oven
Oven that heats with the air circulating naturally.

Convection oven
Oven that uses a fan to circulate the air efficiently throughout the oven and to speed baking a little.

Advantium
Oven heated by three halogen light bulbs that speed baking.

FIGURE 11.16   These double ovens are placed at convenient heights and adjacent to counters where food can be placed when preparing to use the ovens.

A major concern for many is whether or not an oven is self-cleaning. If it is self-cleaning, some consumers will want to know how hot the exterior of the door becomes during the cleaning cycle. Self-cleaning ovens ordinarily are insulated very well, which makes them efficient when they are used for baking. However, the extremely high temperature required for incinerating food particles during the cleaning cycle does require a great deal of energy each time the oven is cleaned.

Surface elements are available as cooktops for installation in a countertop or as part of a range. The choices and features of surface elements are essentially the same for either type. Radiant heating elements are the traditional type of heating element in electric units, and gas burners are the element in gas units. Some electric ranges and cooktops feature **halogen elements** at one or two of the positions. This unique element begins to heat instantly using lightwaves produced by a tungsten filament in a sealed bulb containing some iodine or other halogen. The result of using a halogen burner is a dramatic visual effect because it immediately glows bright red beneath the cooking surface; also, the cooking time is slightly shorter. However, they are more expensive.

Halogen elements
Sealed heating bulbs containing a tungsten filament and a halogen gas (usually iodine) that begins to provide heat instantly.

Refrigerators

Selection of refrigerators should be based on such factors as the space available for installation, capacity needed, design (side-by-side model or other configuration), interior design, and review of such features as frost free and through-the-door water and ice dispensing (Table 11.3). The precise dimensions available for placing a new refrigerator in an existing kitchen need to be known before selecting a refrigerator unless necessary cabinet adjustments fit within the budget. Despite this limitation, it is important that the capacity of the refrigerator selected is adequate to permit shopping once a week.

Refrigerators can be purchased without a freezer unit, but most refrigerators combine the refrigerator and the freezer into a single appliance. Freezers may be located beside, at the top, or at the bottom of a refrigerator. Side-by-side refrigerator/freezer units have adjacent vertical doors, which are convenient for locating desired items. However, the width of the shelves in both units is comparatively narrow, which is a disadvantage if large containers or platters need to be stored. This is the style used for units that have water and ice dispensed through the door. Units with the freezer at either the top or the bottom have wider shelves, but the viewing access in the freezer is not quite as convenient. In units with the freezer at the bottom, the freezer is designed to pull out to facilitate access. The upper position for the freezer may be accessible through a separate door or from within the refrigerator section. Placement of the

TABLE 11.3   Checklist for Selecting a Refrigerator

Feature	Importance	Required[a]
Dimensions	Must fit within space	
Capacity	Must hold a week's foods	
Side-by-side style	Needed for in-door ice/water	
In-door ice/water	Needs water source available	
Freezer top vs. below	Personal preference	
Storage drawers	Produce/meat/butter, cheese	
Shelf design	Adjustable to fit needs	
Exterior design/color	Must blend with kitchen plan	
Energy use	Needs to be efficient	

[a]*Consumer's personal decision.*

freezer does not have a significant influence on energy consumption. Expected energy usage is indicated in information provided by the manufacturer.

Frost-free refrigerators and freezers provide a real convenience for consumers, but this feature is a bit more costly than the simpler models that do not defrost automatically. The individual consumers need to determine the importance of this feature. Another feature that adds to the price is the ice and water dispenser. Consumers need to be sure water can be plumbed to the back of the refrigerator if this item is selected.

Design of the interior space of the refrigerator is of considerable importance. Adjustable shelves add to the flexibility of refrigerator usage. Depth of shelves, both in the interior and on the door, are significant in determining how well food can be stored and accessed. Other features to check include storage compartments for produce, butter, and meat.

Dishwasher

Dishwashers usually are installed under the counter close to the sink, but portable dishwashers also are available (usually at a slightly higher cost because of the wheels and the added hoses and fixtures needed for connecting them at the sink). Although the usual width is 24 inches, a narrower (18 inches) version is available for use in situations where space is at a premium.

Features to check begin with the design of the various racks, baskets, and trays for holding the dishes, pans, and utensils. The efficiency with which they can be loaded has a significant impact on the ease of use, the number of loads that need to be run, and the consumer's overall satisfaction with a dishwasher. There must be adequate space for the washing arm to function without colliding with dishes or other items in the machine when it is operating. If possible, it is helpful to place a few clean dishes in the racks in the display models to determine how well they fit the design.

Check to determine the operating temperature in the wash cycle (140°F is needed for adequate sanitizing). Also compare the cycles and options available in the various models. Some have a timer to program a delay in starting the dishwasher. This feature may be very convenient, depending on lifestyle needs. A water-saving cycle may be of importance to consumers who are living in areas with water restrictions during periods of drought.

The noise level when various dishwashers operate is influenced significantly by the sound insulation in the door. Before a final selection is made, it is wise to hear the machine operating. This is particularly important when the machine will be running while people are in its immediate vicinity.

Color and panel design are visual aspects that are important when selecting a dishwasher. Its general appearance should blend with the decor of the rest of the kitchen and its appliances. Another significant aspect is the energy consumed by this model compared with similar models.

Summary

Kitchen floor plans revolve around the triangle created by the placement of the refrigerator, sink, and cooking area. Depending on the dimensions, door and window placements, and shape, a kitchen may be designed as a galley, single-wall, L-shape, or U-shape type.

Work centers in a kitchen include food storage, preparation, cooking, serving, cleanup, and planning. Placement of major appliances and the sink ideally allow the work centers to be arranged so work flows smoothly from food storage, through preparation and cooking, to serving, and onto the dining table. Key factors in selecting ranges, ovens, cooktops, refrigerators/freezers, and dishwashers were reviewed. The equipment required for preparing and cooking should be stored in the work center where they will be used. Glasses, dishes, flatware, and other serving items need to be stored so they are convenient to the dining area and the dishwasher.

Study Questions

1. Diagram the floor plan of the kitchen in your home. If possible, measure the room and indicate the length of the walls, the actual placement of any doors and windows, and the locations of the sink, refrigerator, and cooking center (countertop, ovens, and microwave, if built in). How would you alter this floor plan to make the kitchen easier and more efficient to work in?

2. In the floor plan developed in the preceding question, where would the food storage be located? Why is this the best place?

3. In the floor plan developed in question 1, where would the preparation center be placed? What would you store in the preparation center? Describe any special storage ideas that would be used.

4. In the floor plan developed in question 1, where would the cooking center be located? Describe the appliances and their placement. What equipment will be stored in the center? Describe any special storage plans you have for this center.

5. In the floor plan developed in question 1, where would the serving center be? Describe the items to be stored and any special storage ideas you have for this center.

6. Describe the cleanup center. How does it interface with the preparation center?

7. Will a planning center be included in this kitchen? If so, describe it and its contents. If not, describe where planning will be done.

8. Draw a floor plan for an ideal kitchen. Indicate the placement of major appliances, the sink, cupboards above and below the counters, any design features of cabinets, location of small appliances, counter surface, and floor covering. Write a critique of your design, including reasons for the decisions.

Selected Websites

http://www.kitchenquest.com/critique/advantium/
Information on the GE Advantium Oven.

http://www.consumersearch.com/www/kitchen/refrigerators/index.html
Consumer Reports reviews of some refrigerators.

http://www.consumersearch.com/www/kitchen/ranges-reviews/fullstory.html
Consumer Reports overview of ranges.

http://www.geappliances.com/products/introductions/trivection/
Information on General Electric's Trivection Oven.

http://www.ehow.com/how_5327_choose-dishwasher.html
Basic information about dishwashers.

http://homechannel.aol.com/aolhome/articles/0,22010,712794,00.html
Kitchen planning.

http://www.extension.umn.edu/distribution/housingandclothing/DK1392.html#Considerations
Basic overview of kitchen remodeling.

http://www.nkba.org/xindustry/planning_guidelines_detail.asp?sec=k
Specific guidelines for kitchen planning.

Bibliography

Hunter, L. 1996. *Kitchens: Your Guide to Planning and Remodeling*. Better Homes and Gardens Books. Meredith Corporation. Des Moines, IA.

Olson, W., et al. 1993. *Kitchen Planning*. North Central Regional Extension Publication No. 497. University of Minnesota. St. Paul, MN.

CHAPTER
12
Time and Energy Management

Individual time plans for meal management vary considerably with each person because a number of factors impinge on the total plan. Family size, ages of individuals, employment demands, and available equipment are key factors influencing time plans.

FACTORS INFLUENCING TIME PLANS

Family Pattern

Family composition needs to be considered when developing time plans for meals, both weekly and for individual meals. A family with one or more small children needs to have a time plan for preparing and serving meals that either provides for meal service at the time the youngsters need to eat or permits meals to be served when child-care demands are minimal. With very young children in the household, time plans should be somewhat more extended and flexible than is true when planning for a situation in which interruptions are not likely to occur during meal preparation.

In some families, time plans need to include the involvement of two or more members of the household. The contributions of assistants may vary widely, from helping to set the table to making a significant part of the meal. When two or more people are working in a kitchen at the same time, the amount of time required for preparation of individual items usually is slightly longer than when only one person is working in the kitchen. This difference is due to the small inefficiencies involved when two people are working in an area where their traffic patterns and work space requirements overlap. However, service of the meal actually is accelerated when two or more people are available to serve and transport food to the table.

An extremely important factor to consider in drafting individual time plans is the speed at which the person works. Inexperienced workers take appreciably more time to prepare foods for cooking than an individual who has developed considerable skill and dexterity in working with food. In addition to the influence of experience, people work at varying speeds. Some move very quickly; others are more deliberate in their actions. The actual cooking times do not reflect this variable, but both preparation and serving time requirements are modified greatly by individual work rates.

Meal Management Goals

For people wishing to emphasize the sociability afforded by gracious meal service, time plans require attention to the preparation of such accessories as table linens, silver or other flatware, centerpieces, and serving dishes (if required for the planned type of service). This may be a particularly important consideration when meals are being planned for company.

If the aesthetic value of food is an important priority, some of the menu items to be prepared are likely to require more preparation time than if they are being served more casually. Special ingredients also may require spending more time than is usually needed for grocery shopping.

When efficient use of time is a top priority for the meal manager, tight time plans should be developed. Ways of utilizing appliances to decrease human time demands can be sought and incorporated in planning.

Schedules for preparing foods, particularly for preparing fruits and vegetables, should be developed to retain nutritive value at maximum levels. Nutritional concerns may influence modes of preparation as well as the selection of fresh ingredients or prepared items. Baking takes longer than frying; steaming requires a bit more time than boiling (Figure 12.1). Stir-frying involves very little cooking time, but a relatively long

FIGURE 12.1 This antique wood-burning stove serves as a reminder of the kitchen timesavers available today.

time is needed to wash and slice all the ingredients. Preparing menu items using basic ingredients requires time to do basic pre-preparation of vegetables or other ingredients, as well as to measure and combine all ingredients for cooking. These steps consume time, whereas prepared foods require no time or just the cooking time. In essence, prepared foods are today's replacement for a helper in the kitchen.

Employment Demands

Schedules for meal preparation for people employed outside the home require special planning. A considerable amount of the preparation may need to be done on weekends or in the evenings during the week. Some may be done before leaving for work. When this is desirable, the items prepared most often in advance are entrées, molded salads, and desserts.

The quality of foods when prepared in advance needs to be considered when thinking about utilizing this approach to meal management. For example, molded salads are easier to serve when they have been prepared the day before than when they are made only a few hours before serving. However, they do become somewhat rubbery when stored in the refrigerator for more than a couple of days. Cakes, cookies, and breads retain their optimum quality for only a day or slightly longer, but they can be frozen for use later in the week. Their quick thawing time makes freezing a very feasible means of storing for later use.

Preparation of large meat cuts, such as ham or a big roast, can be done on weekends to provide an excellent meal when freshly prepared and to yield the leftovers planned for use in various other recipes later in the week. Leftover meats can be prepared in the planned recipes on the weekend and then either refrigerated or frozen, depending on how much time will elapse before they are served. Alternatively, packages of the appropriate amounts of meat can be refrigerated or frozen and then incorporated into the final recipe at the time that meal is prepared.

Schedules for meal preparation during the week may need to include time for packing lunches. Efficiency can be brought into play in this regard. For example, the sandwiches for the week can all be made at one time, packaged individually, and frozen until the lunch is packed. Lettuce, mayonnaise, and other ingredients that would be damaged by freezing need to be added when the lunch is packed (either inserted in the sandwich or bagged and included with the lunch). An assembly-line approach to packing lunches saves considerable time, especially if several have to be packed.

The evening meal usually is the most time-demanding meal of the day, and this preparation occurs at a time when the fatigue level from a day at work may be high. An unhurried time plan may be appropriate in such cases. This permits some relaxation from the time pressures that accompany many jobs. However, in families with young children or with other time commitments after dinner, a more compact and efficient time plan may be required. In other words, the lifestyle of the family significantly influences the time plan for the evening meal.

Equipment

Programmed Oven

The equipment available in the kitchen plays a significant role in determining time plans. Some ovens can be programmed to turn on and/or off at predetermined times. This provides additional flexibility in scheduling meal preparation by people who are away from home during the time oven items need to be baking. When the oven is programmed to turn on several hours after meats or other protein-containing dishes are placed in the oven, food safety must be considered. If the food will be in the oven no more than two hours before baking begins, the food will be safe. However, programmed baking should not be used if the food will be at room temperature longer than two hours.

If an oven can be programmed to shift to a safe holding temperature of 140°F after the baking time has elapsed, protein-containing dishes can be baked at a pre-determined time not to exceed two hours at room temperature. Foods held in the oven at the standing temperature after baking begin to lose moisture and be less palatable. Therefore, this approach is practical only if the total time involved is about $2\frac{1}{2}$ hours longer than the baking time of the dish.

A technological solution to the food safety problem associated with programmed ovens is being developed now, but it will be quite costly. This latest appliance is an electric range that maintains a safe refrigerator temperature until the oven is turned on according to its programmed instructions. With this new range, the problem of microbiological hazards developing during extended storage at room temperature is eliminated.

Microwave Oven

A microwave oven is an appliance that alters time plans greatly (Figure 12.2). The adjustments in scheduling necessitated by its use are related to the number of people to be served and the types of foods being prepared in a microwave oven. Cooking times in a microwave oven are quite short for most foods when done in small quantities. For example, one potato bakes in approximately five minutes in a microwave oven versus an hour in a conventional oven. However, only a little time is saved when six potatoes are baked in a microwave at the same time.

FIGURE 12.2   Microwave ovens are convenient timesavers for warming and thawing foods.

One particularly useful feature of microwave ovens is the automatic defrosting cycle. This cycle automatically turns the power on and off to intersperse periods of energy input with the standing times needed to permit more uniform heat distribution in the thawing product. With this setting, it is possible to thaw 1/2 pound of meat in about four minutes or a 3-pound cut in about 15 minutes. The defrosting cycle also is useful in heating foods that require slower heating than provided when the oven is operated at full power.

One of the initial disadvantages of microwave ovens was their inability to brown the surfaces of baked products and meats. Fortunately, some microwave ovens now are equipped with browning units that provide direct radiant heat to overcome this disadvantage.

With this appliance, considerable flexibility is added to meal management. Dinner for an absent diner can be plated at the same time others are served, held in the refrigerator, and then reheated quickly on the plate in the microwave oven when needed. Family members who are unable to be home at meal times are particularly appreciative of the quality of foods reheated in a microwave oven. The flavors of leftovers are very similar to the original food flavors. Whether the leftovers are from a fancy restaurant meal or from a home-cooked meal, microwave ovens can reheat them to approximate their original quality.

Maintenance of equipment is also an important factor when considering convenience and time management. The microwave oven is a time-saving appliance from the standpoint of cleanup. Because many foods can be served in the same container in which they are heated, microwave cookery reduces the number of cooking utensils used. Furthermore, heating with microwaves avoids the sticking and possible burning of foods that can occur with conventional heating on the range top. Scrubbing and scouring are not required in a microwave oven because the interior walls are never very hot. As a result, splattered food does not burn on the walls and ceiling. A simple wiping of the compartment, door, and gasket is all that is required. The amount of time needed for this maintenance is approximately comparable to the amount of actual time required to maintain a self-cleaning oven. Use of the microwave oven for some cookery ordinarily done on the range top provides additional time saving because of reducing the amount of cleaning needed for the surface units of the range.

It is clear that the microwave oven can save valuable time in both preparation and cleanup when used by small families. However, this type of cookery does have its limitations. The quality of the finished products needs to be considered too. A microwave oven is a useful adjunct to traditional methods of preparing foods, but it is not a satisfactory replacement for a conventional range. Certainly, it is possible to prepare meals efficiently without a microwave oven, whereas preparation of a meal without a conventional range is difficult. Ideally, both a microwave oven and a conventional range are available.

Standing time
Time when magnetron tube in a microwave oven shuts off to allow time for heat to distribute more uniformly through the food.

When constructing a time plan for meals involving microwave cookery, a microwave oven cookbook for the particular brand of oven is a valuable tool. If more than one food is to be prepared in the microwave oven, foods requiring some **standing time** after cooking usually should be prepared first. Foods being prepared in small amounts and those in small pieces should be done last so they will not cool unduly before being served. Usually, it is most practical to plan meals using a combination of range and microwave cookery. Often it is convenient to prepare one or two items in the microwave oven and the remainder of the menu using the range or other appliances.

Pressure Saucepan

Another time-saving piece of equipment is a pressure saucepan. This device saves time in preparing foods requiring relatively long cooking periods in moisture. Examples of foods particularly well suited to preparation in a pressure saucepan include stews, pot roasts, legumes, and potatoes. This device is equipped with a locking lid, tight gasket, and a pressure gauge, as well as a safety vent.

When the food and cooking liquid have been placed in the pan and the lid has been locked in position, heat is applied, building pressure within the tightly sealed pan. The pressure gauge serves as the control point, allowing the cook to regulate the pressure by regulating the amount of heat under the pressure saucepan. The increased pressure in the pan raises the temperature of the water boiling within the pan, which means the food is being cooked at a faster rate than it would be if the boiling point were 212°F. As a result of this higher temperature, it takes less time to cook foods in a pressure saucepan to the desired degree of doneness.

This device is convenient to use whenever time for food preparation is limited, but it is particularly convenient for people living at high elevations. The lower temperature of boiling water in the mountains means that normal cookery methods are distinctly slower than they are at sea level, but a pressure saucepan speeds cooking markedly.

Crock Pot

Collagen
Type of connective tissue in meat that softens and converts to gelatin with extended heating.

A crock pot is another interesting small appliance when considering time management. It is possible to start a meal early in the day and have it ready to eat when it is time for dinner. This very slow method of cooking is particularly effective for preparing dried legumes and for less tender cuts of meat, which require a long time to convert **collagen** to gelatin and make the cut fork tender. Crock pots are designed to heat foods above 140°F (outside the danger zone) and to hold them at a high enough temperature to kill microorganisms without being so hot that the food browns extensively and becomes dry. Pots with two heat settings allow cooking to be done satisfactorily while away from the kitchen for half days or short full days. Although food would become monotonous if crock pots were used frequently, this appliance is very convenient for times when dinner is needed very promptly on a day filled with other activities or work.

Food Processor

From a time-management standpoint, a food processor has merit if recipes require a considerable amount of chopping, slicing, and grating, for this machine does these jobs very effectively. These operations, when done manually, can be rather time consuming. However, food processors are expensive and, in addition, they occupy counter or storage space even when not in use. In small kitchens where space is at a premium, this is one appliance that is not essential. The savings in time need to be weighed against the disadvantages.

Freezer

A standalone freezer is a large appliance that may be a very valuable management tool for some families. Its particular advantage is that it is designed to maintain a temperature of 0°F or lower. This temperature permits safe food storage for extended periods. A significant limitation is that this appliance requires a considerable amount of floor space and an electrical outlet to operate it. These requirements sometimes are met by placing the freezer in the garage, which is likely to be rather inconvenient. Kitchens rarely have the necessary space available.

When adequate freezer space is available, it is feasible to double many recipes, using half of the food at one meal and freezing the remainder for future use. This approach to meal management saves considerable preparation time and also adds the security of having a meal ready for emergencies. Use of the freezer is helpful to households of any size, although small families may be able to operate effectively using only the freezer section of the refrigerator.

Short-term storage in the freezer section of a refrigerator is very satisfactory, and the time-management benefits can be realized even without a standalone freezer. Long-term storage cannot be done satisfactorily in the freezer section of a refrigerator because the temperature is not maintained at a low enough temperature to assure safety during prolonged storage.

People living alone may find that an additional benefit of using the freezer as a management tool is improved nutritional value of meals. Leftovers, either planned or from restaurant dining, can be frozen and reheated at times when the bother of fixing a real meal may seem unappealing. Nourishing frozen leftovers are prepared so easily and quickly that snacking on foods low in nutrition but high in calories may be less likely to happen.

Dishwasher

A dishwasher can serve as a useful timesaver when preparing meals and cleaning the kitchen afterward. The advantage of the dishwasher during meal preparation is that it provides a convenient place to put soiled preparation utensils. By habitually placing soiled items in the dishwasher during meal preparation, the cook can keep counter areas clear of extraneous materials and work more efficiently. It is not necessary to keep shifting equipment from place to place.

During and/or after a meal, dishes can be rinsed and placed directly in the dishwasher as they are brought from the table, thus reducing the time involved in doing the dishes. There also is a psychological value in having any dirty dishes organized before eating. When the kitchen looks clean at the conclusion of a meal, it definitely is easier to clear the table and finish the dishes.

Other appliances also are available for preparing meals, but time-management contributions of most of these are less significant than the ones mentioned here.

TIME PLANNING

Weekly Planning

A weekly overview of the planned menus is helpful in organizing plans for meal preparation. In fact, this weekly plan often can be generated at the time menus are being planned. If sandwiches for bag lunches are being planned on various days of the week, the weekly time plan likely should include a single time for preparing and freezing the sandwiches. Items requiring advance preparation also should be identified from the menu plan, and a time should be determined for preparing them. By pinpointing the foods to be prepared in advance and the time (at least the day) when they actually will be prepared, the meal manager can be sure that production of the various menus planned for the week can be completed without having to make substitutions at the last minute because of poor time management.

When the person primarily responsible for meal preparation works full time outside the home, much of the weekly time plan may focus on skillful use of weekends to ease preparation during the week. However, it may be possible to do short preparation tasks before leaving for work or in the evening. The changes in quality that occur in these foods as a result of the imposed storage time need to be considered when making the weekly time plan. If food quality cannot be maintained satisfactorily during the storage time dictated by the initial draft of the time plan, a more appropriate timeline or a different menu needs to be developed.

The need for a weekly time plan varies with individual circumstances. People who are at home during the day may have flexibility in drafting time plans because they may have time to do some necessary pre-preparation during the day. In contrast, people with full-time jobs or very heavy volunteer commitments outside the home can handle meal preparation responsibilities far more easily if they create and follow a carefully considered weekly plan designed to fit specific preparations into available time slots.

In addition to a time plan for preparing the food, meal managers need to consider what other aspects of kitchen maintenance and food service will be required during the week. If the refrigerator or freezer needs defrosting, this task needs to be planned so it is completed before the food shopping is done. Defrosting is not a major task if automatic defrosting is a feature of a refrigerator, but refrigerators always need to be cleaned before the week's food marketing expedition so they are ready to receive the new inventory.

Maintenance of range tops, ovens, and other equipment also needs to be planned and completed as needed, either at a defined time during the week or on the weekend. Although not required every week, the polishing of silverware and maintenance of table linens and accessories may need to be added to the time plan, particularly if a dinner party or other hosted activity is scheduled during the week. Considerable stress and fatigue can be saved if these types of tasks are completed well in advance of the anticipated need.

Scheduling a Meal

Initial Calculations

When drafting a time plan for a specific meal, the first step is to predict the preparation time, the cooking or baking time, and the serving time required for each menu item. The total time for an item is the sum of these three (preparation, cooking, and serving). Unless these times for each food are known with a good degree of experience, the time plan needs to include a small buffer to allow slightly more time to prepare items that are rather labor intensive.

As experience increases, buffers in the schedule may be shortened and eventually eliminated so the food actually is ready at the appropriate time for service. Time plans can gradually become more accurate and useful if individual time plans are evaluated and appropriate modifications are noted after meals are completed.

The Specific Time Plan

Begin developing the specific time plan for the meal by establishing the time when it is to be served. This time serves as the base point, and the remainder of the time plan is calculated backward from that base.

With information on the intended time for the meal and the time required for preparing and serving each item so it is ready to be placed on the table, a meal manager can translate this information into a specific time plan for the meal. This step is done by determining the clock time when preparation of a specific menu item needs to be started to be ready at serving time. All menu items need to be placed appropriately on this time plan so all foods are ready at the designated time.

Some adjustments are needed if preparation tasks for two or more items overlap on this initial phase of the time plan unless other people are available to do each preparation at the designated time. Changes need to be made when any time overlap exists in the initial draft of the actual time plan. When adjustments are made to accommodate conflicts, any added tasks (e.g., reheating or baking an item) required for actual service of the food that has been rescheduled need to be added to the time plan.

An example of making necessary adjustments might be a time plan that reveals preparation times for muffins and a casserole are scheduled at the same time. Even if there were an overlap for a short period of time, the time plan would need to be adjusted to eliminate the time conflict. A possible solution would be to prepare the casserole earlier and refrigerate it (which is only necessary if it would be standing more than an hour prior to baking). The time for actually baking the casserole would need to be written on the final time plan. However, if a soufflé is being planned, prior preparation of that item is not feasible, and the muffins would need to be prepared and baked in advance of the soufflé. Unless a second oven is available, this would be necessary regardless of preparation time conflicts because the optimal temperatures for baking muffins and soufflés are not the same. Muffins can be reheated quickly at the time of service if they are baked in advance, but reheating should be incorporated into the time plan.

Integration of time plans requires not only knowledge of the effect of time on the quality of various foods but also careful judgment and attention to detail. For example, judgment regarding the timing for the soufflé in the preceding illustration is based on knowledge that the volume of the soufflé would be reduced because of the negative effect on volume of the egg white foam if a delay occurs between creating the foam and baking.

Time must also be planned for setting the table, arranging a centerpiece, assembling serving dishes, warming and/or chilling plates, and serving the food. The time required for these tasks varies, depending on the speed of the worker, the convenience of the kitchen layout, and the method of service being used. To illustrate, it takes longer to arrange salads on individual salad plates in the kitchen and place them on the table than it does to place a salad bowl on the table to be served by the host or hostess or to be passed for individuals to serve themselves.

Decisions regarding the time plan for the actual serving of a meal should be based on the values and goals of the meal manager and/or those of the diners. Saving time by placing all of the food on the table and having diners help themselves as they pass each item may be very important to some people, whereas others may place their priorities differently. Regardless of the decision made regarding the manner of serving, the service mode selected needs to be known so the time plan will be consistent with the requirements of that style. Correct time planning for actual service of food is important if foods are to be served at the peak of their quality.

The last step in preparing the time plan is a check to be certain all food items have been scheduled from preparation to service and the times required for setting the table, serving, and cleaning work areas have all been included.

A sample menu and its time plan for preparation will make these comments come to life. The menu and the proposed timing for preparing this rather traditional meal are outlined next.

Dinner Menu

Oven-Fried Chicken

Baked Potatoes   Peas with Mushrooms

Mixed Green Salad   Biscuits

Lemon Meringue Pie

Milk   Coffee

Preliminary Time Plan

Morning preparation

Make lemon meringue pie

Anticipated Preparation Times

Chicken—10 minutes for rinsing and preparing chicken; 60 minutes for baking

Potatoes—3 minutes for scrubbing and greasing skins; 60 minutes for baking

Biscuits—15 minutes for preparing; 12 minutes for baking in separate oven (15 with chicken)

Peas with mushrooms—8 minutes for washing, slicing, and sautéing mushrooms, 5 minutes for cooking frozen peas

Mixed green salad—8 minutes for washing and tearing greens; 1 minute for tossing with dressing

Coffee—1 minute to assemble; 5 minutes to brew

Setting table—10 minutes (including simple centerpiece)

Serving

3 minutes for pouring milk and placing it on the table
2 minutes for serving butter on a plate and placing it on the table
2 minutes for placing potatoes on individual dinner plates and squeezing open after slitting them
3 minutes for stirring in the sautéed mushrooms
2 minutes for placing napkin and biscuits in a bread basket
3 minutes for serving chicken and peas attractively on plates beside the potato

Actual Time Plan (based on dinner at 6:30 p.m.)

5:00   Wash hands, preheat oven, and assemble recipes
5:12   Scrub potatoes and begin to bake them
5:15   Prepare chicken
5:25   Place chicken in oven with potatoes

5:26   Prepare salad; cover and refrigerate

5:35   Prepare biscuits, cut, arrange on baking sheet; place by oven

5:50   Set table; arrange centerpiece, silver for butter dish, salt and pepper

6:00   Make coffee

6:02   Prepare mushrooms, stirring occasionally while sautéing

6:13   Place biscuits in preheated oven to bake

6:14   Put butter on plate and place on table

6:16   Heat water to boiling and add peas

6:17   Pour milk and place on table

6:20   Add dressing, toss salad, place on salad plates, and arrange on table

6:22   Drain peas, stir together with mushrooms, and place on simmer to keep warm

6:25   Arrange napkin and biscuits in the bread basket and put on table

6:27   Arrange potatoes on individual dinner plates, squeezing open; add meat and peas

6:29   Place pans in sink to soak

6:30   Place plates and seat diners

In this plan, the coffee is ready and being kept warm until dessert. The pie is kept in the refrigerator until the main course has been eaten and the table cleared of all items except those needed with the dessert. If the dishwasher is ready, the plates can be scraped, rinsed, and placed in the dishwasher as they are brought from the table. If a dishwasher is not available, dishes can still be scraped and rinsed when they are brought to the kitchen. They can then be stacked on the counter next to the sink in preparation for washing after dinner.

This suggested time plan is outlined in considerable detail so all of the necessary tasks will be remembered and completed without confusion. As experience is gained, it is not necessary to include the smaller details that will have become habit because of their repetition. However, a general plan for the sequence and timing of all of the foods always helps ensure preparation of a pleasing meal, with food quality high and each item served attractively at the correct temperature.

Cleanup

An important part of meal management is control of cleanup operations, for considerable time can be saved if attention is given to developing habits that minimize cleaning. Here are some ways to make cleanup easier:

1. Control temperature during cooking to reduce spattering in the oven and around surface units.
2. Use pans of appropriate size to prevent spills.
3. Cleanup spatters or spills in the microwave oven and conventional oven after each use so food does not become difficult to remove.
4. Rinse dishes and soak pans as they are soiled so they can be washed without requiring hard scrubbing.
5. Prepare fresh produce on the side of the sink containing the disposer so the trimmings can be washed directly into the disposer and ground up.

SAVING ENERGY

Human Energy

Food preparation does require human energy, for it is a job that involves standing (often for quite a long time), rapid walking, stirring, beating, and chopping. Individual work styles differ markedly. Some people work efficiently and rapidly; others are somewhat meditative and slower in their movements. People with high energy levels and/or sedentary jobs may enjoy standing and walking around the kitchen while preparing meals. Others with lower energy levels may wish to conserve their energy by using a high kitchen stool whenever possible.

The layout of the kitchen (Chapter 11) is an important key to conserving energy during food preparation. If fatigue is a problem during meal preparation, careful thought should be given to seeking a kitchen arrangement that helps conserve human energy. While actually preparing meals, note the trips made to various parts of the kitchen while preparing the food and setting the table. Consider whether different storage placement or other changes would increase efficiency in the kitchen.

Even with an optimal plan, a considerable amount of movement still will be required to prepare a meal. However, steps can be saved by carefully planning the preparation. This detailed planning helps the work to flow smoothly, removing the inefficiencies that inevitably develop when work is being done under time pressures. By assembling all of the ingredients before starting to prepare a recipe, steps and energy can be saved. Efficiently discarding empty containers or other trash avoids congestion during preparation.

Use of a tray is a simple technique for saving many steps. The table can be set with only one trip if a tray is used to assemble and transport all of the items that will be needed. Several glasses, cups, and plates can be carried if a tray is used.

Where possible, using both hands simultaneously usually improves efficiency. Curved, smooth motions are less tiring than many straight or angular moves. Be aware of movements when performing various cutting, slicing, mixing, or other preparation tasks and try to eliminate awkward or extraneous motions.

It is not possible to identify precisely what changes in habits might be most useful to an individual in establishing energy-conserving work habits. If possible, people should review their work patterns frequently to identify inefficiencies and develop ideas for better use of their personal time and energy.

Meal preparation requires workers to assemble ingredients, transform them into menu items, serve them, carry them to the table, clear the table, and clean the kitchen. Each of these aspects can be examined to look for ways to reduce energy expenditure.

BOX 12.1

Food Insights: Induction and Energy

Induction heating is an energy-efficient means of heating food quickly. Cooktops based on induction heating contain one or more coils of ferromagnetic material. When a coil is turned on, the alternating current of electrical energy generates a magnetic field that induces an electric current in a pan placed on the unit, and the pan is heated and the food is cooked quickly. This seemingly magical occurrence requires that the pan must be iron or other magnetic material capable of being affected by the magnetic field generated by the induction unit. A small magnet can be held near a specific pan to see if it is attracted to the pan. If there is a magnetic attraction, the pan is suitable for induction heating.

Among the advantages of induction cooking is that the cooktop unit is not hot when the pan is removed, which is a particularly useful feature if small children are in the kitchen. Cleanup is easy with this type of cooktop because spilled food does not burn onto the unit. A quick swipe cleans the surface. Electrical energy also is saved because the current starts when the unit is turned on and a pan is placed on it, but it stops whenever the unit is turned off or the pan is removed. In addition, induction energy is estimated to be about 84 to 99 percent efficient, compared with about 58 percent efficiency for halogen burners, 47 percent for electric burners, and 40 percent for gas burners.

Appliances and Energy Use

Concern for the amount of energy consumed by household appliances is mounting because of costly utility bills and the recognition of a shortage of oil and other sources of energy for the home. As a result of these problems, consumers are faced with the need to know about energy consumption by various kitchen appliances (Figure 12.3). They can then make intelligent, informed choices when buying and using appliances.

Households differ considerably in the amount of energy used by those living in them. The efficiency of the kitchen appliances (particularly such major appliances as the range, oven, microwave oven, dishwasher, refrigerator, and freezer) significantly influences monthly energy use, particularly electricity. Major appliances are marketed with tags that clearly indicate their power usage so energy efficiency can become an important part in deciding which specific appliance brand and model to buy.

Consumers can help limit energy use by turning off small appliances when they are not being used. Using a heating element that fits the size of the pan is more energy efficient than using a small pan on a large unit. Lids on pans help heat foods efficiently. These techniques are simple, but they do help to keep energy use as low as possible. When cooking with an electric range, consumers can also save some energy by turning the heat off or down somewhat in advance. This is possible because of the residual heat retained in the element.

Based on standard U.S. Government tests

Dishwasher
Capacity: Standard

KitchenAid
Model: KUD01 Series

Compare the Energy Use of this Dishwasher with Others Before You Buy.

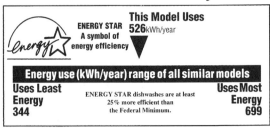

	This Model Uses
ENERGY STAR A symbol of energy efficiency	526 kWh/year

Energy use (kWh/year) range of all similar models

Uses Least Energy 344	ENERGY STAR dishwashes are at least 25% more efficient than the Federal Minimum.	Uses Most Energy 699

kWh/year (kilowatt-hours per year) is a measure of energy (electricity) use. Your utility company uses it to compute your bill. Only standard size dishwashers are used in this scale.

Dishwashers using more energy cost more to operate. This model's estimated yearly operating cost is:

$44 **$27**

when used with an electric water heater   when used with a natural gas water heater

Based on six washloads a week and a 1997 U.S. Government national average cost of 8.31¢ per kWh for electricity and 61.2¢ per therm for natural gas. Your actual operating cost will vary depending on your local utility rates and your use of the product.
Important: Removal of this label before consumer purchase violates the Federal Trade Commission's Appliance Labeling Rule (16 CFR Part 305).
(Part No. 8524580)

FIGURE 12.3   Information regarding energy use by specific kitchen appliance models is available to help consumers in selecting energy-efficient equipment.

Clearly, consumers can exercise some control over their energy use in the kitchen by choosing and using equipment that meets their management goals and needs. Table 12.1 provides information about the energy consumption that can be expected when various electrical kitchen appliances are used. Cooking obviously needs to occur, but the added energy consumed by operating a self-cleaning oven versus using human energy for scrubbing a soiled oven is a choice that consumers make. The answer to self-clean versus personal energy use in maintaining ovens is related to management goals and may be influenced by financial concerns too.

The size of refrigerators and freezers is related to total energy consumption. As seen in Table 12.1, more energy is required to operate a larger versus a smaller refrigerator or freezer. If a large freezer is needed because of the quantities of food a family consumes, the large unit may be a very smart buy. However, a big freezer that has only a small amount of food is a waste of energy.

Energy is a matter of both environmental and economic concern, and the need for thoughtful use and conservation is increasing. All consumers can help meet the challenge by buying kitchen appliances are the right size, are designed to be energy efficient, and that are important to meeting identified meal management goals. Efficient use can also help save power.

TABLE 12.1   Energy Consumption by Selected Kitchen Appliances

Appliance	Electrical Consumption (kwh)[a]
Blender	0.4 kwh/hr
Broiler	1.4 kwh/hr
Coffee maker, automatic	0.2 kwh/pot
Deep fat fryer	1.5 kwh/hr
Dishwasher	1.0 kwh/load
Disposer	0.04 kwh/day regular use
Frying pan	1.2 kwh/hr
Hot plate	1.3 kwh/hr
Microwave oven, full power	1.5 kwh/hr
Mixer	0.13 kwh/hr
Range with oven	3.2 kwh/day regular use
Range, self-cleaning oven	3.3 kwh/day
	5.0 kwh/cleaning
Sandwich grill	1.2 kwh/hr
Toaster	0.04 kwh/serving
Trash compactor	0.2 kwh/load
Waffle iron	0.05 kwh/waffle
Crock pot	0.2 kwh/hr
Food freezer, frostless	
12 cu ft	5.5 kwh/day
20 cu ft	6.1 kwh/day
Food freezer, manual defrost	
12 cu ft	3.2 kwh/day regular use
20 cu ft	4.5 kwh/day
Refrigerator/freezer, frostless	
12 cu ft	4.5 kwh/day
20 cu ft	5.7 kwh/day

[a] *Adapted from Energy Consumption and Your Electric Meter. Los Angeles Department of Water and Power.*

Summary

Time plans are important tools in improving meal management skills. Successful and workable plans need to be developed within the context of the group that is dining, management goals, employment, or other time limitations of the meal manager and any helpers, and the equipment available. Within these identified factors, the week's menus need to be examined and a time plan developed that identifies preparation to be done in advance of the ordinary meal preparation schedule. The time plan for an individual meal needs to be developed by first identifying the timing required to prepare each of the various menu items and then integrating these times into a workable plan that enables the manager and any assistants to complete the total preparation at the time desired, with the food well prepared and served in a manner consistent with the desires of the diners.

Energy management is a companion to time management. Human energy demands and availability need to be considered when preparing time plans. Kitchen layout may need to be reevaluated to conserve human energy. Individual work habits also need to be reviewed and ways explored for reducing energy costs in preparing a meal. The expenditure for operating appliances also should be considered both from the standpoint of cost and the conservation of limited resources.

Study Questions

1. Identify the goals that would be important to you when planning a family dinner on a night during the week. How would they differ from the goals you might set for a dinner with four guests?
2. Plan a dinner menu for a family dinner on a weeknight and indicate what appliances are to be used to prepare the various menu items. Are there any scheduling problems due to equipment limitations that can be anticipated in preparing the menu? If so, what might be a viable solution to the problem(s)?
3. Plan a draft time plan for preparing the dinner menu from question 2.
4. Translate the preliminary plan drafted in question 3 into a time plan for preparing and serving this dinner.
5. Plan a menu for a weekend dinner to which two guests will be invited. Develop the preliminary time plan and the final time plan for this dinner.
6. Sue is planning a baby shower for a friend and will be serving a light lunch to the guests. Suggest an appropriate menu and make a time plan for Sue to follow in preparing the lunch.

Suggested Websites

http://aceee.org/consumerguide/cooking.htm
Suggestions on saving energy when cooking foods.

http://aceee.org/consumerguide/cooking.htm#cooktops
Information on choosing cooktops.

http://aceee.org/consumerguide/topfridge.htm
Information on energy and refrigerators.

http://www.appliance411.com/purchase/
Information about kitchen appliances.

http://www.bhg.com/home/Kitchen-Appliances.html
Overview of buying kitchen appliances.

Bibliography

Freedman, D. H. 1992. Is management still a science? *Harvard Business Review.* 70 (6): 26.

Gregoire, M., and Spears, M. C. 2007. *Foodservice Organizations: A Managerial and Systems Approach* (6th ed.). Prentice Hall. Upper Saddle River, NJ.

Johnson, B. C. 2000. Foodservice benchmarking: practices, attitudes, and beliefs of foodservice directors. *J. Am. Dietet. Assoc.* 100 (2): 175.

Johnson, B. C., and Chambers, J. 2000. Expert panel identifies activities and performance measures for foodservice benchmarking. *J. Am. Dietet. Assoc.* 100 (6): 692.

Konz, S. 1995. *Work Design: Industrial Ergonomics* (4th ed.). Publishing Horizons. Worthington, OH.

Schuster, K. 1997. Benchmarking: How do you measure up? *Food Management.* 32 (8): 42.

SECTION

IV

Service and Hospitality

CHAPTER 13
Setting the Table

INTRODUCTION

An attractive table sets the stage for meals, much as a lovely frame enhances a painting. Specific table settings can be varied to fit not only the meal and menu being served but also the lifestyles and goals of the family or clientele. Some settings may be for casual dining; others may be for festive holidays and parties. Regardless of the occasion, table settings are comprised of table coverings, dinnerware, glassware, and flatware. Opportunities for creating effective table settings arise from the choices available for each of these parts of the settings and the ways they are combined.

With today's time pressures, table appointments and table settings are tailored to individual choices rather than being dictated so much by convention. Simplicity may be the preference for family meals, with occasional parties giving the opportunity for more dramatic or elegant settings. Table settings should fit the situation.

This chapter explores the many choices involved in selecting the various components used in table settings. After consumers have acquired their flatware, dinnerware, glassware, and table coverings, they are ready to create specific table settings. Guidelines for setting attractive tables appropriate to the occasion are discussed in this chapter.

FLATWARE

The usual materials for flatware are silver and stainless steel, although dirilyte may present another option, as mentioned later in this section. Consumers may choose between sterling silver and silver plate if they wish to purchase silver. Stainless steel flatware sometimes is available with wooden handles as an option. Once the material has been decided, choices still need to be made regarding quality and design. Dirilyte choices are very limited.

Silver

Sterling Silver

Silver is fashioned into sterling silver (Figure 13.1) and silver plate. The price of sterling silver is much higher than silver plate because of its greater silver content. Only a small amount of copper is added to almost pure silver to make sterling silver. The copper

FIGURE 13.1   Silver flatware designs range from very ornate (left) to simple (right).

is needed to add strength to flatware; pure silver is too soft to use without alloying it with a harder metal. However, with the addition of copper, sterling silver is both functional and durable. In fact, this type of flatware often is passed from one generation to the next.

Sterling silver is soft enough to scratch, particularly if in contact with a sharp knife blade. However, the usual pattern of wear is the development of numerous shallow scratches that lend a soft patina to used sterling silver. During use, gradual wear occurs, especially on the back of the bowl of spoons and in the same spot on forks. Because sterling silver flatware is made of the same material throughout, this wear is not obvious or of concern.

Silver Plate

Silver plate is made by electroplating individual pieces of flatware that have been stamped from an inexpensive but durable metal. The result is a piece with the surface appearance of sterling silver. However, the plate may gradually be worn from the piece, particularly at the wear points. When the silver plate wears away in places (particularly on the areas of the flatware that rub against plates and table covers), the base metal begins to show, and the worn flatware is no longer pleasant to use.

To extend the useful period of silver plate, some manufacturers reinforce the wear points with extra silver when they fabricate the flatware. This reinforcement effectively extends the period of service provided by silver plate. However, sterling silver has a far longer period of service potentially than can be expected even when silver plate is reinforced. This limitation of silver plate must be considered in relation to the significantly greater cost of sterling silver.

Choice of design in silver flatware should be considered carefully because of the very large investment that may be made and the extended time it will be used. Both sterling and silver plate have available designs ranging from very ornate to extremely simple. Many of the ornate patterns reflect period influences, particularly influences from the French court prior to the French Revolution. Other designs are often motivated by floral or traditional designs.

When choosing a pattern, narrow the selection process to a few designs and then review the shape of the various pieces in each design. Because the weighting of various designs differs, it is wise to try to handle each piece and evaluate how it feels in your hand. Note particularly the feel and weighting of the solid versus hollow-handled table knives.

Because of the investment represented by the purchase of silver, it may be helpful to reconfirm the choice over a period of at least a week or two before making the final decision. It is wise to assemble a place setting of the silver with the dinnerware that may be chosen. The general impression of the two should be mutually supportive, rather than competitive. Any reconsideration of the design options should be done before purchasing the silverware.

It is very important to select the flatware pattern that provides genuine pleasure because this decision often represents a lifetime choice. Its greater durability makes flatware much less likely to be replaced than dinnerware. Because of this factor, many people like to begin selection of tableware with the choice of flatware and then build the design elements from this point.

When sterling silver or silver plate is going to be used only occasionally, it is wise to store it in a felt-lined, relatively airtight case to reduce tarnishing. Compartmentalized bags are relatively inexpensive for this purpose, but a chest lined with felt and divided into appropriate compartments is more convenient to use. When silver becomes tarnished, as it eventually will, it can be polished with silver polish and a soft cloth. Specially treated polishing cloths are available too. No abrasive materials should be used to polish silver.

Stainless Steel

Stainless steel flatware is very durable and easy to care for. Unlike silver, it does not tarnish. Therefore, it is always ready to use. A wide range of qualities is available in stainless steel flatware. Very inexpensive stainless steel is stamped from a thin sheet of metal and may have sharp edges that offend both the mouth and the hand. Finer crafting of stainless steel from a heavy metal sheet results in attractive flatware that is very pleasant to use.

The characteristics of this relatively hard metal make it particularly well suited to crafting into simple designs. Some designs may gain their beauty from the skillful shaping and contouring of the handles; others may be stamped with the designs. As was true with silverware, design choices should be based on individual preference and the effect of the flatware with the dinnerware.

The nature of most stainless steel flatware designs and the qualities of the metal itself create a less formal appearance than presented by silverware. It is particularly well suited to combining with stoneware and earthenware. Although a few very high-quality stainless steel flatware patterns are as formal as fine silverware, most stainless steel flatware suggests a tone that is a bit too informal to use with fine porcelain dinnerware.

Care of stainless steel requires only normal washing procedures. For convenience in setting the table, stainless steel flatware can be stored in a drawer or box equipped with compartments to separate the various types of pieces.

Gold-Colored Flatware

Dirilyte
Alloy of aluminum, copper, and nickel used in making gold-colored flatware.

Another option in flatware is **dirilyte**, a gold-colored metal that is an alloy of aluminum, copper, and nickel. This can be a particularly attractive choice to accompany porcelain trimmed with gold. Dirilyte develops a patina similar to that of sterling silver through use over a period of time. The design options are very limited in this material.

Vermeil
Gold-plated flatware containing some gold in the alloy.

Other options are **vermeil**, a gold-plated flatware or a flatware actually containing some gold in the alloy. When gold is either a part of the alloy or the plating that covers sterling silver, the cost is very high. A somewhat less expensive option is gold-plated stainless steel.

DINNERWARE

Porcelain
Hard, bone, and soft china made from slightly different materials and fired to high temperatures.

Various experts classify dinnerware into slightly different types, making it difficult to know precisely what characteristics can be expected from each. But there is general agreement that **porcelain** is the finest dinnerware because of its strength and quality. Often the terms *porcelain* and *china* are used interchangeably for categorizing this dinnerware. Other possible choices of types of dinnerware are classified as stoneware and earthenware.

Choices between these different categories of dinnerware need to be made in relation to cost, durability, and design features. The purchase of a full set of porcelain represents a large investment. It usually is far more expensive to buy than stoneware or earthenware, although the prices of specific patterns and brands may vary. However, porcelain is much more resistant to chipping and breaking than either stoneware or earthenware. Its durability means that porcelain can be used for many years and even passed from one generation to the next if it is handled with some care. Obviously, the cost of porcelain seems far less indulgent if it can be used for a very long time.

Breakage and chipping may be a problem with earthenware because of the porous nature of the material and the low firing temperature. Stoneware is likely to be able to be used longer than earthenware without requiring replacement. There is so much variation in the prices of different stoneware and earthenware that generalizations cannot be made. The important underlying factor to consider is the predicted chipping and breakage that can be expected if they are selected.

Stoneware and earthenware vary widely in their weight, but they definitely are heavier and look more massive than porcelain. Because of their thickness and rougher texture, stoneware and earthenware impart a less formal flavor to a table setting than porcelain dinnerware. When more than one set of dinnerware is used in a home, the choice often is to have a set of porcelain dinnerware for more formal occasions and either stoneware or earthenware for regular use.

Porcelain (China)

Porcelain is classified into hard (also called hard paste), bone, and soft (soft paste). Hard porcelain is made from kaolin (china clay), feldspar, and quartz in various mixtures and derived from varying sources (Figure 13.2). The kaolin component is not fusible, but the silicates in feldspar do fuse gradually as a result of the very high temperatures used in firing hard porcelains. In hard porcelains, the higher the amount of kaolin used in the formulation, the harder is the product and the more severe its appearance. Hard porcelain made with somewhat less feldspar is well suited to dinnerware because of performance and appearance characteristics.

Bone porcelain also is made from kaolin and feldspar, but bone ash (calcium phosphate) is included in the formula. The added bone ash is helpful in fusing the dinnerware during firing. It contributes to the pleasingly soft, rather than brittle, appearance and also promotes the translucency and durability that are desired in hard paste porcelain.

Soft paste porcelains are characterized by their creamy color and soft look. They are made from white-firing clays mixed with a fusible silicate such as a frit of glass, sand, or finely ground china. Kaolin is not generally included in the formulation. Bone and soft paste porcelains are less brittle than the hard porcelains.

The manufacturing of porcelains is a lengthy process, which begins with the grinding, washing, and mixing of ingredients to be used in the formulation. The ingredients

Bone porcelain
China made from kaolin, feldspar, and bone ash.

FIGURE 13.2   Porcelain patterns may be quite simple (left) or more ornate (right).

are mixed with water to form a "slip." The slip is fairly fluid, allowing it to be poured into a plaster-of-Paris mold. The mold absorbs extra moisture from the slip, and the molded ware becomes hard enough to be removed from the mold and hold its shape. Following drying, the ware is fired to the very high temperatures needed for fusing the silicates.

Underglazed porcelain
Porcelain that has the design applied and fired before it is glazed.

If **underglazed porcelain** is being made, the design is applied to the fired ware before a glaze is applied. This decorated and glazed ware is then fired to fuse the glaze. Underglazed porcelain designs can be washed safely in dishwashers even when precious metals are used in the design because the metal in the design is protected adequately by the glazes and firings involved in manufacturing. It is very important to review the manufacturer's guidelines before using the dishwasher to wash porcelain decorated with gold or platinum. Not all porcelain decorated with gold is made by underglazing.

Underglazed porcelain designs can be identified because of the slight roughness of the glaze above the design. This type of porcelain design is produced in somewhat limited quantities because of the high heat needed for fusing the glaze. Some colors used in designs are altered by such intense heat and become less desirable. Underglazed porcelains are likely to have soft, rather than sharp, outlines in their designs.

Overglazed porcelain
Porcelain that is glazed and fired prior to applying the design and then fired again.

Overglazed porcelain designs also are manufactured. In this process, the glaze is applied and fired before the design is applied and the piece is fired again. The second firing is at a lower temperature than is used for underglazed porcelain, a change that reduces the impact of heat on the design colors. Overglazing is the method of design application used most commonly today.

The advantages are the brighter and sharper design colors and the ease of manufacturing this type. Disadvantages to overglazing are the possible damage to design details because of the greater exposure of the design and the need for a firing to fuse the design into the glaze. The problem with designs (particularly when decals are used for the designs) is greater in inexpensive, carelessly manufactured overglazed china than in high-quality dinnerware. The gold and platinum design details found in many porcelain dinnerware designs are added by the process of overglazing. These metals fuse with the glaze during the final firing. However, loss of these metals does occur very gradually with prolonged use and handling. Overglazed porcelain designs containing gold or platinum should not be washed in the dishwasher.

Stoneware

Stoneware
Dinnerware that is usually heavy and informal.

Stoneware is an interesting possibility for use as informal tableware. Its slightly porous texture imparts a casual mood to the table setting (Figure 13.3). Despite its porosity, this type of ware is reasonably durable as a result of its firing. Often stoneware is very thick and heavy, characteristics well suited to creating a natural, earthy appearance in a table setting. The greater bulk and weight, as well as the slight warping tendency of stoneware, make this a type of dinnerware that is more troublesome and bulky to store than porcelain. Its unique appearance may more than compensate for this disadvantage, however, if an informal setting is being planned.

Earthenware

Earthenware
Somewhat porous dinnerware that is less durable than china.

Earthenware is a rather broad category embracing a variety of products. Ironstone is a fine hard earthenware with good handling characteristics and a fine appearance. Delft is European earthenware typified by blue-and-white designs. This ware, as is often true of earthenware, is susceptible to chipping and breaking.

No set formula of materials can be defined as earthenware. This category can be characterized best as mixtures of clay. The porosity of various brands of earthenware is related to the composition of the clay mixtures used in making them. Earthenware typically is less massive in appearance and weight than stoneware.

FIGURE 13.3   Stoneware is rather heavy dinnerware that often is warped a little, which may tilt stacks of bowls or plates.

BOX 13.1

Food Insights: Lead Alert

Lead has long been a component of some glazes used on pottery, particularly in some countries noted for pottery as folk art. Firing of folk-art pottery often is done in kilns fired to low temperatures. To get the desired melting of some of these glazes, lead was used traditionally in glaze formulas because of its low melting point. Although the artistic effect of lead-based glazes was lovely, pottery that came in contact with food could leach lead into food and accumulate over time in the bodies of people using these dishes.

Workers making pottery with lead-based glazes are at risk of accumulating toxic levels of this potentially harmful metal. States have implemented safety programs and legislation to help promote workers' health by reducing the use of lead in manufacturing. An example of such efforts was Los Angeles County's Occupational Lead Education and Awareness Project (OccLEAD) that works with companies in monitoring lead levels in their workers and the factory. Since 1992, more than 40 ceramics factories have been participating;

As the dangers of lead poisoning from lead-based glazes on pottery became known, shoppers were warned that such pottery could be harmful if used with moist foods, particularly acidic foods. Hot beverages, fruit juices, and foods containing tomato, vinegar, or other acidic ingredients unfortunately are particularly effective in leaching lead from the glaze into the food people eat. Crackers, pretzels, nuts, and other dry foods can be served safely using these dishes, but even these types of food should not be left on them for extended periods.

Problems of lead glazes in Mexican pottery are being addressed by the Lead-Free Pottery Alliance, in cooperation with the Mexican National Foundation for Development of Folk Art, Aid to Artisans, UNESCO, United States Agency for International Development (USAID), and American Express. Lead-free glazes suitable for firing in low-temperature kilns have been developed for making Mexican pottery, and the Mexican National Foundation for Development of Folk Art has developed a simple technique potters can use to decontaminate their kilns. These steps are being taken to help assure that the pottery can be marketed and exported as food-safe, lead-free ceramics. Export marketing opportunities are being developed with international assistance to assist potters in their businesses.

Other Materials

Plastic dinnerware may be the choice of some people with small children, those who are packing picnics, or in other circumstances when dish breakage might present a problem. The characteristics of plastic dishes vary somewhat with the specific products. The feel of the material always is softer than ceramic tableware. Some plastics are able to withstand the high temperatures in dishwashers. Plastic dishes are susceptible to damage by sharp knives, with serrated blades presenting a particular problem. Use of plastic dishes definitely provides an informal appearance to a table.

Stainless steel, pewter, and silver are also possible choices for dinnerware. The price of pewter and silver today makes items containing either of these materials very expensive choices. As mentioned earlier, silver has the added disadvantage of being so soft that it scratches easily and also requires frequent polishing to eliminate unsightly tarnish.

Pewter is much easier to maintain than silver. The soft finish of some of the popular pewter today provides a restful and comfortable ambience to the table. Some people like to use pewter serving pieces or pewter plates (often used as chargers or liners, as explained later) to highlight the table. This approach is less costly than setting the entire table in pewter.

Stainless steel is easy to maintain. Other advantages are its relatively modest cost and attractive designs. For simple service, use of stainless steel serving pieces or plates can be pleasing. Enamelware offers the opportunity for some exciting color choices. Perhaps its greatest limitation is its susceptibility to chipping. Chipped enamelware detracts greatly from the bold, contemporary look that can be achieved by this type of dinnerware.

Wood sometimes is chosen as a material for dinnerware, but its use often is restricted to salad bowls or liners. The appearance of wood provides a soft informality to a table, but the water-absorbing quality of wood causes these dishes to split easily. Therefore, they cannot be washed in a dishwasher or used in a microwave oven. In spite of these limitations, wooden dishes can provide a pleasant accent or change in tableware for occasional service.

Design Choices

The selection of designs for dinnerware is very much a matter of personal preference. In most cases, the dishes are used frequently for many years. Thus it is wise to select a pattern that appeals to those who will be using the dishes, preferably an understated rather than a dramatic design. The latter attracts attention instantaneously but may become boring if used frequently. An evaluation of this aspect of design can best be made by viewing the design several times before deciding to purchase a bold pattern.

The amount of design on a plate is another aspect to consider. It is wise to attempt to envision the plate when food is served on it (Figure 13.4). A striking, very large design covering the entire plate may seem to be competing with the food for the eye's attention. A border design, however, may serve as an attractive frame for the food (Figure 13.5). Many patterns feature a rather simple design in the center of the plate and a border design around the rim.

Some dishes derive part of their design from their contours and shapes. When contouring includes small deep depressions, it may be difficult to wash out particles of food that stick in the crevices if the dishes are to be washed by hand. Other than this difficulty, contouring does not present a problem, and it does afford subtle and pleasing design potential.

The weight and color included in a design are important in creating the visual impression of a dish pattern. Delicate colors and small intricate designs impart a dainty

FIGURE 13.4   The busy design of magnolias on this plate competes with the food.

air to a table. In contrast, strong colors and bold designs contribute a contemporary, somewhat informal mood.

Personality and lifestyle are important factors for consumers to consider when selecting a dinnerware pattern. Greater pleasure and satisfaction are derived when the dishes selected are consistent with personality characteristics and design preferences. When an impulsive choice is made that is inconsistent with usual selections, the dishes will likely bring only limited pleasure to the user.

FIGURE 13.5   This simple, yet elegant border frames food beautifully to enhance the effect of the meal.

Another aspect to consider is whether this will be the only set of dishes. If it is, the choice of colored dishes may cause problems in serving some foods. For example, brick red dishes may match the mood of a cheery, informal occasion. However, if economic realities and space limitations limit the choice to one set of dishes, a somewhat more subtle color or pattern may be appropriate.

Other Selection Factors

Open stock
Dishes that can be purchased individually, rather than as a complete set.

Although the choices of material and design are fundamental to consider when selecting dishes, there are also some other basic matters to review. When buying porcelain, it is important to know whether the pattern being considered is available in **open stock**.

Open stock means that single, specific pieces can be purchased. This is an important question because replacements may be needed for single pieces but seldom involve a complete place setting. When only place settings or complete sets can be purchased, as sometimes is true (particularly in earthenware), replacement of broken pieces may be too costly in proportion to need. This situation causes the inventory to be reduced gradually until it becomes necessary to replace the entire set, an expensive solution in some cases.

Before making a final decision on a pattern, examine the design of the serving pieces. If two designs are about equal in appeal, the design of the serving pieces may become the deciding factor. There is considerable variation in the shape of serving pieces; some of them appear to be very stylish, and others may seem awkward.

Of the pieces in the individual place settings, the cup is the one requiring the most careful examination. Points to consider are the general shape, the ratio of the depth to the width of the cup, and handle design. The general design of the cup should be one that makes the cup easy to use. Square cups require drinking from an awkward corner. Cups that are slightly narrow toward the top also are awkward to use. Shallow cups may be very graceful in design, but the large surface area in relation to the shallow depth causes beverages to cool very quickly. In addition, shallow cups with gracefully sloping sides are more likely to result in spills than are cups with vertical sides.

Handle designs should make the cup easy to hold without risk of tilting or dropping it. Some handles are just the right size to trap a finger when the cup is being set down. Others may be difficult to hold securely because the handle is too small to allow a confident grip.

Coupe design
Dishes with a curved lip rather than a rim.

Some dishes are made in a **coupe design** (curved lip), rather than a traditional rimmed design. The coupe design stacks less firmly than rimmed dishes. This is only a matter of interest when dishes with a coupe design need to be arranged in a high stack. The choice regarding coupe or rimmed design primarily is one of personal preference.

When comparing costs of various patterns being considered, there may be pricing available for place settings, starter sets for two or four place settings, and complete sets with 96 or more pieces. Determine just which pieces are included in the price of a place setting; settings do vary, particularly with regard to the inclusion of any bowls and bread-and-butter plates. In the complete sets, identify just exactly what pieces comprise the place settings and which serving pieces are included.

An important consideration also is what flatware and glassware will be used in concert with the dinnerware. Sometimes dinnerware may be the first item chosen, but family treasures (particularly silverware) may be the table appointment to set the tone for the choice of dinnerware. Bear in mind the design flavor being contributed by each part of the table setting so a coordinated and pleasing arrangement results.

Care of Dinnerware

Dishes need to be handled carefully, whether they are the finest porcelain or the more fragile earthenware. This means that any handling should be cautious to avoid chipping and cracking, whether by hitting against themselves or against faucets or other kitchen hazards. If dishes are being placed in a rack in the dishwasher, they should be positioned so they will not fall against other items and no other dishes and pans will tip into them. When they are being scraped and rinsed in preparation for washing, special care needs to be taken so they are not bumped against the sink or faucet. Dishes washed by hand should be placed securely in a rack for draining.

To avoid difficulties in washing plates, scraping and rinsing promptly are helpful practices. In the event that food does dry on a plate, soaking helps loosen particles. Metal scouring pads and abrasive cleansers should not be used on plates and other dinnerware because of their effect on the glaze. The most abrasive material that can be used safely on dinnerware is a plastic pad, which should be used as little as possible. Adequate and prompt rinsing is the best approach.

Some dishes warp or their designs may deteriorate when washed repeatedly in dishwashers; ordinarily, this is not a problem. If the dishes are antiques, it may be preferable to wash them very carefully by hand. Mild detergents are useful when washing dishes decorated with gold or platinum.

GLASSWARE

Glassware is far more susceptible to breakage than the other components of a table setting. For this reason, it is important to consider carefully the merits of purchasing expensive crystal for individual place settings. Certainly formal settings are enhanced greatly by the addition of graceful **stemware**, but this may be an impractical choice for people who move frequently or are on a tight budget.

Stemware
Footed glassware mounted on a glass stem.

Many families have a set of inexpensive glassware for regular use and more elaborate glassware for formal occasions. All glass is made of silica, in combination with other materials. To produce fine crystal, lead is added to melted silica. The result is a heavy glass of excellent brilliance and a resonant quality when tapped. Lime is an important ingredient in the crafting of less expensive glassware. This formula is well suited to manufacturing pressed glassware.

Early in 1991, warnings were sounded that some of the lead in lead crystal migrates into beverages, leading to the possibility of lead poisoning if fine crystal is used frequently or if crystal decanters are used to store brandy or other alcoholic beverages (Graziano and Blum, 1991). This study indicated that some lead migrated from crystal wine glasses into wine in 20 minutes; 20,000 µg of lead per liter of brandy were measured when lead decanters were used to store brandy for five years. True lead crystal contains between 24 and 32 percent lead oxide.

The actual amount of lead entering alcoholic or fruit juice drinks from crystal varied with the crystal, thus making generalizations difficult. Officials from the U.S. Food and Drug Administration are studying this problem. However, consumers should be alert to the potential problem of using fine lead crystal every day. Occasional use probably is not a hazard, although pregnant women and children should probably avoid regular use of lead crystal.

Design choices in glassware are numerous, with the more formal designs found in stemware (Figure 13.6). The formality of stemware is inappropriate with the heavy nature of stoneware and some earthenware, but it is lovely and in keeping with the mood introduced by the use of fine porcelain and sterling silver. Again, as in keeping with the

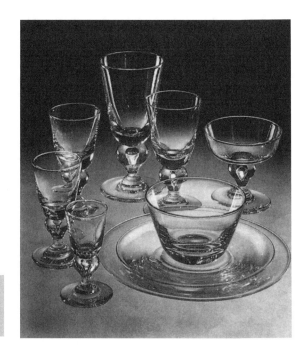

FIGURE 13.6 Stemware highlights a formal table. Crystal stemware is elegant, but less costly stemware can be a practical and satisfying choice.

other items selected for the table, lifestyle should be considered when consumers are choosing glassware.

Glasses of many sizes and shapes are available within the design lines manufactured at both economical and expensive price levels. Select just the specific glasses that ordinarily will be needed for the beverages typically served. For simple meals and informal lifestyles, this could be as limited as glasses for juice and another beverage, such as milk or water. However, other specific glasses are useful in many homes.

After selecting the approximate price range, glassware can be chosen on the basis of color, texture, and design. Tinted glass is rather popular for informal settings, particularly when more than one set of glassware for casual use is being purchased. Rough or coarse textures may be selected to add to the informality of the table, if desired. Conversely, fine crystal with its inner brilliance may be the preferred glass material.

Design in glassware has two components: the basic shape of the glass and the design detail sometimes applied to the surface (Figure 13.7). When considering the basic shape of the glasses, the dimensions in relation to hand size are of importance; a somewhat squatty, broad glass may be awkward to hold. The shape of the glass also influences its center of gravity, a fact that can be of great importance. Glasses with a high center of gravity are likely to tip when they are barely touched. Very tall stemware has this problem unless the foot is quite wide or the lower part of the stem is weighted fairly heavily to lower the center of gravity in the goblet.

Some fine crystal is decorated with cut designs. This adds significantly to the cost of the piece. Inexpensive simulated cut glass is a possible choice when actual cut glass is desired but too expensive. Designs sometimes are engraved on glasses. Engraving of monograms is an example of this type of design. In less-expensive glassware, colorful designs sometimes are applied. These definitely lend an informal air to any occasion when they are used.

FIGURE 13.7   Stemware requires a wide enough foot to avoid easy tipping. Note the cut-glass designs on some of these patterns.

LINENS

The choice of table coverings is important to the general tone of a meal. Coarse-textured fabrics promote a feeling of naturalness and informality. An elaborate lace or fine damask tablecloth requires a traditionally elegant setting. In short, selecting the stage for a meal begins with selection of the table covering.

Place Mats

With today's emphasis on conservation of time and energy, place mats are a practical, very interesting type of table covering to consider. However, place mats reveal a fair expanse of the surface of the table, making the appearance of the table an important consideration. If place mats are placed on a wooden table with an attractive surface, the effect can be very pleasing. The ambience they create can range from formal to decidedly informal, depending on the place mats selected.

The size of place mats varies considerably, but they should be large enough to hold a single place setting comfortably, without crowding the dishes, glasses, and flatware. The usual width of place mats ranges from 18 to 20 inches, with a depth between 12 and 14 inches. If mats are being used on an oval or circular table, a round or oval mat fits the table better than a rectangular mat. Rectangular mats are compatible with the shape of square and rectangular tables. If space permits, a runner of the same fabric may be used down the center of the table. This provides a convenient background for the centerpieces as well as a suitable spot for the serving dishes.

Various types of fabrics are used for place mats. Sometimes backings are added to provide additional protection for the table and to help keep the mats from sliding on a slippery table. For easy care, woven mats or no-iron fabrics are suggested. For elegance, linen and cut-work mats are appropriate.

Tablecloths

Tablecloths are an appropriate choice for any occasion and especially important if the table does not have an attractive surface. Maximum formality is afforded by the choice of a damask cloth. Lace and cut-work cloths also are excellent choices for setting a formal table. The damask cloth affords the opportunity to use a silence cloth or table protector to help avoid damaging the top of a fine table.

Table protectors have the added advantage of reducing the sound of dishes and flatware clattering against the table during a meal. These protective coverings cannot be used with lace or cut-work tablecloths because they show through the cloth. Coarser fabrics and fabrics with bold, bright designs are suitable choices for tablecloths when a casual setting is desired. Often it is possible to find cloths of this type that are made of no-iron or easy-care fabrics. This increased ease of care can be a very important timesaver without detracting from the appearance of a table setting.

The size of the tablecloth should be considered. An overhang of between 12 and 16 inches on all sides of the table is suitable for a tablecloth to be used for a formal table setting. Sometimes a buffet table for a grand occasion may even have the cloth extending almost to the floor. This creates a dramatic appearance but certainly is not appropriate at a formal table where people are seated. For informal meals, an overhang of about 10 inches is suggested.

Napkins

The size of napkins is influenced by the occasion. Small napkins (between 11 and 13 inches square) are appropriate for snacks and breakfast. Luncheon napkins ordinarily are approximately 16 inches square. Dinner napkins may be between 18 and 24 inches square, with the larger size suggested for very formal occasions.

The most formal effect is achieved by using napkins that match the tablecloth or place mats. However, less formal, yet attractive table settings may be created using napkins of a contrasting fabric that complements the fabric of the table covering. Considerable variety and excitement in table settings can be achieved by the creative use of table linens.

Care of Table Linens

Appropriate storage is a key to an efficient table setting. Place mats ideally are stored in drawers or cupboards large enough so the mats can be placed flat. It may be helpful to use heavy cardboard as trays on which to store each pattern of mats. With the use of these trays, several sets of mats can be stacked without wrinkling the mats. This mode of storage also makes it easy to remove the desired set of mats from the stack without disturbing the other mats. Tablecloths can be ready to put on the table without wrinkles if they are stored carefully on rollers or tubes. Napkins can be stored in the same way as place mats.

Good laundering practices are vital to the maintenance of attractive table linens. The care and use directions accompanying the coverings and napkins should be followed. Linen and cotton cloths can be washed in washing machines, using the appropriate temperature control and a suitable detergent.

Some spots on napkins and table coverings can be removed by spraying them before the fabric is placed in the washing machine. Prompt removal of stains is very important to help eliminate the spot. Suggestions for removal of common stains include the following techniques:

Alcoholic beverages—Blot excess liquid with an absorbent towel and soak in cool water. Vinegar rinses at 15-minute intervals may be used for stubborn stains.

Meat drippings and blood—Blot the excess and soak in cold water. Rub by hand with a detergent until the stain is removed before subjecting it to normal laundering.

Candle wax—Solidify the wax with ice and then use a dull table knife to scrape off the extra wax. Then sandwich the waxy area of the cloth between layers of paper towels and press with a warm iron. The heat of the iron will soften the wax, permitting it to be absorbed by the paper towels.

Chocolate and cocoa—Wash and scrub the stain in cold water, using a detergent. Follow this treatment with washing in hot water.

Coffee—Rinse well with cold water. Remove any remaining stain by scrubbing the spot by hand, using cold water and liquid detergent. Rinse this out, and then pour boiling water through the cloth into the sink, holding the container of water approximately 2 feet above the cloth. Care must be taken to avoid splashing hands with the boiling water.

Cream—Before washing in cold water, scrape off any excess. A hot water washing with detergent is the final step.

Egg—Follow the procedure used for removing cream.

Fruit—Wash the spot well in cold water before a second washing in hot water. Persistent stains can be treated with bleach if the fabric can handle this treatment without damage.

Gum—Chill thoroughly with ice and carefully scrape off as much as possible with a dull table knife. Cleaning fluid probably will be needed to sponge the area before it is washed.

Mustard—Treat with liquid detergent before rinsing in cold water. Follow with a washing in hot soapy water.

Rust—Dip the affected area in a solution consisting of a tablespoon of oxalic acid crystals in a cup of very hot water. Continue dipping the fabric until the spots disappear.

Tea—Use the same treatment as for coffee.

Centerpieces

Centerpieces are intended to provide the focal highlight of table settings. They should be designed with an eye to the occasion and with careful consideration of color, line, proportion, and design. They may be very grand and sweeping if they are designed for buffet tables where people will be standing while serving themselves at the table but nobody will be seated at the table.

Less dramatic and lower arrangements are needed for dinner tables where people will be seated. The centerpiece must be low enough that the line of vision is not interrupted between any of the people seated at the table (Figure 13.8). The centerpiece also needs to be proportioned so none of the material in the centerpiece crowds or overhangs plates of food.

Centerpieces can be fashioned using simple decorative objects already available. Flowers are always an excellent choice for a centerpiece. Attractively arranged fruits and/or vegetables are suitable choices any time of the year. The types of materials that can be used appropriately are limited only by the imagination. The creation of an artful centerpiece can be a delightful assignment for creative people, and the result will add significantly to the hospitable mood of the meal.

Candles can be placed a short distance from both ends of an arrangement to enhance the ambience created by the centerpiece. Sometimes they are used as the central focus of a centerpiece. It is appropriate to use matching candles for formal arrangements, but candles also may be grouped for special effects. When candles are a part of a table setting, they should be selected so their flames will be either above or below eye level. Whenever candles are a part of a table setting, they should be lighted while the meal is in progress. They also should be lighted during buffets, receptions, and teas if they are a part of the setting.

FIGURE 13.8   This centerpiece is too massive for the size of the table and interferes with conversation.

SETTING THE TABLE

Cloths and Mats

Table settings provide the opportunity to create truly beautiful settings in which to enjoy the food that has been prepared. A fine meal deserves a presentation that mirrors the attention given to creating the occasion. A little time spent to arrange the linens and tableware carefully and create a pleasing centerpiece helps assure the success of the meal.

Begin by selecting linens that complement the menu and are well suited to the table where they will be placed. Be sure they are clean and neatly pressed. Tablecloths need to be placed so they are straight on the table, with overhangs of equal length on the opposite side and opposite end. Place mats should be arranged carefully at each place. Rectangular mats can be placed parallel to the edge of a rectangular table, either right at the edge or an inch back. Usually, mats should not overhang the edge of the table, although some mats are designed to be placed in that fashion.

Napkins

Formal dinners usually feature a large dinner napkin (18-inch square), either arranged just to the left of the forks or centered on the service plate at each cover. Each napkin is folded in quarters and then once more into eighths. The bottom edge of the napkin should parallel the edge of the table and be 1 inch in from the edge of the table. The open corner of the napkin should be at the lower right corner, an arrangement that makes it convenient to open the napkin in half when placing it on the lap at dinner.

Although this arrangement is considered an excellent choice for arranging the napkin, elaborately folded napkins sometimes are featured in table settings to add to the design elements. This trend has been fostered by the practices of many upscale restaurants that focus on beautifully presented fine food. Napkin folding is rather time consuming until the desired folding techniques are mastered. Some ideas include the fan, triangle, cone, and bishop's hat folds. The steps for executing each of these folds are as follows.

Fan Fold

1. Fold in half by placing the bottom edge even with the top edge.
2. Start with the short edge and crease in 1-inch accordion pleats to within 4 inches of the other edge.
3. Fold in half by turning the left half underneath so the pleats are outside and at the bottom (folded edge is at the left).
4. Turn down the upper right corner and tuck behind the pleat.
5. Holding the tucked-in corner in one hand, place on table, and spread pleats in a fan. The portion with the tucked-in corner serves as a stand at the back to hold the fan upright.

Triangle fold

1. Fold in half to make a rectangle with the fold toward you.
2. Fold the left side of napkin over the right to make a square.
3. Fold in triangle by bringing the lower left corner to the upper right corner.
4. Fold the triangle in half again and stand with the folded edge toward you.

Cone fold

1. Fold the napkin in half to make a triangle with the fold at the left.
2. Fold the top edge down to the bottom edge to make a square.
3. Start rolling tightly from the lower left corner toward the upper right corner, being sure to keep the point of the cone at the left and tightly rolled. The point will end at the upper left corner, and the open end will be at the right.
4. Turn wide end up to form a cuff to hold the napkin together.

Bishop's hat fold

1. Fold in half, bringing the tip toward you to form a triangle.
2. Bring the upper-left and upper-right corners down to meet this point, which causes the folded edges to come together.
3. Bring the top corner down to within 1 inch of the point nearest you.
4. Turn this same corner back up to meet the last fold.
5. Turn the entire napkin over.
6. Bring the bottom corners together.
7. Tuck the right corner inside the left to hold in place.
8. Stand the napkin upright.

Flatware

Cover
Individual place setting.

The pieces of flatware to be placed at each **cover** are dictated by the menu and also by the formality desired for the meal. Usually the minimum pieces are a knife, fork, and spoon (Figure 13.9). The knife is arranged just to the right of the plate, with the sharp side of the knife facing the dinner plate. The spoon is placed just to the right of the knife, and the fork is at the left of the dinner plate. The arrangement of a place setting varies according to the formality and menu for the meal; Figure 13.10 indicates the various options.

All pieces of flatware are arranged perpendicular to the edge of the table with the ends of the handles forming an imaginary line parallel to the edge of the table and in 1 inch. This imaginary line is extended by the napkin, which is also placed 1 inch from the edge of the table just to the left of the fork(s).

Sometimes only a fork and spoon may be the flatware planned at each cover. In this case, the fork may be set to the right of the plate (in the position of the missing

FIGURE 13.9   The silverware is positioned carefully at this place, with the ends of the handles an inch from the edge of the table and the sharp side of the knife blade directed toward the plate. Note also the placement of the goblet just above the knife.

knife), with the spoon just to the right of the fork. The other option is to balance the flatware by placing the fork to the left and the spoon to the right of the dinner plate.

If additional flatware is to be used, the arrangement on both sides of the plate is in the order of intended use, with the item to be used first on either side being placed farthest from the dinner plate. Forks provide a useful illustration of this sequencing

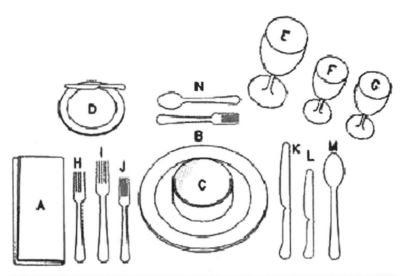

FIGURE 13.10   Guidelines for placing flatware at a place setting according to the menu for formal dinner; for informal meals, only the necessary items are set.

arrangement. The dinner fork is placed immediately to the left of the dinner plate, and a salad fork (when intended for use in eating the salad) is placed to the left of the dinner fork. Sometimes the intention is for the smaller fork to be used for eating the dessert, not the salad. If that is the plan, the salad (dessert) fork is placed immediately to the left of the dinner plate and the dinner fork is placed just to the left of this smaller fork. The diner knows that the smaller fork is to be used for the salad in the first example because its position at the far left indicates it is to be used first. When the smaller fork is the fork closest to the plate, the diner knows it is intended for use when eating the dessert.

Some meals are served with three forks—a smaller one for salad, a dinner fork, and another smaller fork for dessert. These three forks are arranged by placing the larger dinner fork between the two smaller forks, with all three being to the left of the dinner plate. As previously noted, the ends of the handles should be 1 inch from the edge of the table.

Sometimes a soupspoon is needed. Because this spoon is usually needed for the first course, it should be placed just to the right of the teaspoon. Occasionally, a seafood cocktail may be the first course. If so, the small cocktail fork is the utensil placed farthest away from the dining plate on the right side (just to the right of the spoons).

When a bread-and-butter plate is part of the cover, the butter spreader is placed directly on that plate. Usually it is arranged with the handle to the right, the sharper edge of the blade pointed toward the diner, and the knife parallel with the edge of the table in a position near the top of the plate. Other acceptable positions for the butter spreader are (1) at the right edge of the bread-and-butter plate and perpendicular to the table with the sharper edge of the blade pointed to the left, or (2) the tip at the center of the plate and the handle extending toward the right with the knife paralleling the edge of the table.

The European tradition of setting dessert silver above the plate and parallel with the edge of the table is also sometimes used in the United States. When this is done, the fork is placed directly above the dinner plate, and the spoon is above the fork. The handle of the spoon always is directed to the right, but the handle of the fork sometimes is positioned toward the left and sometimes to the right. Either direction for the fork is considered correct. There may even be a need for a fruit or cheese knife for the dessert course. If this knife is needed, it is placed above the fork and below the spoon that are arranged above the dinner plate.

Clearly there are some options for arranging flatware, but here are some key points to check when setting a table:

- The number of pieces of flatware on either side of the plate should give a balanced appearance to the cover.
- The cutting edge of the knife should be directed toward the dinner plate.
- The handles of the flatware should be aligned carefully so they parallel each other, with the bottom of each piece 1 inch from the edge of the table.

Glassware

Glasses for water are placed directly above the tip of the knife. Beverage glasses are positioned to the right of the water glasses and slightly closer to the edge of the table. Each glass needs to be arranged carefully to avoid disturbing the placement of flatware at each cover. Also, the glasses need to be placed so they are easy to pick up without bumping into adjacent glasses or flatware. Special care needs to be given to stemware (footed glassware) so diners are able to lift them without catching on the edge of a plate or flatware. Careful placement of beverage glasses can save spills at a meal.

Dinnerware

Charger
Large plate placed at a
cover to decorate it, but
food is not placed on it.

Liner
Plate placed beneath
a soup bowl or other
small dish to facilitate
serving.

For rather formal meals, a **charger** (service plate) may be placed in position in the center of the individual covers. Soup or seafood cocktail can be served in a crystal or china dish placed atop a **liner** (salad plate), and the two are then placed on the charger. Use of a liner makes it easy to clear the first course while still leaving the charger in position to maintain the beauty of the original setting if another course will precede the entrée.

After this course is eaten, these dishes (including the charger, if present) are cleared, leaving a clear space for the dinner plate to be placed. If a charger is not used, the soup or other appetizer may be served with the liner directly on the table cover in front of the diner.

The salad plate is placed just above the forks unless a bread-and-butter plate is part of the place setting. When both plates are included in the place setting, the bread-and-butter plate is placed directly above the forks, and the salad plate is a bit to the left and somewhat closer to the edge of the table. If space is limited, the bread-and-butter plate can be shifted somewhat closer to the right, with the salad plate a bit closer to it. Eliminate the bread-and-butter plate if the cover is too crowded.

Summary

Table appointments represent important decisions because of their expense and long period of service. Decision making begins with an assessment of the amount of money potentially available for such purposes and the importance of these items to one's lifestyle. Usually it is wise to begin by selecting flatware. In some families, one set is selected for regular use and another set for special occasions. Stainless steel flatware often is chosen for daily use, with sterling silver or silver plate selected for more formal use.

Dinnerware also may be selected for particular uses. Porcelain dinnerware is especially durable and attractive, but it is relatively costly. Stoneware and earthenware are excellent choices for less formal service. Pewter sometimes is used for special effects and so is silver hollow ware, but these items are costly. Wood provides yet another alternative material. Its disadvantage is in relation to its care and durability. Some people prefer plastic tableware because it is relatively indestructible.

Glasses are available in a very wide range of designs, sizes, styles, and prices. It often is possible to purchase more than one type of glassware, thus making greater variety in table settings practical. Very expensive lead crystal stemware can be chosen for special use, but excellent effects can be created for a rather low cost by careful choice of less expensive glassware. Options in glassware include stemware, colored glass, cut glass, and engraved patterns. The design of glasses should be reviewed in relation to the ease of tipping or spilling, simply as a matter of practicality.

Table linens can be selected to suit the occasion. Through skillful choices of colors, patterns, and textures, a wide range of table settings can be created. Place mats are a useful type of table covering because of the ease of care, but greater formality (and better protection of the table surface) can be achieved by using a tablecloth. Napkins of matching or contrasting fabrics and colors also can add to the total impact of a table setting. Small napkins are appropriate for breakfast and lunch; very large ones are desirable for elaborate dinners.

The centerpiece is the focal point for the table. Buffet tables provide the opportunity for dramatic centerpieces. Smaller, lower centerpieces are necessary for meals

FIGURE 13.11   What changes could be made to improve this table setting?

where guests are seated because the view of other diners should not be obscured by any part of the centerpiece. Candles may be a part of the centerpiece, but they should be lighted during the meal if they are on the table.

Careful table setting is a key part of presenting beautiful meals. Creative use of table linens and various styles of folding napkins can provide a lovely background for a table setting that enhances the pleasure of a well-prepared meal (Figures 13.11 and 13.12). A thoughtful look at the appearance of the table at the start of a meal is important in developing an appreciation of table setting as an art.

FIGURE 13.12   Is the silverware placed correctly in this setting? If not, how should the pieces be placed?

Study Questions

1. What flatware type and pattern would be a reasonable choice for newlyweds who have two more years in college before graduation? Explain this recommendation. Might there be other choices that also would meet their situation? Explain.

2. For the couple in question 1, recommend tableware and explain the recommendation.

3. Recommend glassware for a two-income family (with no children) that entertains often. Explain your recommendation.

4. Diagram a cover for a dinner that will include an appetizer, a salad, rolls, entrée, and vegetables (both on the dinner plate), dessert (as a separate course), and wine.

5. Diagram the cover for a family dinner that has a salad served on its own plate but at the same time as the rest of the main course.

6. Examine Figures 13.11 and 13.12, and write the answers to the questions in the captions.

7. Go to a store displaying dinnerware and select the three patterns you like the best. Explain why you chose the type of dinnerware and also why the pattern is a good choice.

Suggested Websites

www.towlesilver.com
Towle Silversmiths website.

www.bestbuysilver.com
Information on various brands of silverware.

www.gorham1831.com
Information on Gorham silver and china.

www.lenox.com
Information on Lenox silver, china, and glassware.

http://www.wedgwoodusa.com/index.asp
Information on Wedgwood china, flatware, and crystal.

www.royaldoulton.com
Information on Royal Doulton dinnerware and crystal.

www.villeroy-boch.com
Information on Villeroy & Boch dinnerware and crystal.

www.waterford.com
Information on Waterford crystal.

www.libbey.com
Information on Libbey tableware for food service and the home.

http://64.78.31.65/pdfs/publications/usaid_leadfree_frontline.pdf
Discussion of efforts to reduce lead from glazes used in Mexican pottery.

Bibliography

Bones, F. M., and Fisher, R. 1998. *Standard Encyclopedia of American Silverplate: Flatware and Hollow Ware: Identification and Value Guide.* Collector Books. Paducah, KY.

Graziano, J. H., and Blum, C. 1991. Lead exposure from lead crystal. *The Lancet* 337 (8734): 141–142.

Rinker, H. L. 1997. *Dinnerware of the 20th Century.* House of Collectibles. New York.

Rinker, H. L. 1997. *Silverware of the 20th Century.* House of Collectibles. New York.

Von Drachenfels, S., and Luscombe, K. 2000. *Art of the Table: A Complete Guide to Table Settings.* Simon & Schuster. New York.

CHAPTER
14
Methods of Meal Service

Family, home, and friends have become the center of many people's lives today, at least partly as a result of the tragic events of September 11, 2001. Food and warm hospitality are an important part of lifestyles. Nevertheless, the busy lifestyles of today have caused much of the ritual and nonessential frills to be replaced by simpler, yet thoughtful meal service. These changes reflect the values and lifestyles in individuals and families. In many homes, all adults are working outside the home, thus limiting the time available for maintaining some of the standards of days past. In addition, household help often is not a part of the picture in homes today.

Daily meals and social occasions in many homes focus on the value of warm hospitality, not on trying to impress others. The result often is less structured dining, less formality, and a style that saves time. However, there still is a desire for graciousness and beauty in dining. Although time and money may present limitations, some formality may be preferred because it heightens the pleasure of a meal.

The method selected for serving has a strong influence on the ambience of a meal. Different styles of service may be used to fit the specific occasion. Part of the pleasure of meal management is using a type of meal service that creates the desired mood.

This chapter presents various types of meal service to facilitate creating a warm and hospitable ambience for the occasion. Adaptations can be made to tailor meal service to suit the diners and meal manager.

INFORMAL STYLES OF MEAL SERVICE

Preferences in styles of meal service differ widely, influenced by the ages being served, socioeconomic status, cultural background, lifestyles, and the physical setting in which the meal is served. Generally, family meals are served rather informally and company meals may be more formal or even very formal in their service. Decisions regarding service should be made before starting the meal. This eliminates confusion during meal service.

Blue-Plate Service

Blue-plate service
Simple method of service; plates for the salad and entrée are filled in the kitchen and placed on the table before guests are seated.

Family service
Dinner plates are stacked in front of the host, who serves them and passes them to the adjacent diner to pass down the table to the hostess or others.

Compromise service
Another name for family service.

One of the simple yet pleasing styles of service that can be handled easily by one person is **blue-plate service**. In this type of service, salad plates will already be served and placed on the table at each cover, water will be poured (and other beverages, if being served) at the beginning of the meal, and any candles will be lighted. At the last minute, individual dining plates are served in the kitchen and quickly placed on each cover (Figure 14.1). The diners then come to the table. When they are seated, the hostess picks up her fork, signaling the others to begin. If second servings are offered, they may be served either by taking diners' plates (one at a time) to the kitchen to replenish the items desired or by bringing serving dishes to the table and passing them.

After all diners have finished the main course, the serving dishes are removed before carrying the individual salad and dinner plates of each diner to the kitchen. Clearing of plates should be done without stacking any plates, which means the salad plate can be removed from the diner's left side and transferred to the right hand before the dinner plate is removed with the left hand (also from the left side of the diner). These two plates are then carried to the kitchen before the next cover is cleared. This process is repeated until only beverages and dessert silver remain on the table. The dessert is then served from the kitchen and beverages are refreshed and/or a new beverage is served.

Family Service

Family service, also referred to as **compromise service**, is another form of service well suited to family meals and dinners for a small group of people. This service is considered

FIGURE 14.1   For blue-plate service, plates are served in the kitchen and placed on the table at each place.

by some to be more gracious than blue-plate service. However, it is done most easily if the meal is served in a dining room where there is a convenient sideboard or service cart where the serving dishes can be placed.

The appetizer course may be in position at the individual covers when diners come to the table, or this course may be served first in the living room. If the appetizer is served at the table, the plates from this course are removed before the main course is brought to the table. Plates are removed from the left (as described in the blue-plate service) and should not be stacked before being carried to the kitchen.

For family service (Figure 14.2), warmed dinner plates are stacked in front of the host, and the serving dishes (accompanied by the required serving silver) are arranged

FIGURE 14.2   For family service, places are set with everything but the dinner plate, which is served by the host and then passed to the diner.

conveniently close to the host's cover. Each plate is served by the host and then passed by diners along the table to the recipient indicated by the host, beginning with the hostess. If the meal is elaborate and requires several items to be served on the plates, the host may ask the person to the left to serve part of the food. However, the host always serves the entrée. After all of the plates have been served, the serving dishes can be removed to the sideboard or cart while the meal is eaten. If second servings are desired, the serving dishes may be passed, or individual plates may be passed back to the host to be replenished. When the main course has been completed, the plates are removed, as described in blue-plate service.

Dessert usually is served at the table, although it can be served in the living room. When served at the table, the dessert dishes, dessert, and appropriate serving silver are placed in front of the hostess. The hostess serves the dessert in the same manner that was used for serving the main course, but the host is designated as the recipient of the first plate. If a hot beverage is to accompany the dessert course, it is served from the right of the diner. At this time, water glasses also are refilled from the right, if necessary. Plates are removed after the diners leave the table.

BOX 14.1

Food Insights: "When in Rome ..."

Meals may be served quite differently in other cultures than they are in a typical American household. In Morocco, hands are rinsed while people are seated around a low table and then diners wipe their wet hands on their large napkins as they prepare to eat. Then they each use their right hand to take some food from the tagine or other serving container placed in the middle of the table so they can reach it easily until they are satisfied. Silverware is not used. Then another dish is brought in. This continues throughout the meal until hands are washed again and wiped on napkins.

In Korea and other Asian countries, shoes are removed before people enter their homes. A low table is used for dining, and diners sit on tatami mats on the floor (Figure 14.3). Several dishes of food are placed in the center of the table so diners can each use chopsticks to transfer some of the food to their plates. Food is eaten using chopsticks.

In China, a lazy Susan in the center of the table makes it easy for each person to take portions of each dish and also to get more of anything desired. People eat with chopsticks, but soup is eaten with a large porcelain spoon shaped with a flat bottom. This is in contrast to the Japanese way of eating soup. They drink the broth by delicately holding the bowl to their lips. Chopsticks are used to eat the noodles or other items in the broth.

FIGURE 14.3   Koreans traditionally remove their shoes to enter a home. Dinner is served on low tables with diners sitting on the floor.

American Service

American service is a very informal style of service, perhaps best described as efficient and without formality. For this type of service, the dinner plates are set in position at each cover when the table is set. When it is time to serve the meal, the food is brought to the table in serving dishes, which can be placed in various spots around the table. The serving silver either is placed on the table where the appropriate dish is placed, or it is in the serving dish.

When everything is ready and the diners have been seated, the person sitting close to a dish lifts that dish and places the desired amount of food on the dinner plate before passing the serving dish to the diner seated to the right. Each diner seated close to a dish follows the same procedure so all food dishes are moving around the table at the same time in a counterclockwise direction. The result is that people are able to serve themselves the amount of food they desire rather quickly, which helps assure that the food for diners will still be hot. When all of the food has been passed, the hostess lifts her fork, which is the signal for all diners to begin eating.

Second helpings are offered simply by passing the serving dishes so diners can help themselves if they desire more food. When everyone is through eating the main course, one or two of the diners can carry the empty plates to the kitchen, beginning with removal of the serving dishes.

Dessert may be plated in the kitchen, with the individual servings carried to each diner by the people who cleared the main course. Alternatively, the hostess may serve the dessert at the table following the procedure described in family service.

Buffet Service

When entertaining a large group of people for dinner, **buffet service** provides a good solution for the efficient service of hot food. The basic part of this service is a buffet table, which is arranged so it is easy for guests to serve themselves as they proceed along the table. This buffet table may be a sideboard or the dining table itself. Arrangement of the food on a buffet table may be limited to serving from one side only. However, both sides of a buffet table can be used if there is sufficient room for diners to pass freely along the buffet. For a big crowd, arranging the buffet table so both sides are mirror images effectively cuts serving time almost in half.

A decision needs to be made regarding seating arrangements for diners while they are eating. If the group fits at the dining table, this arrangement is convenient. Of course, diners cannot be seated at the dining table if it is being used as the buffet table; a sideboard or other suitable large surface will need to be available for the food service.

A suitable seating plan for a buffet may be to set up on card tables or TV trays and chairs arranged so all guests can be seated comfortably with at least a convenient table for the beverage (preferably for the dinner plate, too). Because people will be walking through this seating area while they are carrying plates and beverages, leave sufficient space to walk without bumping into furniture or diners.

When tables are used, individual covers can be set with silverware, napkins, and water glasses. If guests will be using lap trays or sitting where there only is table space for the beverage, individual covers cannot be set; flatware and napkins will need to be placed on the buffet table where diners can pick them up before proceeding to their chairs. For the comfort of guests who are required to juggle plates on their laps while eating, menus featuring an entrée or casserole that does not require any cutting are appropriate. Such menu items can be eaten with a fork, thus avoiding the hazard of trying to cut meat in a precarious situation.

Buffet service often is planned so guests serve themselves as they move along the buffet table. If a menu item is difficult for diners to help themselves to while holding their plates, it may be desirable to have someone serve that item while people are passing along the buffet table. The hostess needs to watch the buffet table and replenish serving dishes that may be depleted when a large group is being served.

Beverages can be placed at the end of the buffet table so they can be picked up after diners have finished serving themselves. However, it is helpful to diners if beverages can be served to them after they are seated. If a large group is being served and help is limited, it is practical to have guests carry their beverages from the buffet area to their seats.

People can begin eating when all of the places are filled at their table or in their seating area. The dinner plates need to be cleared after all people in a dining group have finished the main course. Clearing should be done unobtrusively, in an unhurried manner and without stacking any plates.

After the dinner plates are cleared, dessert may be served in whatever arrangement best fits a particular situation. If the dining space is crowded, simply carrying the dessert (with the appropriate silver on the plate) to guests while they are seated avoids added congestion. If guests are seated at the dining table, the simplest dessert service is to serve the dessert on plates in the kitchen and then carry them to the diners at the table. Coffee or tea may be served to people after they have received their dessert, thus eliminating the need to walk to a beverage station.

An arrangement that works well if space is not too limited is to clear the buffet table of the serving dishes from the main course and reset the table with the dessert, plates, and dessert silverware. Coffee or tea may also be available at the dessert buffet table. Guests can visit the dessert area and serve themselves when they are ready for dessert and a hot beverage.

FORMAL STYLES OF SERVICE

English Service

English service
Formal service; host serves entrée, which is carried by a server to the hostess, who serves the other foods before the server places the plate before the diner.

English service is a rather formal service that requires staff to serve properly. In this method, the host serves the entrée, after which the server carries the plate to the hostess, who serves the vegetables on the plate. She then hands the filled plate to the server, who carries it to the designated person, serving it from the left side of the diner. This method of service is very cumbersome if nobody is available to carry the plates between the host and hostess because each plate has to be passed back and forth the length of the table and then back to the final recipient. Much time and effort are wasted, and the food likely will be cold before everyone is served.

Russian Service

Russian service
Very formal service; servant serves food on the plate at the sideboard and then delivers the plate to a diner.

Russian service is the most formal type of table service. Food is served at the sideboard by servers who then carry the plate to the table and place it before the appropriate person, serving from the left side of the diner. A variation of this method is to have servers place the empty plate for a course before each diner and then offer to serve the food from the serving platter to each diner. Either the server or the diner may transfer the food from the serving dish to the individual's plate.

Russian service consists of more ritual than is found in any of the other styles. At the beginning of the meal, the table is set with an elaborate charger (service plate) at each cover. If soup is to be the first course, the soup and its liner are placed directly on the charger after the guests are seated. When this course is finished, the soup course and charger are removed. The plate for the next course is placed at each cover when the service plate is removed. This procedure means there will always be a plate in front of the diner. This process is followed for all courses through the salad. (Note that the salad is served as a separate course following the entrée.) When the salad plate is removed, the individual covers are empty.

The dessert course is set by first arranging the silver at each place. The dessert is then brought to each diner, serving from the left. Sometimes a course of fresh fruit or candies follows the dessert course. Finger bowls are used in this type of service, provided with the dessert course or immediately after it.

In Russian service, coffee is served in the living room, not at the table. Another difference is that it usually is served as a demitasse. The somewhat more relaxed ambience provided by serving coffee in the living room contrasts with the rather stiff, formal dinner in the dining room.

Russian service has the advantage of having all diners at the table throughout the meal, thus avoiding distractions and interruption of conversation. Unfortunately, at least one server is required for this formal service, and this assistance is not available in most homes today.

Summary

There are different styles of service used today in this country, depending on the occasion and the preferences of those who will be dining. Usually the style of service selected emphasizes convenience and cordial hospitality. Informal styles of service fit the busy lifestyles and the interest in friends and family that characterize American families today. These styles are well suited to many situations because families usually do not have servers to permit the use of formal styles of service.

The methods of service in general use in homes and restaurants today are blue-plate, family, and American service—all are informal styles. Any of these can be used effectively for family meals or small dinner parties.

Buffet service is popular for serving dinner parties or other occasions where a group of people is dining. Various adaptations can be used when serving buffet style. Both sides of the table, with the same foods arranged along each side, can be used when a large group needs to be served. Smaller parties can be served efficiently by arranging the food so diners pass along only one side. Beverages and dessert can be served at the buffet table or brought to diners after they are seated.

English service can be used for family meals and small dinner parties, but it creates a rather formal atmosphere. This style proceeds better if a person is available to wait on the table, although it can be used (albeit somewhat laboriously) without a helper.

Russian service, the most formal type, requires servants to wait on the table. No diners, including the hostess, are expected to leave the table during the entire meal. English and Russian services, with their need for servants, are not compatible with most lifestyles in the United States today.

Study Questions

1. What type of service would be particularly appropriate to use when two family members are dieting to lose weight? Explain why this is a good choice.

2. Describe a suitable service for a family breakfast to be served before people leave for school and work. Why is this plan a good one?

3. A holiday dinner for 12 people is being planned. What type of service would work well for this occasion? Why is it an appropriate style? Describe in detail the total plan for serving and clearing this meal.

4. Describe another style of service that might be used to serve the dinner described in question 3. What are

the advantages of this style compared with the style planned in question 3? The disadvantages?

5. Diagram the arrangement for a buffet table to serve 16 guests. The menu includes a beef roast with horse-radish sauce and gravy accompaniments, garlic mashed potatoes, medley of buttered steamed vegeta-bles, salad of mixed greens, sesame rolls accompanied by butter and jam, birthday cake, and coffee and tea. Describe the appearance of the table, including the linens and centerpiece.

6. Plan the menu and type of service for a birthday party with three of your close friends as guests. Explain the reasons for the menu selected. What influenced your decision on style of service?

Suggested Websites

http://www.tpub.com/content/administration/14163/css/14163_212.htm
Information on meal service.

http://www.hertzmann.com/articles/2004/service/
Discussion of Russian service.

http://www.westernsilver.com/etiquette/place_settings
Information on table settings.

http://home.ivillage.com/entertaining/partyideas/topics/0,4tkq,00.html
Several suggestions for meals and entertaining.

http://entertaining.about.com/od/etiquetteforentertaining/
Suggestions regarding etiquette and dining.

Bibliography

Baldridge, L. 2003. *Letitia Baldridge's New Manners for New Times*. Scribner. New York.

Post, P. 2004. *Emily Post's Etiquette*. 17th ed. Collins. New York.

Post, P. 1998. *Emily Post's Entertaining*. Collins. New York.

Tuckerman, N., and Dunnan, N. 1995. *Amy Vanderbilt's Complete Book of Etiquette*. Doubleday. New York.

CHAPTER 15
Hospitality

The President and Mrs. Laura Bush

request the pleasure of your company

at a Holiday Reception

to be held at

The White House

on Thursday, December 2, 2004

at six o'clock

East Entrance

OVERVIEW

Food is the universal symbol of hospitality. Its service, when done graciously, does much to enrich lives and bring personal satisfaction. The warmth of friendship is enhanced and strengthened by dinners in the home. In this day of rush and stresses, the act of opening one's home to friends is a special event symbolizing sincerity and friendship. This air of hospitality is the cornerstone of wonderful evenings.

The meal preparation and service should serve merely as a background for extending the warmth of the occasion. Truly outstanding meals certainly are to be desired, but they will not be appreciated to the fullest if their preparation has exhausted the hostess or others to the point that hospitality seems strained. Careful planning in advance, including selection of a menu suited to the experience and the limitations of the cook(s), makes it possible to concentrate on hospitality when guests are present.

There are several facets of hospitality when a person entertains guests at a meal. First, invitations need to be issued. At the time of the dinner or party, introductions probably need to be made. The host and hostess have additional social responsibilities at the table, and guests contribute to the occasion as they interact with others throughout the event. When diners are comfortable with their knowledge of table etiquette, they will be able to enjoy the pleasure of the meal without being distracted by concerns about which fork to use or other minor details of dining. These topics are the subjects in this chapter.

INVITATIONS

Invitations for informal dinners often are issued either in person or by phone. This approach, although not as formal as a written invitation, has the advantage of the host knowing for certain that the message has been received and any details have been clarified. It is wise to repeat the details of the date, time, and occasion to be certain the invitation has been received accurately. This verification is important because the guest has no written invitation to which to refer later.

Written invitations need to be mailed at least two weeks before the dinner so there will be adequate time for the mail to reach the guest, who then responds promptly to the host. For informal dinners, a friendly social note stating the occasion for the invitation, the hour, date, and place is all that is needed. If desired, additional information about plans for the event, such as the fact that the dinner is being planned to introduce a visiting friend, can be included. Such invitations are usually written on simple notepaper.

The envelope and salutation are addressed to all of the people in the household who are being invited. Thus the envelope would read Mr. and Mrs. John Doe if the invitation is for a couple. If the adults and children in a family are being invited, the envelope would read The John Doe Family.

Written invitations should be acknowledged with a written response unless the time is short and a telephone number is given (Figure 15.1). The form of the response should be similar to the level of formality in the invitation. For an informal invitation, an informal note accepting or declining the invitation is all that is needed. This acknowledgment is required for all invitations, even when people are not planning to attend.

Even when an invitation does not say RSVP, the abbreviation for *répondez, s'il vous plaît* (French expression that translates literally to respond, if you please), it is important to let the host or hostess know a person's plan regarding the event. If something unforeseen arises and alters the plan to attend, guests must inform the host of the change.

Please respond to

The Social Secretary
The White House

at your earliest convenience
giving date of birth
and social security number

202-456-7788

FIGURE 15.1   The response card accompanying the White House holiday reception invitation. Security requirements prompted the specifics required to attend the reception.

Failure to let the host or hostess know of such a change is extremely rude, especially if the invitation is for dinner; seating and food arrangements for dinners depend on an accurate guest list.

An informal invitation might read as shown in the example here.

Mr. & Mrs. John Public
17 University Place
Columbia, MN 82355

Dear Sue and Bill.

John and I hope that you will be able to join us and a few other friends on Saturday, September 5, at 7 P.M. for dinner and a video of our recent trip.

Sincerely,
Sharon

An appropriate response to this invitation would be the following.

Mr. and Mrs. William Smith
2353 Center Street
Columbia, MN 82355

Dear Sharon,

Bill and I will be pleased to come to your home for dinner and the video on Saturday, September 5, at 7 P.M. We are eager to see your video and learn more about your vacation.

Sincerely,
Sue

Informal teas and parties also require a written invitation. The form for these usually is slightly more formal than the previous example for an informal dinner party. Because the number attending is not as critical as it is for a dinner, a written response is not mandatory. However, a written response is appropriate if time permits. An example of an invitation to an informal tea is the following.

Tea
Honoring Mrs. Jane Doe

Thursday, November   125 South Street,
Two to Four   Yorba Linda

Invitations of this type usually are written on plain informal notes (small notepaper folded in half, with the crease along the top). The invitation is written in longhand on the bottom half of the inside of the notepaper. Sometimes the name of the hostess is printed on the front page of the notepaper, but this is not mandatory. Informal notepaper is useful for writing responses to invitations as well as for writing the invitations. It is convenient to keep a box of notepaper on hand at all times.

Formal invitations are rarely used for parties today, but they are still the correct form for invitations to weddings and receptions. For large events, it is practical to order engraved invitations, but formal handwritten invitations are appropriate for a small but formal dinner. An example of a formal invitation to a dinner might be worded as shown.

Mr. and Mrs. John Smith

Request the pleasure of Mr. and Mrs. Richard Wright's

Company at dinner

Saturday, February the twenty-third

At seven o'clock

2535 West Street

The response to this invitation is written in the same format used in the invitation. Note the use of third person in both the formal invitation and in the response to it.

Mr. and Mrs. Richard Wright
Accept with pleasure
Mr. and Mrs. John Smith's
Kind invitation to dinner
On Saturday, February the twenty-third,
At seven o'clock

As suggested for the response to an informal invitation, small informal notepaper with no decoration of any type is recommended for responding to formal invitations. Although responses for wedding invitations are not mandatory, it is thoughtful to send a formal response to such invitations. However, if the wedding invitation includes an invitation to the reception, a response is required. Invitations to formal teas and receptions should be acknowledged if the recipient will not be able to attend, and it is helpful to the hostess if responses are also sent for acceptance. In short, it is never an error to respond in writing to an invitation, regardless of the occasion.

INTRODUCTIONS

Introductions are an important part of social interactions, and the responsibility for introducing guests in one's home rests with the host and/or hostess. Timeliness of introductions is essential. When a guest arrives who is not acquainted with everyone already present, either the host or hostess should immediately begin to introduce the new arrival to others in the group. If the party is only a small group, introduce each person to the group. In larger gatherings, it is more hospitable to lead the new arrival from group to group for introductions.

Introductions may be stated in several ways. A form generally in practice today is one in which the name of the honored person (the older person or the woman) is named first, followed by a simple statement introducing the other person by name. For example:

Introducing a man and a woman:

> *"Mary Jones, this is Byron Tatum."*

Or

> *"Mary, this is Byron Tatum. Byron, this is Mary Jones."*

Or

> *"Mary, it is my pleasure to introduce Byron Tatum. Byron, this is my friend, Mary Jones."*

Introducing a younger (Mary Jones) and an older woman (Mrs. Jackson):

> *"Mrs. Jackson, this is Mary Jones, my neighbor."*

Following the introduction, it is helpful to the two who have just been introduced to have a bit of information provided that will help the two new acquaintances start a conversation. Simply mentioning a hobby they both happen to share, or some other mutual interest, is sufficient to break the silence that may develop at this point. It may be helpful in advance of a party to identify some topics that would be of conversational interest to those attending the party.

HOST AND HOSTESS ROLES

The responsibilities of the host and hostess, overall, are to ensure the comfort and enjoyment of guests. In families where both a host and hostess are present, the responsibilities traditionally are divided according to the following patterns (Table 15.1). When one person is fulfilling both roles, the major responsibilities need to be coordinated into a single role. In this circumstance, table service should be considered carefully to streamline the labor requirements as much as possible (Figure 15.2). The important guideline for hospitality is to arrange the meal or party so a maximum amount of time is spent with guests and a minimum length of time is spent in the kitchen after the guests arrive.

TABLE 15.1 Roles of the Host and Hostess

Host	Shared	Hostess
Welcome guests		Welcome guests
Help with coats	Introductions	Check food, as needed
Host appetizer course		Prepare appetizers to serve
Promote conversation	Attention to include each guest in table conversation	Contribute to conversation
Lead guests to table		Serve plates[a]
Seat guest of honor		Indicate seating to guests
Serve plates, if planned		Place napkin in lap
Promote conversation		Lift fork to eat
		Adjust to guests' dining[b]
		Clear plates
		Serve dessert, beverages
		Replace napkin on table
Lead guests to living room		Invite guests to living room
	Share in conversation with guests	

[a]Serve food on plates in kitchen and place at each cover on the table if serving blue-plate service; serve food into serving dishes and place on table at host's place for other forms of service.
[b]Eat more slowly or faster, depending on the progress of the slowest guest.

Although roles in families are quite variable today, it is helpful to identify the various aspects of entertaining so individuals or couples are prepared to provide a warm and hospitable setting for the party or dinner. The first responsibility as the party begins is that of welcoming guests, helping them with their coats, and bringing them into the living room to meet other guests and to engage in conversation.

The adults in the hosting family can share this aspect of entertaining, but couples should be sure each guest has been welcomed by both the host and hostess. This requires that meal preparation be under control at the time the party starts, thus

FIGURE 15.2 The hostess at this party replenishes food on the buffet table while guests converse and help themselves.

freeing the cook to be with the guests as much as possible. Trips to the kitchen should be limited only to those essential to achieving the desired meal quality. Ideally, the menu does not require involved preparation near the end of cooking.

If the cook needs to be in the kitchen as serving time comes, it is helpful to the spirit and conviviality of the party to have another person assume much of the responsibility for hosting the appetizer course, if it is being served in the living room. This service can be done easily if the hors d'oeuvres have been arranged on platters and trays for quick transport to the living room. Again, this is a time when careful planning and time management can be used to help free the hostess to enjoy being a part of the party.

Throughout the evening, the conversation is led and supported, when appropriate or necessary, by the host (with some assistance from the hostess). This does not mean the conversation should be monopolized by one or two people, but it does mean that new topics and exciting ideas can be introduced by the hosting family to help make the party stimulating and enjoyable for their guests.

When the appetizer is finished and dinner is ready to be served, everything is placed in readiness for guests to come to the table. The usual practice is for the hostess to indicate the appropriate seat to each guest. Ordinarily, the hostess is seated at the end of the table closest to the kitchen, and the host is at the opposite end. The honored female guest is seated to the host's right, and the honored male guest is seated to the right of the hostess. As much as possible, the remainder of the seating is done by alternating men and women along the sides of the table. The actual seating plan should be decided before the party begins. Place cards can be used to indicate places at the table, but they are not required. Even when they are used, it is helpful if the hostess indicates where people are to sit.

When everyone has reached the designated place, the hostess should be seated (ordinarily with the aid of the gentleman on her right), and the host assists the lady to his right. Male guests may help by seating the woman who is to sit next to them. When all are seated, the hostess unfolds her napkin halfway and places it in her lap. All others at the table follow her lead and also place their napkins (folded in half) in their laps.

BOX 15.1

Food Insights: Resveratrol, Anybody?

Red wine served before or during the meal may be a healthful choice, as well as an interesting topic of conversation because it contains resveratrol. In 2006, researchers working at several universities and the federal Institute of Aging reported that their collaborative work demonstrated that mice on high-calorie diets had better physical condition and lived longer if they received a daily supplement of resveratrol. A similar effect had been observed in fruit flies and other test subjects, but the study on mice represents a big step in the study of this compound.

Unfortunately, red wine and other foods containing resveratrol have very small levels compared with the amount given to the mice in the study. It would be necessary to drink at least 100 glasses of wine daily to reach the level that was tested. Although some people might view that as an interesting challenge, it certainly is not recommended for dinner parties (or any other time).

If the service is the blue-plate type, the hostess promptly lifts her fork as the signal to everyone that it is time to begin eating. If family service is being used, the host immediately begins to carve the meat and serve the plates. When each plate is filled, the host indicates the recipient and passes the plate to the person seated on his right (or left if the diner receiving the plate is on that side). The hostess usually is the first person served. The host may then serve the guest of honor, or he may methodically serve the plate of the person to the left of the hostess (the right side of the table from the host's perspective) and continue serving everyone on the right side. Diners on the left side of the table are then served; the host serves himself last.

When all plates have been served, the serving dishes may be transferred to the sideboard or serving cart, if desired. The salt and pepper and other items to be passed are started by the person seated closest to them and passed to the right (counterclockwise), with the item taken in the right hand and then transferred to the left hand before passing it to the person on the right. This method is used for all items passed by diners at the table.

During dinner, the hostess has the responsibility for being certain that beverage glasses are filled as needed and second servings are offered, if that is the plan for the meal. The hostess also should be alert to the speed with which others are eating and adjust her dining so a guest is not eating alone or having to sit without food while others are still eating. This can be done by conversing or listening intently to the conversation while taking only occasional bites if it is necessary for her to prolong her meal. However, there may be instances when it is necessary to stop eating before she is finished if speed seems to be the mode for all the guests.

No plates should be cleared from the table until all diners have finished eating the course. Although plates can be cleared by passing them to the hostess, who stacks the plates on a cart positioned beside her chair, this becomes a task that disrupts the flow of conversation. A more pleasant atmosphere is maintained by having plates removed from the table by a family member or guest who volunteers. Although a guest would not have served this role in the past, such assistance is perfectly appropriate today. Usually, only one guest and the hostess should clear the table.

The table is cleared by first removing all serving dishes, the salt and pepper, butter, and any other accessory items not needed for the dessert course. After these have been taken to the kitchen, the individual places are cleared, beginning with the guest of honor and continuing until all places are cleared. Each place is cleared from the left of the diner by picking up the dinner plate with the left hand, transferring it to the right hand, and then removing the salad plate with the left hand. If a bread-and-butter plate is part of the cover, the salad plate needs to be placed on the dinner plate in the right hand before the bread-and-butter plate is removed with the left hand. The dishes for one place setting are either carried directly to the kitchen or placed on the sideboard while another cover is removed (so two settings can then be taken to the kitchen).

Unlike the service of food and the removal of plates, both of which are done from the left of the diner, beverages are served and removed from the right. This is convenient because glasses and cups are located on the right side of the individual covers. The cardinal rule of service at the table is to avoid reaching in front of the diner.

Glassware used during dessert is left at each cover. Other glasses, such as an empty milk glass that is not being refilled, are removed (from the right side of the diner) after the main course. This helps maintain an attractive table during the dessert course. Crumbs can then be removed by brushing the table with a folded napkin if a very crumbly food has been served. Otherwise, this probably is not necessary.

Service of the dessert course begins with refilling water glasses and placing the dessert silver if it is not already at each cover. If desired, the dessert silver can be placed on each of the dessert plates before they are brought from the kitchen.

Consistent with the relaxed lifestyle preferred by many today, dessert can be served efficiently by carrying desserts from the kitchen (one in each hand) and serving from the left of each diner, beginning with serving the one in the left hand. The second dessert is transferred to the left hand and served to the next diner (again from the diner's left).

An alternative dessert service is to have the hostess serve the dessert at the table, which creates a rather formal mood. This style of dessert service begins by placing the dessert plates directly in front of the hostess (where her dinner plate had been). The dessert is placed directly above the stack of dessert plates, along with the serving silver. As each plate is served, the hostess passes it to the right, indicating the person who is to receive it. The diners proceed to pass it along the table to that person. After the first side of the table has been served, she then serves the second side.

After the desserts have been served, the coffee or tea may be poured. If cups and saucers are at each cover, the beverage is poured at the table from the diner's right. An alternative is to pour the coffee in the kitchen and carry the cup and saucer to the table, placing it from the diner's right.

At the end of the meal, the hostess places her napkin (without folding it) on the table to the left of her cover. While doing this, she invites guests to move to the living room.

THE ROLE OF GUESTS

Guests also have responsibilities at social occasions. First of all, they need to be sure to respond promptly to invitations. It is rude to the host to ignore this basic courtesy. Another golden rule for guests is to be prompt so food quality is not harmed by late arrivals. When they are leaving, guests should offer a gracious thank you to each of the people giving the party. The next day some expression of appreciation should be made, either in a written note or a phone call or e-mail.

TABLE ETIQUETTE

The cardinal guideline for etiquette at the table is to think of the impact of your actions on the enjoyment of others also dining at the table. By doing this, appropriate actions will happen rather easily. As a simple example, others will enjoy their meal far more if you are careful to chew with your mouth closed at all times, a simple action that has the dual benefits of improving appearance and reducing sound. Similarly, beverages should be drunk silently. Smacking one's lips, slurping, and other noises made with the mouth definitely are annoying to others.

Awareness of the pleasure of others also means thoughtful acts, such as thanking a dinner partner for helping when being seated at the beginning of a meal. If salt and pepper or other items need to be passed, gracious guests are sure to pass them to the person seated on the right, who then continues passing them to the right.

If serving bowls of food or other items are placed near a diner at the table, that person should lift the food dish with its serving silver in it and offer it to the person on the right when the hostess indicates the meal is to begin. Usually, the first person to take food from the dish is the person to whom it is passed. However, if the hostess asks the first person to take some of the food before passing it on, the guest certainly should do just that.

The serving silver is only used to transfer food from the serving dish to one's plate. For example, the butter knife on the butter dish is never used to spread butter on one's roll. As soon as the food is transferred to the dinner plate, the serving silver is replaced in the dish. The serving dish is then passed to the person to the right, who repeats this process.

If a serving dish is heavy or quite large, it is helpful if the person who is passing the food holds the serving container while the person to the right serves a portion of the food on the dinner plate. This same courtesy is then extended to the next person. The last person being served from each dish should place the dish back on the table, thus avoiding perpetual motion and signaling that all is ready for the meal.

Guests should follow the lead of the hostess while at the dining table. When the hostess places her napkin in her lap, guests should follow suit, also unfolding their napkins to half the total dimension and placing them on their laps. At the end of the meal, guests replace their napkins to the left of their covers, being sure they do not touch the dessert plate.

The hostess is the one who provides the cues for when to begin to eat and which silverware to use for various foods. Diners may begin after the hostess starts to eat. When in doubt about the intended procedure, watch the hostess and follow her lead.

Ordinarily, American customs regarding silverware usage are suited to the particular occasion. The preferred style for eating meat in the United States is to cut one bite and transfer the fork from the left to the right hand. The bite is positioned on the fork tines (with the tines pointed upward) before being transported to the mouth. It is not considered good form to spear the bite of meat with the fork tines, but Europeans efficiently spear the bite while holding the fork in the left hand and carry that bite directly to the mouth, using the left hand only. The next bite is cut when the bite in the mouth has been chewed and swallowed. This same procedure is used for any food needing to be cut with a knife.

A soupspoon, if used, should be tipped slightly away from you as it is lifted from the bowl. It is correct to put the soup into the mouth from the near side of the soupspoon. The soupspoon does not actually go into the mouth but rather rests on the lips. From that position, the spoon can be tipped so the soup flows into the mouth. Soup bowls should remain flat on the liner on which they are served. Tipping the bowl is not considered good manners.

Whenever the soupspoon is not being used, it should be placed on the liner (just to the right of the bowl), not in the bowl. This practice is useful because the soupspoon is less likely to drop from the liner than from the soup bowl. At the conclusion of the soup course, the soupspoon is placed again on the liner to the right of the soup bowl. However, if the liner is so small that the spoon may fall when the bowl and liner are removed, the soupspoon should be placed in the bowl.

The same rules apply for using other silverware to eat appetizers. For example, a cocktail fork for a shrimp cocktail should rest on the liner to the right of the cocktail dish, just as the soupspoon is placed on the liner to the right of the soup bowl. If the appetizer is served directly on a plate, the silverware used to eat it should be returned to the diner's appetizer plate. Silverware that has been used is never placed back on the table.

During the main course, the silverware should be positioned on the plate except when it actually is in use. While a diner is chewing a bite, the fork and knife should rest on the dinner plate. When this habit is formed, there will not be a temptation to emphasize a point in the conversation with a fork or knife. Vigorous gestures of this type are inappropriate at the table. During dinner, the knife is placed close to the far edge of the dinner plate, parallel with the edge of the table.

At the conclusion of the meal, the fork and knife should be placed parallel to each other and almost parallel with the edge of the table, with the tip of the knife resting in the plate below the rim. By placing the silver in this manner, the diners send a subtle message that they are through with that course. This placement of silverware is recommended because it reduces the likelihood that the silverware will fall from the plate while the table is being cleared. Silverware placed precariously near the edge of the plate may fall regardless of the care exercised in clearing the plate.

If a salad fork has been used during the meal, the salad fork is placed on the salad plate when it is not in use. The same is true for the butter spreader when it is used; that is, it is replaced on the bread-and-butter plate when not in use. The silverware used for eating the foods served on these special plates always should be placed on the special plate, not on the dinner plate.

Bread and rolls should be broken into smaller portions for buttering and eating. Only these smaller portions are buttered at one time. It is poor form to butter a whole slice of bread or roll, even when it is resting on the plate.

As a general rule, foods served on the dinner plate are to be eaten with the dinner fork. Foods served with a thin sauce or one that will flow too much for service on the dinner plate should be served in a small bowl at each place. This food is eaten with a spoon. Unless a liner is served with the bowl (which usually is not done), the spoon is left in the bowl when it is not being used.

Most foods are eaten with the appropriate silverware, but some very crisp items are best eaten as finger foods. This is true of radishes, celery curls, and carrot sticks, to suggest but a few. However, french fries (unless extremely crisp) are eaten with a fork after being cut to bite size with the fork. Fried chicken should be treated like any other meat unless being eaten at a picnic. It often is considered to be a finger food at picnics, but a knife and fork are the appropriate utensils at regular meals. Bones are left on the plate at all times at meals other than picnics, and even then it is a questionable practice to pick up bones. These comments apply to ribs and any other meat cuts that have a bone included in a serving.

Stemmed glassware is picked up by holding the base of the upper part of the glass with the thumb and two fingers. This gives a secure hold on the glass. The exception to this is when wine is served in stemware. In this case, the glass is held on the stem, not the bowl of the glass. This avoids having wine warmed by heat from the hand.

When holding a cup, the diner places the index finger into the handle, placing the thumb on top of the handle, and placing the third finger beneath the handle. With the use of these three fingers, the cup can be balanced and held securely. If the handle of the cup is tight on the index finger, care must be taken to avoid jerking the cup when it is being replaced on the saucer. In some cups, it may not be possible to extend the index finger into the handle. This is more likely to be a problem for men than for women because of their larger fingers. If the finger could be caught in the handle, do not try to insert it, but instead pick up the cup by grasping the handle securely.

If salads include foods that are difficult to cut with the salad fork, it is appropriate to use the dinner knife to cut the food. After the food has been cut, the knife is replaced on the dinner plate. The bite that has been cut is picked up on the fork (held in the right hand) and carried to the mouth.

If a finger bowl is provided, it is used without any flourishes. The fingers of one hand are dipped (not immersed) in the water, and that hand is wiped unostentatiously on the napkin. The same procedure is used to clean the fingers of the other hand. If the mouth needs moistening, the mouth is rubbed lightly with the moistened fingers of one hand, and then blotted lightly with the napkin. Usually, this is not necessary if the meal has been eaten with some care.

Everyone at the table has the responsibility to contribute to and maintain a pleasant conversation. Topics of interest to the group should be featured. Emotionally charged topics definitely should be avoided. Remember, the dinner table is a time for promoting comradeship and fellowship, not for settling the affairs of state. This should not be construed to mean that intellectual subjects are banned from the table. Stimulating and interesting topics are ideal.

The voice level of all participants also is important. Mumbling and very loud voices are difficult to accommodate during a meal. Strive for a well-modulated voice and speak distinctly. If the conversation begins to be inappropriate at the table, the host or hostess has the primary responsibility for shifting topics. However, guests also can help modify the conversation.

When food is pleasing, it certainly is appropriate to make an enthusiastic comment or to compliment the person who prepared it. If an unfamiliar food is served, it is expected that all people at the table will at least sample it. Wary comments prior to sampling are inappropriate. Comments of appreciation are welcome if they are sincere. If the new food is difficult to appreciate at first, simply allow the food to remain on the plate. Explanations or comments are inappropriate.

Summary

Practices of etiquette vary in different parts of the country and in different groups. The best guideline in a new situation is to observe the hostess and follow her lead. When hosting a party or dinner at home, emphasis should be placed on providing a comfortable setting for guests. This means planning a setting that is relaxing and pleasant for those attending. Compatible guests, careful and thorough preplanning and preparation, and attention to guests' needs ensure a successful party. Specific suggestions for invitations, hosting, and dining included in this chapter need to be considered in the context of specific situations and applied as appropriate.

Study Questions

1. Write an invitation to a dinner party at your home. What decisions need to be made before writing the invitation? What information needs to be stated on it?

2. What would be an appropriate response to an invitation to each of the following: (a) Sunday brunch at a friend's home, (b) a wedding and reception, (c) a dinner party celebrating a 10th wedding anniversary of friends?

3. How would you introduce each of the following combinations at a party: (a) Helen Jones (age 5) to Susan Chan (age 18); (b) William White (age 22) to a group of five men standing together at the party; (c) Clara Martinez (age 25) to Susan Brown (age 50)?

4. How would you eat each of the following: (a) very crisp bacon, (b) clam chowder, (c) spaghetti, (d) T-bone steak, (e) chicken leg, (f) barbecued ribs?

5. Identify at least five topics that a host might plan to use as possible ideas for dinner conversation. Indicate why each of these would be good for the particular occasion.

6. You are hosting a dinner party. Explain briefly how you would handle each of the following circumstances:
   a. Jane calls to say she is stuck in traffic and will be about 45 minutes late.
   b. John arrives after Pete and Barbara are already there, but he does not know them.
   c. The timer is beeping in the kitchen.

Suggested Websites

http://www.epicurious.com/cooking/how_to/video/
Videos on various techniques on food and entertaining.

http://www.westernsilver.com/etiquette.htm
Useful information on etiquette of dining.

http://entertaining.about.com/od/dinnerparties/
Information on presenting special dinner parties.

http://www.evite.com/
Invitations and party planning help.

http://busycooks.about.com/library/lessons/bldi
Basic guidelines for planning and presenting a dinner party.

http://www.collegejournal.com/successwork/onjob/
20061019-meehan.html
Perspectives on entertaining at dinners.

http://home.ivillage.com/entertaining/partyideas/
0,,s6c1,00.html

Ideas for entertaining and dinner parties.

http://www.medicalnewstoday.com/medical
news.php?newsid=55691

Overview of Harvard University collaborative study
on effects of resveratrol on mice.

Bibliography

Baldridge, L. 2003. *Letitia Baldridge's New Manners for New Times*. Scribner. New York.

Baur, J., et al. 2006. Resveratrol improves health and increases survival of mice on a high-calorie diet. *Nature* DOI 10: 1038.

Post, P. 1998. *Emily Post's Entertaining*. HarperCollins. New York.

Post, E. 1999. *Emily Post's Essentials: Everyday Etiquette*. HarperCollins. New York.

Post, P. 2004. *Emily Post's Etiquette*. 17th ed. HarperCollins. New York.

Tuckerman, N., and Dunnan, N. 1995. *Amy Vanderbilt's Complete Book of Etiquette*. Doubleday. New York.

CHAPTER
16
Special Occasions

Holidays, parties, dinners, receptions, and special outings are the types of social occasions in which food occupies a place of prominence in the festivities. These events warrant special planning, with attention given to the setting, logistics for service, appearance of the plates and platters with their garnishes, and overall quality of preparation of the food. These are opportunities for making a spectacular centerpiece, for using cherished serving pieces, and enjoying the more elaborate menus that crowded schedules often do not permit. In short, food for special occasions can be a very satisfying medium for creative expression.

PLANNING SPECIAL MENUS

Defining the Occasion

Start planning the event by defining the central theme or idea. What is the reason for the gathering? Who is to be invited? How many guests will be attending? Decide on the degree of formality (possibilities range from an extremely casual beach picnic to a formal dinner party). Perhaps the event is to be a family Thanksgiving dinner, with various family members contributing to the menu. Maybe the occasion is a New Year's Eve party for 10 friends. Suppose the event is a bridge party at home, and the hostess is to provide the entrée. All sorts of events can trigger the opportunity to plan something a bit special and offer a chance to be the creative chef.

Once the occasion has been defined, the actual menu-planning task is simplified. The food selections need to be:

1. Consistent with the formality of the event
2. Able to be prepared in appropriate quantities using available equipment
3. Available and seasonal
4. Affordable (consistent with the budget for the event)
5. Pleasing combinations from the perspectives of flavor, color, aroma, shape, and texture

Although this sounds complex, this list can be checked off quite quickly before making the final decision to include specific items on the final menu.

Sources of Ideas

Menu plans for entertaining are easiest to develop if sources are available to stimulate the flow of creative ideas. Books, magazines, and newspapers, as well as some websites, can trigger many thoughts to begin to build a plan. Some recipes or articles might be so appropriate that they can be used with minor adaptations; others may stimulate the development of original concepts. Magazines and food sections of newspapers can be helpful in suggesting ideas appropriate to the time of year or the holiday.

Menu planning definitely is simplified when a collection of cookbooks is at hand. This collection should have at least one general-purpose cookbook that contains recipes for all parts of a meal. Added interest can be found in specialty cookbooks; cookbooks featuring the recipes for a particular country or region may be the inspiration for a party menu. Sometimes cookbooks filled with recipe ideas for using an appliance (such as a wok or microwave oven) may stimulate menu ideas.

Television shows featuring gourmets and chefs can be the means of finding some new ideas and techniques that will add interest to menu planning. A jotted note during the program and recipes prepared on the show can be tools for moving forward with menu plans. The visual presentation of these programs can give useful tips for serving and garnishing, as well as for shopping for ingredients and preparing the food.

BOX 16.1

Food Insights: Culinary Cultural Clashes

As concerns about such topics as the environment, cultural identity, and food safety arise, food practices commonly accepted in other countries may conflict with laws in some American cities. A recent example flared in Glendale, California, when restaurants were barred from grilling outdoors. Some neighbors were complaining about the aromas permeating through their area throughout the day, and they wanted the ban enforced. This struck an ethnic nerve among Armenians, who comprise about 40 percent of Glendale's population. They relished eating shish kebabs grilled outdoors over mesquite and rushed to their tables, embodying a wonderfully fragrant and tasty reminder of their native land. Grilling indoors simply fails to develop the characteristic aroma and flavor of kebabs they remember. Who knows how this problem may resolve itself. Perhaps free kebabs once a week to all living within the range of the aromas may be the answer. At the moment, people are seeking a compromise.

One of the biggest restaurant owners is trying to find a way to move his giant outdoor rectangular steel grill indoors from the parking lot and then figure out how to use it without smoking out all his customers—clearly a giant challenge.

Several years ago Peking duck created quite a flurry when the Los Angeles County Health Department issued citations to Chinese restaurants because these ducks were not being prepared and held at temperatures required by departmental regulations. The fact that Peking duck has been a Chinese delicacy for many centuries and the Los Angeles version of Peking duck was being made exactly according to tradition carried no weight with the local authorities. Even though nobody in Los Angeles had been reported as having an illness caused by eating Peking duck, rules are rules. The problem caused such turmoil that a compromise finally was reached and Peking duck is available, albeit with very minor changes from the traditional procedures. Peace has returned to Chinatown in Los Angeles.

Personal recipe files can be invaluable in planning for a special occasion. These files can be developed continually by collecting recipes from friends, restaurants, or other contacts. Try to get recipes for dishes that are particularly appealing, and add them to the files. One convenient way to store these recipes is in a file box or notebook. Computers are very effective for filing recipes, but they do require that the recipe be entered accurately into a computer recipe file, a task that may not always be done in a timely fashion.

People who take entertaining seriously may find it helpful to maintain a permanent record of special occasions, including the date, people who attended, the menu (including the specific location of each recipe), and any special comments regarding the menu and table setting. This record is useful in avoiding repetition of menu items for specific guests. A computer is very useful in maintaining this record and provides easy access to the information when other events are being planned. A useful part of this record is a list of guests and friends, complete with information about food allergies, favorite foods, and items that perhaps should be avoided. A quick check of this resource before beginning to plan the menu will identify foods to emphasize or eliminate from consideration, according to the specific information about each of the guests.

Selecting the Menu

A decision on the meal's entrée is usually the best place to begin planning the menu. This decision requires that a choice be made first between a recipe that features meat (or other flesh food) or a casserole or similar entrée. This basic decision directs the search

FIGURE 16.1 An outdoor barbecue featuring grilled chicken, broccoli with lemon butter, rice and mushroom pilaf, and hot French baguette with butter is geared toward a special evening with friends.

toward appropriate recipes and eliminates many recipes, thus saving a good deal of time. When cost is important, choice of a casserole of some type is helpful because meats, poultry, or fish usually are the greatest single expense in a meal. Casseroles typically augment a limited amount of meat with less expensive ingredients, yet the results can be gourmet quality. Choice of a meat, poultry, or fish—perhaps served with a flavorful sauce or garnish—is also appropriate for special meals (Figure 16.1).

With today's emphasis on healthy food choices, selection of a fish or poultry entrée is certainly appropriate; occasional use of such red meats as beef, veal, pork, or lamb can create a festive meal. Consider whether a sauce is desirable to accompany the entrée. Another important question is whether or not time is available to roast or prepare the entrée. Remember, a large cut of meat or a large fowl requires that cooking begin well in advance of the actual serving time. Such items are impractical unless someone is available to start cooking at the appropriate time. When a recipe has been selected, write it on the menu and indicate the cookbook or other source of the recipe, being sure to also include the page number.

Once the entrée has been chosen, the rest of the menu needs to be planned to coordinate with that choice. One key question is to decide the number of courses to be served. Often an appetizer is a good way to stimulate conversation and help people shift into a sociable, relaxed frame of mind. The appetizer can be hors d'oeuvres served in the living room or on the patio. This arrangement works well if some final preparations need to be done in the kitchen just before serving.

Sometimes it may be more convenient to serve the appetizer at the table after everyone is seated. This option requires more plate clearing and table service, however. Regardless of the choice made regarding the location, the selection of the appetizer or hors d'oeuvres should be made with the general plan for the meal firmly in mind. A fairly hearty start is appropriate to accompany a light main course. However, a large or filling appetizer before a heavy entrée reduces the pleasure of the other courses.

There are no rules about the number of courses that should be planned; nor is the sequence of service defined. The salad in a meal perhaps provides the best illustration of the freedom available in menu planning. Sometimes a platter of crudités (perhaps celery sticks, radish roses, or carrot curls) and a dip for them might be served as an appetizer in the living room. This array or other similar fare could be considered the salad, if desired.

Another scenario might have the salad served as the first course at the table, and yet another alternative is to have it accompany the main course. Some people prefer to serve the salad as a separate course following the main course. The choice is left to the discretion of the person planning the menu. This is one of the reasons that menu planning is such a creative challenge.

Salads provide a great opportunity for adding contrasts to a meal. Food mixtures in salads can run the gamut of nature's color palette, just as they may include textural contrasts from soft to crisp and chewy. They may even accent a cool background with a suggestion of warmth, such as adding slivers of hot chicken or bacon to salad greens. The hot dressing used in making fresh spinach salad is yet another illustration of contrasting temperatures in salads. Because of the vast range of possibilities in salads, this particular menu item can be chosen to enhance and even rectify shortcomings that may be found in a menu.

Usually the main course consists of the meat or other entrée, at least one vegetable, and a starch-rich food, which might be potatoes in some form, rice, or some other grain. Because these items are presented simultaneously, it is particularly important to consider the total impact of these foods from the perspective of all of the senses. Colors and shapes should be planned to appeal to the eye, flavors and aromas must please the nose and palate, and the textures need to provide satisfying contrasts. Try to visualize all of these aspects when deciding on a menu, and then consider how these choices mesh with the appetizer, salad, and/or dessert choices. Sharp contrasts are not essential, but some variation is desirable.

Trends in dining are continually evolving, which means that ideas regarding menu planning are always going to keep changing. Health issues clearly dominate menu planning at the present time. No longer do special meals mean agony afterward for diners who eat everything on too large a menu. With the emphasis on weight control and reduced levels of fat in food, dessert may even be deleted in special meals. However, dessert remains the reason for dining for many people, and leaving it out at a special meal could be an unsatisfactory choice. A pleasing compromise might be a serving of an especially appealing fruit, or perhaps a fruit cup without whipped cream (or with the whipped cream passed so that each person can add a dollop of the desired size). Traditional pastries and cakes are other options for this course. A tempting way of increasing milk intake is to serve crème caramel, flan, or a pudding for dessert.

Naming Recipes

Creative names for various menu items can add considerable interest to a menu. It is more exciting to share a recipe with guests if the name of the dish is "Coquilles St. Jacques" rather than simply "Baked Scallops" or "Scallops in Cream Sauce."

Vocabulary is an important aspect of menu writing. The names of recipes invoke images of the food to be presented and help create the ambience sought in a particular meal. Notice the difference in expectations between "Buttered Carrots" and "Parsley Lemon Carrots," for example. Even coining a descriptive word, such as "Lemonnaise," is a perfectly acceptable way of developing recipe names. Foreign words, especially French, add an international dimension and a degree of sophistication too.

Table 16.1 presents a mini-vocabulary of some of the types of words that might be helpful in menu writing. It is by no means exhaustive. In addition to drawing on ideas from cookbooks, menus from quality restaurants, with their various sauces (Table 16.2) and creative dishes, can be the inspiration for other ideas. Jot these ideas

TABLE 16.1　*Mini-Vocabulary for Menu Writing*

Á la	In the style of
Antipasto	Italian hors d'oeuvres (e.g., mushrooms, pimiento, olives, provolone cheese, sausage)
Au gratin	Crumb and/or grated cheese topping, baked to brown
Au jus	Served with the unthickened meat juices
Blanquette	Veal, lamb, or chicken stew (French recipe for white stew of veal, white mushrooms, and white onions)
Boeuf	Beef
Bouquet garni	Herb bouquet used to flavor soups and sauces
Brochette	Broiled on a skewer
Cappucino	Mixture of espresso coffee and hot milk
Cassoulet	Stew of dried beans, sausages, and other meats
Chantilly	Containing whipped cream
Chiffonade	Finely shredded vegetables; also a French dressing containing parsley, pimiento, onion, and egg
Compote	Stewed fruit
Coq au vin	Chicken with red wine sauce
Coupe	Ice cream served in a stemmed glass
Crème fraîche	Matured, thickened cream (not sour), >30 percent fat
Du jour	Of the day
Flambé	Flamed with a high-proof alcohol
Florentine	Served with or on spinach
Franconia potato	Pared potatoes roasted to a pleasing brown beside an oven roast of meat
Frittata	Omelet topped or filled with tasty filling
Glacé	Fruits cooked in heavy sugar syrup
Grecque	Greek; added olive oil and cold rice
Julienne	Matchlike sticks of vegetables
Lyonnaise	Sautéed with onions
Meunière	Flour-dipped fish sautéed in butter, lemon, and parsley
Nicoise	Tomatoes, garlic, onions, olive oil, anchovies, capers
Pilaf	Browned rice or other grain, seasoned, pine nuts
Ragout	Meat, poultry, or beef stew with seasonings
Risotto	Italian rice dish
Roulade	Thin boneless meat rolled with ground meat filling
Roux	Paste of butter and flour used as the base for thickening soups, gravies, and some sauces
Sauté	Cooked quickly in small amount of oil
Semolina	Finely milled durum wheat flour for pastas
Vinaigrette	Oil and vinegar and herb marinade or salad dressing

down and keep adding to this vocabulary of menu planning as opportunities arise. A small notebook or a developing list in the computer can provide ready access when words are needed.

Writing a Menu

After the courses and recipes have been planned, it is time to write the menu into a form that is functional. Try writing it in the format used by many fashionable restaurants. List each course separately, with the title of the main food for the course centered on the line and the accompaniments (if any) written on the next line and set over to either the left or right margin of the menu. Be sure to include the names of any sauces and accompaniments so the entire menu is revealed, including beverages. This formal presentation of the menu makes it easy to see just what items are to be prepared and helps assure that part of the dinner is not found languishing in the refrigerator awaiting service after the guests have left. Here are examples of written menus.

TABLE 16.2   Selected List of Sauces

Allemande	Velouté sauce with cream, egg yolk, and lemon juice
Bearnaise	Yellow sauce: egg yolk, vinegar, butter, onion, spices
Béchamel	White sauce: butter, flour, chicken stock, cream, mushrooms
Beurre noir	Brown butter sauce: vinegar, parsley, salt, pepper
Bordelaise	Brown sauce with red wine and flavorings
Bourguignonne	Red wine sauce with bacon, mushrooms, onion
Crème	Cream sauce; béchamel sauce with added cream
Espagnole	Brown sauce with some tomato
Hollandaise	Yellow sauce: lemon juice, butter, spices heated gently with egg yolk to thicken
Italienne	Brown sauce with tomatoes, mushrooms, ham, seasonings
Madère	Brown sauce with Madeira wine
Maître d'hôtel	Yellow sauce: lemon juice, butter, parsley, salt, pepper
Marinara	Tomato-based sauce
Mornay	Sauce made with thick cream, eggs, cheese, seasonings
Mousseline	Whipped cream and Hollandaise sauce
Newberg	Yellow sauce: eggs, sherry, cream
Piquante	Brown sauce with pickles and capers
Rémoulade	Mayonnaise with anchovies, pickles, capers, herbs
Tartar	Mayonnaise with chopped green onions, chives, sour pickles
Velouté	White sauce made with chicken or veal stock

Easter Brunch

Fresh Fruit Salad

Quiche Alsace

Bran Muffinettes   *Zucchini Carnival*

Raspberry Sorbet in White Chocolate Nest

Coffee

50th Birthday Feast

Appetizers

Baby New Potatoes with Salmon and Horseradish

Asparagus Spears & Goat Cheese Wrapped with Prosciutto

Dinner

Roast Loin of Pork

Mashed Sweet Potatoes with Balsamic Splash

Sautéed Spinach with Garlic

Dessert

Jennifer's Pumpkin Cheesecake

Coffee

EVALUATING THE MENU

Once the menu has been written, an evaluation of the plan is needed so that any weaknesses can be corrected before shopping for the ingredients. The following check points provide a good basic checklist for menu evaluation; other items may be added, if desired.

Mini Evaluation Checklist

1. *Does an ingredient appear in more than one place in the menu?*

   Unique seasonings and key ingredients in recipes are most effective when they appear in only one item in the menu.

2. *Is there more than one food high in fat?*

   Fat content should generally be fairly low with no more than one item being fried or otherwise high in fat.

3. *Is there more than one food with a strong flavor?*

   Brussels sprouts and creamed onions on the same menu vie for the palate.

4. *Are the anticipated flavors compatible?*

   Chutney with curry is an example of a flavor combination that has proven popular, and such Italian favorites as oregano and basil are essential to many pasta sauces.

5. *Are there textural contrasts between the foods in the meal?*

   Crisp radish roses with a mixed greens salad are a suitable contrast with a main course that includes mashed potatoes, for example.

6. *Does the menu include temperature contrasts?*

   Hot rolls provide a pleasing shift from a chilled salad.

7. *Are the taste sensations varied so a meal provides some piquancy rather than an overall impression of sweet or acid?*

   Chinese sweet and sour pork illustrates this range of taste possibilities in a single sauce, but this variety also can be provided at various points in the meal rather than just in a single dish.

8. *Is the seasoning intensity appropriate to the people who will be eating the meal?*

   If small children are to be included, the hot and spicy dishes that accent such cuisines as Thai may be too intense; a very bland menu may be boring to people who are accustomed to extensive use of peppers and other very hot and/or spicy ingredients.

9. *Are the colors of the food being served at the same time pleasing and interesting to the eye?*

   An all-white menu of sliced breast of turkey, mashed potatoes, and cauliflower may not offend the eye, but it certainly lacks excitement and visual interest.

10. *Has the presentation of each of the dishes been visualized, and have necessary garnishes been planned?*

    The impressions of food that the diner's eye interprets are the early messages that herald this is a special meal. Thoughtful, beautiful presentations are a hallmark of quality.

The 10 points just listed focus on the food itself. However, there are some other perspectives to be evaluated. These practical considerations, essential to successful preparation of the menu, include the following:

1. Are the ingredients available at an acceptable price?
2. Is the equipment available that is required for preparation?
3. Can the food be prepared within the time available?

BUFFETS

Buffet service is an excellent, in fact almost mandatory, choice for serving a large group of people (Figure 16.2). The arrangements for such meals work very well when the serving facilities and the size of the group are considered carefully during the planning. Decisions that need to be made include where people will sit and what physical arrangements for dining are required. If space permits, the easiest arrangement is to have card tables set up and chairs provided at each table, an arrangement that allows each guest to be seated comfortably for dining. There has to be enough floor space for the tables and the chairs (including the space occupied by the diners, with the chairs pushed back comfortably from the tables), plus space to pass between the tables. Unless this can be arranged, another seating plan is required.

One optional seating plan might be to provide TV trays for each guest. This arrangement allows guests to sit on the existing furniture, which saves some space. Card tables and chairs need to be inventoried and the necessary number made available. If plans include having some people sit on upholstered living room chairs, it is essential to consider whether they will be able to eat comfortably with this arrangement.

FIGURE 16.2 Buffet service is an ideal way to feed a large group at a picnic.

If people will be sitting in chairs around the living room, it is necessary for the beverage service to be carefully planned. It is certainly not enjoyable to have to try to juggle a beverage while eating. Small occasional tables or TV trays are possible solutions to this problem. Their placement will need to be planned so each guest has easy access to a table holding the beverage.

When card tables are used, the setting for each card table should be planned with as much care as would be exercised for setting a dinner table, but the size of the centerpiece needs to be scaled to the size of the table. A single flower in a small vase may be the right touch for the center of the table. A set of salt-and-pepper shakers should be placed on each table. The silverware and napkins should be set carefully at each cover. Place cards may be placed on the tables if desired. The cups and saucers may be on the table when the party begins, or they may be placed later when dessert is being served.

The buffet table should be arranged for ease of service. The usual practice is to place the plates at one end of the table, with the entrée being placed next to the plates (Figure 16.3). The entrée is served by the host or by a guest invited to do the honors unless the party is being served with additional help. If available, a helper can do the carving and serving of the entrée.

Usually, guests serve the remainder of the food themselves. They then move into the dining area planned for the party and are seated.

When occasional tables are to be used for beverages, it may be necessary to arrange them as guests are returning from the buffet tables. The practice regarding such arrangements has to be geared to suit the room where the guests are dining. A crowded party may require placement after some guests are seated.

The hostess may invite guests to return to the buffet table for additional food, if that is the plan. However, the serving dishes should all have been replenished before guests return. It also is appropriate to circulate in the dining area, offering additional water or other beverages to those needing a refill during dinner.

After the main course has been completed, the dishes are cleared and dessert is served. If coffee or tea is being served at this time, the accompaniments for the beverage are placed on each table or are passed to each guest, depending on the number of tables.

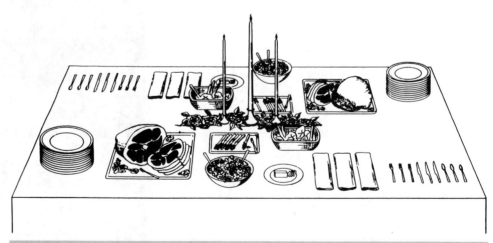

FIGURE 16.3   Diagram of a buffet arrangement planned to serve diners on both sides of the table.

Sometimes guests are invited to return to the buffet table for their dessert and beverage service. This procedure allows dishes to be cleared from the dining tables while guests are in the buffet line for dessert. After dessert and coffee have been completed in a leisurely manner, the tables may be cleared and the dishes carried to the kitchen.

If the party is to continue for an extended time after the dinner, it may be wise to collapse the folding tables and restore the living room to the normal arrangement to facilitate conversation. This may disrupt the party, so tables usually are left standing or just shifted out of the way unless the uncluttered floor space is needed for people to be able to move around the room more easily.

HOLIDAY OCCASIONS

Dinners

Holidays spell enjoyment for families because they afford an opportunity to socialize and be together. Although this is a pleasant and comfortable occasion, it also is an event that brings large family groups together for a bountiful and festive dinner (Figure 16.4). Such an occasion deserves careful preplanning so the person(s) responsible for the dinner can also be a part of the gathering.

Because of the complexity of holiday feasts, it is wise to plan a meal that allows a reasonable amount of pre-preparation of food (consistent with available and appropriate food storage facilities). Desserts, salads, and rolls that can be prepared in advance are very important aids in easing the complexity of the dinner preparation on the holiday itself. The freezer can be a real asset when foods can be prepared ahead of time.

The holiday table and the method of service should be planned at least a few days prior to the dinner so necessary accessories can be assembled without the need for a last-minute shopping expedition. It is desirable to seat everybody at a single table if they will fit comfortably with extra table leaves added. An auxiliary serving table might

FIGURE 16.4 Buffet table for a dinner celebrating Independence Day.

also be helpful. If more than one table is needed, the tables should be arranged to afford conviviality and conversation for all of the family.

These special arrangements may require linens that are only used occasionally. Time is saved when preparing the meal itself if the necessary linens have been identified and are ready to be placed on the table. Meals proceed far more smoothly if the table can be set for the dinner well in advance of the meal (ideally the evening before). This relieves time pressures, thus providing a good situation for creating a truly beautiful table setting with carefully arranged covers and a lovely centerpiece.

With the logistics involved in preparing a large meal for a group of people, food safety must be kept in mind. For example, attractive as it may seem from a time-management standpoint, one must not yield to the impulse to stuff the turkey the evening before it is to be roasted. However, preparation of the stuffing and refrigeration in a bowl overnight until it is time to stuff and roast the turkey is safe and efficient.

Informal Entertaining

Holidays are a time when friends and neighbors often drop by. The hospitality of the season encourages much more informal and congenial times than seem to be able to be crowded into calendars at other times during the year. In anticipation of this situation, it is wise to plan ahead, with the aid of the freezer, so some tempting food always is available for planned or unexpected guests.

Fruit breads, fruitcake, and many different types of cookies can be baked well in advance of the season and frozen in tight containers so they are in prime condition when thawed and served. Similarly, special rolls and coffee rings can be placed in the freezer. A wide range of foods of this type can be prepared ahead and stored in the freezer for holiday use.

The point is to anticipate the need and have the foods prepared well in advance so the holidays can be a time of enjoyment rather than of the unusual pressures in the kitchen. Along with this approach, it is wise to purchase appropriate napkins, candles, and other decorative items that may be a part of the holiday needs. Extra coffee and tea also are convenient to have in the cupboard at such times.

RECEPTIONS

The Receiving Line

Receptions usually are planned for guests to have an opportunity to meet an honored guest or guests. To ensure that each guest is able to meet the honoree(s), a receiving line is formed in a convenient place, usually fairly close to the entry, yet a sufficient distance from the door so the entrance to the room is not obstructed. The first person in the line is the hostess. The others in the line are arranged according to the occasion. If there is an organization sponsoring the reception, the usual practice is to have the officers in the line, with the president of the group immediately preceding the honored guest. This position enables the president to introduce each guest to the honoree.

Probably the most frequent social occasions for receptions are weddings. The bride's mother is the first person in the receiving line at a wedding reception. The sequence of the remainder of the line is the groom's father, groom's mother, bride's father, two bridesmaids, maid or matron of honor, bride, groom, and the remaining bridesmaids. The line should be arranged so the bride is on the groom's right, unless he is in a military uniform.

The bride's mother is the first person in line because she presumably knows many of the guests and will be able to greet them by name and welcome them. If she does not know a guest, she introduces herself to the guest; the guest should respond by saying her or his name. She can then introduce the guest by name to the groom's father.

Persons in the receiving line shake hands with each guest. After a brief conversation, the person in the receiving line introduces the guest to the next person in the line. It is important to speak names very clearly when introducing the guest to the next person in the line. Otherwise, guests may end up with surprising names by the time they meet the last person in the receiving line.

Guests passing along the receiving line should be sure to introduce themselves to people in the line if they have not been introduced. A brief comment by the guest as each introduction is made is appropriate. At a wedding reception, it is appropriate to greet the bride with a friendly greeting of "best wishes." It is correct to congratulate the groom. Prolonged conversation is inappropriate in the receiving line and should be saved for a later time. Otherwise, guests may have to wait too long as they attempt to traverse the receiving line.

Hospitality

When a guest has come to the end of the receiving line, a friend of the hostess or members of the group hosting the reception should usher the guest to the table for refreshments. If a hostess is pouring the beverage at the reception table, she will hand the beverage (on a plate) to the guest; otherwise, the guest takes a plate from the table. The guest will then select the food desired from the platters, placing them on the plate. Silverware, if needed, and a napkin also are picked up at the table.

When the guest has finished at the serving table, a host or hostess engages the guest in conversation and then makes the appropriate introductions to a compatible group. After the guest has been assimilated into a group, the hosting person returns to the table area to host the next guest similarly. Someone needs to be assigned to remove plates when guests are through eating. Guests may be invited to help themselves at the table again, however, before plates are removed.

The length of time a guest should stay at a reception varies considerably with the occasion and with the people involved. It is proper to stay approximately 20 minutes at a formal reception, but stimulating conversation and a sufficiently large room encourage lingering, which is perfectly acceptable. Cues regarding the length of time to stay should be observed, but there is no need to limit a stay to 20 minutes if there is space for all and if it is apparent that the hosts wish to have guests stay longer. At wedding receptions, guests usually are expected to stay for the cake cutting and the throwing of the bride's bouquet and garter, as well as for dancing and/or music.

The Serving Table

The serving table for a reception affords exciting opportunities for elaborate floral displays or other showy centerpieces (Figure 16.5). A large arrangement can be placed in the center of the table if service is to be on both sides, or it can be at the back of the table if service will proceed along only one side.

The decision regarding the use of one or both sides of the table is determined by the number of people to be served. A very large reception can become extremely congested if service is limited to one side. A small reception in a home may flow more smoothly if the table is placed against a wall and service is limited to one side.

The serving table may be arranged with a beverage at each end of the table if two beverages are to be served. In this case, guests will be invited to start at the end of the table where their preferred beverage is being poured. Some plates and cups are positioned at the end of the table convenient to the beverage service. Additional plates

FIGURE 16.5 The buffet table at a reception can feature a tall, dramatic centerpiece because people will be standing while passing along the table.

and cups can be brought as needed, but big stacks of plates and cups should not be placed on the table. The beverage should be placed in a pot or punch bowl on the serving tray. Food platters and their serving silver are positioned conveniently for guests to help themselves after they have their beverage. Napkins and silverware are arranged so they are in a convenient spot for guests to help themselves.

The food planned for the reception table varies greatly with the occasion. It often is appropriate to plan a rather simple table, with only two or three platters of refreshments. The refreshments themselves are usually scaled to be delicate in appearance and size. Particular attention should be given to making each individual item as attractive as possible.

The focus is on daintiness. Sandwiches are appropriate, but they are prepared as finger sandwiches, not as half a slice of bread. Pinwheel and ribbon sandwiches are popular styles. Cookies are made in small sizes. Cakes sometimes are prepared as petit fours, rather than being cut into slices.

Often a reception table features something sweet and something slightly salty or savory. Sweet items may be pastries, cookies, or cakes; salty items usually are crackers or dip items, sandwiches, and/or nuts. Emphasis at reception tables is on food that provides a beautiful experience but not a dinner.

Sometimes at weddings and a few other occasions, dinner is intended to be a part of the reception. If this is the plan, the dinner can be organized by following the procedures outlined for presenting a guest dinner. However, help usually will need to be hired for the occasion.

When planning a reception without using additional help, it is necessary to assign various tasks to family and group members, or special friends may be invited to help. It is considered an honor to be asked to serve the beverage at the serving table. Friends also may be asked to serve as hosts at the door when people first arrive or as hosts to take guests to the receiving line, from the receiving line to the serving table, and from the serving table to conversational groups. It is less of an honor to collect the soiled dishes. When possible, children or hired help may do this task.

The person who is to serve the beverage at a reception table is seated at the end of the table, with the beverage arranged on the tray directly in front and the plates and cups placed within easy reach. Pouring is done by first placing a cup directly in front on the tray. The beverage is then poured, the cup is placed on a plate, and the plate (with its cup of beverage) is handed to the guest. If the beverage being poured is coffee, the person who is pouring first asks if cream and/or sugar may be desired and adds them if they are requested. A similar technique is used if the beverage is tea, which is accompanied by sugar and slices of lemon. Of course, nothing is added if the guest does not wish anything. If a large number of people need to be served, it is more efficient to place the beverage accompaniments adjacent to the beverage service so guests can help themselves.

INFORMAL TEAS

When friends drop in for informal conversation, it is pleasant to serve a beverage and perhaps light refreshment in the living room. This is done most graciously by preparing a tray in the kitchen and then pouring and serving from a table in the living room. A teacart is ideal for this type of service, but a tray can be used and then placed on the coffee table in the living room.

The tray or cart is arranged with the necessary number of cups and saucers (or plates), the beverage accompaniments, silverware, napkins, the beverage, and a plate of cookies or other food, if food is being served. The hostess pours the beverage and asks the guest what accompaniments are to be added. The beverage and its plate or saucer, any necessary silverware, and a napkin are then handed to the guest. When each guest has been served, the hostess offers the platter of food to each guest. When beverage refills are needed, the pot is taken to the kitchen and refilled with hot beverage before the hostess offers to replenish the guests' beverage.

Sometimes it may be more convenient to pour the beverage in the kitchen. When this is done, the cup, saucer or plate, silverware, and napkin are carried directly to the guest. Cream and sugar, or other appropriate accompaniments, are arranged on a small tray and offered to each person. The hostess then offers food to each guest. After the hostess is seated, she begins to eat, and the guests follow her lead.

Summary

Special occasions should be enjoyable to both guests and hosts. With adequate planning and pre-preparation, the party proceeds smoothly and is a pleasure for all. By giving careful thought to the serving requirements and coordinating the menu with the limitations of the situation, a very successful event can be staged.

Emphasis is directed toward doing as much preparation as is practical and appropriate to achieving safe, high-quality food products in advance. Of necessity, preparation for many items needs to be done the day of the party. A good time plan helps ensure that these preparations go smoothly and nothing is forgotten.

Guests and hosts alike have responsibilities for helping make the social occasion a success. Suggestions for the people at parties were included in this chapter. Although the success of the party is related directly to the planning and efforts of the host and hostess, guests also are important to the quality of the occasion. Active participation in conversation and assistance in serving (if that is helpful to the hostess) are ways of helping the event move well. Only a few examples of occasions have been given here. When planning events, the important thing is to plan the occasion to meet the expectations of the group and to stage it at a level of formality appropriate to the occasion.

Study Questions

1. What five specific sources might be useful in planning the menu for a buffet dinner to be served on Christmas Eve?

2. Based on the ideas found in question 1, plan the menu and evaluate it using the criteria stated in this chapter.

3. Sketch the buffet table to show the placement of all food items, plates, and any other items for the table. Indicate the traffic pattern for guests at the buffet table.

4. Describe the number of guests and the plans for their dining arrangements.

5. Plan a dinner for six people, including the menu, a plan for the table setting, and a time plan for preparing the food.

6. Plan the food for a formal tea with approximately 30 guests. Explain why each item was chosen. Describe the service and plans for seating and hospitality throughout the tea.

Suggested Websites

http://www.batmitzvahs.org
Suggestions for bar mitzvahs.

http://www.vtliving.com/party
Tips on planning different kinds of parties.

http://www.partydirectory.com/guide/partylnk.htm

Directory of web sites for party planning.

http://www.divinecaroline.com/browse/home-and-food/entertaining/special_occasions
Ideas for entertaining on special occasions.

Bibliography

Baldridge, L. 2003. *Letitia Baldridge's New Manners for New Times*. Scribner. New York.

Post, P. 1998. *Emily Post's Entertaining*. Collins. New York.

Post, E. 1999. *Emily Post's Essentials: Everyday Etiquette*. HarperCollins. New York.

Post, P. 2004. *Emily Post's Etiquette*. 17th ed. HarperCollins. New York.

Tuckerman, N., and Dunnan, N. 1995. *Amy Vanderbilt's Complete Book of Etiquette*. Doubleday. New York.

CHAPTER 17

Manners in the Cultural Milieu

INTRODUCTION

Manners are constantly evolving, as can be seen easily by reading a few pages in the early editions of Emily Post's books on manners. The transition from her era of very formal manners and concern about so-called proper behavior to today's casual style of manners has taken place with little notice. However, the corporate world now is recognizing the importance of manners, and employees are even taking classes to learn manners that formerly were learned at home.

Certainly, business dealings have always relied to some extent on the ability of people to interact effectively, but the dramatic increase in the global marketplace has added the complication of cultural differences. Misunderstandings that occur in business discussions may be traced to the fact that the same action may be interpreted quite differently, depending on the cultures of the participants.

THE BASIS OF MANNERS

Manners may feel like a list of do's and don'ts that need to be memorized to avoid problems in the workplace and at home. The reality is that manners are intended to help people interact in a way that creates as positive a feeling as possible between the people involved. Even if there is a difference of opinion, manners can help people resolve issues.

Good manners begin when you think about the other person before your own interests. Be aware of others involved in the meeting or conversation. Take time to recognize what is important to them. If time is a priority, then efficient conversation in a calm voice and without digressions is appropriate. Some people prefer a more casual and leisurely style. Clearly you would need to adjust your end of the conversation if you are to be effective in interacting with these two very different situations. Even the closure would require an awareness of whether a brief statement or a friendlier farewell is appropriate. The important matter in terms of manners is that you tailor your behavior to optimize the rapport and results while still retaining your personality.

DAILY LIVING

Greeting People

Accepted ways of greeting people vary with the setting and the people involved. In a business setting, a rather brief, firm handshake is expected. Both people have a pleasant expression and look each other in the eye. This greeting may be followed by some pleasant conversation. In a less formal meeting, good friends may greet each other with a casual handshake or a short hug. The important thing is that the greeting is comfortable for both people.

If other people are also there, it is appropriate to greet each person and say something to help create a pleasant gathering. If some people do not know each other, introductions need to be made by the person who knows one or both of them. It is helpful not only to give names but also to mention some topic or information that may provide an opportunity for conversation.

Cell Phones

Of course cell phones are an important means of communication, but callers need to remember that the whole world is not their private phone booth. Conversations should be done away from other people and at a decibel level that avoids broadcasting

---

BOX 17.1

Cultural Overtones: Greeting

People from other countries and cultures have their own traditions for meeting and greeting people. Some of these differences are described here.

Asians do not consider physical contact to be appropriate; bowing with eyes directed downward and hands at one's side is preferable to a handshake. Sometimes a simple, friendly "hello" is the best greeting. Women often cover their mouth with their hand when smiling. Outward displays of affection between sexes are inappropriate, although people of the same sex may sometimes hold hands as a symbol of friendship.

Middle Easterners of the opposite sex do not touch each other. Men may shake hands, but the shake is brief. It is not unusual for men to embrace and/or kiss each other on the cheek or to walk holding hands.

People from India, Sri Lanka, Bangladesh, and Southeast Asia usually greet and say farewell to each other by saying "**Namasté**" while touching the palms of their hands together in front of their chest and giving a gentle nod of the head.

Namasté
Pronounced "nahm-uh-STAY"; greeting accompanied by touching palms in front of the chest in a prayer-like position and a slight head nod.

---

conversations into other people's space. Lines at a post office are not the spot to close business deals or chat about last night's activities.

Rules on cell phone manners are based on recognizing the rights of others, not just your own. Now that virtually everybody has one, it is not necessary to impress others around you that you have your very own cell phone. Use it only when the call is necessary and then do your call in a private space.

It is rude to carry on a phone conversation while you are walking, dining, or doing other activities with somebody else. The message to people with you is that you do not value their company. To expect them to be respectfully quiet while you chat shows lack of respect for your companion(s). Do your call later.

Talking on the phone while driving can be not only annoying to others but also costly. Cell phone calling has been demonstrated to be the cause of many accidents, and poor driving (perhaps slowing other traffic or wandering out of a lane) is seen all too often. Other drivers are inconvenienced and/or put at risk because of the phone call some stranger is choosing to make while driving.

Last but not least, cell phones need to be checked to be sure they are turned off while attending classes, concerts, and other gatherings where the ring of the phone and any conversation is intrusive and totally distracting. To fail to do the simple act of turning off a cell phone at such times is extremely rude and unacceptable.

SOCIAL INTERACTIONS

Body Language

Conversations while standing usually are simple, comfortable social occasions. However, some people tend to shout quite loudly, whereas others may be so soft spoken that they can barely be heard. If the listener has to ask you to repeat what you have said, be sure to speak directly to that person, and raise the sound level a bit while watching to see if you are being heard. It may also help to speak a bit slower.

BOX 17.2

Cultural Overtones: Body Language

Body language may communicate quite differently from one culture to another. For example, many people from Asia and Mexico may avoid direct eye contact and consider staring to be rude. This may be disconcerting to Americans who view eye contact as a sign of attention and understanding, but they also consider staring to be rude.

Beware of hand movements because they may have very different connotations to various cultural groups. A friendly good-bye wave may be interpreted by Southeast Asians as a gesture saying "come here." They also may view the gesture of beckoning to someone with a finger as a signal calling a pet, and our positive signal of thumbs up may be interpreted as an obscene gesture.

Even the space between people talking together varies with the culture. Be aware of the private space that others need when you are talking with them and accommodate them by talking at a somewhat closer or more distant position.

Time

Time is a commodity that all people have in common—24 hours each day. However, individuals may view time in very different ways. The common complaint is that there never is enough time to do everything, but the reality is that some people accomplish a great deal and others may have spent their day to meet different priorities. Regardless of personal choices, there are times when people gather for a meeting, dining, sporting events, and other types of programs.

The time at which individuals arrive at any gathering can be a matter of importance, particularly at meetings, classes and lectures or concerts, and dinners in people's homes. The people who are always on time for these occasions are showing respect for the value of everyone's time. It is rude to expect others to wait until you arrive before things can start. Of course, sometimes an accident may make it impossible to be prompt, but a regular habit of tardiness says to others that you think your time is more important than theirs. This can be a lethal message on the job, and it can also be a strong negative in interpersonal relationships in all aspects of life.

Communication

When invited to a party, the guest has the responsibility of promptly accepting or declining the invitation so the host will know if you are coming. Then it is assumed you will be there at the time indicated. In the event that an accident is causing you to be late or to have to cancel, phone your host immediately. These communications are a

---

BOX 17.3

Cultural Overtones: Time

Punctuality may be next to godliness in corporate America, but the attitude toward time is very different in some other cultures (e.g., Latin Americans value warm hospitality more than the clock). If it takes a little longer to say farewell before going to a meeting, that is viewed as being a wiser choice than being rude by rushing away. Clearly, it is difficult to mesh this aspect of daily living if a person has a foot in each of these worlds.

great help to the host or hostess and also show your appreciation of the effort being made to entertain you.

Traditions vary regarding a hostess gift, but often it is appropriate to bring flowers or a small gift to show your pleasure at being included.

An appreciative farewell to the host and hostess at the end of the party is the prelude to leaving. That is followed up the next day by a thank you note. Depending on the occasion, a phone call or e-mail the next day may be made to express your thanks.

DINING

At the Table

People should gather at the table and seat those who may need assistance before seating themselves. Then diners unfold their napkins halfway and place them in their laps. When everybody has finished eating, diners place their napkins on the table at the left side of their cover. Then everybody leaves the table at the same time.

Meals are particularly enjoyable when those who are dining together include a pleasant, interesting conversation as part of the experience. Complimentary remarks to the person who prepared the meal are always appreciated. Share the conversation with all who are at the table, and introduce a new topic of interest to diners who may be reticent. All diners have the responsibility of participating in the conversation. Dinner is an important opportunity for family members and/or friends to share experiences and ideas.

Manners, whether at family meals or special occasions, should be based on consideration of the dining pleasure of all people at the table. If food is in serving bowls or on platters, it should have serving silver on it so people can use it to serve themselves. The serving silver is replaced on the serving dish and passed to the next person. The silver that people have been using while eating should never be used when removing food from a serving dish.

Diners use only the silverware at their personal setting, and that silverware should be placed on the plate after being used until it is used again in the meal. Chewing is done with lips closed, and unnecessary sounds are avoided. Attention is on the conversation not on dining manners or social faux pas. Even when a conversation is dynamic, silverware should not be waved in the air to make a point. Used silverware is always placed on plates, not on the table. Knives are used for cutting and are never licked or used to carry food to the mouth.

Restaurant Dining

When arriving at a restaurant, the gentleman or person leading the group should approach the hostess or maitre d' to request a table for the party. The lady follows the hostess when the party is being seated. Others follow, gentlemen behind ladies in the group. Men hold chairs and seat ladies before they seat themselves.

Some women prefer to have their escorts give their order to the waiter. Otherwise, women should place their orders before the men in the group. However, servers sometimes find it more convenient if they control the sequence, and this usually is a satisfactory arrangement.

Presentation of the bill may be awkward unless one person is clearly hosting the dinner. Sometimes a group simply divides the bill by the number of people after a tip has been added to the bill and each person or couple pays the appropriate amount to the person in the party who is acting as the group's comptroller. If that convenient arrangement is not acceptable to some, each person or couple can pay the part that is theirs, but they must be sure to calculate their share of the tax and tip and add those

---

BOX 17.4

Cultural Overtones: Dining

Although Americans consider such noises as slurping or belching at the dining table to be rude, that is not the interpretation in some other cultures. If a Japanese person makes a slurping noise while eating, it is considered a sign of appreciation. In Saudi Arabia and the Philippines, a belch gives a message that the food was good. Lip smacking is interpreted as a sign of approval in Hong Kong.

Diners in Jordan, Egypt, Thailand, and the Philippines can send a quiet message that the meal was good by leaving a little food on their plates. Mixed messages are carried by cleaning one's plate: In Japan a clean plate says the food was good; in Cambodia it says the diner wants more; and in Indonesia, it is considered rude to leave any food on the plate. Because of the possible confusion, be alert to the potential problem and try to note what others are doing.

---

items to their share of the bill. It is not fair to let someone else in the party be responsible for that part of the bill.

When leaving the restaurant, a brief conversation and farewell is appropriate outside the restaurant. If the restaurant is crowded, lingering conversations inside cause unnecessary congestion in the restaurant. The most important thing at the end of the meal is to be sure to thank the host and/or hostess for the evening. If you have been a guest, be sure to remember it is appropriate to host a similar party or a dinner at your home so they can enjoy your hospitality.

Summary

Manners are based on being aware of those around you and behaving in ways that show respect for their needs, as well as your own. Appropriate guidelines in matters of daily living were discussed for greeting people and using cell phones. Social interactions at work and outside the workplace are influenced by body language and the value placed on time. Manners for dining at home and in restaurants were also discussed in this chapter. Some cultural differences related to manners were highlighted to raise awareness of the importance of appreciating other cultures and respecting their manners, too.

Suggested Websites

http://www.emilypost.com/
Information on manners.

http://www.bsu.edu/students/careers/students/
interviewing/dining/
Overview of dining etiquette.

http://www.japan-guide.com/e/e622.html
Guide to Japanese etiquette.

http://www.executiveplanet.com/index.php?title=Main_
Page#Guidelines_for_business_etiquette
Guidelines for business etiquette in many foreign countries.

Bibliography

Dresser, N. 2005. *Multicultural Manners*. Wiley. New York.

Post, P. 2004. *Emily Post's Etiquette*. 17th ed. HarperCollins. New York.

Post, P. 2006. *Excuse me, but I was next . . .* HarperCollins. New York.

Whitmore, J. 2005. *Business Class: Etiquette Essentials for Success at Work*. St. Martin's Press. New York.

Appendices

Appendix A

Meat Carving

a

b

Rolled rib roast. (a) Insert the fork firmly 1 inch below the top of the roast. Slice across the grain from the right side. (b) Lift the slice with the knife to the side of the platter or to another hot serving platter.

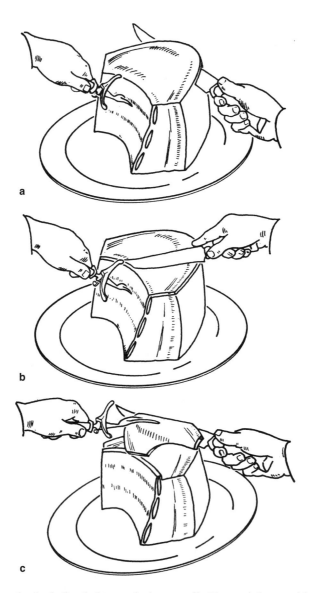

Standing rib roast. (a) Insert the fork firmly beneath the top rib. From right outside edge, slice across the grain toward the left hand. (b) Release the slice by cutting closely along the rib with the tip of the knife. (c) Lift the slice with the blade of the knife to the side of the platter or to an auxiliary platter.

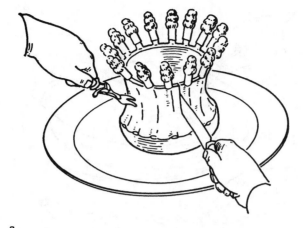

a

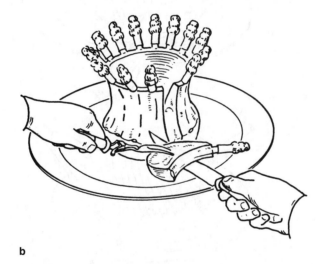

b

Lamb crown roast. (a) Steady the roast with the fork and slice down toward the platter between each pair of ribs. (b) Lift the slice on the knife blade, using the fork to steady it.

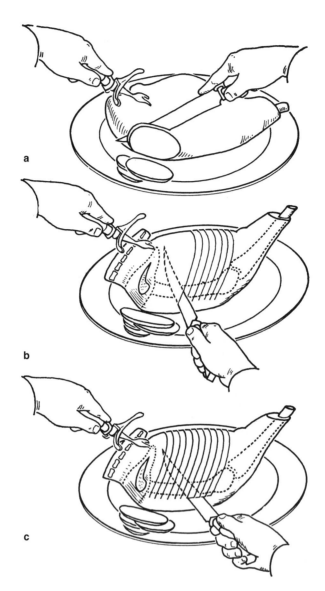

Leg of lamb. (a) Remove several slices from the thin side parallel to the length of the lamb leg. (b) Turn the leg so the surface just cut rests on the platter. Make parallel slices down to the leg bone, starting at the shank end of cushion. (c) Loosen the slices by cutting under them along the leg bone.

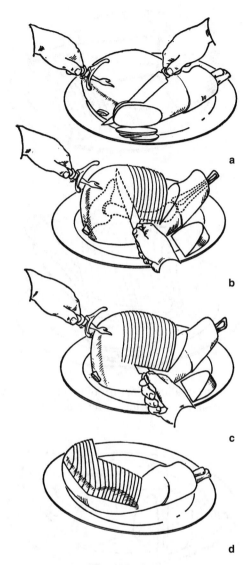

a

b

c

d

Baked whole ham. (a) Remove several slices from the thin side parallel to the length of ham. (b) Turn the ham to rest on the surface just cut. Hold firmly with the fork and slice down the leg bone, beginning at the shank end of the cushion. (c) Release the slices by cutting along the leg bone at right angles to the slices. (d) For more servings, turn the ham to the original position and slice at right angles to the bone.

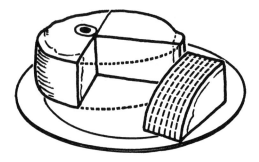

Carving center-cut ham slice.

Picnic shoulder. Remove the slices from smaller side; turn to stand on this surface and slice to the bone, starting at the shank end. Release the slices by cutting along arm bone.

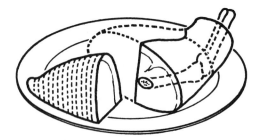

Half ham (shank half). Remove the cushion, turn on the cut surface, and slice, beginning at the large end. Separate remaining section from the shank, remove the bone, turn, and slice.

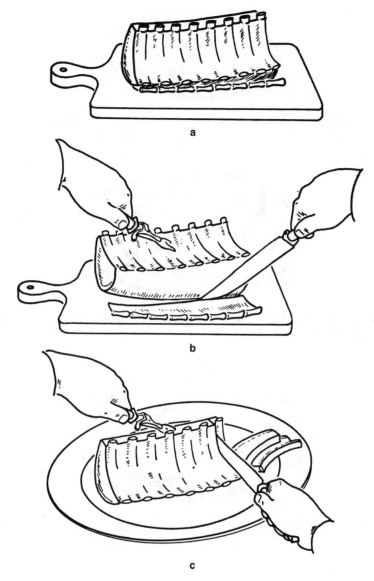

Pork loin roast. (a) Have the retailer saw across base of ribs to loosen backbone of the roast. (b) Remove the backbone before the roast is brought to the table. (c) Insert the fork firmly in the top of the roast. Cut closely against both sides of each rib. Alternate slices will be boneless.

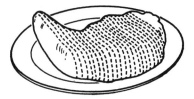

Beef tongue. Make the first slice beginning at the tip end of the tongue. Continue to make thin slices parallel to the first one.

Beef brisket. Make the slices in rotation from three faces that are started on the round side. The slices should be thin and at a slight angle.

Cushion lamb shoulder. Cut the slices from ⅜ to ¼ inch thick through the meat and dressing.

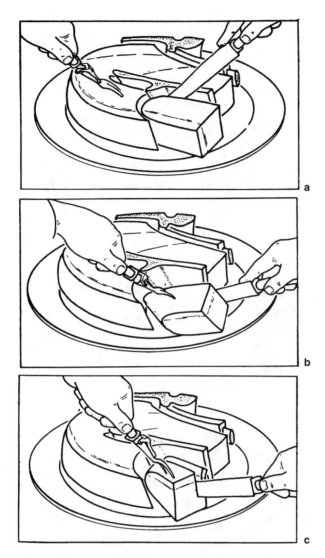

Blade pot roast. (a) Separate the section on the near side from the meat and bone. (b) Turn the piece just separated so the cut surface is down and the grain runs parallel to the platter. (c) Hold the meat with the fork and slice from the top side down to the platter.

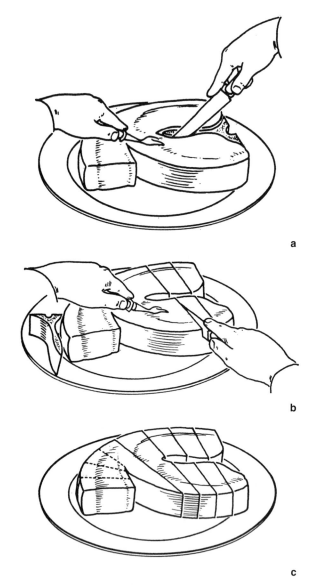

Porterhouse steak. (a) Remove the bone by cutting around it with the knife. (b) Cut across the full width of the steak, making wedge slices, narrowest on the tenderloin side. (c) Serve the flank end last if additional servings are needed.

Appendix B

Turkey Carving

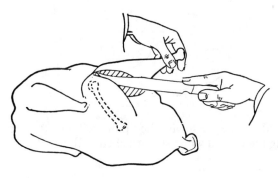

(a) Turn the turkey on its side so the back is toward you. Remove the drumstick by grasping the lower end and pulling forward as the knife cuts through the joint, separating it from the thigh.

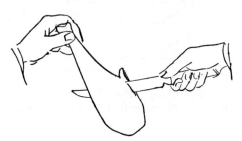

(b) Hold the drumstick upright and remove the slices by carving toward the platter and parallel to the bone.

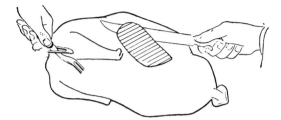

(c) Take thin slices from outside of the thigh until the the bone is exposed.

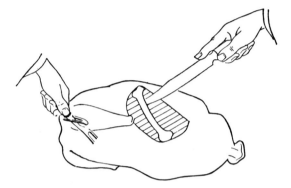

(d) Loosen the meat on each side of the thigh with the tip of the knife; then remove the bone with the tines of the fork. Slice the remaining thigh meat while still attached to the bird.

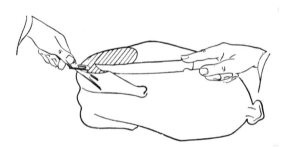

(e) Slicing the breast with the grain: Remove lengthwise slices from the breast and wing until the joint where the wing joins the body is exposed. Secure the fork in the wing and, with knife, unjoint it from the body.

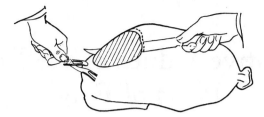

(f) Continue to remove thin lengthwise slices from the breast until the white meat on this side is entirely carved.

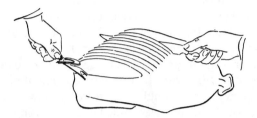

(g) Slicing the breast across the grain: First remove the wing by cutting down toward the backbone from a point about 1 to 1 $\frac{1}{12}$ inches above point where the wing seems to join the body. This should hit the joint exactly. Cut the breast into diagonal slices by starting at the point where the wing was removed, and make the first slice at a slant of about 45 degrees. Continue making slices parallel to this first one until the keel bone is reached. Each slice may be removed from the bone as it is cut, or the entire group of slices may be loosened and removed at one time.

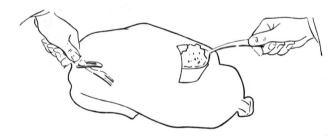

(h) Slice the thin skin under the thigh with the tip of the knife to make an opening large enough for a serving spoon to remove the dressing.

Appendix C

Nutritive Values of the Edible Parts of Food

The source of these data is *Nutritive Value of Foods*, Home and Garden Bulletin 72, revised, U.S. Department of Agriculture, Washington, D.C. Data for some cooked and prepared foods are taken from Church and Church, *Food Values of Portions Commonly Used—Bowes and Church*, Ninth Edition, Lippincott, Philadelphia.

The abbreviation for trace (tr) is used to indicate fatty acid and vitamin values that would round to zero with the number of decimal places carried in these tables. For other components that would round to zero, a zero is used.

Dashes show that no basis could be found for inputting a value, although there was some reason to believe a measurable amount of the constituent might be present.

Other abbreviations used are as follows:

average	oz-ounce
c-cup	%-percent
diam-diameter	pc-piece
hp-heaping	qt-quart
jc-juice	sc-section
lb-pound	serv-serving
lg-large	sl-slice
lv-leaves	sm-small
med-medium	sq-square
tbsp-tablespoon	

TABLE C.1   Nutritive Values of the Edible Parts of Food

Food	Weight, gm	Approximate Measure	Food Energy, Cal.	Protein, gm	Fat (total lipid), gm
Almonds, shelled	142	1 c	850	26	77
Apple, raw	150	1 med	70	tr	tr
Apple brown betty	230	1 c	345	4	8
Apple butter	20	1 tbsp	37	tr	tr
Apple juice, bottled or canned	249	1 c	120	tr	tr
Applesauce, sweetened	254	1 c	230	1	tr
Apricots:					
raw	114	3 apricots	55	1	tr
syrup pack	259	1 c	220	2	tr
dried, uncooked	150	1 c	390	8	1
dried, cooked	285	1 c	240	5	1
Asparagus:					
fresh, cooked	175	1 c	35	4	tr
canned, green	96	6 spears	20	2	tr
Bacon:					
broiled or fried	16	2 sl	100	5	8
Canadian, cooked	21	1 sl	65	6	4
Banana, raw	150	1 med	85	1	tr
Beans:					
baked, with tomato sauce, with pork	261	1 c	320	16	7
baked, with tomato sauce, without pork	261	1 c	310	16	1
green snap, fresh cooked	125	1 c	30	2	tr
green snap, canned	239	1 c	45	2	tr
Lima, fresh, cooked	160	1 c	180	12	1
red kidney, canned	256	1 c	230	15	1
wax, canned	125	1 c	27	2	tr
Beef, cooked:					
cuts, braised, simmered, pot-roasted	72	2.5 oz, lean	140	22	5
cuts, braised, simmered, pot-roasted	85	3 oz, lean and fat	245	23	16
hamburger, ground lean	85	3 oz	185	23	10
hamburger, regular	85	3 oz	245	21	17
rib roast	51	1.8 oz, lean	125	14	7
rib roast	85	3 oz, lean and fat	375	17	34
round	78	2.7 oz, lean	125	24	3
round	85	3 oz, lean and fat	165	25	7
steak, sirloin	56	2 oz, lean	115	18	4
steak, sirloin	85	3 oz, lean and fat	330	20	27
Beef, canned:					
corned beef	85	3 oz	185	22	10
corned beef hash	85	3 oz	155	7	10

(*continued*)

TABLE C.1　Nutritive Values of the Edible Parts of Food (continued)

	Fatty Acids										
	Unsaturated										
Saturated (total), gm	Oleic, gm	Linoleic, gm	Carbohydrate, gm	Calcium, mg	Iron, mg	Vitamin A Value, IU	Thiamin mg	Riboflavin, mg	Niacin, mg	Ascorbic Acid, mg
6	52	15	28	332	6.7	0	0.34	1.31	5.0	tr
—	—	—	18	8	0.4	50	0.04	0.02	0.1	3
4	3	tr	68	41	1.4	230	0.13	0.10	0.9	3
—	—	—	9	3	0.1	0	tr	tr	tr	tr
—	—	—	30	15	1.5	—	0.01	0.04	0.2	2
—	—	—	60	10	1.3	100	0.05	0.03	0.1	3
—	—	—	14	18	0.5	2,890	0.03	0.04	0.7	10
—	—	—	57	28	0.8	4,510	0.05	0.06	0.9	10
—	—	—	100	100	8.2	16,350	0.02	0.23	4.9	19
—	—	—	62	63	5.1	8,550	0.01	0.13	2.8	8
—	—	—	6	37	1.0	1,580	0.27	0.32	2.4	46
—	—	—	3	18	1.8	770	0.06	0.10	0.8	14
3	4	1	1	2	0.5	0	0.08	0.05	0.8	—
—	—	—	3	4	—	0	0.18	0.03	1.1	0
—	—	—	23	8	0.7	190	0.05	0.06	0.7	10
3	3	1	50	141	4.7	340	0.20	0.08	1.5	5
—	—	—	60	177	5.2	160	0.18	0.09	1.5	5
—	—	—	7	62	0.8	680	0.08	0.11	0.6	16
—	—	—	10	81	2.9	690	0.08	0.10	0.7	9
—	—	—	32	75	4.0	450	0.29	0.16	2.0	28
—	—	—	42	74	4.6	tr	0.13	0.10	1.5	—
—	—	—	6	45	2.1	150	0.05	0.06	0.5	6
2	2	tr	0	10	2.7	10	0.04	0.16	3.3	—
8	7	tr	0	10	2.9	30	0.04	0.18	3.5	—
5	4	tr	0	10	3.0	20	0.08	0.20	5.1	—
8	8	tr	0	9	2.7	30	0.07	0.18	4.6	—
3	3	tr	0	6	1.8	10	0.04	0.11	2.6	—
16	15	1	0	8	2.2	70	0.05	0.13	3.1	—
1	1	tr	0	10	3.0	tr	0.06	0.18	4.3	—
3	3	tr	0	11	3.2	10	0.06	0.19	4.5	—
2	2	tr	0	7	2.2	10	0.05	0.14	3.6	—
13	12	1	0	9	2.5	50	0.05	0.16	4.0	—
5	4	tr	0	17	3.7	20	0.01	0.20	2.9	—
5	4	tr	9	11	1.7	—	0.01	0.08	1.8	—

Food	Weight, gm	Approximate Measure	Food Energy, Cal.	Protein, gm	Fat (total lipid), gm
Beef, dried or chipped	57	2 oz	115	19	4
Beef and vegetable stew	235	1 c	210	15	10
Beef pot pie	227	1 pie, 4 $\frac{1}{4}$" diam	560	23	33
Beer, av 3.6% alcohol	240	1 c	100	1	0
Beets, cooked, diced	165	1 c	50	2	tr
Beet greens, cooked	100	$\frac{1}{2}$ c	27	2	tr
Beverages, carbonated:					
cola type	240	1 c	95	0	0
ginger ale	230	1 c	70	0	0
Biscuit, enriched flour	38	1, 2 $\frac{1}{2}$" diam	140	3	6
Blackberries, raw	144	1 c	85	2	1
Blueberries, raw	140	1 c	85	1	1
Bluefish, baked or broiled	85	3 oz	135	22	4
Bouillon cubes	4	1 cube	5	1	tr
Brains, all kinds, raw	85	3 oz	106	9	7
Bran, raisin	28	$\frac{2}{3}$ c	99	2	tr
Bran flakes, 40%	28	1 oz	85	3	1
Brazilnuts, shelled	140	1 c	915	20	94
Bread:					
Boston, enriched	48	1 sl	100	3	1
cracked-wheat	23	1 sl	60	2	1
French or Vienna, enriched	454	1 lb	1,315	41	14
Italian, enriched	454	1 lb	1,250	41	4
raisin, enriched	23	1 sl	60	2	1
rye, American	23	1 sl	55	2	tr
rye, pumpernickle	454	1 lb	1,115	41	5
white, enriched	23	1 sl	60	2	1
white, unenriched	23	1 sl	60	2	1
whole wheat	23	1 sl	55	2	1
Breadcrumbs, dry	88	1 c	345	11	4
Broccoli, cooked	150	1 c	40	5	tr
Brussels sprouts, cooked	130	1 c	45	5	1
Buckwheat flour, light	98	1 c	342	6	1
Butter:					
stick, $\frac{1}{8}$	14	1 tbsp	100	tr	11
pat or square	7	1 pat	50	tr	6
Buttermilk, cultured, skim	246	1 c	90	9	tr

(continued)

TABLE C.1 Nutritive Values of the Edible Parts of Food (continued)

| | *Fatty Acids* | | | | | | | | | | |
| | **Unsaturated** | | | | | | | | | | |
Saturated (total), gm	**Oleic, gm**	**Linoleic, gm**	**Carbohydrate, gm**	**Calcium, mg**	**Iron, mg**	**Vitamin A Value, IU**	**Thiamin mg**	**Riboflavin, mg**	**Niacin, mg**	**Ascorbic Acid, mg**
2	2	tr	0	11	2.9	—	0.04	0.18	2.2	—
5	4	tr	15	28	2.8	2,310	0.13	0.17	4.4	15
9	20	2	43	32	4.1	1,860	0.25	0.27	4.5	7
—	—	—	9	12	tr	—	0.01	0.07	1.6	—
—	—	—	12	23	0.8	40	0.04	0.07	0.5	11
—	—	—	6	118[1]	3.2	6,700	0.08	0.18	0.4	34
—	—	—	24	—	—	0	0	0	0	0
—	—	—	18	—	—	0	0	0	0	0
2	3	1	17	46	0.6	tr	0.08	0.08	0.7	tr
—	—	—	19	46	1.3	290	0.05	0.06	0.5	30
—	—	—	21	21	1.4	140	0.04	0.08	0.6	20
—	—	—	0	25	0.6	40	0.09	0.08	1.6	—
—	—	—	tr	—	—	—	—	—	—	—
—	—	—	1	14	3.1	0	0.20	0.22	3.7	15
—	—	—	22	0	1.0	0	0.10	—	1.1	0
—	—	—	23	20	1.2	0	0.11	0.05	1.7	0
19	45	24	15	260	4.8	tr	1.34	0.17	2.2	—
—	—	—	22	43	0.9	0	0.05	0.03	0.6	0
—	—	—	12	20	0.3	tr	0.03	0.02	0.3	tr
3	8	2	251	195	10.0	tr	1.26	0.98	11.3	tr
tr	1	2	256	77	10.0	0	1.31	0.93	11.7	0
—	—	—	12	16	0.3	tr	0.01	0.02	0.2	tr
—	—	—	12	17	0.4	0	0.04	0.02	0.3	0
—	—	—	241	381	10.9	0	1.05	0.63	5.4	0
tr	tr	tr	12	16	0.6	tr	0.06	0.04	0.5	tr
tr	tr	tr	12	16	0.2	tr	0.02	0.02	0.3	tr
tr	tr	tr	11	23	0.5	tr	0.06	0.03	0.7	tr
1	2	1	65	107	3.2	tr	0.19	0.26	3.1	tr
—	—	—	7	132	1.2	3,750	0.14	0.29	1.2	135
—	—	—	8	42	1.4	680	0.10	0.18	1.1	113
—	—	—	78	11	1.0	0	0.08	0.04	0.4	0
6	4	tr	tr	3	0	460[2]	—	—	—	0
3	2	tr	tr	1	0	230[2]	—	—	—	0
—	—	—	13	298	0.1	10	0.09	0.44	0.2	2

[1] *Calcium may not be usable because of presence of oxalic acid.*
[2] *Year-round average.*

Food	Weight, gm	Approximate Measure	Food Energy, Cal.	Protein, gm	Fat (total lipid), gm
Cabbage:					
raw	100	1 c	25	1	tr
cooked	170	1 c	35	2	tr
Chinese, raw	100	1 c	15	1	tr
Cakes:					
angelfood	40	2" sc, $\frac{1}{12}$ of 8" diam	110	3	tr
chocolate, chocolate icing	120	2" sc, $\frac{1}{16}$ of 10" diam	445	5	20
cupcake, with chocolate icing	50	1, 2 $\frac{3}{4}$" diam	185	2	7
cupcake, without icing	40	1, 2 $\frac{3}{4}$" diam	145	2	6
fruit cake, dark	30	1 pc, 2" × 2" × $\frac{1}{2}$"	115	1	5
plain, with chocolate icing	100	2" sc, $\frac{1}{16}$ of 10" diam	370	4	14
plain, without icing	55	1 pc, 3" × 2" × 1 $\frac{1}{2}$" diam	200	2	8
pound	30	1 sl, 2 $\frac{3}{4}$" × 3" × $\frac{5}{8}$"	140	2	9
sponge	40	2" sc, $\frac{1}{12}$ of 8" diam	120	3	2
Candy:					
butterscotch	5	1 pc	21	0	tr
caramels	28	1 oz	115	1	3
chocolate almond bar	32	1 bar	176	3	12
chocolate, milk	28	1 oz	150	2	9
chocolate cream	13	1 pc	51	1	2
fondant	11	1 av	4	—	—
fudge, plain	28	1 oz	115	1	3
hard	28	1 oz	110	0	tr
marshmallow	28	1 oz	90	1	tr
peanut brittle	25	1 pc	110	2	4
Cantaloupe, raw	385	$\frac{1}{4}$ of 5" melon	60	1	tr
Carrots:					
raw	110	1 c, grated	45	1	tr
cooked	145	1 c, diced	45	1	tr
Cashew nuts	135	1 c	760	23	62
Cauliflower:					
raw	100	1 c	25	2	tr
cooked	120	1 c	25	3	tr
Celery:					
raw	100	1 c, diced	15	1	tr
cooked	65	$\frac{1}{2}$ c, diced	12	1	tr

[3]*If the fat used in the recipe is butter or fortified margarine, the vitamin A value for chocolate cake with fudge icing will be 490 IU; 100 IU for fruit cake; 300 IU for plain cake without icing; 220 IU per cupcake; 400 IU for plain cake with icing; 220 IU per cupcake with icing; and 300 IU for pound cake.*

(continued)

TABLE C.1 Nutritive Values of the Edible Parts of Food (continued)

| | *Fatty Acids* | | | | | | | | | | |
| | **Unsaturated** | | | | | | | | | | |
Saturated (total), gm	Oleic, gm	Linoleic, gm	Carbohydrate, gm	Calcium, mg	Iron, mg	Vitamin A Value, IU	Thiamin mg	Riboflavin, mg	Niacin, mg	Ascorbic Acid, mg
—	—	—	5	49	0.4	130	0.05	0.05	0.3	47
—	—	—	7	75	0.5	220	0.07	0.07	0.5	56
—	—	—	3	43	0.6	150	0.05	0.04	0.6	25
—	—	—	24	4	0.1	0	tr	0.06	0.1	0
8	10	1	67	84	1.2	190^3	0.03	0.12	0.3	tr
2	4	tr	30	32	0.3	90^3	0.01	0.04	0.1	tr
1	3	tr	22	26	0.2	70^3	0.01	0.03	0.1	tr
1	3	1	18	22	0.8	40^3	0.04	0.04	0.2	tr
5	7	1	59	63	0.6	180^3	0.02	0.09	0.2	tr
2	5	1	31	35	0.2	90^3	0.01	0.05	0.1	tr
2	5	1	14	6	0.2	80^3	0.01	0.03	0.1	0
1	1	tr	22	12	0.5	180^3	0.02	0.06	0.1	tr
—	—	—	4	1	0.1	0	0	tr	tr	0
2	1	tr	22	42	0.4	tr	0.01	0.05	tr	tr
—	—	—	16	68	0.9	40	0.03	0.16	0.3	tr
5	3	tr	16	65	0.3	80	0.02	0.09	0.1	tr
—	—	—	9	—	—	—	—	—	—	—
—	—	—	10	—	—	—	—	—	—	—
2	1	tr	21	22	0.3	tr	0.01	0.03	0.1	tr
—	—	—	28	6	0.5	0	0	0	0	0
—	—	—	23	5	0.5	0	0	tr	tr	0
—	—	—	18	10	0.5	7	0.02	0.12	1.2	0
—	—	—	14	27	0.8	$6,540^4$	0.08	0.06	1.2	63
—	—	—	11	41	0.8	12,100	0.06	0.06	0.7	9
—	—	—	10	48	0.9	15,220	0.08	0.07	0.7	9
10	43	4	40	51	5.1	140	0.58	0.33	2.4	—
—	—	—	5	22	1.1	90	0.11	0.10	0.6	69
—	—	—	5	25	0.8	70	0.11	0.10	0.7	66
—	—	—	4	39	0.3	240	0.03	0.03	0.3	9
—	—	—	2	33	0.3	0	0.03	0.02	0.2	3

[4]*Value based on varieties with orange-colored flesh; for green-fleshed varieties value is about 540 IU per $1/2$ melon.*

Food	Weight, gm	Approximate Measure	Food Energy, Cal.	Protein, gm	Fat (total lipid), gm
Cheese:					
blue or Roquefort type	28	1 oz	105	6	9
Camembert	28	1 oz	84	5	7
Cheddar or American	17	1" cube	70	4	5
Cheddar or American	112	1 c, grated	445	28	36
Cheddar, process	28	1 oz	105	7	9
foods, Cheddar	28	1 oz	90	6	7
cottage, creamed	225	1 c	240	31	9
cream	15	1 tbsp	55	1	6
Limburger	28	1 oz	97	6	8
Parmesan	28	1 oz	110	10	7
Swiss	28	1 oz	105	8	8
Cherries:					
raw, sweet, with stems[5]	130	1 c	80	2	tr
canned, red, sour, pitted, heavy syrup	260	1 c	230	2	1
Chicken:					
broiled	85	3 oz, flesh only	115	20	3
canned, boneless	85	3 oz	170	18	10
creamed	118	$\frac{1}{2}$ c, sm serv	208	18	12
fryer, breast, fried	94	$\frac{1}{2}$ breast, with bone	155	25	5
fryer, leg, fried	59	with bone	90	12	4
pot pie	227	1 pie, 4 $\frac{1}{4}$" diam	535	23	31
roasted	80	2 sl, 3" × 3" × $\frac{1}{4}$"	158	23	7
Chili con carne (no beans)	255	1 c	510	26	38
Chili sauce	17	1 tbsp	20	tr	tr
Chocolate:					
bitter or baking	28	1 oz	145	3	15
sweet	28	1 oz	150	1	10
Chocolate-flavored milk drink	250	1 c	190	8	6
Chocolate syrup	20	1 tbsp	50	tr	tr
Clams:					
raw	85	3 oz	65	11	1
canned, solids and liquid	85	3 oz	45	7	1
Cocoa beverage with milk	242	1 c	235	9	11
Coconut:					
dried, sweetened	62	1 c, shredded	340	2	24
fresh	97	1 c, shredded	335	3	34
Coleslaw	120	1 c	120	1	9

[5]*Measure and weight apply to entire vegetable or fruit including parts not usually eaten.*

(*continued*)

TABLE C.1 Nutritive Values of the Edible Parts of Food (continued)

Fatty Acids

| Saturated (total), gm | Unsaturated | | Carbohydrate, gm | Calcium, mg | Iron, mg | Vitamin A Value, IU | Thiamin mg | Riboflavin, mg | Niacin, mg | Ascorbic Acid, mg |
	Oleic, gm	Linoleic, gm								
5	3	tr	1	89	0.1	350	0.01	0.17	0.1	0
—	—	—	1	29	0.1	286	0.01	0.21	0.3	0
3	2	tr	tr	128	0.2	220	tr	0.08	tr	0
20	12	1	2	840	1.1	1,470	0.03	0.51	0.1	0
5	3	tr	1	219	0.3	350	tr	0.12	tr	0
4	2	tr	2	162	0.2	280	0.01	0.16	tr	0
5	3	tr	7	212	0.7	380	0.07	0.56	0.2	0
3	2	tr	tr	9	tr	230	tr	0.04	tr	0
—	—	—	1	165	0.2	358	0.02	0.14	0.1	0
—	—	—	1	325	0.1	297	tr	0.20	0.1	0
4	3	tr	1	262	0.3	320	tr	0.11	tr	0
—	—	—	20	26	0.5	130	0.06	0.07	0.5	12
—	—	—	59	36	0.8	1,680	0.07	0.06	0.4	13
1	1	1	0	8	1.4	80	0.05	0.16	7.4	—
3	4	2	0	18	1.3	200	0.03	0.11	3.7	3
—	—	—	7	83	1.1	328	0.04	0.18	3.8	tr
1	2	1	1	9	1.3	70	0.04	0.17	11.2	—
1	2	1	tr	6	0.9	50	0.03	0.15	2.7	—
10	15	3	42	68	3.0	3,020	0.25	0.26	4.1	5
—	—	—	0	16	1.7	0	0.06	0.14	7.2	0
18	17	1	15	97	3.6	380	0.05	0.31	5.6	—
—	—	—	4	3	0.1	240	0.02	0.01	0.3	3
8	6	tr	8	22	1.9	20	0.01	0.07	0.4	0
6	4	tr	16	27	0.4	tr	0.01	0.04	0.1	tr
3	2	tr	27	270	0.4	210	0.09	0.41	0.2	2
tr	tr	tr	13	3	0.3	—	tr	0.01	0.1	0
—	—	—	2	59	5.2	90	0.08	0.15	1.1	8
—	—	—	2	47	3.5	—	0.01	0.09	0.9	—
6	4	tr	26	286	0.9	390	0.09	0.45	0.4	2
21	2	tr	33	10	1.2	0	0.02	0.02	0.2	0
29	2	tr	9	13	1.6	0	0.05	0.02	0.5	3
2	2	5	9	52	0.5	180	0.06	0.06	0.3	35

Food	Weight, gm	Approximate Measure	Food Energy, Cal.	Protein, gm	Fat (total lipid), gm
Cookies:					
plain and assorted	25	1 cooky, 3" diam	120	1	5
wafers	10	2 wafers, 2 $\frac{1}{8}$" diam	49	1	2
Corn:					
fresh, cooked	140	1 ear, 50 long	70	3	1
canned	256	1 c	170	5	2
Corn flakes	28	1 oz	110	2	tr
Corn grits:					
enriched, cooked	242	1 c	120	3	tr
unenriched, cooked	242	1 c	120	3	tr
Corn muffin, enriched	48	1 med, 2 $\frac{3}{4}$ diam"	150	3	5
Cornmeal, white or yellow, dry:					
enriched	145	1 c	525	11	2
unenriched	118	1 c	420	11	5
Crabmeat, canned	85	3 oz	85	15	2
Crackers:					
Graham	14	2 med	55	1	1
saltines	8	2 crackers	35	1	1
soda, plain	11	2 crackers	50	1	1
Cranberry sauce, sweetened	277	1 c	405	tr	1
Cream:					
half-and-half	15	1 tbsp	20	tr	2
heavy or whipping	15	1 tbsp	55	tr	6
light or coffee	15	1 tbsp	30	tr	3
Cucumber, raw	50	6 sl	5	tr	tr
Custard, baked	248	1 c	285	13	14
Dandelion greens, cooked	180	1 c	60	4	1
Dates, fresh and dried	178	1 c	490	4	1
Doughnut, cake type	32	1 doughnut	125	1	6
Eggs:					
raw, whole	50	1 med	80	6	6
boiled	100	2 med	160	13	12
scrambled	64	1 med	110	7	8
Farina, enriched, cooked	238	1 c	100	3	tr
Fats, cooking, vegetable	12.5	1 tbsp	110	0	12

[6]*Based on yellow varieties; white varieties contain only a trace of cryptoxanthin and carotenes, the pigments in corn that have biological activity.*
[7]*Vitamin A value based on yellow product; white product contains only a trace.*
[8]*Iron, thiamine, riboflavin, and niacin are based on the minimal level of enrichment specified in standards of identify promulgated under the Federal Food, Drug, and Cosmetic Act.*
[9]*Based on recipe using white cornmeal; if yellow cornmeal is used, the vitamin A value is 140 IU per muffin.*

(continued)

TABLE C.1   Nutritive Values of the Edible Parts of Food (continued)

Fatty Acids

	Unsaturated									
Saturated (total), gm	Oleic, gm	Linoleic, gm	Carbohydrate, gm	Calcium, mg	Iron, mg	Vitamin A Value, IU	Thiamin, mg	Riboflavin, mg	Niacin, mg	Ascorbic Acid, mg
—	—	—	18	9	0.2	20	0.01	0.01	0.1	tr
—	—	—	7	—	—	—	—	—	—	—
—	—	—	16	2	0.5	310^6	0.09	0.08	1.0	7
—	—	—	40	10	1.0	690^6	0.07	0.12	2.3	13
—	—	—	24	5	0.4	0	0.12	0.02	0.6	0
—	—	—	27	2	0.7^8	150^7	0.10^8	0.07^8	1.0^8	0
—	—	—	27	2	0.2	150^7	0.05	0.02	0.5	0
2	2	tr	23	50	0.8	80^9	0.09	0.11	0.8	tr
tr	1	1	114	9	4.2^8	640^7	0.64^8	0.38^8	5.1^8	0
1	2	2	87	24	2.8	600^7	0.45	0.13	2.4	0
—	—	—	1	38	0.7	—	0.07	0.07	1.6	—
—	—	—	10	6	0.2	0	0.01	0.03	0.2	0
—	—	—	6	2	0.1	0	tr	tr	0.1	0
tr	1	tr	8	2	0.2	0	tr	tr	0.1	0
—	—	—	104	17	0.6	40	0.03	0.03	0.1	5
1	1	tr	1	16	tr	70	tr	0.02	tr	tr
3	2	tr	tr	11	tr	230	tr	0.02	tr	tr
2	1	tr	1	15	tr	130	tr	0.02	tr	tr
—	—	—	2	8	0.2	tr	0.02	0.02	0.1	6
6	5	1	28	278	1.0	870	0.10	0.47	0.2	1
—	—	—	12	252	3.2	21,060	0.24	0.29	—	32
—	—	—	130	105	5.3	90	0.16	0.17	3.9	0
1	4	tr	16	13	0.4^{10}	30	0.05^{10}	0.05^{10}	0.4^{10}	tr
2	3	tr	tr	27	1.1	590	0.05	0.15	tr	0
4	5	1	1	54	2.3	1,180	0.09	0.28	0.1	0
3	3	tr	1	51	1.1	690	0.05	0.18	tr	0
—	—	—	21	10	0.7^{11}	0	0.11^{11}	0.07^{11}	1.0^{11}	0
3	8	1	0	0	0	—	0	0	0	0

[10]Based on product made with enriched flour. With unenriched flour, approximate values per doughnut are: iron, 0.2 mg; thiamine, 0.01 mg; riboflavin, 0.03 mg; niacin, 0.2 mg.

[11]Iron, thiamine, riboflavin, and niacin are based on the minimum levels of enrichment specified in standards of identity promulgated under the Federal Food, Drug, and Cosmetic Act.

Food	Weight, gm	Approximate Measure	Food Energy, Cal.	Protein, gm	Fat (total lipid), gm
Figs, dried	21	1 fig	60	1	tr
Fig bars	16	1 sm	55	1	1
Fishsticks, breaded, cooked	227	10 sticks	400	38	20
Fruit cocktail, canned	256	1 c	195	1	1
Gelatin, dry, plain	10	1 tbsp	35	9	tr
Gelatin dessert:					
plain	239	1 c	140	4	0
with fruit	241	1 c	160	3	tr
Gingerbread	55	1 pc, 2" × 2" × 2"	175	2	6
Grapefruit:					
raw, white	285	$\frac{1}{2}$ med, 4 $\frac{1}{4}$" diam	55	1	tr
raw, white	194	1 c, sc	75	1	tr
juice, canned	247	1 c, unsweetened	100	1	tr
juice, dehydrated, water added	247	1 c	100	1	tr
Grapes:					
Concord, Niagara	153	1 c	65	1	1
Muscat, Thompson, Tokay	160	1 c	95	1	tr
Grape juice, bottled	254	1 c	165	1	tr
Grapenut flakes	28	1 oz	110	3	tr
Gravy, meat, brown	18	1 tbsp	41	tr	4
Haddock, fried	85	3 oz	140	17	5
Heart, beef, lean, braised	85	3 oz	160	27	5
Herring:					
Atlantic, broiled	85	1 med	217	21	14
smoked, kippered	100	$\frac{1}{2}$ fish	211	22	13
Honey, strained or extracted	21	1 tbsp	65	tr	0
Honeydew melon	150	1 wedge, 20 × 6 $\frac{1}{2}$"	48	1	0
Ice cream, plain	71	1 sl, or $\frac{1}{8}$ qt brick	145	3	9
Ice milk	187	1 c	285	9	10
Jams and preserves	20	1 tbsp	55	tr	tr
Jellies	20	1 tbsp	55	tr	tr
Kale, cooked	110	1 c	30	4	1
Kohlrabi, cooked	75	$\frac{1}{2}$ c	23	2	tr
Lamb:					
chop, cooked	137	1 chop, 4.8 oz	400	25	33
leg, roasted	71	2.5 oz, lean	130	20	5
shoulder, roasted	64	2.3 oz, lean	130	17	6
Lard	14	1 tbsp	125	0	14
Lemon	106	1 med	20	1	tr

(*continued*)

TABLE C.1 Nutritive Values of the Edible Parts of Food (continued)

| Fatty Acids | | | | | | | | | | |
Saturated (total), gm	Unsaturated Oleic, gm	Linoleic, gm	Carbohydrate, gm	Calcium, mg	Iron, mg	Vitamin A Value, IU	Thiamin mg	Riboflavin, mg	Niacin, mg	Ascorbic Acid, mg
—	—	—	15	26	0.6	20	0.02	0.02	0.1	0
—	—	—	12	12	0.2	20	0.01	0.01	0.1	tr
5	4	10	15	25	0.9	—	0.09	0.16	3.6	—
—	—	—	50	23	1.0	360	0.04	0.03	1.1	5
—	—	—	—	—	—	—	—	—	—	—
—	—	—	34	—	—	—	—	—	—	—
—	—	—	40	—	—	—	—	—	—	—
1	4	tr	29	37	1.3	50	0.06	0.06	0.5	0
—	—	—	14	22	0.6	10	0.05	0.02	0.2	52
—	—	—	20	31	0.8	20	0.07	0.03	0.3	72
—	—	—	24	20	1.0	20	0.07	0.04	0.4	84
—	—	—	24	22	0.2	20	0.10	0.05	0.5	92
—	—	—	15	15	0.4	100	0.05	0.03	0.2	3
—	—	—	25	17	0.6	140	0.07	0.04	0.4	6
—	—	—	42	28	0.8	—	0.10	0.05	0.6	tr
—	—	—	23	—	1.2	0	0.13	—	1.6	0
—	—	—	2	—	0.2	0	0.15	0.01	tr	—
1	3	tr	5	34	1.0	—	0.03	0.06	2.7	2
—	—	—	1	5	5.0	20	0.21	1.04	6.5	1
—	—	—	0	—	1.2	130	0.01	0.15	3.3	0
—	—	—	0	66	1.4	0	tr	0.28	2.9	0
—	—	—	17	1	0.1	0	tr	0.01	0.1	tr
—	—	—	13	26	0.6	60	0.08	0.05	0.3	34
5	3	tr	15	87	0.1	370	0.03	0.13	0.1	1
6	3	tr	42	292	0.2	390	0.09	0.41	0.2	2
—	—	—	14	4	0.2	tr	tr	0.01	tr	tr
—	—	—	14	4	0.3	tr	tr	0.01	tr	1
—	—	—	4	147	1.3	8,140	—	—	—	68
—	—	—	5	35	0.5	tr	0.03	0.03	0.2	28
18	12	1	0	10	1.5	—	0.14	0.25	5.6	—
3	2	tr	0	9	1.4	—	0.12	0.21	4.4	—
3	2	tr	0	8	1.0	—	0.10	0.18	3.7	—
5	6	1	0	0	0	0	0	0	0	0
—	—	—	6	18	0.4	10	0.03	0.01	0.1	38

Food	Weight, gm	Approximate Measure	Food Energy, Cal.	Protein, gm	Fat (total lipid), gm
Lemon juice, fresh	15	1 tbsp	5	tr	tr
Lettuce:					
head, Iceberg	454	1 head, 4 $\frac{1}{4}$" diam	60	4	tr
leaves	50	2 lg	10	1	tr
Lime juice, fresh	246	1 c	65	1	tr
Liver:					
beef, fried	57	2 oz	130	15	6
calf, cooked	72	2 sl, 3" × 2 $\frac{1}{4}$" × $\frac{3}{8}$"	147	16	7
pork, fried	74	2 sl, 3" × 2 $\frac{1}{4}$" × $\frac{3}{8}$"	170	18	7
Lobster:					
boiled or broiled	334	1($\frac{3}{4}$ lb) + 2 tbsp butter	308	20	25
canned	85	$\frac{1}{2}$ c	75	15	1
Macaroni:					
enriched, cooked	130	1 c	190	6	1
unenriched, cooked	130	1 c	190	6	1
Macaroni & cheese, baked	220	1 c	470	18	24
Mackerel, canned	85	3 oz	155	18	9
Malted milk beverage	270	1 c	280	13	12
Mangos	100	1 sm	66	1	tr
Margarine:					
stick, $\frac{1}{8}$	14	1 tbsp	100	tr	11
pat or sq	7	1 pat	50	tr	6
Metrecal	237	8 oz	225	18	5
Milk:					
whole	244	1 c	160	9	9
nonfat, skim	246	1 c	90	9	tr
dry, nonfat, instant	70	1 c	250	25	tr
condensed	306	1 c	980	25	27
evaporated	252	1 c	345	18	20
Molasses:					
light	20	1 tbsp	50	—	—
blackstrap	20	1 tbsp	45	—	—
Muffins, white, enriched	48	1 med, 2 $\frac{3}{4}$" diam	140	4	5
Mushrooms, canned	244	1 c	40	5	tr
Mustard greens, cooked	140	1 c	35	3	1

[12]*Iron, thiamine, riboflavin, and niacin are based on the minimum levels of enrichment specified in standards of identity promulgated under the Federal Food, Drug, and Cosmetic Act.*

(continued)

TABLE C.1 Nutritive Values of the Edible Parts of Food (continued)

Fatty Acids

	Unsaturated										
Saturated (total), gm	Oleic, gm	Linoleic, gm	Carbohydrate, gm	Calcium, mg	Iron, mg	Vitamin A Value, IU	Thiamin mg	Riboflavin, mg	Niacin, mg	Ascorbic Acid, mg
—	—	—	1	1	tr	tr	tr	tr	tr	7
—	—	—	13	91	2.3	1,500	0.29	0.27	1.3	29
—	—	—	2	34	0.7	950	0.03	0.04	0.2	9
—	—	—	22	22	0.5	30	0.05	0.03	0.3	80
—	—	—	3	6	5.0	30,280	0.15	2.37	9.4	15
—	—	—	3	5	9.0	19,130	0.13	2.39	11.7	15
—	—	—	8	10	15.6	12,070	0.25	2.30	12.4	10
—	—	—	1	80	0.7	920	0.11	0.06	2.3	0
—	—	—	0	55	0.7	—	0.03	0.06	1.9	—
—	—	—	39	14	1.4[12]	0	0.23[12]	0.14[12]	1.9[12]	0
—	—	—	39	14	0.6	0	0.02	0.02	0.5	0
11	10	1	44	398	2.0	950	0.22	0.44	2.0	tr
—	—	—	0	221	1.9	20	0.02	0.28	7.4	—
—	—	—	32	364	0.8	670	0.17	0.56	0.2	2
—	—	—	17	9	0.2	6,350	0.06	0.06	0.9	41
2	6	2	tr	3	0	460[13]	—	—	—	0
1	3	1	tr	1	0	230[13]	—	—	—	0
—	—	—	28	500	3.8	1,250	0.50	0.75	3.8	25
5	3	tr	12	288	0.1	350	0.08	0.42	0.1	2
—	—	—	13	298	0.1	10	0.10	0.44	0.2	2
—	—	—	36	905	0.4	20	0.24	1.25	0.6	5
15	9	1	166	802	0.3	1,090	0.23	1.17	0.5	3
11	7	1	24	635	0.3	820	0.10	0.84	0.5	3
—	—	—	13	33	0.9	—	0.01	0.01	tr	—
—	—	—	11	137	3.2	—	0.02	0.04	0.4	—
1	3	tr	20	50	0.8	50	0.08	0.11	0.7	tr
—	—	—	6	15	1.2	tr	0.04	0.60	4.8	4
—	—	—	6	193	2.5	8,120	0.11	0.19	0.9	68

[13]*Based on the average vitamin A content of fortified margarine. Federal specifications for fortified margarine require a minimum of 15,000 IU of vitamin A per pound.*

Food	Weight, gm	Approximate Measure	Food Energy, Cal.	Protein, gm	Fat (total lipid), gm
Noodles:					
enriched, cooked	160	1 c	200	7	2
unenriched, cooked	160	1 c	200	7	2
Oats, puffed	28	1 oz	115	3	2
Oatmeal, cooked	236	1 c	130	5	2
Oils, salad, corn	14	1 tbsp	125	0	14
Okra, cooked	85	8 pods	25	2	tr
Olives:					
green, pickled	16	4 med	15	tr	2
ripe, pickled	10	3 sm	15	tr	2
Onions:					
raw	110	1 onion, 2 $\frac{1}{2}$" diam	40	2	tr
cooked	210	1 c	60	3	tr
young green	50	6 onions	20	1	tr
Orange:					
navel	180	1 med	60	2	tr
other varieties	210	1 med	75	1	tr
sections	97	$\frac{1}{2}$ c	44	1	tr
juice, fresh	247	1 c	100	1	tr
juice, frozen	248	1 c	110	2	tr
juice, dehydrated, water added	248	1 c	115	1	tr
Orange and grapefruit juice, frozen	248	1 c	110	1	tr
Ocean perch, breaded, fried	85	3 oz	195	16	11
Oyster meat, raw	240	1 c	160	20	4
Oyster stew	230	1 c with 3–4 oysters	200	11	12
Pancakes:					
white, enriched	27	1 cake, 4" diam	60	2	2
buckwheat	27	1 cake, 4" diam	55	2	2
Papayas, raw	182	1 c	70	1	tr
Parsley, raw, chopped	3.5	1 tbsp	1	tr	tr
Parsnips, cooked	155	1 c	100	2	1
Peaches:					
raw	114	1 med	35	1	tr
raw	168	1 c, sliced	65	1	tr
canned, syrup pack	257	1 c	200	1	tr
dried, cooked	270	1 c	220	3	1
frozen	340	12-oz carton	300	1	tr

[14]Iron, thiamine, riboflavin, and niacin are based on the minimum levels of enrichment specified in standards of identity promulgated under the Federal Food, Drug, and Cosmetic Act.

(continued)

TABLE C.1   Nutritive Values of the Edible Parts of Food (continued)

Fatty Acids

| | Unsaturated | | | | | | | | | |
Saturated (total), gm	Oleic, gm	Linoleic, gm	Carbohydrate, gm	Calcium, mg	Iron, mg	Vitamin A Value, IU	Thiamin, mg	Riboflavin, mg	Niacin, mg	Ascorbic Acid, mg
1	1	tr	37	16	1.4[14]	110	0.23[14]	0.14[14]	1.8[14]	0
1	1	tr	37	16	1.0	110	0.04	0.03	0.7	0
tr	1	1	21	50	1.3	0	0.28	0.05	0.5	0
tr	1	1	23	21	1.4	0	0.19	0.05	0.3	0
1	4	7	0	0	0	—	0	0	0	0
—	—	—	5	78	0.4	420	0.11	0.15	0.8	17
tr	2	tr	tr	8	0.2	40	—	—	—	—
tr	2	tr	tr	9	0.1	10	tr	tr	—	—
—	—	—	10	30	0.6	40	0.04	0.04	0.2	11
—	—	—	14	50	0.8	80	0.06	0.06	0.4	14
—	—	—	5	20	0.3	tr	0.02	0.02	0.2	12
—	—	—	16	49	0.5	240	0.12	0.05	0.5	75
—	—	—	19	67	0.3	310	0.16	0.06	0.6	70
—	—	—	11	32	0.4	180	0.08	0.03	0.3	48
—	—	—	23	25	0.5	490	0.22	0.06	0.9	127
—	—	—	27	22	0.2	500	0.21	0.03	0.8	112
—	—	—	27	25	0.5	500	0.20	0.06	0.9	108
—	—	—	26	20	0.2	270	0.16	0.02	0.8	102
—	—	—	6	28	1.1	—	0.08	0.09	1.5	—
—	—	—	8	226	13.2	740	0.33	0.43	6.0	—
—	—	—	11	269	3.3	640	0.13	0.41	1.6	—
tr	1	tr	9	27	0.4	30	0.05	0.06	0.3	tr
1	1	tr	6	59	0.4	60	0.03	0.04	0.2	tr
—	—	—	18	36	0.5	3,190	0.07	0.08	0.5	102
—	—	—	tr	7	0.2	300	tr	0.01	tr	6
—	—	—	23	70	0.9	50	0.11	0.13	0.2	16
—	—	—	10	9	0.5	1,320[15]	0.02	0.05	1.0	7
—	—	—	16	15	0.8	2,230[15]	0.03	0.08	1.6	12
—	—	—	52	10	0.8	1,100	0.02	0.06	1.4	7
—	—	—	58	41	5.1	3,290	0.01	0.15	4.2	6
—	—	—	77	14	1.7	2,210	0.03	0.14	2.4	135[16]

[15]Based on yellow-fleshed varieties; for white-fleshed varieties value is about 50 IU per 114-gm peach and 80 IU per cup of sliced peaches.
[16]Average weight in accordance with commercial freezing practices. For products without added ascorbic acid, value is about 37 mg per 12-oz carton and 50 mg per 16-oz carton; for those with added ascorbic acid, 139 mg per 12-oz carton and 186 mg per 16-oz carton.

Food	Weight, gm	Approximate Measure	Food Energy, Cal.	Protein, gm	Fat (total lipid), gm
Peanuts, roasted	9	1 tbsp	55	2	4
Peanut butter	16	1 tbsp	95	4	8
Pears:					
raw	182	1 med	100	1	1
canned, syrup pack	255	1 c	195	1	1
Peas, green:					
fresh, cooked	160	1 c	115	9	1
canned	249	1 c	165	9	1
Pecans, chopped	7.5	1 tbsp	50	1	5
Peppers, green, raw	62	1 med	15	1	tr
Pickles:					
dill	135	1 pickle, 40" long	15	1	tr
relish	13	1 tbsp	14	tr	tr
sour	30	1 sl, 1 $\frac{1}{2}$" diam $\times$ 10	3	tr	tr
sweet	20	1 pickle, 2 $\frac{3}{4}$" long	30	tr	tr
Pies:					
apple	135	$\frac{1}{7}$ of 9" pie	345	3	15
cherry	135	$\frac{1}{7}$ of 9" pie	355	4	15
custard	130	$\frac{1}{7}$ of 9" pie	280	8	14
lemon meringue	120	$\frac{1}{7}$ of 9" pie	305	4	12
mince	135	$\frac{1}{7}$ of 9" pie	365	3	16
pumpkin	130	$\frac{1}{7}$ of 9" pie	275	5	15
Pie crust, plain, baked	135	1, 9" crust	675	8	45
Pimentos, canned	38	1 med	10	tr	tr
Pineapple:					
raw	140	1 c, diced	75	1	tr
canned, syrup pack	260	1 c, crushed	195	1	tr
canned, syrup pack	122	2 sm sl + 2 tbsp jc	90	tr	tr
juice, canned	249	1 c	135	1	tr
Pizza, cheese	75	5 $\frac{1}{2}$" sector	185	7	6
Plums:					
raw	60	1 plum, 20" diam	25	tr	tr
canned, syrup pack	122	3 plums + 2 tbsp jc	100	tr	tr
Popcorn, popped	14	1 c	65	1	3
Pork:					
chop, cooked	98	1 chop, 3.5 oz	260	16	21
ham, cured	85	3 oz	245	18	19
ham, fresh, lean	107	2 sl, 2" $\times$ 1 $\frac{1}{2}$" $\times$ 1"	254	40	9
boiled ham	57	2 oz	135	11	10

(continued)

TABLE C.1   Nutritive Values of the Edible Parts of Food (continued)

Fatty Acids

	Unsaturated									
Saturated (total), gm	Oleic, gm	Linoleic, gm	Carbohydrate, gm	Calcium, mg	Iron, mg	Vitamin A Value, IU	Thiamin mg	Riboflavin, mg	Niacin, mg	Ascorbic Acid, mg
1	2	1	2	7	0.2	—	0.03	0.01	1.5	0
2	4	2	3	9	0.3	—	0.02	0.02	2.4	0
—	—	—	25	13	0.5	30	0.04	0.07	0.2	7
—	—	—	50	13	0.5	tr	0.03	0.05	0.3	4
—	—	—	19	37	2.9	860	0.44	0.17	3.7	33
—	—	—	31	50	4.2	1,120	0.23	0.13	2.2	22
tr	3	1	1	5	0.2	10	0.06	0.01	0.1	tr
—	—	—	3	6	0.4	260	0.05	0.05	0.3	79
—	—	—	3	35	1.4	140	tr	0.03	tr	8
—	—	—	3	2	0.2	14	0	tr	tr	1
—	—	—	1	8	0.4	93	tr	0.02	tr	2
—	—	—	7	2	0.2	20	tr	tr	tr	1
4	9	1	51	11	0.4	40	0.03	0.02	0.5	1
4	10	1	52	19	0.4	590	0.03	0.23	0.6	1
5	8	1	30	125	0.8	300	0.07	0.21	0.4	0
4	7	1	45	17	0.6	200	0.04	0.10	0.2	4
4	10	1	56	38	1.4	tr	0.09	0.05	0.5	1
5	7	1	32	66	0.6	3,210	0.04	0.15	0.6	tr
10	29	3	59	19	2.3	0	0.27	0.19	2.4	0
—	—	—	2	3	0.6	870	0.01	0.02	0.1	36
—	—	—	19	24	0.7	100	0.12	0.04	0.3	24
—	—	—	50	29	0.8	120	0.20	0.06	0.5	17
—	—	—	24	13	0.4	50	0.09	0.03	0.2	8
—	—	—	34	37	0.7	120	0.12	0.04	0.5	22
2	3	tr	27	107	0.7	290	0.04	0.12	0.7	4
—	—	—	7	7	0.3	140	0.02	0.02	0.3	3
—	—	—	26	11	1.1	1,470	0.03	0.02	0.5	2
2	tr	tr	8	1	0.3	—	—	0.01	0.2	0
8	9	2	0	8	2.2	0	0.63	0.18	3.8	—
7	8	2	0	8	2.2	0	0.40	0.16	3.1	—
—	—	—	0	7	2.5	0	0.69	0.33	5.4	0
4	4	1	0	6	1.6	0	0.25	0.09	1.5	—

Food	Weight, gm	Approximate Measure	Food Energy, Cal.	Protein, gm	Fat (total lipid), gm
Potatoes:					
baked	99	1 med	90	3	tr
French fried	57	10 pc	155	2	7
hash-browned	100	½ c	241	3	12
mashed	195	1 c with milk	125	4	1
mashed	195	1 c with milk & butter	185	4	8
Potato chips	20	10 chips	115	1	8
Pretzels	5	5 sm sticks	20	tr	tr
Prunes:					
dried, uncooked	32	4 prunes	70	1	tr
dried, cooked, syrup	270	1 c (17–18 prunes)	295	2	1
juice, canned	256	1 c	200	1	tr
Puddings:					
chocolate	144	½ c	219	5	7
lemon snow	130	1 serv	114	3	tr
tapioca	132	½ c	181	5	5
vanilla	248	1 c	275	9	10
Pumpkin, canned	228	1 c	75	2	1
Radishes, raw	40	4 sm	5	tr	tr
Raisins, dried	160	1 c	460	4	tr
Raspberries, red, raw	123	1 c	70	1	1
Rhubarb, cooked, sugar added	272	1 c	385	1	tr
Rice:					
parboiled, cooked	176	1 c	185	4	tr
puffed	14	1 c	55	1	tr
white, cooked	168	1 c	185	3	tr
Rice flakes	30	1 c	115	2	tr
Rolls:					
plain, enriched	38	12 per lb	115	3	2
plain, unenriched	38	12 per lb	115	3	2
sweet	43	1 roll	135	4	4
Rutabagas, cooked	100	½ c	38	1	tr
Rye flour, light	80	1 c	285	8	1
Salads:					
apple, celery, walnut	154	3 hp tbsp, 2 lv lettuce	137	2	8
carrot & raisin	134	3 hp tbsp, 2 lv lettuce	153	2	6

(continued)

TABLE C.1   Nutritive Values of the Edible Parts of Food (continued)

Fatty Acids

Saturated (total), gm	Unsaturated		Carbohydrate, gm	Calcium, mg	Iron, mg	Vitamin A Value, IU	Thiamin mg	Riboflavin, mg	Niacin, mg	Ascorbic Acid, mg
	Oleic, gm	Linoleic, gm								
—	—	—	21	9	0.7	tr	0.10	0.04	1.7	20
2	2	4	20	9	0.7	tr	0.07	0.04	1.8	12
—	—	—	32	18	1.2	30	0.08	0.06	1.7	7
—	—	—	25	47	0.8	50	0.16	0.10	2.0	19
4	3	tr	24	47	0.8	330	0.16	0.10	1.9	18
2	2	4	10	8	0.4	tr	0.04	0.01	1.0	3
—	—	—	4	1	0	0	tr	tr	tr	0
—	—	—	18	14	1.1	440	0.02	0.04	0.4	1
—	—	—	78	60	4.5	1,860	0.08	0.18	1.7	2
—	—	—	49	36	10.5	—	0.02	0.03	1.1	4
—	—	—	37	147	0.2	196	0.05	0.22	0.2	0
—	—	—	27	4	0.1	0	tr	0.02	tr	10
—	—	—	28	151	0.6	195	0.05	0.21	0.6	0
5	3	tr	39	290	0.1	390	0.07	0.40	0.1	2
—	—	—	18	57	0.9	14,590	0.07	0.12	1.3	12
—	—	—	1	12	0.4	tr	0.01	0.01	0.1	10
—	—	—	124	99	5.6	30	0.18	0.13	0.9	2
—	—	—	17	27	1.1	160	0.04	0.11	1.1	31
—	—	—	98	212	1.6	220	0.06	0.15	0.7	17
—	—	—	41	33	1.4[17]	0	0.19[17]	0.02[17]	2.0[17]	0
—	—	—	13	3	0.3	0	0.06	0.01	0.6	0
—	—	—	41	17	1.5[17]	0	0.19[17]	0.01[17]	1.6[17]	0
—	—	—	26	9	0.5	0	0.10	0.02	1.6	0
tr	1	tr	20	28	0.7	tr	0.11	0.07	0.8	tr
tr	1	tr	20	28	0.3	tr	0.02	0.03	0.3	tr
1	2	tr	21	37	0.3	30	0.03	0.06	0.4	0
—	—	—	9	55	0.4	330	0.07	0.08	0.9	36
—	—	—	62	18	0.9	0	0.12	0.06	0.5	0
—	—	—	16	32	0.8	355	0.08	0.08	0.4	5
—	—	—	28	48	1.5	4,708	0.08	0.08	0.5	6

[17]*Iron, thiamine, and niacin are based on the minimum levels of enrichment specified in standards of identity promulgated under the Federal Food, Drug, and Cosmetic Act. Riboflavin based on unenriched rice. When the minimum level of enrichment for riboflavin specified in the standards of identity becomes effective the value will be 0.12 mg per cup of parboiled rice and of white rice.*

Food	Weight, gm	Approximate Measure	Food Energy, Cal.	Protein, gm	Fat (total lipid), gm
fruit, fresh	195	3 hp tbsp, 2 lv lettuce	174	2	11
gelatin with fruit	188	1 sq, 2 lv lettuce	139	2	6
gelatin with vegetable	164	1 sq, 2 lv lettuce	115	2	6
lettuce, tomato, mayonnaise	115	4 lv lettuce, 3 sl tomato	80	2	6
potato	123	½ c, French dressing	184	2	11
Salad dressings:					
blue cheese	16	1 tbsp	80	1	8
commercial, plain	15	1 tbsp	65	tr	6
French	15	1 tbsp	60	tr	6
home cooked, boiled	17	1 tbsp	30	1	2
mayonnaise	15	1 tbsp	110	tr	12
Thousand Island	15	1 tbsp	75	tr	8
Salmon, pink, canned	85	3 oz	120	17	5
Sardines, Atlantic	85	3 oz	175	20	9
Sauerkraut, canned	235	1 c	45	2	tr
Sausage:					
bologna	227	8 sl	690	27	62
frankfurter, cooked	51	1 frankfurter	155	6	14
liverwurst	30	1 sl, 3" diam × ¼"	79	5	6
pork, links or patty, cooked	113	4 oz	540	21	50
Vienna	18	1 av, 2" × ¾" diam	39	3	3
Scallops, fried	145	5–6 med pc	427	24	28
Shad, baked	85	3 oz	170	20	10
Sherbet, orange	193	1 c	260	2	2
Shortbread	16	2 pc, 58 per lb	78	1	3
Shrimp, canned	85	3 oz	100	21	1
Syrups, table blends	20	1 tbsp	60	0	0
Soups:					
bean	250	1 c	170	8	6
beef	250	1 c	100	6	4
beef noodle	250	1 c	70	4	3
beef bouillon, broth, consomme	240	1 c	30	5	0
chicken	250	1 c	75	4	2
chicken noodle	250	1 c	65	4	2
clam chowder	255	1 c	85	2	3
cream, mushroom	240	1 c	135	2	10

(*continued*)

TABLE C.1	Nutritive Values of the Edible Parts of Food (continued)

Fatty Acids

	Unsaturated									
Saturated (total), gm	Oleic, gm	Linoleic, gm	Carbohydrate, gm	Calcium, mg	Iron, mg	Vitamin A Value, IU	Thiamin mg	Riboflavin, mg	Niacin, mg	Ascorbic Acid, mg
—	—	—	21	45	0.8	685	0.08	0.09	0.4	32
—	—	—	22	23	0.5	391	0.04	0.05	0.3	16
—	—	—	15	24	0.5	1,977	0.04	0.06	0.3	8
—	—	—	7	20	0.8	1,115	0.06	0.07	0.5	19
—	—	—	21	21	0.8	243	0.07	0.04	0.8	16
2	2	4	1	13	tr	30	tr	0.02	tr	tr
1	1	3	2	2	tr	30	tr	tr	tr	—
1	1	3	3	2	0.1	—	—	—	—	—
1	1	tr	3	15	0.1	80	0.01	0.03	tr	tr
2	3	6	tr	3	0.1	40	tr	0.01	tr	—
1	2	4	2	2	0.1	50	tr	tr	tr	tr
1	1	tr	0	167[18]	0.7	60	0.03	0.16	6.8	—
—	—	—	0	372	2.5	190	0.02	0.17	4.6	—
—	—	—	9	85	1.2	120	0.07	0.09	0.4	33
—	—	—	2	16	4.1	—	0.36	0.49	6.0	—
—	—	—	1	3	0.8	—	0.08	0.10	1.3	—
—	—	—	1	3	1.6	1,725	0.05	0.34	1.4	0
18	21	5	tr	8	2.7	0	0.89	0.39	4.2	—
—	—	—	0	2	0.4	0	0.02	0.02	0.6	0
—	—	—	19	41	3.1	0	0.09	0.17	2.3	0
—	—	—	0	20	0.5	20	0.11	0.22	7.3	—
—	—	—	59	31	tr	110	0.02	0.06	tr	4
—	—	—	11	2	tr	0	0.01	tr	tr	0
—	—	—	1	98	2.6	50	0.01	0.03	1.5	—
—	—	—	15	9	0.8	0	0	0	0	0
1	2	2	22	62	2.2	650	0.14	0.07	1.0	2
2	2	tr	11	15	0.5	—	—	—	—	—
1	1	1	7	8	1.0	50	0.05	0.06	1.1	tr
0	0	0	3	tr	0.5	tr	tr	0.02	1.2	—
1	1	tr	10	20	0.5	—	0.02	0.12	1.5	—
tr	1	1	8	10	0.5	50	0.02	0.02	0.8	tr
—	—	—	13	36	1.0	920	0.03	0.03	1.0	—
1	3	5	10	41	0.5	70	0.02	0.12	0.7	tr

[18]*Based on total contents of can. If bones are discarded, value will be greatly reduced.*

Food	Weight, gm	Approximate Measure	Food Energy, Cal.	Protein, gm	Fat (total lipid), gm
pea, green	245	1 c	130	6	2
tomato	245	1 c	90	2	2
vegetable with beef broth	250	1 c	80	3	2
vegetable-beef	203	1 serv, 3 from can	64	6	2
Soy flour, medium fat	88	1 c	232	37	6
Spaghetti:					
enriched, cooked	140	1 c	155	5	1
unenriched, cooked	140	1 c	155	5	1
in tomato sauce	250	1 c with cheese	260	9	9
Italian style	292	1 serv, with meat sauce	396	13	21
Italian style	302	1 serv, as above with grated cheese	436	15	24
Spinach	180	1 c	40	5	1
Squash:					
summer, cooked	210	1 c	30	2	tr
winter, cooked	205	1 c	130	4	1
Strawberries:					
raw	149	1 c	55	1	1
frozen	284	10-oz carton	310	1	1
Sugar:					
brown	14	1 tbsp	50	0	0
maple	15	1 pc, 1 $\frac{1}{4}$" × 1" × $\frac{1}{2}$"	52	—	—
white, granulated	12	1 tbsp	45	0	0
white, powdered	8	1 tbsp	30	0	0
Sweet potatoes:					
baked	110	1 med, 5" × 2"	155	2	1
candied	175	1 sm, 3 $\frac{1}{2}$" × 2 $\frac{1}{4}$"	295	2	6
Tangerine	114	1 med	40	1	tr
Tomatoes:					
raw	150	1 med	35	2	tr
canned	242	1 c	50	2	tr
Tomato juice, canned	242	1 c	45	2	tr
Tomato catsup	17	1 tbsp	15	tr	tr
Tongue, beef, simmered	85	3 oz	210	18	14
Tuna, canned, drained	85	3 oz	170	24	7

(*continued*)

TABLE C.1   Nutritive Values of the Edible Parts of Food (continued)

Fatty Acids

Saturated (total), gm	Oleic, gm	Linoleic, gm	Carbohydrate, gm	Calcium, mg	Iron, mg	Vitamin A Value, IU	Thiamin mg	Riboflavin, mg	Niacin, mg	Ascorbic Acid, mg
1	1	tr	23	44	1.0	340	0.05	0.05	1.0	7
tr	1	1	16	15	0.7	1,000	0.06	0.05	1.1	12
—	—	—	14	20	0.8	3,250	0.05	0.02	1.2	—
—	—	—	6	5	0.5	2,340	0.03	0.04	0.8	—
—	—	—	33	215	11.4	100	0.72	0.30	2.3	0
—	—	—	32	11	1.3[19]	0	0.19[19]	0.11[19]	1.5[19]	0
—	—	—	32	11	0.6	0	0.02	0.02	0.4	0
2	5	1	37	80	2.2	1,080	0.24	0.18	2.4	14
—	—	—	39	27	2.1	901	0.12	0.12	3.0	24
—	—	—	40	99	2.2	1041	0.12	0.16	3.0	24
—	—	—	6	167	4.0	14,580	0.13	0.25	1.0	50
—	—	—	7	52	0.8	820	0.10	0.16	1.6	21
—	—	—	32	57	1.6	8,610	0.10	0.27	1.4	27
—	—	—	13	31	1.5	90	0.04	0.10	0.9	88
—	—	—	79	40	2.0	90	0.06	0.17	1.5	150
—	—	—	13	12	0.5	0	tr	tr	tr	0
—	—	—	14	27	0.5	—	—	—	—	—
—	—	—	12	0	tr	0	0	0	0	0
—	—	—	8	0	tr	0	0	0	0	0
—	—	—	36	44	1.0	8,910	0.10	0.07	0.7	24
2	3	1	60	65	1.6	11,030	0.10	0.08	0.8	17
—	—	—	10	34	0.3	350	0.05	0.02	0.1	26
—	—	—	7	20	0.8	1,350	0.10	0.06	1.0	34[20]
—	—	—	10	15	1.2	2,180	0.13	0.07	1.7	40
—	—	—	10	17	2.2	1,940	0.13	0.07	1.8	39
—	—	—	4	4	0.1	240	0.02	0.01	0.3	3
—	—	—	tr	6	1.9	—	0.04	0.25	3.0	—
—	—	—	0	7	1.6	70	0.04	0.10	10.1	—

[19]*Iron, thiamine, riboflavin, and niacin are based on the minimum levels of enrichment specified in standards of identity promulgated under the Federal Food, Drug, and Cosmetic Act.*

[20]*Year-round average. Samples marketed from November through May average around 15 mg per 150-gm tomato; from June through October, around 39 mg.*

Food	Weight, gm	Approximate Measure	Food Energy, Cal.	Protein, gm	Fat (total lipid), gm
Turkey, roasted	100	3 sl, 3" × 2 ½ × ¼"	200	31	8
Turnips, cooked, diced	155	1 c	35	1	tr
Turnip greens, cooked	145	1 c	30	3	tr
Veal:					
chop, loin, cooked	122	1 med	514	28	44
cutlet, broiled	85	3 oz	185	23	9
roast	85	3 oz	230	23	14
Vinegar	15	1 tbsp	2	0	—
Waffles, baked	75	1 waffle, ½" × 4 ½" × 5 ½"	210	7	7
Walnuts, English	8	1 tbsp, chopped	50	1	5
Watermelon:					
raw	100	½ c cubes	28	1	tr
raw	925	1 wedge, 4" × 8"	115	2	1
Wheat:					
puffed	28	1 oz	105	4	tr
shredded	28	1 oz	100	3	1
Wheat flakes	28	1 oz	100	3	tr
Wheat flours:					
all-purpose or family, enriched	110	1 c, sifted	400	12	1
all-purpose or family, unenriched	110	1 c, sifted	400	12	1
cake or pastry flour	110	1 c, sifted	365	8	1
self-rising, enriched	110	1 c	385	10	1
whole wheat	120	1 c	400	16	2
Wheat germ	68	1 c	245	18	7
White sauce, medium	265	1 c	430	10	33
Yeast, brewer's, dry	8	1 tbsp	25	3	tr
Yogurt	246	1 c	120	8	4

(*continued*)

TABLE C.1   Nutritive Values of the Edible Parts of Food (continued)

Fatty Acids

Unsaturated

Saturated (total), gm	Oleic, gm	Linoleic, gm	Carbohydrate, gm	Calcium, mg	Iron, mg	Vitamin A Value, IU	Thiamin mg	Riboflavin, mg	Niacin, mg	Ascorbic Acid, mg
—	—	—	0	30	5.1	tr	0.08	0.17	9.8	0
—	—	—	8	54	0.6	tr	0.06	0.08	0.5	33
—	—	—	5	267	1.6	9,140	0.21	0.36	0.8	100
—	—	—	0	7	3.5	0	0.17	0.26	5.8	0
5	4	tr	—	9	2.7	—	0.06	0.21	4.6	—
7	6	tr	0	10	2.9	—	0.11	0.26	6.6	—
—	—	—	1	1	0.1	—	—	—	—	—
2	4	1	28	85	1.3	250	0.13	0.19	1.0	tr
tr	1	3	1	8	0.2	tr	0.03	0.01	0.1	tr
—	—	—	7	7	0.2	590	0.05	0.05	0.2	6
—	—	—	27	30	2.1	2,510	0.13	0.13	0.7	30
—	—	—	22	8	1.2	0	0.15	0.07	2.2	0
—	—	—	23	12	1.0	0	0.06	0.03	1.3	0
—	—	—	23	12	1.2	0	0.18	0.04	1.4	0
tr	tr	tr	84	18	3.2[21]	0	0.48[21]	0.29[21]	3.8[21]	0
tr	tr	tr	84	18	0.9	0	0.07	0.05	1.0	0
tr	tr	tr	79	17	0.5	0	0.03	0.03	0.7	0
tr	tr	tr	82	292	3.2[21]	0	0.49[21]	0.29[21]	3.9[21]	0
tr	1	1	85	49	4.0	0	0.66	0.14	5.2	0
1	2	4	32	49	6.4	0	1.36	0.46	2.9	0
18	11	1	23	305	0.5	1,220	0.12	0.44	0.6	tr
—	—	—	3	17	1.4	tr	1.25	0.34	3.0	tr
2	1	tr	13	295	0.1	170	0.09	0.43	0.2	2

[21]_Iron, thiamine, riboflavin, and niacin are based on the minimum level of enrichment specified in the standards of identity promulgated under the Federal Food, Drug, and Cosmetic Act._

Index